PROGRESS IN DESERT RESEARCH

PROGRESS IN DESERT RESEARCH

edited by
Louis Berkofsky
and
Morton G. Wurtele

ROWMAN & LITTLEFIELD
PUBLISHERS

ROWMAN & LITTLEFIELD

Published in the United States of America in 1987
by Rowman & Littlefield, Publishers
(a division of Littlefield, Adams & Company)
81 Adams Drive, Totowa, New Jersey 07512

Library of Congress Cataloging-in-Publication Data

Progress in desert research.

   "Proceedings of the "UCLA-BGU conference held
at the Jacob Blaustein Institute for Desert
Research, Ben-Gurion University of the Negev,
Sede Boqer Campus, Israel, September 1984".
   Includes bibliographies and index.
   1. Deserts—Congresses.   I. Berkofsky, Louis.
II. Wurtele, Morton G.
GB611.P738   1986   551.4   86-21926
ISBN 0-8476-7480-0

90   89   88   87
10   9   8   7   6   5   4   3   2   1
Printed in the United States of America

Contents

Tables and Figures

Tables

Figures

Preface

The UCLA-Ben Gurion University of the Negev interdisciplinary conference on "Desert Research," held at Sede Boqer, Israel in September 1984, was the third in a series of conferences under the UCLA-BGU Exchange Program. The conferences are held both at UCLA and at BGU approximately annually. The Desert Research conference included twenty-two participants from BGU and seven from UCLA.

UCLA and Ben-Gurion University of the Negev have enjoyed a beneficial exchange relationship since the signing of a formal agreement in 1980, which provides for the exchange of faculty and students, cooperative sponsorship of conferences, and other activities of joint interest.

UCLA is so well known that it needs no description. Its location and involvement with problems of semi-arid zones make it an ideal partner for joint programs with BGU.

Ben-Gurion University of the Negev was founded in 1969, with the main campus in Beer Sheva, the capital of the Negev. There are now about 6,000 students. A second campus, inaugurated in 1976, is situated 55 kilometers south of Beer Sheva, at Sede Boqer. Sede Boqer overlooks the starkly beautiful Wadi Zinn, the largest canyon in the Negev. This outpost boasts the Ben-Gurion Research Institute, which houses the personal papers of David Ben-Gurion, and the Jacob Blaustein Institute for Desert Research. The location of these two campuses in the Negev, a desert region, makes BGU an ideal place for research related to desert development, and, indeed, BGU's founding charge included the mandate to coordinate the development of the Negev. It was within this framework that the Jacob Blaustein Institute for Desert Research, which investigates interdisciplinary aspects of the Negev leading to future settlement, arose.

The UCLA—BGU Exchange Program, under the direction of Professor Samuel Aroni of the Graduate School of Architecture and Urban Planning at UCLA, has been highly active since its outset. A steady flow of visiting faculty and students in both directions has served to cement interinstitutional bonds. Exchange visits from UCLA faculty members from architecture, economics, education, history, medicine, and other disciplines, and a similarly diverse succession of visiting faculty from BGU have also spawned joint research projects.

It is hoped that publication of this book will inspire other researchers to tackle the enormously important and exciting problems of the desert.

PARTICIPANTS

University of California, Los Angeles

Sam Aroni, architecture
John A. Dracup, hydrology
Paul M. Merifield, remote sensing
Yale Mintz, meteorology
Kenneth A. Nagy, physiological ecology
Park S. Nobel, biology
Arthur Wallace, desert agriculture
Morton G. Wurtele, meteorology

Ben-Gurion University

Philip U. Alkon, wildlife ecology
Oran E. Aviv, meteorology
Louis Berkofsky, meteorology
Hendrik J. Bruins, desert agriculture
A. Alan Degen, physiological ecology
Michael Evenari, botany
David Faiman, solar energy
Daniel Feuermann, solar energy
Isaac Gilead, archaeology
George Gutman, meteorology
Lev N. Gutman, meteorology
Arie Issar, hydrogeology
Norman S. Kopeika, electrical engineering
Jonathan B. Laronne, geography
Shimshon Lerman, plant pollution
Berry Pinshow, physiological ecology
Amos Richmond, biology
Arieh Rogel, desert agriculture
Uriel N. Safriel, ecology
Moshe Shachak, ecology
Abraham N. Seidman, meteorology
Chaim Tsoar, geography
Aaron Yair, geomorphology
Abraham Zangvil, meteorology

PART I

DESERT AGRICULTURE, ANCIENT AND CONTEMPORARY

ONE

Run-off Farming Management and Climate

HENDRIK J. BRUINS, MICHAEL EVENARI,
AND ARIEH ROGEL

ABSTRACT

Climate is not a rigid standard factor in agricultural production. Even in more humid regions, fluctuations and abnormal climatic behavior should be taken into account in agricultural planning and management. Run-off farming makes agricultural production possible in arid zones where simple rain-fed agriculture would be out of the question. However, run-off farmers have to cope with drought years, as arid regions are characterized by great yearly fluctuations in the amount of run-off producing precipitation. In the Central Negev highlands, in the 100mm winter rainfall zone, shortage of run-off water is a severe limiting factor in agricultural production every three to four years. This average figure is based upon data from the Avdat, Shivta, and Wadi Mashash experimental run-off farms, obtained during the period 1960–84. Consequently, viable run-off desert farming depends upon the ability to stockpile enough water, food, or money during the good years for the drought years. The forming of reserve stocks are considered an indispensable part of proper run-off farming management. Future research should place emphasis on system synthesis through either of these realistic model farms: 1. Profitable run-off farming production systems, based on a money economy; or 2. Autarkic run-off farming production systems, based on a food economy.

INTRODUCTION

"We live in a world that is increasingly vulnerable to climatic shocks." This statement by Lamb (1982, xviii), one of the world's leading climatologists, is in sharp contrast to the more established opinion among many scientists and historians that climate can be viewed as constant. The first long records of weather observations seemed to give credit to the latter view. However, as noted by Lamb (ibid.,), from about 1950 the climatic tendencies have changed. Extreme variations in the weather patterns occurred in many parts of the world, breaking instrumental records.

Agriculture is very dependent upon the weather. Farm management and agricultural planning are to a considerable extent based upon the "average" climate, deduced from a standard period of 30 years of weather observations. However, the increased amplitude of climatic variations during the last few decades went beyond the expected standard norm. As a result, food production was seriously affected in many parts of the world, yields being below target.

Arid and semi-arid regions are particularly susceptible to climatic fluctuations. The drier the climate, the larger the interannual variability of the precipitation. Many arid zones of the world are entirely dependent upon rainfall for their food production or livelihood. Alternative, controllable water resources such as deep ground water or desalinated sea water are not easily made available, due to economic or technical constraints. A better and more efficient agricultural use of the local rainfall is often the only feasible way to improve food production in these regions. As such, run-off farming can be a viable agricultural system in arid regions (Evenari et al. 1961, 1971). It has been estimated by Le Houérou and Lundholm (1976) that about three to five percent of the arid zones can be developed through run-off farming. This figure is comparable, in terms of total area, to the potential of common irrigation farming. For that reason alone, more attention should be paid to run-off farming in arid zone development by the international community. In view of the variant usage of the term in the literature, run-off farming is defined here as agriculture in arid lands by means of run-off rainwater from any type of catchment or ephemeral stream.

LIMITS OF TRADE AND FINANCE

It is sometimes argued that malnutrition (famine) is an economic problem: if undernourished people in developing countries only had more money in their pockets, they would be able to buy food. Some experts even advocate that agriculture in dry regions should be abandoned altogether, due to the rationalization of agriculture and world trade. Huge areas in a favorable humid climate ought to concentrate on just one or two crops which supposedly grow best there. World trade should do the rest to bring this food to every home. These are all very nice arguments, but they are unrealistic for the world in which we live. The one-crop economy depends in essence on a forecast constancy of climate. When even in an individual year the weather conditions go beyond the expected range, the consequences may be catastrophic. As pointed out by Lamb (1981), the one-crop economy was at the root of many of the greatest famines of the past. In recent years, climates in many parts of the world have shown an increased range of variability. This ought to be a cause of concern for agricultural planners. Notwithstanding agricultural technological improvements, increased use of fertilizers and new seed varieties, world grain reserves by 1975 had fallen to less than a quarter of what they were in 1961. Lamb (ibid.) points to the climatic behavior as the main cause.

Millions of people in developing countries, situated in arid zones, cannot easily be reached by transported food from elsewhere. The necessary infrastructure is just not existent. There are no grocery stores in most parts of the countryside, where people simply can buy food, if only they have money. In fact, where can they earn money, if no other job is available than in subsistence agriculture or pastoralism? Finance and trade cannot sufficiently rectify the imbalance of food abundance in one part of our planet and malnutrition or hunger somewhere else. This is the harsh reality. The risks are indeed very high for a recipient country to be largely dependent upon food that is grown thousands of miles away. Climatic, economic, or political upheavals can torpedo the life line of imported food. Therefore, local food production in arid regions should be increased, not abolished.

THE SHIVTA, AVDAT, AND WADI MASHASH EXPERIMENTAL RUN-OFF FARMS

Run-off farming was practiced in the Central Negev desert during the reign of King Solomon (tenth century B.C.) and later during the Nabatean-Byzantine period (about A.D. 100–700) when the peak of its development was reached (Evenari et al., 1958; Cohen 1976; Negev 1981). Experience and knowledge of run-off farming in the region disappeared with the ancient Byzantine farmers during the Early Arab period. More than a thousand years later, Evenari, Shanan, and Tadmor (1961, 1971, and 1982) started anew to learn the principles and possibilities of run-off agriculture in the Negev desert. In 1958 an ancient run-off farm system was reconstructed near Shivta. The farm contains seven terraced fields situated in a little wadi. (A wadi is an ephemeral stream or arroyo.) Well-designed spillways allow the run-off water to flow from one terrace to the next. The total cultivable area is 0.7 hectares, dependent for its water supply upon run-off rainwater from a natural catchment of 17 hectares. Already during its first year, the Shivta Desert Farm has yielded promising results, as fruit trees started to grow well under run-off farming conditions. This initial success was crucial for further development and it was decided that a second farm experiment, on a larger scale and in a different watershed, was warranted. Thus the experimental run-off farm near Avdat was established in 1959, about 18 km southeast of the Shivta farm. Fourteen terraced fields were reconstructed altogether at the Avdat farm, albeit somewhat different from the ancient configuration. The total cultivable area is 2.6 hectares, situated in a loessial valley plain with silt-loam soils. A southern watershed of about 35 hectares provides run-off rainwater for the farm via seven conduit channels situated on the hill slopes. A large eastern watershed, including terraced wadis and farm units that were not reconstructed, may also contribute run-off water into the fields via a wadi inlet, In addition to the ancient systems, micro-catchments were layed out on Pleistocene terraces of Wadi Zin. The size of the micro-catchments, a relatively new concept in run-off farming, ranges from 0.1 to 0.0016 hectare. In 1976, an area of six hectares was prepared for run-off farming on a loessial valley plain 1.5km west of the Avdat farm. These large fields were also farmed in the past during the Nabatean-Byzantine period. A major part of the run-off for this area is derived from Wadi Avdat via a new 750 meter long diversion channel. Pistachio orchards, almond trees, and a recreational desert park were established on this new area. The Avdat experimental run-off farm has demonstrated, since its reconstruction in 1960, that a variety of fruit trees, field crops, pasture plants, and vegetables can be grown in the Central Negev desert with run-off agriculture (Evenari et al. 1982).

In 1970, a larger experimental run-off farm was set up at Wadi Mashash, 34km north of Avdat, in a very wide valley plain of this wadi and its various tributaries. The size and geomorphology of the plain provides the opportunity to test different run-off systems next to each other. About 3000 micro-catchments of 0.025 hectare in size were layed out on the somewhat more elevated part of the plain. The micro-catchments were planted with fruit trees, mainly almond but also olive and pistachio trees. In connection with the tributaries of Wadi Mashash, another run-off system was set up at various lower parts of the flood plain: the liman system. A liman, from the Greek word *limne* meaning lake, is an arable piece of land surrounded by a check-dam. The liman harvests the run-off floodwaters of a tributary wadi. Altogether ten hectares of limans were established and planted with orchards of mainly olive trees, as well as almond and fig trees, and grapevines. More recently, a number of limans were planted with potential fuel and pasture trees to study their biomass production and management. In the broad stream bed of Wadi Mashash pasture is grown on an area of 60 hectares. Here, grazing experiments are performed with sheep to study the carrying capacity of pasture under run-off cultivation conditions.

Knowledge and experience of run-off agriculture, acquired at the Avdat, Shivta, and Wadi Mashash experimental farms, has been successfully applied in a number of developing countries, e.g. Afghanistan, Kenya, Botswana, Niger, Upper Volta (Evenari et al. 1982).

RUN-OFF FARMING MANAGEMENT AND CLIMATIC VARIABILITY

Based on 25 years of experimental run-off agriculture in the Negev desert, some conclusions regarding general management are attempted here. Proper management is dictated by a fairly large number of factors of a necessarily local nature. These include environmental, agricultural, eco-nomical, and sociological factors. The success or viability of a run-off farm depends likewise upon its proper integration within a certain society. A viable run-off farm in a developing country may be uneconomical under a much higher living standard. The trend of run-off farming for Israeli conditions is mainly towards cash crop orchards of pistachios, almonds, and olives. Food is at present relatively cheap in Israel and easy to purchase all over the country. Hence it is financially more lucrative for farmers to grow cash crops for the local market or export, and to buy basic food products in the shops.

In developing countries the situation may be quite different. Many arid zones are characterized by a chronic lack of food, which is scarce, relatively more expensive and not easy to purchase in the countryside. Under such conditions, there is often no alternative but subsistence farming or pastoral-ism. It has been demonstrated that run-off farming, including pastoral production systems based on run-off water, can make significant improve-ments in food supply and farm income in these circumstances (Nessler 1980).

Whether the purpose of run-off agriculture is to produce cash crops or to maintain subsistence farming, the greatest challenge in proper farm man-agement is the climatic variability of the arid zones. Table 1.1 shows the annual rainfall and available run-off data of the Avdat, Shivta, and Wadi Mashash farms. Each year is a hydrological year, running from October to September, since the calender year cuts the rainy season. The first rains may fall in October and the last rains in April, but the typical rainfall months are usually December, January, February, and March. The average annual precipitation, measured by standard rain gauges, for th Avdat, Shivta, and Wadi Mashash farms is 86.8mm, 88.3mm and 117.2mm, respectively for the periods 1960–84, 1960–76, and 1970–84. The present evaluation of the rainfall and available run-off data focuses attention on the major problem of run-off farming in arid regions: the number of drought years with insufficient run-off water for adequate argricultural production. It is easy to distinguish between a very good and a very bad year, but it is rather difficult to draw the dividing line between a moderately bad year and a year in which agricultural production is just above the limit of economic or nutritional survival. The size of the farm should be taken into account in relation to the amount of people depending upon it. Considering run-off water management, the incoming run-off water might be spread over all the fields or only over some of them. In the latter case, the amount of water might be sufficient to harvest good yields from part of the farm, whereas spreading the same amount of run-off water over all the fields would result in a total crop failure due to lack of moisture. The type of crops and the time and sequence of the run-off floods in a certain year can also determine success or failure without changing the actual amount of rainfall and run-off. Data like these are of course not available in a comparable manner from year to year, due to the pioneering and experimental character of the farms in which emphasis and

Table 1.1 Annual Rainfall and Available Runoff Data

Rainy season	Avdat farm			Shivta farm			Wadi Mashash Limans		
	Rainfall (mm)	Runoff water (m³)	Drought year	Rainfall (mm)	Runoff water (m³)	Drought year	Rainfall (mm)	Runoff water (m³/ha)	Drought year
1960-61	70.0	1,932		102.5	594				
1961-62	64.7	4,471		50.6	280	x			
1962-63	29.5	792	x	24.8	44	x			
1963-64	183.3	51,875		145.3	6,293				
1964-65	144.2	6,115		160.8	9,444				
1965-66	91.5	6,905		67.1	1,297				
1966-67	80.7	1,827		94.4	2,285				
1967-68	86.9			75.4					
1968-69	70.3			73.2					
1969-70	58.4			43.6		x			
1970-71	82.0		x	115.2			142.0	7,000	
1971-72	162.6			172.4			207.0	10,000	
1972-73	53.5		x	41.0		x	55.0	0	x
1973-74	132.6			105.8			180.5	4,000	
1974-75	84.9			77.7			93.0	3,000	
1975-76	77.1			62.6		x	79.5	0	x
1976-77	64.1		x				101.0	2,000	
1977-78	68.0						75.0	1,500	
1978-79	56.0		x				90.7	5,000	
1979-80	100.6						166.0	16,500	
1980-81	100.8						120.7	10,000	
1981-82	68.8		x				75.5	0	x
1982-83	124.2						170.0	3,500	
1983-84	29.3		x				84.5	0	x
Average	86.8	10,560		88.3	2,891		117.2	4,464	
Drought year frequency (once every…years)			3.4			3.2			3.5

crop type vary. Therefore, the present evaluation of the number of run-off drought years cannot be absolute but is a reasonable approximation.

At the Avdat experimental run-off farm, about seven out of 24 years can be classified as drought years; on the average every 3.4 years. The Shivta run-off farm experienced about five drought years during 16 years of measurements; an average of every 3.2 years. At the Wadi Mashash run-off farm, four out of 14 years can be classified as run-off drought years; an average of every 3.5 years. Thus, in the present climatic regime of the Central Negev highlands, in the 100mm winter rainfall zone, shortage of run-off water is a severe limiting factor in agricultural production every three to four years. From a farm management point of view, it is a must to overcome these run-off drought years before viable run-off farms can be established.

With the availability of high-technology, a more affluent country, might supplement the lack of run-off water during drought years or times of severe moisture stress with water from alternative sources like deep groundwater, as suggested by Issar (1981). A controllable additional water source seems obviously the ideal solution. In some developing countries, however, it might be a problem to set up and maintain such a system. Even rich countries may find it difficult to explore alternative water sources. In many arid regions it is, at least for the time being, economically out of the question to use another water source than rain. What then can be done in situations where no water but run-off is available for agricultural production? How shall they cope with drought years? The most obvious solution is the formation of stockpiles and reserves during the favorable years for use during the dry years. Possible stockpiles can be grouped in three categories: water, food, and money.

Water

This precious liquid is the main limiting factor in agricultural production during run-off drought years. As far as perennials like fruit trees are concerned, experience from the Shivta, Avdat, and Wadi Mashash farms indicates that suitable varieties can survive by drawing upon the deeper soil water during drought years. This water can be considered as a reserve stock, deeply infiltrated into the soil during a wet year when large amounts of run-off water ponded the fields. Storage of run-off in the deeper soil parts is only possible if the rainwater harvesting catchment area is sufficiently large to supply plentiful quantities of run-off water to the fields during good years. The run-off receiving field must be surrounded by dams high enough to allow at least 30cm of water to accumulate on its surface to enable deep water penetration. The soil should have a good water storage retention capacity.

Larger catchments, though less efficient than micro-catchments from a hydrological viewpoint (Shanan 1975), seem to be preferable in desert regions from an agronomic outlook as far as fruit trees are concerned. Both at the Wadi Mashash and Avdat farms, fruit trees in micro-catchments are inferior to those planted in fields attached to larger catchments. The latter systems are able to produce copious amounts of run-off water in good years, stored in the subsoil as a reserve for bad years. This property seems to be missing in current micro-catchment designs, which appears to be a critical disadvantage in very dry arid zones with drought years occurring regularly. In a wetter arid climate, this disadvantage is outweighed by the beneficial property of micro-catchments to produce run-off more often than larger catchments. In a desert region, micro-catchments may be better suited for annual crops, although new designs might also make them more suitable for trees. However, the advantage of large catchments for trees in terms of deep water storage to overcome drought years in deserts is illustrated by a unique example from southwestern Libya. In Beni Walid there are beautiful olive groves in an area where precipitation is on the average 70mm per year. A large catchment basin concentrates run-off floodings and this system has been working continuously for almost 2000 years! (Le Houérou and Lundholm 1976).

Apart from natural storage of water in the subsoil, it is a great asset for viable run-off farming when additional amounts of run-off water can be stored in cisterns, tanks, or ponds. Enormous quantities of run-off water flow by in good years and some of it ought to be stored in man-made constructions for use as supplementary irrigation in periods of drought. This greatly enhances the viability of run-off farms. An interesting and stimulating example in this respect comes from Karnataka in India, where about 50 dugout field ponds have been constructed for lifesaving or supplemental irrigation during moisture stress periods (Verma 1978).

Food

In countries or regions where food is scarce and relatively costly, run-off farming should be directed foremost to food crop production. Cereals and pulses are the most important food types, the former making up about 75 percent of the world's diet. It is of great importance to develop durable food production systems for run-off farming in developing countries.

The genetic variability within each crop should be studied with respect to suitability for water-harvesting agriculture, in which drought stress is a recurring phenomena. Modern cultivars were generally bred for improved environments in more humid regions, whereas land-races evolved under much harsher conditions. The comparative performance of species and cultivars should be tested in run-off farming environments. Studies on genetic variability and drought resistance in cereals (Blum 1978; Poiarkova and Blum 1983) and pulses (Westphal 1974) provide relevant information for Southwest Asia and Africa.

In low-input and labor-intensive run-off agriculture, suited for the family farm in developing countries, mixed cropping of cereals and legumes may offer greater production and stability. In combination with proper crop rotation, durable food production systems may thus be achieved in which some control over soil fertility, weeds, pests, and moisture regime is attained. The balance between plant density and an environment under stress, in terms of water supply and soil fertility, is very delicate. The plant density has to be adapted to the unique environment of water harvesting agriculture (Blum, pers. com. 1984).

The integration of food crop cultivation and livestock husbandry may also improve production stability and long term viability of run-off farming in a significant way. This is indicated by investigations on dry farming in the northern Negev (Van Keulen et al. 1982). Food production in run-off farming systems takes place in marginal arid environments and ought to be based on a diversified footing.

In a subsistence or food economy, farm management should be aimed at the formation of buffer food stockpiles during the good years as a reserve for the bad drought years. The handling and proper storage of food is of prime importance in this respect (Hall 1970). Post-harvest losses due to rodents or pests are just as bad as crop failures due to droughts.

Money

When the infrastructure and economic situation in a country is such that agricultural surplusses and cash crops can be marketed, while food can be purchased easily, then money becomes an important factor as a reserve to overcome drought years in run-off farming systems. Translated in the situation of the Central Negev desert: in one good year enough money must be earned for two years, if no additional water reserves are available for periods of moisture stress or droughts. Although a run-off drought year occurs here on the average every three to four years, the accompanying table shows intervals during which there is a significant lack of run-off water every other year. Realistic run-off farm management ought to base its planning more upon the bad intervals than on average periods of good years.

PALEOCLIMATE AND PAST RUN-OFF
FARMING MANAGEMENT

The question arises whether the climate during past periods of run-off farming in the Negev was different than at present. What is the relationship between climatic and agricultural history and how did the ancient farmers and related urban settlements cope with the situation of crop failure? A detailed treatise on these and related matters is given by Bruins (1986).

For much of the Latest Pleistocene (ca 100,000 to 15,000 B.P.), the amount of precipitation was considerably higher in the Negev than at present, as deducted from proxy climatic indicators (Begin et al. 1974; Bruins 1976; Bruins and Yaalon 1979; Issar and Bruins 1983). Within the last 2000 years, variations in the level of the Dead Sea (Klein 1981) reflect relatively distinct humid periods of more than 100 years duration, as well as dry intervals. Climate is not exactly constant with time but has its own history of variations, fluctuations, and changes. A rather unexplored paleo-climatic realism with many nuances exists in between the simplistic climatic determinism of Huntington (1911) and the view that the climate during historical times was both constant and the same as today. How is it today? In many parts of Africa today a drought of truly catastrophic proportions exists which began around 1968. The preceding part of the twentieth century has been considerably more humid in Africa (Unesco 1984). For farmers and pastoralists in these drought stricken areas, the climate today is not the same as in the recent past.

The H.D. Colt archaeological expedition discovered in 1935 unique papyrus documents from the sixth and seventh centuries A.D. while excavating at the ancient Negev town of Nitzana (Nessana or Auja). Situated in the western part of the run-off farming region of the Central Negev, Nitzana was one of the six Nabatean-Byzantine towns in the area. The Nitzana papyri mention the growing and importance of wheat and barley in local water-harvesting agriculture during the sixth and seventh centuries A.D. This is outstanding information, because it implies a rainfall-runoff amount and seasonable distribution of the run-off water suitable for the production of these annual food crops. Due to the particular growing season and short life cycle, wheat and barley are more sensitive than perennial fruit trees to yearly rainfall-run-off patterns. Although barley is more drought-resistant than wheat, the latter is surprisingly the predominant cereal crop in the Nitzana papyri. Wheat is mentioned in 13 documents in connection with: sale and salary, requisitions, food tax, donations, receipt accounts, sowing and yield amounts, a threshing floor. Only two documents mention barley (Kraemer 1958; Mayerson 1955, 1960).

The important general conclusion of the combined historical and archaeological data is the fact that run-off farming was viable as an agricultural system in the Central Negev highlands for many centuries during the Nabatean-Byzantine period, and also during the tenth century B.C. (Israelite II period). Somehow, the ancient farmers and inhabitants of the region managed to cope with drought years and crop failures. It seems likely that food storage played a significant role in this respect.

SUGGESTIONS FOR FUTURE RESEARCH

Emphasis should be placed upon system synthesis, incorporating all elements and aspects of run-off farming, to investigate the proper functioning and management of independent water harvesting agricultural systems. The climatic variability of the arid zones is the most difficult factor to be overcome in this connection. Research of individual aspects should not be carried out at random, but with reference to their position in a particular run-off farming system as a whole. System synthesis and integrated research of agricultural production is exemplified by the work of De Wit (1968, 1979).

Two basic types of realistic model run-off farms are envisaged:

1. *Profitable run-off farming production systems, based on a money economy*. Mechanized agricultural equipment, chemical fertilizers, and a modern infrastructure are considered to be available. Water is a limiting factor, hence the necessity to use run-off water in regional development. Financial profitability is the only standard to measure success or failure.

2. *Autarkic run-off farming production systems, based on a food economy*. This type is envisaged for developing countries and remote desert regions. Storage of both run-off water and food is essential to cope with drought years. Viability in this system is measured by its ability to operate in an autarkic way and to produce enough food for the people who depend upon it.

REFERENCES

Begin, Z. B., A. Ehrlich and Y. Nathan. 1974. Lake Lissan, the Pleistocene precursor of the Dead Sea. *Bull. Geol. Survey*. Ministry of Comm. and Ind., State of Israel. 63.

Blum, A. 1979. Genetic improvement of drought resistance in crop plants: a case for sorghum. In Mussell, H. and Stamples, R. C. (eds.) *Stress Physiology in Crop Plants*. Wiley-Interscience Div., New York, N.Y. pp. 430–45.

Bruins, H. J. 1986. *Desert Environment and Agriculture in the Central Negev and Kadesh-Barnea during Historical Times*. Nijerk, Holland: Midbar Foundation.

Bruins, H. J. 1976. The origin, nature and stratigraphy of paleosols in the loessial deposits of the northwestern Negev (Netivot, Israel). *M.Sc. thesis*, Jerusalem: The Hebrew University, Dept. of Geology.

Bruins, H. J. and D. H. Yaalon 1979. Stratigraphy of the Netivot section in the desert loess of the Negev (Israel). In Pecsi, M. (ed.) *Studies on Loess. Acta Geol. Acad. Sci. Hung.* 22(1–4): 161–69.

Cohen, R. 1976. Excavations at Horvat Haluquim. *Atiqot* 11:34–50.

de Wit, C. T. 1968. Plant production. *Misc. Papers Landb. Hogeschool*. Wageningen 3:25–50.

———. 1979. The efficient use of labour, land and energy in agriculture. *Agricultural Systems* 4:279–87.

Evenari, M., Y. Aharoni, L. Shanan, and N. H. Tadmor, 1958. The ancient desert agriculture of the Negev, III: Early Beginnings. *Israel Expl. Journal* 8:231–268.

Evenari, M., L. Shanan, N. H. Tadmor, and Y. Aharoni. 1961. Ancient agriculture in the Negev. *Science* 133: 979–96.

Evenari, M., L. Shanan, and N. H. Tadmor. 1971. *The Neqev: The challenge of a desert*. Boston: Harvard University Press. 1982 second enlarged edition.

Hall, D. W. 1970. Handling and storage of food grains in tropical and subtropical areas. *FAO Agric. Devel. Paper*. 90.

Huntington, E. 1911. *Palestine and its transformation*. Boston.

Issar, A. 1981. The reclamation of a desert by the combination of ancient and modern water systems. *Outlook on Agriculture* 10: 393–96.

Issar, A. S. and H. J. Bruins. 1983. Special climatological conditions in the deserts of Sinai and the Negev during the latest Pleistocene. *Palaeogeogr., Palaeoclimat., Palaeoecol.* 43: 63–72.

Klein, C. 1981. The influence of rainfall over the catchment area on the fluctuations of the level of the Dead Sea since the 12th century. *Israel Meteor. Res. Paper* 3: 29–58.

Kraemer, C. J. 1958. *Excavations at Nessana. Volume 3. Non-literary Papyri*. New Jersey: Colt Archaeological Inst., Princeton University Press.

Lamb, H. H. 1982. Climate, history and the modern world. London and New York: Methuen.

Le Houerou, H. N. and B. Lundholm. 1976. Complementary activities for the improvement of the economy and the environment in marginal dry lands. In A. Rapp. H. N. Le Houerou, and B. Lundholm (eds.) Can desert encroachment be stopped? *Ecological Bull*. Swedish Nat. Sci. Res. Council, NFR. 24: 217–229.

Mayerson, P. 1955. Arid zone farming in antiquity: A study of ancient agricultural and related hydrological practices in southern Palestine. *Ph.D. thesis*. New York Univ., Univ. Microfilms Int., London.

———. 1960. The ancient agricultural regime of Nessana and the Central Negev. London: Colt Archeological Institute, British School of Archaeology, Jerusalem.

Negev, A. 1981. Les Nabatéens au Negev, le Christianisme au Negev, la vie économique et sociale à l'époque Byzantine: *Le Monde de la Bible* 19:4–46.

Nessler, U. 1980. Ancient techniques aid modern arid zone agriculture. *Kidma: Israel Journal of Development* 20.

Poiarkova, H. and A. Blum 1983. Land-races of wheat from the Northern Negev in Israel. Euphytica 32: 257–71.

Shanan, L. 1975. Rainfall and runoff relationships in the Avdat region of the Negev desert. *Ph.D. thesis*, Hebrew University, Jerusalem.

UNESCO. 1984. Climate, drought and desertification. *Nature and Resources*. Unesco 20: 2–8.

Van Keulen, H., R. W. Benjamin, N. G. Seligman, and I. Noy Meir. 1982. Actual and potential production from semi-arid grasslands–Phase II. *Joint Dutch-Israeli Research Project, Final Technical Report and Annotated Bibliography*. ARO, Bet Dagan; Hebrew University, Jerusalem; CABO, Wageningen; Agricultural University, Wageningen.

Verma, B. 1978. Run-off water for black soils of Karnataka. *Indian Farming*. July.

Westphal, E. 1974. Pulses in Ethiopia, their taxonomy and agricultural significance. *Agric. Res. Rep*. 815. Wageningen.

TWO

Problems and Challenges of Egyptian Agriculture: Contemporary Subtropical Arid Land Agriculture in Egypt

ARTHUR WALLACE

ABSTRACT

Egypt has had an irrigated cultivated agriculture on arid lands for at least five milleniums. It presently cultivates about 2.44 million hectares of desert lands. This is mostly in the Nile River Valley and delta, but with some desert oases. Ancient methods of agriculture are still in use. Since 1967, with the advent of the Aswan High Dam, more land reclamation projects have been undertaken mostly to use water from the Nile River for irrigation of nearby lands. Mistakes similar to those made with large irrigation schemes in antiquity have been made in Egypt so that the 360,000 hectares of reclaimed lands are only marginally productive. Salinity and water-logging are severe problems. Moreover, the net gain in land for agriculture has been minimal because of increased urbanization. Governmental controls of the main crops grown in Egypt has led to artificial priorities among farmers which are preventing the farmers from achieving an agricultural sufficiency. Major emphasis is currently given to livestock production, even though there are few real advantages for Egypt to do so, and there are formidable difficulties, partly the result of the desert. Current livestock prices in Egypt are on the average 15 percent over world prices, however. Simultaneously, prices in Egypt for wheat, rice, corn, and cotton are well below world prices. Egypt's comparative advantages of climate, water, land resources (even in a desert), and people should

(The Laboratory of Biomedical and Environmental Sciences is operated for the U.S. Department of Energy by the University of California under contract No. DE-ACO3-76-SF00012)

make it possible to at least double the production of these four main crops plus that of fruits and vegetables. Egyptian farms are small with an average size much less than one hectare. Major constraints need to be overcome to achieve food sufficiency, and these are in the realms of the technical, social, economic, political, and medical. New land reclamation projects are proposed to put 200,000 hectares of desert land under new cultivation, although water will be available for 840,000 hectares. Reasons for the difference are economical, unavailability of more good soil, and lack of basic and applied research which can solve the problems involved. Space technology is being used to identify areas of the desert which may be suitable for agriculture.

OVERVIEW OF EGYPTIAN AGRICULTURE

An understanding of the status of agriculture in Egypt is essential to an evaluation of contemporary desert agriculture in Egypt. Egyptian agriculture poses a real challenge. Egypt has an enormous supply of fresh water. Although it has a tremendous amount of unused land, it has a relatively limited amount of good land on which to use its large supply of water (Elgabaly et al. 1969). Discharge from the Aswan High Dam is a constant 55×10^9 cubic meters of water per year distributed reasonably equally throughout the year (Elgabaly et al., 1969). With some 2.5 million hectares of land under irrigation, approximately 22,000 cubic meters are available per hectare (Office of Intern. Corp. and Devel. 1979). Most of the land is double-cropped and some is triple-cropped (El Tobgy 1976) per year so that about 10,000 cubic meters are available per hectare per crop season. Since ground water tables have risen considerably since 1968 when the Aswan High Dam went into operation, too much water is probably available, although all of it does not go directly into irrigation—much is lost by inefficiency of the delivery systems. Incidentally, Egypt has a population of around 46 million persons, and its agricultural productivity makes for less than 50 percent self-sufficiency.

Israel has 1.3×10^9 cubic meters of water available for irrigation. The water is used on about 0.4 million hectares of land which are nearly all double-cropped, except for perennial crops. Israel has a population of about 4.5 million and is agriculturally self-sufficient. Efficiency of water use in agriculture then is about eight times more in Israel than in Egypt. Efficiency here would be defined as percent of yearly food and fiber needs for a person per cubic meter of water used in agriculture. The contrast is shown in Table 2.1.

At least in part, the limiting factors or constraints on Egyptian agriculture can be identified through a comparison of management practices in Israel and Egypt. It is not possible for the purposes of this chapter to develop a comprehensive set of comparisons because insufficient information is available to the author. Perhaps the most obvious differential, however, is that

Table 2.1 Comparative Efficiency of Irrigation Water Use in Egypt and Israel

	Egypt	Israel	Egypt-Israel ratio
Hectares in farming	2.4×10^6	0.4×10^6	6.00
Water available per hectare, m^3	22,600	3,400	6.65
Agricultural self-sufficiency, %	50	100	0.50
Population, number of persons	45×10^6	4.5×10^6	10.00
Self-sufficiency per hectare, number of persons	9.38	11.25	0.83
Number of self-sufficient persons per 1000 m^3 water	0.42	3.31	0.127[a]

[a] Relative water use efficiency is 7.9:1 in favor of Israel.

Israeli irrigation systems are modern, largely computer-operated, and highly efficient. On the other hand, most of those in Egypt are many centuries old, sometimes in poor condition, and never were more than 50 percent efficient in terms of water delivered to the crop.

In 1978, the author directed Egypt's attention to both a national salt balance and a national evapo-transpiration balance (Wallace and Hassan 1978). Even though the figures used were crude estimates, it was apparent that a net build-up of water table and of salt burden was occurring on the agricultural land (Hassan et al. 1979; Arab Repub. of Egypt 1977). If this is correct and not reversed, then Egypt could eventually lose most of its agriculture in the Nile River Valley. The calculations are in dire need of refinement because of the critical nature of their implications.

Egypt has some 2.44 million hectares of land in irrigated cultivation (U.S. Foreign Agric. Econ. Rept. No. 120, 1976; U.S. Dept. Agric. and Office Intern. Corp. and Devel., 1979). In 1985, Egypt expected to have five million hectares of crops under cultivation due to double- and triple-cropping, even though some of the land was in permanent crops like fruit trees and sugar cane (U.S. Foreign Agric. Econ. Rept. No. 120, 1976; U.S. Dept. Agric. and Office Intern. Coop. and Develop., 1979). (See Figure 2.1 and Tables 2.2 and 2.3.) The traditional cropping pattern in Egypt is for cotton, rice, maize in Northern Egypt; and sorghum in Southern Egypt in the summertime, and for clover and wheat in the winter. Some three percent of the land is used for winter vegetables, and some 13 percent is used for winter horsebeans, lentils, and onions. Summer vegetables occupy about 6 percent of the land, while year-round sugarcane uses about five percent, and fruit trees about six percent.

Cotton occupies the land for about eight months of the year, so a partial crop of catch-crop clover is used in rotation where one or two cuttings of clover are taken before plowing for cotton. Some winter vegetables also are in rotation with cotton. About 27 to 29 percent of the land grows cotton in the summertime.

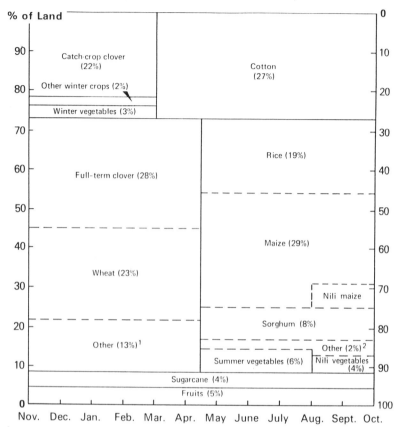

Figure 2.1 Typical crop rotation systems in use in Egypt and proportionate averages of crops in the systems for 1972–1974. (Adapted from U.S. Foreign Agric. Econ. Rept. No. 120 1976).

Full-term clover is grown for about six months in the winter on about 30 percent of the land. Land then goes to either rice or maize for the summer. Usually full-term clover is planted for the next winter, followed by rice or maize, or wheat is grown followed by rice or maize, then full clover back to rice or maize, followed by catch-crop clover to cotton, so that rotations involve cotton every two or three years (U.S. Foreign Agric. Econ. Rept. No. 120 1976; El Tobgy 1976).

Production of crops per unit of land is generally above world average, but not really for good irrigated land (Min. of Ag. of Egypt 1982). Although Egypt has been increasing its agricultural productivity in recent years, its use of farm commodities has increased tremendously simultaneously, so that its food security gap has been steadily increasing (Min. of Ag. of Egypt, 1982). Study groups have concluded that the potential for expanding the

Table 2.2 Area, Yield, Production, and Farm Value of Major Crops and Old Lands, 1972-74 Average, and 1985 Projected (one feddan = 0.42 hectares or 1.04 acres)

	Area (1,000 feddans)		Yield in metric tons per feddan		Production (1,000 metric tons)		Production per capita (in pounds)		Value[a] per $ million LE	
	1972-74	1985	1972-74	1985	1972-74	1985	1972-74	1985	1972-74	1985
Nonforage field crops										
Cotton (lint)	1,535	1,700	0.30	0.37	462	628	29	30	148	202
Wheat	1,289	1,275	1.38	1.81	1,778	2,312	111	110	125	162
Maize	1,647	950	1.53	2.15	2,523	2,047	158	98	144	117
Sorghum	484	275	1.71	2.31	826	635	52	30	—	—
Rice	1,061	1,200	2.19	2.62	2,327	3,141	146	150	151	204
Sugarcane	203	280	36.10	45.70	7,336	12,802	459	610	55	96
Other[b]	653	800	2.19	2.48	1,428	1,983	89	95	—	—
Vegetables	764	1,170	7.21	10.42	5,511	12,196	345	582	—	—
Citrus	139	170	6.10	10.00	848	1,700	53	81	—	—
Other fruits[c]	120	130	5.00	7.25	599	942	38	45	—	—
Forage crops							Tons per AU[d]			
Catch-crop clover	1,230	1,600	12.0	15.0	14,710	24,000	2.7	4.5	—	—
Full-term clover	1,597	1,100	24.0	30.0	38,345	33,000	7.1	6.1	—	—
Maize and sorghum	—	1,100	—	18.0	—	19,800	—	3.7	—	—
Total	10,722	11,750							623	781
Cropping ratio	1.9	2.1							—	—

— means not reported.
[a] Based on export or import prices at Alexandria, adjusted to farm level equivalent. Unit prices for 1985 were held constant at 1972-74 level.
[b] Chiefly horsebeans and lentils.
[c] Excludes dates for which no land area is calculated.
[d] Metric tons per animal unit. The number of animal units in 1985 was assumed to be the same as in 1972-74 (5,375,000).

Table 2.3   Area and Production of Crops 1973-1975

Crop	1973		1975	
	Area	Production	Area	Production
	1,000 feddans	1,000 metric tons	1,000 feddans	1,000 metric tons
Catch-crop clover	1,284	NA	1,124	NA
Full-term clover	1,590	NA	1,688	NA
Clover seed	(187)[b]	43	(183)	44
Seed Cotton	1,600	1,543	NA	NA
Wheat	1,229	1,836	1,394	2,032
Maize	1,654	2,507	1,830	2,782
Millet	486	853	489	775
Barley	84	96	96	118
Rice (paddy)	997	2,274	1,053	2,423
Horsebeans	270	273	246	234
Sugarcane	198	7,349	NA	NA
Lentils	74	62	58	39
Lupins	9	6	8	5
Chickpeas	8	6	6	4
Sesame	36	21	33	17
Groundnuts	29	26	32	28
Flax seed	40	19	54	27
Fennugreek	26	20	32	24
Onions[a]	45	528	44	572
Garlic	14	206	12	127
Vegetables	799	5,572	NA	NA
Fruits (including dates)	263	1,818	285	1,653

NA means not available.

[a]Production includes onions interplanted with other crops for which no area is estimated.
[b]Part of full-term clover.

Source: Derived from Ministry of Agriculture data.

Egyptian agricultural sector is great, and that the rapidly widening gap between production and utilization of food can be considerably reduced (Min. of Ag. of Egypt 1982). This corresponds with studies elsewhere (Food Task Force, Univ. Ca. 1974, Nat. Acad. of Sci., 1975a, AAAS 1975b; Chou et al. 1977; Duncan 1977). Many problems or constraints currently prevent Egypt from realizing its agricultural development potential. These constraints may be grouped into four broad categories: policy, technological, resource, and institutional (U.S. Foreign Agric. Econ. Rept. No. 120, 1976; Min. of Ag. of Egypt 1982).

Historically, the agricultural sector in Egypt has been a major contributor to the Egyptian economy. By the early 1970s, however, the relative contribution of agriculture to government revenues and foreign exchange earnings was declining. Since the October War of 1973, Egypt's economic situation has changed dramatically. Petroleum, remittance from workers abroad, and tourism have become the major earners of foreign exchange. Compared to other activities, agriculture has had the slowest growth, increasing by an average of only 2 percent annually between 1975 and 1980, while growth in the services sector averaged more than 8 percent and petroleum 30 percent (Min. of Ag. of Egypt 1982).

Investment in the Egyptian agricultural sector has not been optimal. Land reclamation, which received 40 percent of available funds, has given very low returns. This is due to many reasons, including lack of micronutrients, lack of drainage, government operations rather than private sector, and poor market facilities. Other funds have been used mainly for infrastructural improvement, including the Aswan High Dam, irrigation canals, and drainage facilities. At the farm level in the old lands, relatively little investment in new technology has occurred in contrast to the situation in Israel. Farmers have not been encouraged to save or to invest because set prices and other controls have limited the profitability of farming (U.S. Foreign Agric. Econ. Rept. No. 120, 1976; Min. of Ag. of Egypt 1982; El Tobgy 1976). This urban subsidization by the agricultural sector has been very critical.

Likewise, growth in the supply of food and agricultural products in Egypt has been slow. A 25 percent gain in the value of agricultural output was experienced between 1970 and 1981 (Min. of Ag. of Egypt 1982). Over the same period, crop output value expanded 16 percent, while animal product value grew 42 percent. Production of traditional field crops, such as cotton, rice, wheat, and sorghum, showed little increase; but output of animal products, berseem clover, maize, fruits, and vegetables expanded. These production shifts were related to government policies, farmer response to prices, consumer demand, and technical constraints. Livestock prices are well above world prices—they are at least 115 percent. Field crop prices are generally well below world prices.

The Ministry of Agriculture oversees farm production and influences farm output through crop quotas, fixed crop rotations, administered prices, input allocations, and technical assistance (El Tobgy 1976). Government intervention in agriculture has been characterized by mixed goals: earning a surplus for governmental use from the farm sector through low producer prices, acquiring cheap food for urban distribution which subsidizes the urban population at the expense of the rural, insuring production of profitable export crops which earns foreign exchange, protecting farmers against world price fluctuations, and encouraging adoption of new technology. The policies lead to distortion of economic processes of supply and demand that result in inefficiency.

Agricultural land area is limited mainly to the Nile Valley and delta, with a few oases and some arable land in Sinai. The cultivated area is 2.44 million hectares—three percent of the total land area. The entire crop area is irrigated, except for some rain-fed areas on the Mediterranean coast used mostly for grazing. Land reclamation of 380,000 hectares over the last three decades has been offset by land lost to urbanization of approximately 295,000 hectares (Min. of Ag. of Egypt 1982).

Land holdings are fragmented, with the average size of operating farm units being one hectare (El Tobgy 1976; U.S. Foreign Agric. Econ. Rept. No. 120, 1976). Many farms are half a hectare or smaller. Land tenure is divided among legal owners, renters, and sharecroppers, in order of magnitude. Small farms present special problems (Norman 1978; League for Intern. Food Educ. 1975c). Even so, most of the world's food is produced on small farms (Chou et al. 1977; Univ. of Calif. Food Task Force 1974), and Egypt's small farms will undoubtedly continue.

The government maintains fixed producer prices for a number of crops. Because of distortions resulting from price regulations, farmers have often preferred to cultivate less regulated crops, including vegetables, fruits, and berseem clover.

Per capita consumption of many agricultural commodities in Egypt has increased significantly, especially since 1974. In fact, in the six-year period from 1974 to 1980, per capita utilization of wheat increased 38 percent, sugar 69 percent, maize 24 percent, red meat 38 percent, white meat 67 percent, dairy products 41 percent, and fish 76 percent (Min. of Ag. of Egypt 1982). This rapid increase in demand for food is due to a number of factors, including a high rate of population growth, a shift in population from rural to urban areas, increasing income, and substantial government subsidies for food. Some corruption adds to the demand.

Egypt is becoming increasingly reliant upon food imports to meet its needs and upon foreign assistance to finance them. In 1974 the value of agricultural imports exceeded exports for the first time. The figures rose quickly, and by 1981 Egypt was importing some 48 percent of its staple food commodities. In 1981 the value of agricultural imports exceeded exports by some three billion dollars (Min. of Ag. of Egypt 1982).

While the value of Egypt's agricultural imports is growing, agricultural exports are falling (Min. of Ag. of Egypt 1982). In fact the volume of the three most profitable exports—cotton, rice, and oranges—declined over the last decade. Government policies usually require that the domestic demand be met before commodities can be exported.

AGRICULTURAL DEVELOPMENT POTENTIALS

Egypt has the potential to develop significant export markets, especially for horticultural crops (Wallace 1978). Evaluations of Egyptian agriculture have often emphasized Egypt's unusually favorable land, water, and climatic resources, along with the relatively high levels of agricultural productivity which these resources have enabled the country to achieve. These assessments show yields of most Egyptian crops to be substantially above average world yields, and also to compare very favorably with those of more developed regions of the world (Min. of Ag. of Egypt 1982).

Many have assumed from such comparisons that opportunities for further increasing productivity per unit of land must be limited. Such views have been reinforced by crop yields during the past decade which, with few exceptions, have tended to level off or, in several instances, to decline (Min. of Ag. of Egypt 1982).

Ample evidence suggests that despite relatively high levels of productivity by world standards, or even by those of more developed nations, Egypt's potential for further increasing agricultural output on existing arable lands is enormous (Wallace 1975, 1976, 1984). Such increases would be in excess of whatever gains might be realized by bringing additional lands under production through reclamation. Improving old lands needs more attention than reclamation of new.

Yield comparisons with other agricultural areas of the world often fail to take into account the truly unique nature of Egyptian agriculture. In almost no other country is the agricultural system so completely based on irrigation. In no other country is the total cropland so abundantly supplied with high quality irrigation water. This uniqueness is further enhanced by the deep, rich alluvial soils throughout the Nile River and delta area (Elgabaly et al. 1969). Finally, no country can claim more optimal climatic conditions for agriculture.

To obtain a meaningful comparison of potential Egyptian agricultural productivity, comparisons should be made with other areas where conditions are similar. Perhaps the most useful comparison would involve Egypt's productivity against that achieved under irrigated conditions in the United States. Average yields in comparable areas in the US are substantially greater than those in Egypt. This suggests that the productivity of Egyptian crops has by no means attained full potential, especially considering that Egypt's overall environment for crop production is generally superior to that under average irrigated conditions in the US.

Perhaps the most current and meaningful information available for improvement of crops is the data accumulated from large-scale field demonstrations carried out by the Ministry of Agriculture and US-AID as part of the rice research and training, the major cereal improvement, the citrus project, and the agricultural assistance projects. The real basis for the potential yield increase of perhaps 200 percent is in combining the various agriculturally related disciplines to simultaneously overcome all limiting factors in this arid environment (Wallace 1984).

Extensive demonstrations under farm conditions, involving thousands of hectares, have indicated a potential with current technology and know-how for increasing yield of cereals by 50 to 70 percent and certain vegetables by 170 to 260 percent. With the broad scope and scale of these demonstrations, the yields realized represent levels that could be achieved by average Egyptian farmers within a few years provided the various constraints presently limiting production were appropriately addressed and removed (Wallace 1984). This would bring Egyptian agriculture more in line with Israeli agriculture.

Certainly a strong, well-conceived, and viable research program can be expected to develop the technology needed to increase yields far above the levels which are now obtained.

The needed elements in such a research program must not only take into account the conduct of agriculture in a desert environment, but also a myriad of interactions involving water, soil, salt, nutrients, microbiota, and climate. Failures in the newly reclaimed lands resulted from the omission of such research endeavors, but the lessons learned can be applied towards a vast improvement in even the old agricultural lands of Egypt.

Perhaps an even greater potential to increase the economic returns of Egyptian agriculture and even add to food security lies in the possibilities of export of Egyptian horticultural crops (Wallace 1978). The favorable off-season winter climate of Egypt should make for a much greater horticultural export industry. At the present time, such export from Egypt is insignificant. For export, from each hectare of land, it should be possible to purchase back, for example, wheat from several hectares from other countries, such as the United States. Such potential does not exist for livestock because of limited land in Egypt. For livestock production, Egypt must import much of its feed, a procedure which is very inefficient in terms of food security.

LESS CERTAIN POTENTIAL FOR
NEW LAND RECLAMATION

The potentials for bringing additional land into production and expanding existing livestock enterprises (horizontal expansion) are not nearly as encouraging as prospects for increasing productivity of existing cropping areas and livestock operations (vertical expansion).

With only three percent of Egypt's land base under cultivation, there is obviously space for agricultural expansion. Water is available for some expansion. Appropriate soils that could be developed at reasonable costs, however, are extremely scarce. Most desert soils are not conducive to agriculture. Although the water supply might support 840,000 hectares of reclaimed lands, the possibility of bringing more than 200,000 to 400,000 hectares additionally into cultivation is unlikely because suitable soil is not available (Min. of Ag. of Egypt 1982).

In the 1960s, considerable emphasis was placed on efforts to develop new lands, and more than 380,000 hectares were reclaimed (Elgabaly et al, 1969; U.S. Foreign Agric. Econ. Rept. No. 120, (see Figure 2.2). The Ministry of Agriculture now indicates that only 200,000 of these hectares are "above marginal production" (Min. of Ag. of Egypt 1982). This reclaimed area, which constitutes approximately 13 percent of the total cultivated land in Egypt, currently accounts for only about two percent of total agricultural production (El Tobgy 1976).

Despite the disappointing history of reclamation efforts, the potential exists—given the application of the appropriate technology and suitable management—for producing acceptable yields of high value, speciality crops on newly reclaimed desert lands (Min. of Ag. of Egypt 1982; Bishay and McGinnies 1979). However, the management must be in the hands of qualified persons and must be associated with research efforts.

The relatively high levels of agricultural productivity, permitted by Egypt's unusually favorable land, water, and climatic resources, support one of the most dense livestock populations in the world—about one animal unit (cow equivalent) per 0.4 hectare. Since the fact that the country already falls far short of producing enough food to meet human needs, and since there is limited availability of arable land, the desirability of expanding the production of animal products is questionable. The present level of resources devoted to animal production cannot even be justified, since import of animal feed is involved.

In this type of situation in other parts of the world, priority is normally given to producing from a given land area the staple food commodities that would generate the most energy and provide the best nutrition for humans. Converting large quantities of grain to meat or animal products and using large areas of fertile land to grow forages indicate an unwise allocation of scarce resources (Min. of Ag. of Egypt 1982).

With the severe food deficits that currently confront Egypt and the likelihood that the situation will be even more acute in the future, the strategy of continuing those policies which have favored expanded production of meat and animal products at the expense of crops needed for domestic consumption or export, appears unwise. Egypt's comparative advantages do not lie in the production of animal products. As long as Egypt is in a deficit situation with respect to concentrates for poultry and fish, the relative merit of importing meat directly, instead of the concentrates, should be considered.

Although the potential for further agricultural development in Egypt is significant, many constraints limit the realization of this potential. These constraints are policies, institutions and organizations, resources, technology and medical.

Policies

Agricultural policies used by the government have acted to seriously constrain the growth of Egyptian agriculture. Prices for many agricultural commodities are fixed at low levels. This seriously discourages farmers, as it gives no encouragement for increasing production and actually promotes the inefficient allocation of resources and the inequitable distribution of income. Government pricing of major agricultural inputs, such as seed, pesticides, fertilizer, and water, has also been a part of Egypt's overall agricultural programs. Although such subsidies partially offset the income transfer effects of set commodity prices, they also contribute to unwise uses of resources and to black markets (Min. of Ag. of Egypt 1982).

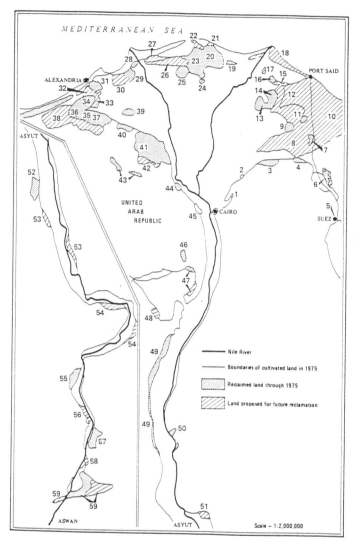

Figure 2.2   Areas of reclaimed land and proposed reclaimed land in Egypt
(Adapted from U.S. Foreign Agric. Econ. Rept. No. 120 1976).

Institutions and Organizations

The institutions and organizations related to the agricultural sector in Egypt
are complex. Four ministries (Agriculture, Irrigation, Land Reclamation,
and Supply) are directly involved in various aspects of food production and
others are indirectly involved. The result is overlapping of duties and
conflicting policies. If the agricultural sector is to meet its potential, all
aspects of the sector should be considered within a unified framework for
planning and executing programs (Min. of Ag. of Egypt 1982).

East of delta	West of delta (contd)
1. El Gab alasfar	31. Abiss
2. Enshass	32. Nubaria prolongation
3. Elmoulak	33. Elhager
4. Elmanaief	34. Elnahda
5. Elswissa	35. North Tahrir sector
6. El Bohairat elmorra	36. Mariut
7. Elverdan	37. Mechanized farm
8. Elsalhia	38. West of Nubaria
9. Baher-elbaker	39. Ferhassh
10. Wadi Tema	40. Elbustan
11. South Port Said	41. Eltahaddy
12. Hessania Valley	42. Elentelaak
13. Elkasabi and Berket san	43. South Tahir and Elfathe
14. Abo-elakhdar	
15. Elmatereia	**Middle Egypt**
16. Elserow	44. Wardan
17. Faraskour	45. Elmansouria
18. Ezbet el Burg	46. Kom-osheen
	47. El Fayoum
Middle of delta	48. Quta
19. Elsatamony	49. Samalout
20. Hafir shehab eldin	50. Tall elamarna and der abuhenness
21. Prolongation of hafir shehab eldin	51. Asyut
22. Baltem and Kashaa	52. West of Tahta
23. West Tira and El Mansour	53. Sohag
24. Elgawia	
25. Shalma	**Upper Egypt**
26. Elborullus	54. Kena
27. Elsenania	55. Esna
	56. Elsaida
West of delta	57. Elradisia and Wadi Abadi
28. Elboseilli	58. Aswan
29. Edko and Halle elgamal	59. Komombo
30. Barsik	

Source: U.S. Foreign Agric. Econ. Rept. No. 120, 1976, 38–39.

The universities are awarding large numbers of degrees in agriculture. Many students, however, receive little laboratory or field training. The laboratories are generally overcrowded and poorly equipped. Many more agricultural graduates than can be effectively used are now employed within the government. This leads to inability to help farmers.

Resources

The resources upon which Egyptian agriculture is based are poorly cared for. Land is being lost to urbanization and to brick-making. Other land is not cultivated because it is the property of speculators. Some land is becoming lost to salinization and waterlogging (Hassan et al. 1979). Such catastrophe is common in arid-land agriculture. Water is used ineffectively (land not level, flow rates incorrect, reliance on basin irrigation, lack of water drainage); new land is developed which tends to salinize old land; small farms have little mechanization; there is inflexibility in the supply and distribution of agricultural inputs; and labor is expensive due to migrations to the cities where people get subsidized food. These are some ways in which the agricultural resources are being eroded. The world's new knowledge on irrigation (Taylor et al. 1983) is mostly not used.

Technology

As mentioned, the agriculture of Egypt is still mostly done with ancient technology. The potential for improvement is enormous. Only by coordinated research and development can the farmers take advantage of new technology. The scientific resources are mostly available, but financial, social, and political constraints are formidable. Export marketing is one area in great need of new technology if Egypt is to reach its potential. Export quality of crops is lacking. A list of constraints to crop marketing follows (Min. of Ag. of Egypt 1982):

Farm-to-market roads and transportation.

Containers and packing.

Lack of adequate off-loading at Egyptian ports.

Storage and refrigeration.

Sanitation.

Grades and standards.

Satellite wholesale markets.

Facilities for preparing and handling products from animals.

Food and vegetable processing plants.

Difficulties of internal food distribution by the government.

Poor performance of government export marketing organizations.

Poor performance by food processing organizations.

Concentration of power to a few in the wholesaling of fresh fruits and vegetables.

Government price policies.

Import tariffs on equipment used in the marketing system.

Lack of government monitoring of the marketing sector.

Medical

The parasitic disease schistosomiasis has plagued rural Egypt for thousands of years (Eckholm 1978). It is now spreading over the world. The irrigation canals create ideal environments for the snails that carry the parasites—blood flukes that are transmitted from the water to the skin of those who swim or wade in the water and then from the skin to the liver. Infections generally last a lifetime and debilitate and kill the host at age 40 to 50. This disease is a major barrier to Egyptian agriculture.

FUTURE LAND RECLAMATION

With Egypt's rapidly exploding population, the country, for political reasons, must continue to move out into the desert. Some new cities have been built or are under construction (Ramadan 10 and Sadat City are examples). A large number of new villages have been built also. As mentioned, water will be available to cultivate at least 840,000 new hectares, or even more if research application can decrease the amount of water currently used in the present agriculture. Three major problems limit the amount of new desert land that can go into reclamation. These are the high costs of reclamation, the unavailability of good land, classes III and IV (class I is most useful and class VIII least useful) mostly are available (U.S. Foreign Agric. Econ. Rept. No. 120, 1976), and the lack of the research, both basic and applied, necessary to cope with the problems associated with reclamation. Sabadell (1979) outlined essential research needs. It has been suggested that the needed research should be undertaken at least 20 years before the beginning of a reclamation project. Even so, Egypt is planning to put about 200,000 hectares of new land into reclamation projects within one or two decades (Shata 1979).

Badran et al. (1979) reviewed the status of and possibilities for further land reclamation in Egypt. They envisioned the development of more than one million hectares of land which is the sum of that already reclaimed (50 percent of it is not cultivated due to problems) and the 840,000 hectares for which water is available. The authors pointed out the extreme difficulty of irrigation in Egypt. The ratio between precipitation and evapo-transpiration potential is less than 0.03 for most of the country, and varies from 0.2 to 0.5 along the northern coast. This indicates also the great probability of salt build-up since there is virtually no rainfall for leaching in most of the country. This emphasizes the need for caution and special research associated with such agriculture. The amelioration of deteriorated soils is recognized to be as much a part of land reclamation as the development of new land. During the past 30 years, Egypt has carried out extensive projects in the reclamation of deserts in areas bordering the Nile River and delta and along the northern coast. It intends to continue.

New areas for reclamation include the Sinai (with ground water, rain runoff, and canals of Nile River water going under the Suez Canal [Said 1979]; along the northwestern Mediterranean coast; enlargement of the Fayoum (partly with reuse of drainage water); enlargement of the Kom Ombo area; and expanding agriculture in the western desert oases with underground water. There is even consideration of an irrigation project in the western desert near the Sudanese border with water from Lake Nasser. This South New Valley in the western desert can be reclaimed with over 500,000 new hectares.

Many of Egypt's land reclamation projects have suffered because they have used old technology, traditional crops have been grown, and the projects have been used primarily as a means of giving occupation to landless people. Thorne (1970) cautioned that spending taxpayers' money to reclaim desert lands with new irrigation systems being used for primitive agriculture can never be justified. This is what Egypt has done in the past, but the future plans are different.

El-Baz (1979) has reported in some detail the potential of the Western Desert for land reclamation. Space photographs and images provide a useful tool in identifying areas with characteristics suitable for agriculture. Some of the oases are already in use for agriculture (Siwa, Wadi El Natrun, Kharga, Fayoum, Dakhla). Others can be developed, but moving-sand dunes are an obstacle. There are some unused underground water resources in the western-desert—enough for a total of 210,000 hectares of irrigated land (Seddik and Shafei 1979).

The northern coast of Egypt does get sufficient rainfall (150mm per year near Alexandria) for some grazing of livestock. Ayyad (1979) has conducted a multi-year study of this ecosystem as part of the world-wide International Biological Program of the 1970s. Ayyad reports:

> "These ecosystems have limited carrying capacities: limited potentials of material cycling and energy flow, and limited abilities to absorb changes, particularly those effectuated by inputs of materials and energy. If land-use practices exceed the carrying capacity of an ecosystem, the dynamic balance that gives it apparent stability will be upset, the ecosystem functioning will be impaired, and damage in the form of soil erosion, salinization, outbreaks in phytophageous insects, rodents, and weeds . . . etc., may be irreparable."

CONCLUSION

Egypt is facing formidable problems in endeavoring to maintain and expand its efforts in desert agriculture. Sophisticated research followed with applicable modern technology are essential to the solution of problems. Salinity in an almost rainless country in which agriculture is done on class III and IV lands (much of it originally saline), and in which the elevation gradients are small so as to impede drainage, is becoming a horrendous problem. The traditional agriculture currently used cannot cope with it. Water-logging in the relatively fertile Nile River Valley and rising water tables will continue unless the evapo-transpiration relationships associated with irrigation are controlled. Since agriculture must essentially pay its own way, cropping patterns must be used from which it is possible to pay the necessarily high costs of desert agriculture. Egyptian agriculture has often failed to do this.

Deserts are fragile, and careful long-time planning and adequate financing are requisite for success in expanding agriculture into the desert lands of Egypt. With multidisciplinary approaches, however, present productivity of some of the old lands can be doubled.

REFERENCES

Anonymous. 1974. A Hungry World: The Challenge to Agriculture. *General Report* by University of California Food Task Force, University of California.

———. 1975a. Agricultural Production Efficiency. *National Academy of Science*, Washington, D.C.

———. 1975b. Food: Politics, Economics, Nutrition and Research (report). *American Association for Advancement of Science*, Washington, D.C.

———. 1975c. Small Scale Intensive Food Production (report). *League for International Food Education*.

———. 1976. Egypt: Major Constraints to Increasing Agricultural Productivity. *U.S. Foreign Agricultural Economic Report No. 120*.

———. 1977. Control of Waterlogging and Salinity in the Areas West of the Noubaria Canal. *Arab Republic of Egypt, Technical Briefing Note*, Egypt 73/048.

———. 1979. Egyptian Agriculture and the U.S. Assistance Program. Technical Assistance Report No. 2, *U.S. Department of Agriculture and Office International Cooperative and Development*.

———. 1982. Strategies for Accelerating Agricultural Development. *Ministry of Agriculture of Arab Republic of Egypt and U.S. Agency for International Development in Cooperation with International Agricultural Development Services and U.S. Department of Agriculture* (summary report).

Ayyad, M. A. 1979. An overview of the Samdene project. In *Advances in Desert and Arid Land Technology and Development*, Vol. 1:97–103. Eds. A. Bishay and W. C. McGinnies. Harwood Academic Publishers, New York.

Badran. S., S. A. Kandeel, M. H. Lakany, M. T. Omran, A. B. El-Sayed, and M. L. El-Osta. 1979. Possibilities of land reclamation in desert areas: review of present and future status. In *Advances in Desert and Arid Land Technology and Development*, Vol. 1:41–53. Eds. A Bishay and W. C. McGinnies. Harwood Academic Publishers, New York.

Bishay, A., and W. C. McGinnies, eds. 1979. *Advances in Desert and Arid Land Technology and Development*, Vol. 1. Harwood Academic Publishers, New York.

Chou, M., D. P. Harmon, Jr., H. Kahn, and S. H. Wittwer. 1977. *World Food Prospects and Agricultural Potential*. Praeger Publishers, New York.

Duncan, E. R. ed. 1977. *Dimensions of World Food Problems*. Iowa State University Press, Ames.

Eckholm, E. 1978. Schistosomiasis: A disease of the poor and of development. *Ceres* Jan./Feb. 37–41.

El-Baz, F. 1979. The western desert of Egypt, its problems and potential. In *Advances in Desert and Arid Land Technology and Development*, Vol. 1:67–84. Eds. A. Bishay and W. C. McGinnies, Harwood Academic Publishers, New York.

Elgabaly, M. M., I. M. Gewaifel, M. N. Hassan, and B. G. Rozanov. 1969. *Soils and Soil Regions of U.A.R. Research Bulletin* No. 21, Alexandria University, Egypt.

El-Tobgy, H. A. 1976. *Contemporary Egyptian Agriculture*, 2nd ed. Ford Foundation, New York.

Hassan, M. H., S. Marei, M. Motagalli, H. El-Abd, and Z. Arnaout. 1979. Salinity hazard and waterlogging in the area west of Noubaria Canal. In *Advances in Desert and Arid Land Technology and Development* Vol. 1:85–95. Eds. A. Bishay and W. C. McGinnies, Harwood Academic Publishers, New York.

Norman, W. B. 1978. Farming systems: Research to improve the livelihood of small farmers. *American Journal Agricultural Economics* 60:813–35.

Sabadell, J. E. 1979. Arid lands development strategies: Research needs. In *Advances in Desert* and Arid Land Technology and Development Vol. 1:105–12. Eds. A. Bishay and W. C. McGinnies, Harwood Academic Publishers, New York.

Said, R. 1979. The development of Sinai. In Advances in Desert and Arid Land Technology and Development Vol. 1:55–58. Eds. A. Bishay and W. C. McGinnies, Harwood Academic Publishers, New York.

Seddik, M. M., and S. Shafei. 1979. Water resources and land reclamation in Egypt. In Advances in Desert and Arid Land Technology and Development Vol. 1:201–210. Eds. A Bishay and W. C. McGinnies, Harwood Academic Publishers, New York.

Shata, A. A. 1979. Application of geoscientific knowledge to evaluation of land and water resources in some desert areas of Egypt. In Advances in Desert and Arid Land Technology and Development Vol. 1:183–200. A. Bishay and W. C. McGinnies, Harwood Academic Publishers, New York.

Taylor, H. M., W. R. Jordan, and T. R. Sinclair, eds. 1983. Limitations to Efficient Water Use in Crop Production. American Society Agronomy, Madison, Wis.

Thorne, W. 1970. Agricultural production in irrigated areas. In Arid Lands in Transition, ed. H. Dregne. Pub. No. 90:31–55. American Association for the Advancement of Science, Washington, D.C.

Wallace, A. 1975. Need for an integrated plan for development of Egypt between 1975 and 2000 A.D., the agricultural and related sectors. Egyptian Journal of Horticulture 2:133–43.

———. 1976. Need for an integrated plan for development of Egypt between 1975 and 2000 A.D., the agricultural and related sectors. Reply to O. A. El-Kholei. Egyptian Journal of Horticulture 3:245–46.

———. 1978. More horticulture will improve the economy of Egypt. Egyptian Journal of Horticulture 5:201–4.

———. 1984. The next agricultural revolution. Communications Soil Science Plant Analysis 15:191–97.

Wallace, A., and M. N. Hassan. 1978. Some environmental effects of the Aswan High Dam. Egyptian Journal of Horticulture 5:205–12.

THREE

Root-Soil Interface Mechanisms that Provide the Adaptability of Plant Species to Arid Calcareous Soils and Some Effects of Stress on Those Mechanisms

ARTHUR WALLACE

ABSTRACT

Plant species that grow naturally in hot arid environments with harsh soils of high pH do so only because they are adapted to periods of heat and of drought; but also to a continuing extremely low solubility of native soil iron, which is one of the essential mineral elements for all living organisms. Plants that grow naturally in deserts, and some other species that will grow in desert lands if water and nutrients and sometimes soil organic matter are supplied, have elaborate and successful mechanisms at the root surface which enable the plant to obtain iron. The mechanisms are genetically controlled, are plastic within a species, and can be manipulated by plant breeding. Microorganisms undoubtedly serve a role in providing iron to higher plants, but the extent is not known. These microorganisms also have parallel mechanisms for obtaining iron. Evidence indicates a multiplicity of mechanisms for different desert plants. These mechanisms have really never been studied as yet. They are subject to stress, and the interactions are as yet little known. Elucidation of the processes is vital to understanding and manipulating succession, productivity, revegetation, and ecosystem stability in deserts.

INTRODUCTION

Iron is essential to all living organisms. Plants must obtain their supply of it from the soil, but in aerated alkaline soils highly buffered at pH values over seven because of calcium carbonate in the soil and exchangeable Na on the soil, the solubility of both Fe^{3+} and Fe^{2+} is vanishingly low (Lindsay 1979). Soils generally maintain a Fe^{3+} activity of around 10^{-21} M at pH 8; for Fe^{2+} at pH 8 and pe + pH of 10, the activity is about 10^{-10} M (Lindsay 1979). A limiting value for plant uptake of Fe^{2+} is around 10^{-9} M or greater (Schwab 1981), even though this level is insufficient by one or two orders of magnitude for maximum growth.

Iron then is extremely insoluble in soil; and even though plentifully supplied naturally in soil, is often a major limiting factor for plant growth in arid soils (Lindsay 1979). Agricultural plants introduced into arid soils are often susceptible to severe iron deficiency (Nelson et al. 1982). Survival is often impossible. It must be concluded that those plants which are native to arid soils, that is, to desert or near desert conditions, are extremely iron-efficient; a condition in plants genetically controlled which makes it possible for those plants to obtain iron from soil (Brown 1977; Nelson et al. 1982). After drought tolerance, iron efficiency is the most important characteristic of plants native to arid lands.

STATUS OF RESEARCH ON THE SUBJECT

Research in this field of iron-stress response mechanisms is relatively new. A fourth international interdisciplinary symposium was held in 1985 in Nebraska. The proceedings of three prior symposia (1979, 1981, 1983) have been published (Wallace and Berry 1981; Nelson et al. 1982; James et al., 1984). Controversy in the field relates to the fact that there undoubtedly are several different physiological mechanisms involved, depending upon plant species. All of the studies have thus far been made with agricultural plants. None have been made with plants native to adverse desert soil conditions in terms of iron availability.

SIX DIFFERENT ROOT MECHANISMS INVESTIGATED

1. Excretion of H^+ by plant roots to the external medium due to greater cation uptake than anion uptake (Wallace et al. 1968; Brown 1977; Lindsay 1984; Bienfait et al. 1982b; Fleming and Foy 1982; Johnson 1982; Hershey and Paul 1984; Varanini and Maggioni 1982). This not only makes both Fe^{3+} more soluble thermodynamically, but also lowers the redox (pe + pH) making possible the reduction of Fe^{3+}; Fe^{2+} is more soluble in soil (Lindsay 1979).

2. Excretion of H^+ by plant roots in the form of organic acids (Young and Terry 1984).

3. Production of specialized roots which can excrete H^+ not always the result of differential cation-anion uptake, so that the whole root system need not do this (Landsberg 1982, 1984; Romheld et al. 1982). Wallace and Mueller (1978) have shown that only part of a root system need be engaged in iron uptake for a plant to obtain a more than sufficient quantity.

4. Plant roots produce and excrete reductants which reduce Fe^{3+} to Fe^{2+} (Brown and Ambler 1973), which form is more readily involved in iron uptake (Olsen et al. 1982; Brown 1977; Hether et al. 1984; Kannan et al. 1984).

5. Plant roots themselves enzymatically reduce Fe^{3+} to Fe^{2+} without the need of external reductant (Uren 1982; Bienfait et al. 1982a, 1982b, 1984; Sijmons and Bienfait 1984; Barrett-Lennard et al. 1983; Campbell and Redinbaugh 1984).

6. Plant roots produce siderophores such as hydroxamates or catechols, which chelate iron (Fe^{3+} in this case) and which subsequently function in the absorption of the iron by the roots (Nomoto et al. 1981; Takemoto et al. 1978; Mino et al. 1983; Reid et al. 1984; Peters and Warren 1970; Nielands 1977; Raymond 1977, Rodriquez et al. 1984).

Reasons why more than one mechanism, according to plant species, is involved, relate to other plant characteristics. For example, species belonging to *Gramineae* seem to produce and excrete siderophores in contrast to other plant species (Takemoto et al 1978; Nomoto et al 1981; Takagi et al. 1984). Production and uptake of siderophores in grasses is specific (Romheld and Marschner 1986). Species of *Gramineae* take up more anions than cations, especially when nitrogen is taken up as nitrate. This would result in excretion by roots of OH^- or HCO_3^- and in an alkaline root surface environment unfavorable to the reduction of Fe^{3+} or to its solution. High pH would result in higher redox (pe + pH). These are the species for which researchers are finding evidence for siderophore mechanisms in contrast to species in which cation uptake exceeds anion uptake under which the root surface boundary can be acidic.

Siderophores have been most studied for microorganisms which seem to have specific siderophores for a species which are nonfunctional for other species as a means of transporting iron to or inside the organism (Allnutt and Bonner 1984; Cline et al. 1984; Reid et al. 1984; Winkelmann and Huschka, 1984; Smith and Neilands 1984).

Many studies have given inconclusive results about the benefits that rhizosphere microorganisms may have in making iron available for higher plants. It is of interest, however, that a soil leachate was quite capable of supplying iron to a higher plant grown in a nutrient solution that was provided with other needed elements, except for iron (Wallace 1966). The form of iron in the leachate was not determined.

Synthetic chelating agents commonly used to provide iron sources for higher plants somewhat mimic the action of siderophores, although the organic chemistry of siderophores is generally more complex than that of the synthetic chelating agents.

Especially for plant species (or varieties, for there is genetic variability within species) having H^+ associated Fe^{3+} reduction at the root surface (McDaniel and Brown 1982; Williams et al. 1982; Coyne et al. 1982; Fleming and Foy 1982; Kannan 1982), the onset of an iron stress elicits a physiological response within the plant (Landsberg 1982, 1984). The chain of events has been called an iron-stress response, and the process an iron-stress-response mechanism. Whether the response is quantitative or qualitative is not fully understood, but qualitative aspects seem to be involved (Wallace and Collaborators 1971).

Wallace et al. (1968, 1969, 1971) in studies with tobacco plants, observed that depriving plants of iron resulted in an increased tendency for H^+ production in the external nutrient solution, and it was shown to be the result of excess cation uptake over anion uptake. This event was followed by the production of riboflavin and root excretion of it to the external medium. After two or three days with intense yellow color in the solution, the color then disappeared, yellow leaves soon became green, and their iron concentration increased even though no additional iron had been applied to the external solutions. The iron had been moved from the roots to the shoots. Root concentration of iron in an inactive state is usually quite high and can be a source of iron when plants are under stress.

Whether or not riboflavin is a reductant or more like a siderophore is not known. The compounds most often considered as candidates for iron reductants in the external medium are phthalic acid, caffeic acid, chlorogenic acid, and others (Hether et al. 1984; Olsen et al. 1982; Kannan et al. 1984). Barrett-Lennard et al. (1983) do not believe that the concentration of such reductants can be large enough to meet the needs of plants. But research involving different plant species with variable iron-stress responses will inevitably result in differences of opinion.

Bienfait's group (1982a, 1982b, 1984) has produced evidence for enzymatic reduction of iron in root membranes. Wallace (1983) has suggested that root membrane potentials of around -200 mv are such that reduction of Fe^{3+} is inescapable while it is being transported.

Bicarbonate, which interferes with the iron-stress response mechanism, is a most important inducer of iron chlorotic plants (Fleming et al. 1984; Romheld et al. 1982; Wallace and Wallace 1984). Levels of bicarbonate which induce iron chlorosis are those which swamp out the effect of the H^+-producing capacity of the root. Plants which rely upon siderophores as part of the iron-gathering process appear not to be affected by the bicarbonate complication (Fleming et al. 1984; Chaney 1984; Coulombe et al. 1984). Bicarbonate production in wet calcareous soils is associated with poor aeration in which respiratory CO_2 is retained in the soil solution (more easily when soil is cold) to dissolve $CaCO_3$.

This would indicate the favorability of grasses as dominant species in calcareous arid ecosystems. The next choice would perhaps be oxalate plants which are so mostly because of a large excess of cation over anion uptake. In any event, plants adapted to the arid deserts must have efficient mechanisms for iron mobilization from soil. This is an aspect of ecophysiology of primary importance.

RESEARCH NEEDS AND ELUCIDATION OF STRESS INTERACTIONS

A most urgent need exists for developing an understanding of how roots of desert plants function in iron mobilization from soil and of how soil microorganisms may be involved in the process. The recent forward thrust in this field is largely confined to agricultural plants, but the most rewarding searches can be with those species best adapted to the harsh soil conditions of the desert. Life is fragile in deserts. The soil system is extremely fragile in deserts. We do not know if the iron-stress responses associated with desert plants are a fragile or a strong link in the life system of deserts. In many plant species, however, it is a weak link and is subject to many stresses (Kohno et al. 1984; Romheld et al. 1982; Landsberg 1982; Chaney and Coulombe 1982; Fleming et al. 1984; Young and Terry, 1984; Wallace and Wallace 1984).

Shrubs and trees affected with iron-deficiency chlorosis usually slowly die over a period of a few years. This happens even though the stress which caused the deficiency was temporary and no longer exists. Known stresses which induce the iron chlorosis condition are excess soil water (producing bicarbonate); excesses of heavy metals; severe root pruning due to animals or machines or microbes; loss of topsoil; excess phosphorus, and others. How these stresses influence the physiological processes involved is largely unknown.

Since the ability of plants to adapt to such extreme iron insolubility conditions as found in arid calcareous deserts is such a prodigious feat, rivaling drought and heat resistance in importance, research on the phenomenon is of considerable moment, especially when there are sincere commitments and diligent efforts to protect and preserve natural ecosystems.

The full range of iron-stress responses in desert plants needs to be evaluated, both from physiological and ecological points of view. The role of rhizosphere organisms need to be considered. The role of stresses on the processes needs consideration. Of special importance is the need for new information on the effects of revegetation onto disturbed lands with supplemental information in relationship with iron-stress responses. Such information could lead to the manipulation of such responses. Also needing elucidation is the role of the fertile-island structure of arid deserts on the behavior of iron-stress responses.

There is an additional aspect of these mechanisms. Other trace elements than iron appear to be simultaneously mobilized. Young and Terry (1984) report that iron and cobalt appear to be taken up by a common mechanism in sugar beet. There is good reason to believe that the uptake of the actinide, Pu, likewise is related to that of iron (Wallace et al. 1978). This is an added dimension to the value of studies in the area.

REFERENCES

Allnutt, F. C. T., and W. D. Bonner, Jr. 1984. Characteristics of iron uptake from hydroxamate siderophores by *Chlorella vulgaris* and the correlation between uptake and reduction. *Journal of Plant Nutrition* 7:427–35.

Barrett-Lennard, E. C., H. Marschner, and V. Romheld. 1983. Mechanism of short term FeIII reduction by roots: Evidence against the role of secreted reductants. *Plant Physiology* 73:893–98.

Bienfait. H. F., J. Duivenvoorden, and W. Verkerke. 1982a. Ferric reduction by roots of chlorotic bean plants: Indications for an enzymatic process. *Journal of Plant Nutrition* 5:451–56.

Bienfait, H. F., A. M. van den Bliek, and R. J. Bino. 1982b. Different regulations on ferric reduction and acidification of the medium by roots of Fe-stressed plants in a 'Rhizostat.' *Journal of Plant Nutrition* 5:447–50.

Bienfait, H. F., A. M. van den Bliek, and N. T. Mesland-Mul. 1984. Measurement of the extracellular mobilizable iron pool in roots. *Journal of Plant Nutrition* 7:659–65.

Brown, J. C. 1977. Genetically controlled chemical factors involved in absorption and transport of iron by plants. *Advances in Chemistry Series* 162:93–103.

Brown, J. C., and J. E. Ambler. 1973. "Reductants" released by roots of Fe-deficient soybeans. *Agronomy Journal* 65:311–24.

Campbell, W. H., and M. G. Redinbaugh. 1984. Ferric-citrate reductase activity of nitrate reductase and its role in iron assimilation by plants. *Journal of Plant Nutrition* 7:799–806.

Chaney, R. L. 1984. Diagnostic practices to identify iron deficiency in higher plants. *Journal of Plant Nutrition* 7:47–67.

Chaney, R. L., and B. A. Coulombe. 1982. Effect of phosphate on regulation of Fe-stress response in soybean and peanut. *Journal of Plant Nutrition* 5:469–87.

Cline, G. R., C. P. P. Reid, P. E. Powell, and P. J. Szaniszlo. 1984. Effects of a hydroxamate siderophore on iron absorption by sunflower and sorghum. *Plant Physiology* 76:36–39.

Coulombe, B. A., R. L. Chaney, and W. J. Wiebold. 1984. Use of bicarbonate in screening soybeans for resistance to iron chlorosis. *Journal of Plant Nutrition* 7:411–25.

Coyne, D. P., S. S. Korban, D. Knudsen, and R. B. Clark. 1982. Inheritance of iron deficiency in crosses of dry beans (*Phaseolus vulgaris* L.). *Journal of Plant Nutrition* 5:575–85.

Fleming, A. L., R. L. Chaney, and B. A. Coulombe. 1984. Bicarbonate inhibits Fe-stress response and Fe uptake-translocation of chlorosis-susceptible soybean cultivars. *Journal of Plant Nutrition* 7:699–714.

Fleming, A. L., and C. D. Foy. 1982. Differential response of barley varieties to Fe stress. *Journal of Plant Nutrition* 5:457–68.

Hershey, D. R., and J. L. Paul. 1984. Iron nutrition of the broadleaf evergreen shrub, *Euonymus japonica* Thumb. Journal Plant Nutrition 7:641–57.

Hether, N. H., R. A. Olsen, and L. L. Jackson. 1984. Chemical identification of iron reductants exuded by plant roots. *Journal of Plant Nutrition* 7:667–76.

James, D. W., J. C. Brown, V. D. Jolley, G. W. Miller, S. D. Nelson, F. Stewart, D. R. Walker, and A. Wallace, eds. 1984. Proceedings of second intern. symposium on iron nutrition and interactions in plants. *Journal of Plant Nutrition* 7:1–864.

Johnson, G. V. 1982. Application of high performance liquid chromatography in the characterization of iron-stress response. *Journal of Plant Nutrition* 5:499–514.

Kannan, S. 1982. Genotypic differences in iron uptake and utilization in some crop cultivars. *Journal of Plant Nutrition* 5:531–42.

Kannan, S., and S. Ramani. 1984. Effects of some chemical treatments on the recovery from chlorosis in Fe deficiency-stressed sorghum cultivars. *Journal of Plant Nutrition* 7:631–39.

Kannan, S., S. Ramani, and A. V. Patankar. 1984. Excretion of dibutyl phthalate by sorghum roots under Fe-stress: Evidence of its action on chlorosis recovery. *Journal of Plant Nutrition* 7:1717–29.

Kohno, Y., C. D. Foy, A. L. Fleming, and D. T. Krizek. 1984. Effect of Mn concentration on the growth and distribution of Mn and Fe in two bush bean cultivars grown in solution culture. *Journal of Plant Nutrition* 7:547–66.

Landsberg, E.-Ch. 1982. Transfer cell formation in the root epidermis: A prerequisite for Fe-efficiency? *Journal of Plant Nutrition* 5:415–32.

————. 1984. Regulation of iron-stress-response by whole-plant activity. *Journal of Plant Nutrition* 7:609–21.

Lindsay, W. L. 1979. *Chemical Equilibria in Soils*. John Wiley & Sons, New York.

————. 1984. Soil and plant relationships associated with iron deficiency with emphasis on nutrient interactions. *Journal of Plant Nutrition* 7:489–500.

McDaniel, M. E., and J. C. Brown. 1982. Differential iron chlorosis of oat cultivars—A review. *Journal of Plant Nutrition* 5:545–52.

Mino, Y., T. Ishida, N. Ota, M. Inoue, K. Nomoto, T. Takemoto, H. Tanaka, and Y. Sugiura. 1983. Mugineic acid-iron(III) complex and its structurally analogous cobalt(III) complex: Characterization and implication for absorption and transport of iron in gramineous plants. *Journal of American Chemical Society* 105:4671–76.

Nelson, S. D., A. Wallace, J. C. Brown, G. W. Miller, W. L. Lindsay, and V. D. Jolley, eds. 1982. Proceedings of 1st Intern. Symposium on iron nutrition and interactions in plants. *Journal of Plant Nutrition* 5 (4–7):229–1001.

Nielands, J. B. 1977. Siderophores: Biochemical ecology and mechanism of iron transport in enterobacteria. *Advances in Chemistry Series* 162:3–32.

Nomoto, K., Y. Yoshioka, M. Arima, S. Fushiya, S. Takagi, and T. Takemoto. 1981. Structure of 2'-deoxymugineic acid, a novel amino acid possessing an iron-chelating activity. *Chimia* 35:249–50.

Olsen, R. A., J. C. Brown, J. H. Bennett, and D. Blume. 1982. Reduction of Fe^{3+} as it relates to Fe chlorosis. *Journal of Plant Nutrition* 5:433–45.

Peters, W. J., and R. A. J. Warren. 1970. The mechanism of iron uptake in *Bacillus subtilus*. *Canadian Journal of Microbiology* 16:1285–91.

Raymond, K. N. 1977. Kinetically inert complexes of the siderophores in studies of microbial iron transport. *Advances in Chemistry Series* 162:33–53.

Reid, C. P. P., D. E. Crowley, H. J. Kim, P. E. Powell, and P. J. Szaniszlo. 1984. Utilization of iron by oat when supplied as ferrated synthetic chelate or as ferrated hydroxamate siderophore. *Journal of Plant Nutrition* 7:437–47.

Rodriguez, R. K., D. J. Klemm, and L. L. Barton. 1984. Iron metabolism by an ectomycorrhiza fungus, *Cenococcum graniforme*. *Journal of Plant Nutrition* 7:459–68.

Romheld, V., and H. Marschner. 1986. Evidence for a specific uptake system for iron phytosiderophores in roots of grasses. *Plant Physiology* 80:175–80.

Romheld, V., H. Marschner, and D. Kramar. 1982. Responses of Fe deficiency in roots of "Fe-efficient" plant species. *Journal of Plant Nutrition* 5:489–98.

Schwab, A. P. 1981. Stability of Fe chelates and the availability of Fe and Mn to plants as affected by redox. Ph. D. Dissertation. Colorado State University, Fort Collins, Colo.

Sijmons, P. C., and H. F. Bienfait. 1984. Mechanism of iron reduction by roots of *Phaseolus vulgaris* L. *Journal of Plant Nutrition* 7:687–93.

Smith, M. J., and J. B. Neilands. 1984. Rhizobactin, a siderophore from *Rhizobium meliloti*. *Journal of Plant Nutrition* 7:449–58.

Takagi, S., K. Nomoto, and T. Takemoto. 1984. Physiological aspect of mugineic acid, a possible phytosiderophore of graminaceous plants. *Journal of Plant Nutrition* 7:469–77.

Takemoto, T., K. Nomoto, S. Fushiya, R. Ouchi, G. Kusano, H. Hikino, S. Takagi, Y. Matuura, and M. Kakudo. 1978. Structure of mugineic acid, a new amino acid possessing an iron-chelating activity from root washings of water-cultured *Hordeum vulgare* L. *Proceedings Japanese Academy Series B* 54:469–73.

Wallace, A. 1966. Growth of bush bean plants in leachates from soil, P. 91. In *Current Topics on Plant Nutrition*. A. Wallace ed. Los Angeles, Calif.

————. 1969. Root excretions of higher plants and possible implications on the iron nutrition of higher plants. *Indian Journal of Horticulture* 26:47–50.

————. 1982. Excretion of riboflavin by iron deficiency plants. 1982. *Journal of Plant Nutrition* 5:543–44.

————. 1983. Root membrane potentials, obligatory need for reduction of Fe+++, excess chelating agents and pe + pH. *Journal of Plant Nutrition* 6:531.

Wallace, A., and collaborators. 1971. Root excretions in tobacco plants and possible implications on the iron nutrition of higher plants. In *Regulation of the Micronutrient Status of Plants by Chelating Agents and Other Factors* pp. 136–39. A. Wallace ed., Los Angeles, Calif.

Wallace, A., E. Frolich, and A. El-Gazzar. 1968. Some effects of iron deficiency on iron uptake and root excretion to tobacco, pp. 385–96. *Intern. atomic energy symposium on isotopes and radiation in soil organic-matter studies*, Vienna, Austria.

Wallace, A., and R. T. Mueller. 1978. Complete neutralization of a portion of calcareous soil as a means of preventing iron chlorosis. *Agronomy Journal* 70:888–90.

Wallace, A., E. M. Romney, and J. Kinnear. 1978. *Soil, plant, food chain relationships of the transuranium elements: Selected annotated bibliography.* UCLA #12–1135 NUREG/CR–0158.

Wallace, A., and G. A. Wallace. 1984. Cation-anion uptake balance and proton efflux in plant efficiency for iron. *Journal of Plant Nutrition* 7:847–52.

Williams, E. P., R. B. Clark, Y. Yusuf, W. M. Ross, and J. W. Maranville. 1982. Variability of sorghum genotypes to tolerate iron deficiency. *Journal of Plant Nutrition* 5:553–67.

Winkelmann, G., and H. Huschka. 1984. A study on the mechanism of siderophore transport: A proton symport. *Journal of Plant Nutrition* 7:479–87.

Uren, N. C. 1982. Chemical reduction at the root surface. *Journal of Plant Nutrition* 5:515–20.

Varanini, Z., and A. Maggioni. 1982. Iron reduction and uptake by grapevine roots. *Journal of Plant Nutrition* 5:521–29.

Young, T. F., and N. Terry. 1984. Specificity of iron transport in iron-stressed sugar beet plants: Evidence for preferential accumulation of cobalt in the presence of iron. *Canadian Journal of Botany* 62:207–10.

FOUR

Photosynthesis and Productivity of Desert Plants

PARK S. NOBEL

INTRODUCTION

Deserts are generally characterized as regions of low plant productivity, usually about 0.1 kg dry weight m^{-2} ground area year^{-1} (Noy-Meir 1973; Leith and Whittaker 1975; 1 kg m^{-2} = 10 Mg ha^{-1} = 10 metric ton ha^{-1}). Indeed, the term "desert" can be defined as regions of such low productivity and thus can include tundra and even oceans. Here, however, deserts will refer to regions where lack of water is the main factor limiting productivity on a yearly basis. Although productivity is low in deserts, instantaneous photosynthetic rates per unit leaf area for certain species of desert plants can be quite high, e.g., the desert annual *Cammissonia claviformis* can have a net photosynthetic CO_2 uptake rate of 55 μmol m^{-2} s^{-1} (Mooney, Ehleringer, and Berry 1976; Longstreth, Hartsock, and Nobel 1980) and the perennial desert bunchgrass *Hilaria rigida* can have a rate of 67 μmol m^{-2} s^{-1} (Nobel 1980a). By comparison, maximum photosynthetic rates of agronomic plants that have been selected and systematically bred are only 20 to 50 μmol m^{-2} s^{-1} (Zelitch 1971; Black 1973; Radmer and Kok 1977; Nobel 1983). The low productivity of deserts is a reflection of a low leaf area index (total leaf area per unit ground area) as well as short periods for maximal photosynthesis, both of which are reflections of the low rainfall of deserts.

Deserts occur in regions that annually receive less than about 250mm precipitation, which represent approximately 30 percent of the earth's land area (Noy-Meir 1973; Walter 1973). Although names and geographical definitions vary somewhat, four deserts are recognized here for North America (Chihuahuan, Great Basin, Mojave, and Sonoran), one in South America (Atacama-Peruvian), two in Africa (Namib-Kalahari and Sahara), seven in Asia (Arabian, Gobi, Iranian, Negev, Takla-Makan, Thar, and Turkestan), and the Australian Desert (McGinnies, Goldman, and Paylore 1977; Smith and Nobel 1986). Plants will be divided into seven groups: (1)

poikilohydric cryptogams (non-seed plants); (2) ephemeral (mainly annual) vascular plants; (3) perennial grasses; (4) deciduous shrubs and trees; (5) succulents; (6) phreatophytes; and (7) evergreen shrubs and trees. These groups are not necessarily mutually exclusive, and hence are presented mainly to help organize the information on photosynthetic rate and productivity. Greater detail on the plant communities and photosynthetic aspects can be found in a recent review by Smith and Nobel (1986). Special attention will here be focused on desert succulents, and a new way of relating their CO_2 uptake abilities to productivity under field conditions will be discussed.

PLANT GROUPS

The seven plant groups will next be described from morphological, physiological, and geographical perspectives. Illustrations of representative species are taken from the author's main research areas in the Mojave and Sonoran Deserts.

Cryptogams

Cryptogams (lichens, mosses, lycopods, and ferns) can be quite abundant in some deserts, particularly coastal deserts in which cover by other plants is low or essentially absent. Such species are generally poikilohydric, the plants tolerating repeated and prolonged dehydration but becoming photosynthetically active upon rehydration. Lichens are the dominant life form in much of the Atacama-Peruvian Desert and the Namib portion of the Namib-Kalahari Desert. Favorable moisture for net CO_2 uptake may occur for only 10 to 20 days per year for lichens in the Sonoran Desert (Nash et al. 1982) but up to 200 days in the Negev Desert (Kappen et al. 1979), leading to the greater relative lichen abundance in the latter desert. Indeed, dewfall can lead to substantial annual productivity for lichens in the Negev Desert (Evenari et al. 1975), while mosses, lycopods, and ferns generally require rainfall.

Ecophysiological characteristics of cryptogams can be quite different from other plants. In many deserts, cryptogams can occur mainly on poleward-facing slopes or shaded microhabitats. For instance, in the Sonoran Desert the fern *Notholaena parryi* (see Figure 4.1) occurs on the sides of rock outcroppings where no direct sunlight reaches it (Nobel 1978). Lichens can show a great heat tolerance, especially when dry. The Negev Desert lichen *Ramalina maciformis* tolerates heating to 65°C when dry, but is more susceptible to heat stress when wet (Lange 1969). The resurrection lycopod *Selaginella lepidophylla* will not recover when rehydrated at temperatures above 45°C (Eickmeier 1979). Many desert cryptogams can exist in a dehydrated state for a year or more, but then resume protein synthesis and other metabolic functions within hours of rehydration. Also, desert crypto-

Figure 4.1 *Notholaena parryi*, a small desert fern that grows in shaded regions under rock overhangs. Site is in the northwestern Sonoran Desert at Agave Hill in the University of California Philip L. Boyd Deep Canyon Desert Research Center (33°38′N, 116°24′W, 850 m elevation) near Palm Desert, California.

gams show a greater conservation of enzyme activity upon desiccation than do closely related mesic species.

Ephemerals

Ephemerals tolerate prolonged dry periods generally as a seed, but also wet season activity can begin from a bud that is often below the soil surface, such as for many perennial forbs. In most deserts they are best represented by annuals that germinate and grow predominantly in the wet season. They often produce very showy and colorful flowers that carpet extensive areas, as can occur for the California poppy, *Eschscholzia californica* (see Figure 4.2). The vegetation of the extremely hot and arid Arabian and Saharan Deserts consists predominantly of ephemerals.

Winter annuals in the deserts of North America are exclusively of the C_3 photosynthetic pathway, while summer annuals germinate after the first heavy rains of summer and usually employ the C_4 pathway (Mulroy and Rundel 1977). In keeping with this, both photosynthesis and growth are optimal for winter annuals near temperatures of 25°C, while optimal temperatures for summer annuals can be above 40°C (Pearcy et al. 1971).

The period for stomatal opening and hence net CO_2 uptake by desert ephemerals is highly dependent on the period of water availability, which is

Figure 4.2   *Eschscholzia californica*, an annual poppy occurring in the
Mojave Desert and many other regions of California.

generally short. They tend to have short leaf durations, which allows desert
ephemerals to avoid water stress. Indeed, some species can complete their
life cycle from germination to the setting of viable seed in less than four
weeks (Mulroy and Rundel 1977). Several desert annuals also track the sun,
some facing the sun and thereby increasing photosynthesis (Mooney and
Ehleringer 1978; Ehleringer 1983) and others avoiding the sun and thereby
lessening water stress (Forseth and Ehleringer 1983). Another interesting
feature of desert ephemerals such as *Mesembryanthemum crystallinum*,
which occurs in arid coastal regions, is that photosynthetic metabolism can
shift from C_3 during the early, wet part of the growing season to the water-
conserving CAM (Crassulacean acid metabolism) during the ensuing dry
periods (Winter and von Willert 1972; Winter et al. 1978).

Perennial Grasses

Perennial grasses are particularly prevalent in deserts with predominantly
summer rainfall, such as the Chihuahuan Desert of North America, the Thar
(Indian) Desert, and the northern parts of the Australian Desert. Grasses in
such regions use mainly the C_4 photosynthetic pathway, while C_3 grasses
predominate in the Mediterranean-climate coastal regions of northern Africa
and Australia as well as in the cool, winter-precipitation Great Basin Desert
of North America. The optimal temperature for photosynthesis is generally

near 20°C for C_3 desert grasses and 35°C for C_4 desert grasses. Temperatures above 40°C can induce summer dormancy in the C_3 Great Basin species, *Agropyron spicatum* (De Puit and Caldwell 1975). On the other hand, the shallow rooted C_4 bunchgrass *Hilaria rigida* (see Figure 4.3) can have an optimal temperature for photosynthesis of 43°C when grown under hot conditions (Nobel 1980a). Hence, C_3 desert grasses tend to be most productive in the cooler winter and spring, while C_4 grasses have maximum activity in the summer and early fall. However, the C_4 *H. rigida* responds to both winter/spring rainfall and late summer rainfall in the Sonoran Desert, and thus it can have a bimodal pattern of productivity (Nobel 1980a).

Perennial grasses become dormant during dry periods, which can begin sooner if there is intense competition for soil water (Robbercht, Mahall, and Nobel 1983). However, desert perennial grasses can obtain water from soil that is too dry (-5 MPa) for most plant groups (Cunningham, Balding, and Syvertsen 1974; Doley and Trivett 1974; Christie 1975; Detling, Parton, and Hunt 1978). Indeed, positive net photosynthesis is maintained by such grasses even in leaves that have a very low water content (leading to leaf water potentials below -5 MPa in some cases), although grasses do not have appreciable internal water storage and productivity can be very low in dry years. In addition to leaves, net CO_2 uptake can also occur in stems and sheaths of grasses, which can be the principal photosynthetic surfaces just prior to dormancy (Caldwell et al. 1981).

Figure 4.3   *Hilaria rigida*, a common perennial bunchgrass of the Sonoran and Mojave Deserts. Same site as Figure 4.1. Note the shallow roots with a mean depth of 9 cm.

Deciduous Shrubs and Trees

Deciduous woody plants tend to be common in deserts that consistently have rainfall in certain seasons. For instance, C_3 winter-deciduous shrubs are secondary dominants in the Chihuahuan Desert with its predictable summer rainfall and C_3 drought-deciduous shrubs are secondary dominants in the Mojave and Sonoran Deserts as well as in the Thar Desert. Drought-deciduous woody plants act like mesic plants during wet seasons and become essentially dormant in dry seasons. They reach their greatest importance in microhabitats where extra seasonal soil moisture is available, such as in washes or where run-on water occurs.

A seasonal leaf polymorphism can occur, e.g., wet-season leaves of *Encelia farinosa* (see Figure 4.4) are fairly large and green while the dry-season leaves are smaller and highly reflective (Smith and Nobel 1978; Ehleringer and Mooney 1978). The decreases in leaf size are mainly a response to the declining water potential, while increases in reflectivity are more a response to irradiance. Increases in pubescence cause the increases in reflectivity for *E. farinosa* (Smith and Nobel 1978; Ehleringer 1982). Although this pubescence reduces the photosynthetically active radiation reaching the mesophyll, the enhanced reflectivity leads to less radiation intercepted and lower leaf temperatures, which can lead to higher photosynthetic rates during the hot, dry periods (Ehleringer and Mooney 1978). For the desert

Figure 4.4   Flowers on *Encelia farinosa*, a small drought-deciduous shrub. Same site as Figure 4.1. Apparatus attached to the barrel cactus, *Ferocactus acanthodes*, was used to measure CO_2 and water vapor exchange.

deciduous shrub *Hyptis emoryi*, leaf area can vary from 0.5cm² for a sun leaf to 40cm² for a shade leaf (Nobel 1976a). The small sun leaves have no advantage in the shade and indeed have a much lower total productivity than shade leaves there, while the large shade leaves overheat in the sun and thus are surpassed in photosynthetic rates by sun leaves for exposed locations of the canopy (Smith and Nobel 1977, 1978). In particular, the small sun leaves have high convective exchange and hence remain close to air temperature, while the large shade leaves can be 5 to 10°C above air temperatures in exposed locations (Smith 1978).

Many drought-deciduous woody plants have green stems that can enhance overall productivity, e.g., *Cercidium microphyllum* (see Figure 4.5). Although for many species green stems appear mainly to be a means of

Figure 4.5   A drought-deciduous tree, *Cercidium microphyllum*, acting as a nurse-plant for *Carnegiea gigantea* in the northern Sonoran Desert just south of Flagstaff, Arizona. From A. G. Gibson and P. S. Nobel, *The Cactus Primer*, Harvard Univ. Press, 1986; used by permission.

avoiding any net CO_2 loss during drought periods, for *Cercidium floridum* the photosynthetic contribution of stems can match that of the leaves (Adams, Strain, and Ting 1967; Adams and Strain 1968). Most drought-deciduous woody plants can maintain net CO_2 uptake to fairly low leaf water potentials (-4 MPa), and the Negev Desert shrub *Artemisia herba-alba* can have a positive net CO_2 uptake for extremely dry leaves (-12 MPa; Kappen et al. 1972)—indeed the driest for any higher plant.

Succulents

Agaves and cacti in the New World and the aloes and euphorbs in the Old World are leaf and stem succulents coping with the low rainfall, high radiation, and often high temperature conditions of deserts. These plants comprise a significant portion of the vegetation only in hot, arid regions, such as the Sonoran Desert, the Atacama-Peruvian Desert of Chile and Peru, and the Namib part of the Namib-Kalahari Desert. The only common succulent of the Negev Desert, *Caralluma negevensis*, occurs in sheltered moist microhabitats and has a net productivity only during the wet winter season (Lange et al. 1975).

The major importance of succulents in the Sonoran Desert is in large measure because of the bimodal annual rainfall and the frost-free winters. Specifically, long dry seasons can inhibit seeding establishment for *Agave deserti* (see Figure 4.6) and *Ferocactus acanthodes* (see Figure 4.4) (Jordan and Nobel 1979, 1981). Also, freezing temperatures limit the northern and high elevation distribution of several species of Sonoran Desert agaves and cacti (Nobel 1980 b,c; Nobel and Smith 1983). Indeed, nurse plants such as *C. microphyllum* (see Figure 4.5) often are critical for protecting cacti from freezing damage caused by cold nighttime skies near the northern part of their ranges (Nobel 1980d).

Desert succulents possess CAM, which generally leads to 5 to 20 times more CO_2 uptake per unit of water lost than for C_3 or C_4 plants. Stomatal opening by CAM plants occurs predominantly at night, when the tissue temperatures are much lower and hence the water vapor concentration drop from tissue to air is less than during the daytime. The lower force on water reduces transpiration and hence conserves water. As another adaptation to arid environments, the water storage of succulents extends the period for stomatal opening and net CO_2 uptake past that when water can be taken up from the soil during drought, e.g., by 8 days for *A. deserti* (Nobel 1976b) and up to 50 days for *F. acanthodes* (Nobel 1977).

The CO_2 taken up at night by CAM plants is incorporated into malate, which progressively increases during the nighttime, leading to acidity increases in the chlorenchyma. During the daytime, the malate is decarboxylated, leading to CO_2 release within the photosynthetic tissue (the stomates are closed during the daytime and hence the CO_2 is not lost from the plant). Many CAM plants, especially leaf succulents, are capable of fixing

Figure 4.6 *Agave deserti*, a common leaf succulent of the Sonoran Desert. Same site as for Figure 4.1. The group illustrated was one of five whose monthly leaf unfolding and seasonal productivity was examined in the field.

some exogenous CO_2 in the light, usually when exposed to more mesic conditions.

The CO_2 uptake at night is related to the total daily photosynthetically active radiation (PAR) received during the daytime. In fact, 90 percent of maximal nocturnal CO_2 uptake occurs at a total daily PAR of about 20 mol of photons m^{-2} plant surface area day^{-1} (Nobel 1980e, 1982a, 1986). This is the average PAR incident on vertical surfaces at various latitudes and seasons for clear days (Nobel 1982b, 1986). Hence, even in the high radiation desert environment, CAM plants are on the verge of being PAR limited, because shading by mountains, other plants, or clouds can reduce nocturnal CO_2 uptake and hence productivity. Since they require high PAR, desert succulents tend to occur in open habitats where competition for light is not too severe. However, successful seedling establishment can require sheltered microhabitats, where a sacrifice in carbon gain because of the reduced PAR is made in exchange for thermal protection.

Desert CAM plants tend to have a low temperature optimum for nocturnal CO_2 uptake, 10 to 15°C (Nobel and Hartsock 1984), although some plants can have a higher temperature optimum, and temperature acclimation can occur. Indeed, the optimal temperature for nine desert CAM plants was 12°C when grown at a nighttime temperature of 10°C, which shifted to 20°C when grown at a high nighttime temperature of 30°C (Nobel and Hartsock 1981). The low temperature optimum for nighttime CO_2 uptake is generally accompanied by a high temperature optimum for daytime internal decarboxylation of organic acids, and so desert productivity by CAM plants tends to be enhanced by marked daily oscillations in temperature.

Another thermal aspect of desert succulents is their tolerance to extreme temperatures. As indicated above, they do not tolerate very low temperatures, but their tolerance of high temperatures is unsurpassed by other vascular plants. Specifically, out of 30 species of agaves and cacti tested (Nobel and Smith 1983; Smith, Didden-Zopfy, and Nobel 1984), nearly all could tolerate one hour at 60°C or higher. Indeed, two species of *Ferocactus* could withstand the extremely high temperature of 69°C, and high temperature damage is relatively rare on desert succulents in the field.

Phreatophytes

Phreatophytic woody plants tap into a permanent water supply and thereby avoid the water stresses characteristic of deserts. *Prosopis glandulosa* (see Figure 4.7), *Tamarix chinensis*, and *Populus fremontii* are common in the deserts of North America, while *Prosopis tamarugo* occurs in the Atacama-Peruvian Desert in regions with extremely little recorded rainfall (Mooney et al. 1980; Felker 1981). Many desert phreatophytes have small, xeromorphic leaves, which causes leaf temperatures to be similar to air temperatures. Leaf water potentials can vary substantially during the daytime, especially during times of high evaporative demand (Nilsen et al. 1983). This

Figure 4.7 *Prosopis glandulosa*, a phreatophyte growing in Death Valley, California, the hottest region in North America.

can greatly reduce stomatal opening and photosynthesis near midday, but the availability of soil water allows phreatophytes to rehydrate relatively rapidly and hence photosynthesis can recover in the late afternoon (Strain 1970). Thus, phreatophytes maintain photosynthetic activity during dry periods and hence have a potentially high productivity in desert regions with an appropriate water table (Felker 1981).

Evergreen Shrubs and Trees

By maintaining green xeromorphic leaves and photosynthetic activity year round, evergreens exhibit extreme tolerance of drought (Mooney 1980). They are often quite common in deserts, e.g., the dominant plant of the Great Basin Desert is the evergreen *Artemisia tridentata*, while the evergreen *Larrea tridentata* (see Figure 4.8) has the greatest biomass in the

Figure 4.8   *Larrea tridentata*, an evergreen shrub that is the dominant plant of the Sonoran Desert and also occurs extensively in the Mojave and Chihuahuan Deserts. Site near East Mesa, California.

other three North American Deserts. (The name *Larrea divaricata* has also been applied to the North American species, which is here recognized as *L. tridentata* in keeping with the current preference.) Another C_3 evergreen, *L. divaricata*, occurs in hot desert regions of South America, while the dominant true evergreen of the Negev Desert is the leafless C_4 evergreen shrub, *Hammada scoparia*. Many desert evergreens are halophytes, meaning they can also tolerate high salinity.

Evergreens can tolerate very low plant water potentials over extended periods and also generally tolerate high tissue temperatures. For instance, *L. tridentata* can maintain net CO_2 uptake down to plant water potentials of -8 MPa (Odening, Strain, and Oechel 1974). Other evergreens tend to control water loss by stomatal closure during the dry season, as occurs for *Artemisia tridentata* (De Puit and Caldwell 1973), *Atriplex hymenelytra* (Scanchez-Diaz and Mooney 1979), *Nerium oleander* (Björkman, Downton, and Mooney 1980), and *Yucca brevifolia* (Smith, Hartsock, and Nobel 1983). The latter species, which is a C_3 tree characteristic of the Mojave Desert, had a fairly uniform distribution of PAR over both sides of the opaque leaves that occur in rosettes born at the apices of trunks or branches. It also showed temperature acclimation so that leaf temperatures through the midday period were near the optimum for net CO_2 uptake in all but the hottest months of the year (Smith, Hartsock, and Nobel 1983). Most desert evergreens actually have near-vertical leaves and so are not PAR-saturated during the midday period.

Evergreens from cool regions such as the Great Basin Desert have broad temperature response curves with optimal temperatures for net CO_2 uptake near 20°C (De Puit and Caldwell 1973), while evergreens from warm regions such as the Australian Desert can have optimal temperatures over 35°C (Hellmuth 1971). Although most evergreens are C_3, many of the C_4 evergreens are photosynthetically active at relatively low temperatures (Caldwell, Osmond and Nott 1977), while *L. tridentata* and other C_3 evergreens can perform well at relatively high leaf temperatures (Mooney, Björkman, and Collatz 1978). The small leaves of most desert evergreens ensure that leaf temperatures remain close to air temperatures. Even though evergreens are highly tolerant of water stress, productivity is substantially reduced during the dry season. However, by maintaining some photosynthetic activity year round, they are able to take advantage of small precipitation events during dry periods.

MAXIMAL PHOTOSYNTHETIC RATES

Now that the various plant groups occurring in deserts have been introduced, the maximal photosynthetic rates occurring under moist conditions, optimal temperatures, and saturating PAR will be presented for each group. This will serve as a prelude for discussion of community productivity considered in the next section and the environmental productivity index in the last section.

Table 4.1 summarizes the maximal photosynthetic rates (photosynthetic capacities) for the various plant groups. Data represent field values under optimal conditions supplemented with data obtained in laboratory studies. The lowest values occur for cryptogams. For lichens this reflects the fact that the photosynthetically active algal component is only 5 to 10 percent of the thallus by weight (Bewley and Krochko 1982), and for mosses and lycopods it reflects the thin leaves, which are often only one or two cells thick in mosses and somewhat thicker in lycopods like *Selaginella*. Ferns have stomates (as do lycopods) and a more typical leaf thickness, leading to their higher photosynthetic rates among the cryptogams (see Table 4.1).

In contrast to cryptogams, the highest photosynthetic rates occur for desert ephemerals, where the typical maximal rates of about 35 to 70 μmol m^{-2} s^{-1} (see Table 4.1) surpass those of nearly all cultivated plants (Zelitch 1971; Black 1973; Radmer and Kok 1977; Nobel 1983). One reason is that a very large fraction of the leaf surface area is occupied by stomatal pores, leading to a high stomatal conductance (Körner, Scheel, and Bauer 1979;

Table 4.1 Summary of Maximal Photosynthetic Rates per Unit Leaf Area for Desert Plants

Plant group	Typical range of maximal photosynthetic rates (μmol CO_2 m^{-2} s^{-1})	Comment
Cryptogams lichens, mosses, lycopods	~1	photosynthesis usually expressed per unit mass; very little information is available
ferns	5–8	data are for *Notholaena parryi*
Ephemerals	35–70	most studies are on Mojave and Sonoran Desert annuals; *Amaranthus palmeri*, which can occur in deserts, can reach 81 μmol m^{-2} s^{-1}
Perennial grasses	30–40	*Hilaria rigida* can reach 67 μmol m^{-2} s^{-1}
Deciduous shrubs and trees	10–40	*Encelia farinosa* can reach 44 μmol m^{-2} s^{-1}
Succulents	5–11	data refer to maximal nocturnal CO_2 uptake rates
Phreatophytes	8–20	
Evergreen shrubs and trees	5–20	*Larrea tridentata* can reach 27 μmol m^{-2} s^{-1}

Source: Smith and Nobel (1985), which should be consulted for more details, including original references.

Longstreth, Hartsock, and Nobel 1980; Nobel 1983). Also, desert annuals have high amounts of ribulose-1,5-bisphosphate carboxylase and other photosynthetic enzymes per unit leaf area (Mooney et al. 1981; Werk et al. 1983). Many desert annuals, especially C_4's, do not PAR saturate even at full sunlight (a PAR of 2000 μmol photons $m^{-2} s^{-1}$). Desert perennial grasses have moderately high photosynthetic capacities (see Table 4.1); most are C_4 and do not PAR saturate at full sunlight.

Maximal photosynthetic capacities for deciduous woody plants vary considerably, from less than 10 μmol $m^{-2} s^{-1}$ for *Artemisia herba-alba* and *Zygophyllum dumosum* of the Negev Desert (Kappen et al. 1972; Schulze et al. 1973) to over 30 μmol $m^{-2} s^{-1}$ for *Ambrosia dumosa*, *Lycium* spp., and *Encelia farinosa* of the Mojave and Sonoran Deserts (Cunningham and Strain 1969; Bamberg et al. 1975; Ehleringer and Björkman 1978). For *E. farinosa*, the hot season increase in reflectivity caused by increases in pubescence leads to less PAR reaching the chlorenchyma and hence lower photosynthetic rates for optimal water and temperature conditions at full sunlight (Ehleringer and Mooney 1978). Desert succulents have relatively low CO_2 uptake capacities, which here refers to nocturnal CO_2 uptake for these CAM plants (see Table 4.1). Part of the lower rate reflects the approximately 10-fold lower stomatal frequencies than for C_3 and C_4 plants, which leads to low maximal stomatal conductances for desert succulents (Osmond, Winter, and Ziegler 1982). Maximal CO_2 uptake rates of 11 μmol $m^{-2} s^{-1}$ occur for both *Agave americana* (Nobel and Hartsock 1981) and *Opuntia ficus-indica* (Nobel and Hartsock 1984). Most phreatophytes have only moderate maximal rates of photosynthesis (see Table 4.1), but because of year round access to water they can have substantial annual productivity. Evergreens also have the possibility for year round CO_2 uptake, but they have relatively low photosynthetic capacities, surpassing only ferns and succulents among desert vascular plants. *Larrea tridentata* can have a substantial CO_2 uptake rate of 27 μmol $m^{-2} s^{-1}$ (Mooney, Björkman, and Collatz 1978), which may account for its great success in the hot deserts of North America.

ANNUAL PRODUCTIVITY

The various plant groups will next be compared with respect to annual dry weight produced per unit ground area per year. Such measurements are time-consuming and have not been made for many species. Also, expressing data per unit ground area is much more difficult than per unit leaf area or even per plant. In particular, it is often ambiguous which ground area should be considered for a particular plant, unless the plants of a particular species occur in extensive monospecific stands or the roots have been carefully excavated.

Although very few measurements have been made for cryptogams, their annual productivity is apparently low. For two lichens from the Negev

Desert, productivity reached only 0.01kg m^{-2} y^{-1} (see Table 4.2). For ephemerals, the entire annual productivity occurs within a short growing season. Nevertheless, ephemerals can have a substantial productivity, e.g., *Amaranthus palmeri* produced a total dry weight of 0.5kg m^{-2} in only a four-week growing season (Ehleringer 1983). Just as photosynthetic rates vary, productivities of deciduous shrubs vary, but can reach 0.2kg m^{-2} y^{-1} (Table 4.2). Perennial grasses can have large monospecific stands and hence have been studied more than most other groups; their productivities can also be 0.2kg m^{-2} y^{-1} (see Table 4.2).

Although succulents are often reputed to be slow-growing, they actually can have substantial annual productivities. Indeed, *Agave deserti* produced 0.7kg m^{-2} y^{-1} above-ground dry weight and *Opuntia ficus-indica* produced 0.3kg m^{-2} y^{-1} (see Table 4.2). However, with three irrigations per year, *O.*

Table 4.2   Annual Productivities of Various Desert Plants

Group and species	Desert	Annual rainfall (mm)	Annual productivity (kg m^{-2}y^{-1})	Reference
Cryptogams				
Diploschistes calcareus, Ramalina maciformis	Negev	50–80	0.01	Kappen et al. 1975
Ephemerals				
Amaranthus palmeri	Sonoran	~300	0.49	Ehleringer 1983
mixed	Negev	163	0.27	Evenari et al. 1976
Deciduous shrubs and trees				
Artemisia herba-alba	Sahara	300	0.18	Rodin, Bazilevich, and Miroshnichenko 1972
A. namanganica	Turkestan	~90	0.17	Litvinova 1972
Halocnemum strobilaceum	Arabian	~150	0.13	Bazilevich, Rodin, and Gorina 1972
Perennial grasses				
Bouteloua eriopoda	Chihuahuan	310	0.19	Sims, Singh, and Lauenroth 1978
Hilaria rigida	Sonoran	360	0.23	Robberecht, Mahall, and Nobel 1983
mixed	Great Basin	270	0.12	Pearson 1965
Succulents				
Agave deserti	Sonoran	450	0.71	Nobel 1984a
Opuntia ficus-indica	Argentina	300	0.27	Braun, Cordero, and Ramacciotti 1979
Phreatophytes				
Prosopis glandulosa	Sonoran	70	0.8–1.3	Sharifi, Nilsen and Rundel 1982
P. tamarugo	Atacama	1	0.60	Salinas and Sanchez 1971
Evergreen shrubs and trees				
Larrea tridentata	Chihuahuan	310	0.25	Szarek 1979

Note: Data represent total above-ground dry weight produced per unit ground area in essentially monospecific stands.

ficus-indica in central Chile produced $1.3kg\ m^{-2}\ y^{-1}$ (Acevedo, Badilla, and Nobel 1983), which is in the range for many crop plants. The substantial productivities of CAM succulents in arid regions with relatively little water loss indicates that future economic exploitation is feasible in such regions. Phreatophytes such as *Prosopis glandulosa* and *P. tamarugo* can have year round photosynthetic activity and hence fairly high productivities, ranging from 0.6 to $1.3kg\ m^{-2}\ y^{-1}$ (Table 4.2). The evergreen *Larrea tridentata* has a modest productivity of almost $0.3\ kg\ m^{-2}\ y^{-1}$.

ENVIRONMENTAL PRODUCTIVITY INDEX

Since annual productivity is time-consuming to measure in the field and has rarely been predicted for field conditions, a new approach for examining the physical factors that influence productivity was devised and tested for the common succulent of the Sonoran Desert, *Agave deserti* (Nobel 1984). Since *A. deserti* (see Figure 4.6) has been studied in detail over the past ten years, its responses to water status, temperature, and PAR are basically known (Nobel 1976b; Nobel and Hartsock 1978, 1981; Jordan and Nobel 1979; Woodhouse, Williams, and Nobel 1980, 1983). Monthly field values were thus obtained for these three physical parameters over the course of a year. Using the effects of these three parameters on net CO_2 uptake determined individually in the laboratory, productivity could thus be estimated for the field. Specifically, a value could be assigned to indices for water status, temperature, and PAR; a value of 1.00 indicated that the particular environmental factor was not limiting net CO_2 uptake over a 24-hour period. The monthly unfolding of new leaves from the central spike of the basal rosette of *A. deserti* allowed accurate determination of productivity in the field without destructive harvesting of the plants (Nobel 1984a).

Gas Exchange Pattern of Agave deserti

As is typical of CAM plants, net CO_2 uptake by *A. deserti* occurred primarily at night (see Figure 4.9). At dusk, net CO_2 uptake increased rapidly as the stomates opened. The gradual decrease in CO_2 uptake beginning near midnight was accompanied by some stomatal closure and the buildup of considerable acidity in the green tissues of the leaf. At dawn the stomates re-opened slightly and the net CO_2 uptake increased (see Figure 4.9), presumably representing a short spurt of net C_3 photosynthesis (Nobel 1976b). After a couple of hours in the light, the stomates closed almost entirely and a net CO_2 loss occurred from the plant (see Figure 4.9). This CO_2 loss reflected the high concentration of CO_2 within the chlorenchyma as the malate stored during the previous night was decarboxylated. Integration of the net CO_2 uptake over the entire 24-hour period represented in Figure 4.9 indicates a net gain of 206 mmol $CO_2 m^{-2}$ day^{-1} under the conditions employed.

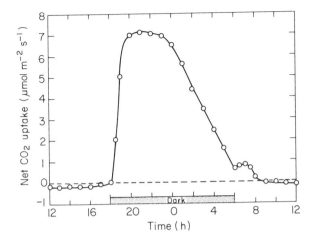

Figure 4.9   Net CO_2 uptake by *Agave deserti* over a 24-hour period. Plants were well-watered, day/night air temperatures were 25°C/15°C, and the total daily PAR was 16 mol m^{-2} day^{-1} (Nobel 1984).

Water Status Index

The influence of precipitation on soil water potential at a field site for *A. deserti* in the northwestern Sonoran Desert has been monitored since 1975 (Nobel 1977; Nobel 1985). Thus, periods can be identified when soil water is available to *A. deserti*, which has shallow roots with an average depth of only 8cm (Nobel 1976b). To determine the water status index based on laboratory responses of *A. deserti* to drought (soil water potential less than −0.4 MPa in the root zone), the following criteria were used: (1) for wet conditions, water status index = 1.00; (2) for drought periods (soil water potential below −0.4 MPa) up to 9 days, water status index = 0.68 (average of fraction of maximal net CO_2 uptake for well-watered plants and plants droughted for 9 days); (3) for drought periods of 9 to 33 days, water status index = 0.18; and (4) for drought periods greater than 33 days, water status index = 0.00 (no net CO_2 uptake was observed for *A. deserti* droughted for 33 days; Nobel 1984).

Based on the rainfall patterns in 1983 and 1984 (see Figure 4.10A), two periods of higher water status index occurred (see Figure 4.10B). The large wet period in the late summer, when the water status index reached essentially unity, was preceded and followed by droughts, when it was essentially zero. The unusually wet period in August helped lead to a high soil water potential well into the fall and was accompanied by considerable plant growth. The winter of 1983 was typically wet, causing a high water status index well into the spring, while the winter of 1984 was uncharacteristically dry (see Figure 4.10).

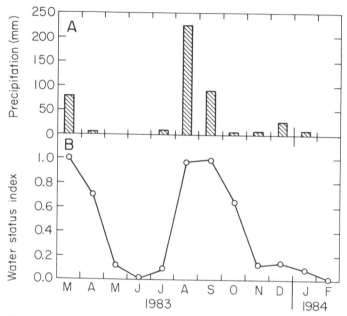

Figure 4.10   Monthly precipitation (A) and water status index (B) for *A. deserti*. Same site as for Figure 4.1.

Temperature Index

Nighttime temperature has a greater influence on net CO_2 uptake by CAM plants than does daytime temperature (Nobel and Hartsock 1978). Since the average nighttime leaf temperatures of *A. deserti* closely ($\pm$ 1°C) matched the minimum nighttime air temperatures measured at the meteorological station, the temperature index was based on average monthly minimum nighttime air temperatures (see Figure 4.11A). Using these monthly temperatures, the effect of temperature on net CO_2 uptake could be determined. In particular, the response of the total daily net CO_2 uptake by *A. deserti* (see Figure 4.9) to day/night temperatures was determined in the laboratory (Nobel 1984). Temperature turns out to be only a secondary influence on net CO_2 uptake by *A. deserti*, as the temperature index varied only from 0.67 to 0.98 (see Figure 4.11B).

PAR Index

The effect of PAR on net CO_2 uptake by *A. deserti* must include the effects of the orientations of both surfaces of all leaves, shading from leaves on the same plant and other plants, blockage of sunlight by topographical features, and cloudiness. For the field site, attenuation of PAR by clouds was based on attenuation of shortwave radiation at a nearby site (see Figure 4.12A). The total daily PAR averaged over the leaf surfaces of *A. deserti* on clear days was

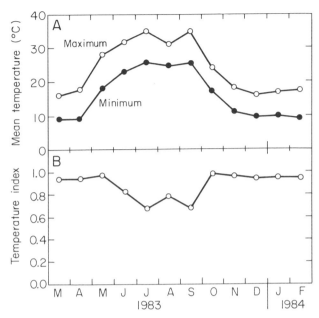

Figure 4.11   Monthly average daily temperatures (A) and temperature index (B)
for *A. deserti*. Same site as for Figure 4.1.

measured as 9.6 mol m^{-2} on 19 January and 20.6 mol m^{-2} on 22 August,
which was validated by a simulation model taking into consideration the
geometrical and environmental factors for this species (Woodhouse, Williams, and Nobel 1980). The plants considered in the field had no shading by
other plants, similar to the *A. deserti* for which the PAR model was
validated, and so the model could be used to extrapolate to other times of the
year. Hence, seasonal variations in cloudiness as well as the sun's trajectory
(see Figure 4.12A) were used to predict the PAR on the leaf surfaces, which
then determined the PAR index (see Figure 4.12B) based on the effects of
total daily PAR on total daily net CO_2 uptake (Nobel 1984). The PAR index
varied from 0.53 in January to 0.90 in June (see Figure 4.12B), indicating the
importance of the seasonal changes in the sun's trajectory.

Environmental Productivity Index

The product of the monthly indices for water status (Fig. 4.10B), temperature (Fig. 4.11B), and PAR (Fig. 4.12B) was assumed to represent the
influence of these three physical factors on net CO_2 uptake by *A. deserti*.
This product, the environmental productivity index (see Figure 4.13A),
indicates the fraction of maximum CO_2 uptake expected each month.
Although this approach assumes limitations by each factor to be multiplica-
tive and hence does not include interactions between them, it still allows an

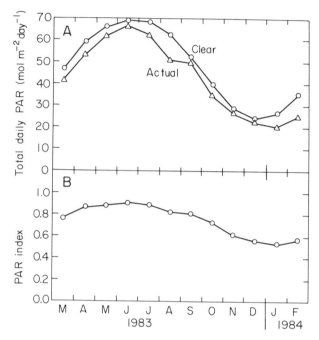

Figure 4.12 Monthly averages of total daily PAR on a horizontal surface (A) simulated for clear days (Clear) and actual values based on measured attenuation of shortwave irradiation (Actual) and PAR index (B) at the field site for *A. deserti*. Clear values were based on simulations (Nobel 1980e; Geller and Nobel 1984). Same site as for Figure 4.1.

assessment of which months might be more favorable for productivity and which environmental factors have the major influence on such productivity. The environmental productivity index exceeded 0.5 in March–April and August–September 1983 (see Figure 4.13A), periods when the water status index was quite favorable (≥ 0.7).

The monthly unfolding of new leaves (see Figure 4.13B) was well correlated with monthly values of the environmental productivity index (see Figure 4.13A). Indeed a maximum of 50 and 51 leaves unfolded on the 50 field plants in March and August, respectively, months that had the highest values of the environmental productivity index. For the one-year study period, 93 percent of the variation in monthly leaf production could be accounted for by monthly variations in the environmental productivity index (see Figure 4.13).

The average of the environmental productivity index for *A. deserti* for the relatively wet period from 9 June to 30 October was 0.36. Since the maximum net CO_2 uptake over a 24-hour period for *A. deserti* under optimal conditions is 285mmol m^{-2}, net CO_2 uptake over the 143-day wet period would be 14.7 mol m^{-2} leaf area [(0.36) (285 × 10^{-3} mol m^{-2} day^{-1}) (143

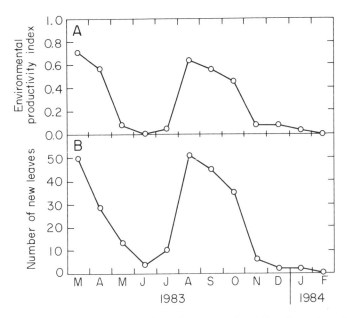

Figure 4.13   Monthly environmental productivity index (A) and number of leaves newly unfolding for 50 plants of *A. deserti* (B). The plants were examined at the end of each month at the same site as for Figure 4.1.

days)]. Ten plants of *A. deserti* were monitored in each of five groups in the field (Nobel 1984). For these groups, the average leaf area index was 1.77 (leaf area of these thick opaque leaves here refers to total leaf area of both sides and ground area refers to that explored by the roots for each group of plants). Hence, the net CO_2 uptake per unit ground area was 26 mol m^{-2} for the June to October period. If all this CO_2 represented carbohydrate, gross productivity would be 0.78kg m^{-2}; of this, 23 percent was consumed by respiration in the roots, stem, and folded leaves and 7 percent went to root growth (Nobel 1984). Hence, the net predicted increase in aboveground dry weight would be 0.55kg m^{-2} over the 143-day wet period. Based on regressions of leaf size on dry weight, the measured fraction of the plants represented by leaves, roots, stems, folded leaves, and dead leaves, and leaf morphology at the beginning and end of the wet period (Nobel 1984), the change in aboveground dry weight was calculated to be 0.53 kg m^{-2}. This excellent agreement (within 4 percent) between productivity measured from conventional dry weight analysis and that predicted from physiological responses lends credibility to use of an environmental productivity index to estimate plant growth in the field for *A. deserti* and other CAM plants. Appropriate modification of the approach should prove useful for analyzing the effect of physical factors on the monthly productivity of other types of plants, especially for regions with highly variable environments such as deserts.

ACKNOWLEDGMENTS

The author gratefully thanks Deborah O. Raphael for assistance in preparing Table 4.2. Financial support was provided by U.S. Department of Energy contract DE-AM03-76-SF00012.

REFERENCES

Acevedo, E., I. Badilla, and P. S. Nobel. 1983. Water relations, diurnal acidity changes, and productivity of a cultivated cactus, *Opuntia ficus-indica*. *Plant Physiology* 72: 775–80.

Adams, M. S., and B. R. Strain. 1968. Photosynthesis in stems and leaves of *Cercidium floridum:* Spring and summer diurnal response and relation to temperature. *Oecologia Planatarum* 3: 285–97

Adams, M. S., B. R. Strain, and I. P. Ting. 1967. Photosynthesis in chlorophyllous stem tissue and leaves of *Cercidium floridum:* Accumulation and distribution of ^{14}C from $^{14}CO_2$. *Plant Physiology* 42: 1797–99.

Bamberg, S. A., G. E. Kleinkopf, A. Wallace, and A. Vollmer. 1975. Comparative photosynthetic production of Mojave desert shrubs. *Ecology* 56: 732–36.

Bazilevich, N. I., L. E. Rodin, and A. I. Gorina. 1972. Productivity and biogeochemistry of succulent communities on solonchaks. In *Eco-Physiological Foundation of Ecosystems Productivity in Arid Zone, International Symposium USSR,* Ed. L. E. Rodin. Nauka, Leningrad. Pp. 203–7.

Bewley, J. P., and J. E. Krochko. 1982. Desiccation-tolerance. In *Encyclopedia of Plant Physiology.* N. S., Vol. 12B, Ed. O. L. Lange, P. S. Nobel, C. B. Osmond, and H. Ziegler. Springer-Verlag, Berlin. Pp. 325–78.

Björkman, O., W. J. S. Downton, and H. A. Mooney. 1980. Response and adaptation to water stress in *Nerium oleander. Carnegie Institution of Washington Year Book* 79: 150–57.

Black, C. C. 1973. Photosynthetic carbon fixation in relation to net CO_2 uptake. *Annual Review of Plant Physiology* 24: 253–86.

Braun, W. R. H., A. Cordero, and J. Ramacciotti. 1979. Productividad ecológica y valor forrajero de tunales *(Opuntia ficus-indica)* de los Llanos, provincia de la Rioja. *Cuaderno Técnico. IADIZA.* 1–79; 29–37.

Caldwell, M. M., C. B. Osmond, and D. L. Nott. 1977. C_4 pathway photosynthesis at low temperature in cold-tolerant Atriplex species. *Plant Physiology* 60: 157–64.

Caldwell, M. M., J. H. Richards, D. A. Johnson, R. S. Nowak, and R. S. Dzurec. 1981. Coping with herbivory: Photosynthetic capacity and resource allocation in two semiarid Agropyron bunchgrasses. *Oecologia* 50: 14–24.

Christie, E. K. 1975. Physiological responses of semiarid grasses. III Growth in relation to temperature and soil water deficit. *Australian Journal of Agricultural Research* 26: 447–58.

Cunningham, G. L., F. R. Balding, and J. P. Syvertsen. 1974. A net CO_2 exchange model for C_4-grasses. *Photosynthetica* 8: 28–33.

Cunningham, G.L., and B.R. Strain. 1969. An ecological significance of seasonal leaf variability in a desert shrub. *Ecology* 50: 400–408.

De Puit, E. J., and M. M. Caldwell. 1973. Seasonal pattern of net photosynthesis of *Artemisia tridentata*. *American Journal of Botany* 60: 426–35.

———. 1975. Gas exchange of three cool semi-desert species in relation to temperature and water stress. *Journal of Ecology* 63: 835–58.

Detling, J. K., W. J. Parton, and H. W. Hunt. 1978. An empirical model for estimating CO_2 exchange of *Bouteloua gracilis* (H.B.K.) Lag. in the shortgrass prairie. *Oecologia* 33: 137–47.

Doley, D., and N. B. A. Trivett. 1974. Effects of low water potentials on transpiration and photosynthesis in Mitchell grass *(Astrebla lappacea)*. *Australian Journal of Plant Physiology* 1: 539–50.

Ehleringer, J. 1982. The influence of water stress and temperature on leaf pubescence development in *Encelia farinosa*. *American Journal of Botany* 69: 670–75.

———. 1983. Ecophysiology of *Amaranthus palmeri*, a Sonoran Desert summer annual. *Oecologia* 57: 107–12.

Ehleringer, J. R., and O. Björkman. 1978. A comparison of photosynthetic characteristics of Encelia species possessing glabrous and pubescent leaves. *Plant Physiology* 62: 185–90.

Ehleringer, J. R., and H. A. Mooney. 1978. Leaf hairs: Effects on physiological activity and adaptive value to a desert shrub. *Oecologia* 37: 183–200.

Eickmeier, W. G. 1979. Photosynthetic recovery in the resurrection plant *Selaginella lepidophylla* after wetting. *Oecologia* 39: 93–106.

Evenari, M., E.-D. Schulze, L. Kappen, U. Buschbom, and O. L. Lange. 1975. Adaptive mechanisms in desert plants. In *Physiological Adaptation to the Environment*. Ed. F.J. Vernberg, Intext Educational New York. Pp. 111–27.

Evenari, M., E.-D. Schulze, O. L. Lange, L. Kappen, and U. Buschbom. 1976. Plant production in arid and semi-arid areas. In *Water and Plant Life: Problems and Modern Approaches*. Eds. O. L. Lange, L. Kappen, E.-D Schulze. Springer-Verlag, Berlin. Pp. 439–51.

Felker, P. 1981. Use of tree legumes in semiarid regions. *Economic Botany* 35: 174–86.

Forseth, I. N., and J.R. Ehleringer. 1983. Ecophysiology of two solar tracking desert winter annuals III. Gas exchange responses to light, CO_2 and VPD in relation to long-term drought. *Oecologia* 57: 344–51.

Geller, G. N., and P. S. Nobel. 1984. Cactus ribs: Influences on PAR interception and CO_2 uptake. *Photosynthetica*. 18: 482–94.

Hellmuth, E. O. 1971. Ecophysiological studies on plants in arid and semi-arid regions in Western Australia. 4. Comparison of field physiology of host *Acacia grasbyl* and its hemiparasite *Amyema nestor* under optimal and stress conditions. *Journal of Ecology*. 59: 225–59.

Jordan, P. W., and P. S. Nobel. 1979. Infrequent establishment of seedlings of *Agave deserti* (Agavaceae) in the northwestern Sonoran Desert. *American Journal of Botany*. 66: 1079–84.

———. 1981. Seedling establishment of *Ferocactus acanthodes* in relation to drought. *Ecology* 62: 901–6.

Kappen, L., O. L. Lange, E.-D. Schulze, M. Evenari, and U. Buschbom. 1972. Extreme water stress and photosynthetic activity of the desert plant *Artemisia herba-alba* Asso. *Oecologia* 10: 177–82.

———. 1975. Primary production of lower plants (lichens) in the desert and its physiological basis. In *Photosynthesis and Productivity in Different Environments*. Ed. J. P. Cooper, Cambridge University Press. Cambridge. Pp. 133–43.

———. 1979. Ecophysiological investigations on lichens of the Negev Desert. VI. Annual course of the photosynthetic production of *Ramalina maciformis* (DEL.) BORY. *Flora* 168: 85–108.

Körner, C.H., J.A. Scheel, and H. Bauer. 1979. Maximum leaf diffusive conductance in vascular plants. *Photosynthetica* 13: 45–82.

Lange, O. L. 1969. Experimentell-ökologische Untersuchungen an Flechten der Negev-Wüste. I. CO_2-Gaswechsel von *Ramalina maciformis* (DEL). BORY unter kontrollierten Bedingungen im Laboratorium. *Flora* 158: 324–59.

Lange, O. L., E.-D. Schulze, L. Kappen, M. Evenari, and U. Buschbom. 1975. CO_2 exchange pattern under natural conditions of *Caralluma negevensis*, a CAM plant of the Negev desert. *Photosynthetica* 9: 318–26.

Leith, H., and R. H. Whittaker. (Eds.) 1975. Primary productivity in the biosphere. In *Ecological Studies*, vol. 14. Springer-Verlag, New York.

Litvinova, W. P. 1972. Productivity of high mountain deserts. In *Eco-Physiological Foundation of Ecosystems Productivity in Arid Zone, International Symposium USSR*. Ed. L.E. Roden. Nauka, Leningrad. Pp. 143–48.

Longstreth, D. J., T. L. Hartsock, and P. S. Nobel. 1980. Mesophyll cell properties for some C_3 and C_4 species with high photosynthetic rates. *Physiologia Plantarum* 48: 494–98.

McGinnies, W. G., B. J. Goldman, and P. Paylore. 1977. *Deserts of the World: An Appraisal of Research into their Physical and Biological Environments*. University of Arizona Press, Tucson.

Mooney, H. A. 1980. Seasonality and gradients in the study of stress adaptation. In *Adaptation of Plants to Water and High Temperature Stress*, Ed. N. C. Turner and P. J. Kramer. John Wiley & Sons, New York. Pp. 279–94.

Mooney, H. A., O. Björkman, and G. J. Collatz. 1978. Photosynthetic acclimation to temperature in the desert shrub, *Larrea divaricata*. I. Carbon dioxide exchange characteristics of intact leaves. *Plant Physiology* 61: 406–10.

Mooney, H. A., and J. R. Ehleringer. 1978. The carbon gain benefits of solar tracking in a desert annual. *Plant, Cell and Environment* 1: 307–11.

Mooney, H. A., J. Ehleringer, and J. A. Berry. 1976. High photosynthetic capacity of a winter annual in Death Valley. *Science* 194: 322–24.

Mooney, H. A., C. Field, S. L. Gulmon, and F. A. Bazzaz. 1981. Photosynthetic capacity in relation to leaf position in desert versus old-field annuals. *Oecologia* 50: 109–12.

Mooney, H. A., S. L. Gulmon, P. W. Rundel, and J. Ehleringer. 1980. Further observations on the water relations of *Prosopis tamarugo* of the northern Atacama desert. *Oecologia* 44: 177–80.

Mulroy, T. W. and P. W. Rundel. 1977. Annual plants: Adaptations to desert environments. *BioScience* 27: 109–14.

Nash, T. H., III, T. J. Moser, C. C. Bertke, S. O. Link, L. L. Sigal, S. L. White, and C. A. Fox. 1982, Photosynthetic patterns of Sonoran desert lichens. I. Environmental considerations and preliminary field measurements. *Flora* 172: 335–45.

Nilsen, E. T., M. R. Sharifi, P. W. Rundel, W. M. Jarrell, and R. A. Virginia. 1983. Diurnal and seasonal water relations of the desert phreatophyte *Prosopis glandulosa* (honey mesquite) in the Sonoran Desert of California. *Ecology* 64: 1381–93.

Nobel, P. S. 1976a. Photosynthetic rates of sun *versus* shade leaves of *Hyptis emoryi* Torr. *Plant Physiology* 58: 218–23.

————. 1976b. Water relations and photosynthesis of a desert CAM Plant, *Agave deserti*. *Plant Physiology* 58: 576–82.

————. 1977. Water relations and photosynthesis of a barrel cactus, *Ferocactus acanthodes*, in the Colorado Desert. *Oecologia* 27: 117–33.

————. 1978. Microhabitat, water relations, and photosynthesis of a desert fern, *Notholaena parryi*. *Oecologia* 31: 293–309.

————. 1980a. Water vapor conductance and CO_2 uptake for leaves of a C_4 desert grass, *Hilaria rigida*. *Ecology* 61: 252–58.

————. 1980b. Morphology, surface temperatures, and northern limits of columnar cacti in the Sonoran Desert. *Ecology* 61: 1–7.

————. 1980c. Influences of minimum stem temperatures on ranges of cacti in southwestern United States and central Chile. *Oecologia* 47: 10–15.

————. 1980d. Morphology, nurse plants, and minimum apical temperatures for young *Carnegiea gigantea*. *Botanical Gazette* 141: 188–91.

————. 1980e. Interception of photosynthetically active radiation by cacti of different morphology. *Oecologia* 45: 160–66.

————. 1982a. Interaction between morphology, PAR Interception, and nocturnal acid accumulation in cacti. In *Crassulacean Acid Metabolism*, Ed. I. P. Ting and M. Gibbs. American Society of Plant Physiologists, Baltimore, MD. Pp. 260–277.

————. 1982b. Orientation, PAR interception, and nocturnal acidity increases for terminal cladodes of a widely cultivated cactus, *Opuntia ficus-indica*. *American Journal of Botany* 69: 1462–69.

————. 1983. *Biophysical Plant Physiology and Ecology*. W. H. Freeman. San Francisco.

————. 1984. Productivity of *Agave deserti*: Measurement by dry weight and monthly prediction using physiological responses to environmental parameters. *Oecologia*. 64: 1–7.

————. 1985. Environmental responses of agaves—A case study with *Agave deserti*. In *Biologia y Aprovechamiento Integral del Henequen y otros Agaves*, Ed. C. Cruz, L. del Castillo, M. Robert, and R. N. Ondarza. CONACYT Y CICY, Mexico. Pp. 55–66.

————. 1986. Form and orientation in relation to PAR interception by cacti and agaves. In *On the Economy of Plant Form and Function*. 1983 Cabot Symposium, Ed. T. J. Givnish. Cambridge University Press, Cambridge, Pp. 83–103.

Nobel, P. S., and T. L. Hartsock. 1978. Resistance analysis of nocturnal carbon dioxide uptake by a Crassulacean acid metabolism succulent, *Agave deserti*. *Plant Physiology* 61: 510–14.

Nobel, P. S., and T. L. Hartsock. 1981. Shifts in the optimal temperature for nocturnal CO_2 uptake caused by changes in growth temperature for cacti and agaves. *Physiologia Plantarum* 53: 523–27.

————. 1984. Physiological responses of *Opuntia ficus-indica* to growth temperature. *Physiologia Plantarum* 60: 98–105.

Nobel, P. S., and S. D. Smith. 1983. High and low temperature tolerances and their relationships to distribution of agaves. *Plant, Cell and Environment* 6: 711–19.

Noy-Meir, I. 1973. Desert ecosystems: Environment and producers. *Annual Review Ecology and Systematics* 4: 25–51.

Odening, W. R., B. R. Strain, and W. C. Oechel, 1974. The effect of decreasing water potential on net CO_2 exchange of intact desert shrubs. *Ecology* 55: 1086–95.

Osmond, C. B., K. Winter, and H. Ziegler, 1982. Functional significance of different pathways of CO_2 fixation in photosynthesis. In *Encyclopedia of Plant Physiology*. N. S., Vol. 12B. Ed. O. Lange, P. S. Nobel, C. B. Osmond, and H. Ziegler. Springer-Verlag, Berlin Heidelberg New York. Pp. 479–547.

Pearcy, R. W., O. Björkman, A. T. Harrison, and H. A. Mooney. 1971. Photosynthetic performance of two desert species with C_4 photosynthesis in Death Valley, California. *Carnegie Institution of Washington Year Book* 70: 540–50.

Pearson, L. C. 1965. Primary production in grazed and ungrazed desert communities of eastern Idaho. *Ecology* 46: 278–85.

Radmer, R. and B. Kok. 1977. Photosynthesis: Limited yields, unlimited dreams. *BioScience* 27: 599–605.

Robberecht, R., B. E. Mahall, and P. S. Nobel. 1983. Experimental removal of intraspecific competitors—Effects on water relations and productivity of a desert bunchgrass, *Hilaria rigida*. *Oecologia* 60: 21–24.

Rodin, L. E., N. I. Bazilevich, and Y. M. Miroshnichenko. 1972. Productivity and biogeochemistry of *Artemisieta* in the Mediterranean area. In *Eco-Physiological Foundation of Ecosystems Productivity in Arid Zone, International Symposium USSR*. Ed. L. E. Rodin. Nauka, Leningrad. Pp. 193–98.

Salinas, H. E., and S. C. Sanchez. 1971. *Informe Tecnico*. 38. Instituto Forestal, Sección Silvicultura, Santiago, Chile.

Sanchez-Diaz, M.F. and H.A. Mooney. 1979. Resistance to water transfer in desert shrubs native to Death Valley, California. *Physiologia Plantarum* 46: 139–46.

Schulze, E.-D., O. L. Lange, L. Kappen, U. Buschbom, and M. Evenari. 1973. Stomatal responses to changes in temperature at increasing water stress. *Planta* 110: 29–42.

Sharifi, M. R., E. T. Nilsen, and P. W. Rundel. 1982. Biomass and net primary production of *Prosopis glandulosa* (Fabaceae) in the Sonoran Desert of California. *American Journal of Botany* 69: 760–67.

Sims, P. L., J. S. Singh, and W. K. Lauenroth. 1978. Comparative structure and function of ten western North American grasslands. I. Abiotic and vegetational characteristics. *Journal of Ecology* 66: 251–85.

Smith, S. D., B. Didden-Zopfy, and P. S. Nobel. 1984. high-temperature responses of North American cacti. *Ecology* 65: 643–51.

Smith, S. D., T. L. Hartsock, and P. S. Nobel. 1983. Ecophysiology of *Yucca brevifolia*, an arborescent monocot of the Mojave Desert. *Oecologia* 60: 10–17.

Smith, S. D. and P. S. Nobel. 1986. Deserts. In *Topics in Photosynthesis. Volume 7, Photosynthesis in Contrasting Environments*. Ed. N. R. Baker and S. P. Long. Elsevier Biomedical Press, Amsterdam. Pp. 13–62.

Smith, W. K. 1978. Temperatures of desert plants: Another perspective on the adaptability of leaf size. *Science* 201: 614–16.

Smith, W. K., and P. S. Nobel. 1977. Temperature and water relations for sun and shade leaves of a desert broadleaf, *Hyptis emoryi*. *Journal of Experimental Botany* 28: 169–83.

———. 1978. Influence of irradiation, soil water potential, and leaf temperature on leaf morphology of a desert broadleaf, *Encelia farinosa* Gray (Compositae). *American Journal of Botany* 65: 429–32.

Strain, B.R. 1970. Field measurements of tissue water potential and carbon dioxide exchange in the desert shrubs *Prosopis julifera* and *Larrea divaricata*. *Photosynthetica* 4: 118–22.

Szarek, S. R. 1979. Primary production in four North American deserts: indices of efficiency. *Journal of Arid Environments* 2: 187–209.

Walter, H. 1973. *Vegetation of the Earth*. English Universities Press, London.

Werk, K. S., J. Ehleringer, I. N. Forseth, and C. S. Cook. 1983. Photosynthetic characteristics of Sonoran Desert winter annuals. *Oecologia* 59: 101–5.

Winter, K., U. Lüttge, E. Winter, and J. H. Troughton. 1978. Seasonal shift from C$_3$ photosynthesis to Crassulacean acid metabolism in *Mesembryanthemum crystallinum* growing in its natural environment. *Oecologia* 34: 225–37.

Winter, K., and von Willert, D. J. 1972. NaCl-induzierter Crassulaceensäurestoffwechsel bei *Mesembryanthemum crystallinum*. *Zeitschrift für Pflanzenphysiologie* 67: 166–70.

Woodhouse, R. M., J. G. Williams, and P. S. Nobel. 1980. Leaf orientation, radiation, interception, and nocturnal acidity increases by the CAM plant *Agave deserti* (Agavaceae). *American Journal of Botany* 67: 1179–85.

Woodhouse, R. M., J. G. Williams, and P. S. Nobel. 1983. Simulation of plant temperature and water loss by the desert succulent, *Agave deserti*. *Oecologia* 57: 291–97.

Zelitch, I. 1971. *Photosynthesis, Photorespiration, and Plant Productivity*. Academic Press, New York.

FIVE

Halotolerant Microalgae:
A Future Crop for Arid Lands

AMOS RICHMOND

ABSTRACT

Fresh water is already used to the point of exhaustion in many arid lands, particularly in Israel but also in many other parts of the world, barring further development of conventional agriculture in these areas. Potentially however, many such regions may support intensive primary production, being endowed with abundant solar irradiance and high temperature throughout the year.

A demand is thus being formulated for a new kind of agriculture that will be based on the use of sea or brackish water, resources which are not suitable for most of the conventional agricultural crops but which are available and even abundant in many arid regions. Algaculture of halotolerant algae thus represents a natural agrotechnology to be considered for such regions.

Microalgae have scarcely been exploited by mankind, either as food or as a source for chemicals. Yet, there are many advantages for microalgal agriculture, particularly in warm regions where only brackish or sea water are available.

The warm-water cyanobacteria *Spirulina*, which is indigenous in brackish and alkaline waters, may serve as a model algal crop. To date, its cost of production is prohibitive for general use as feed or food, but its potentially high yields of protein per unit water promise interesting commercial possibilities in the future.

INTRODUCTION

Fresh water is already used to the point of exhaustion in many arid lands, particularly in Israel and in the US, barring further development of conventional agriculture in these areas. Potentially, however, many such regions may support intensive agricultural production, being endowed with abundant solar irradiance and high temperature throughout the year.

A demand is thus being formulated for a new kind of agriculture that will be based on sea or brackish water, resources which are not suitable for conventional agricultural crops but which are available in many arid regions. Algaculture of halotolerant algae thus represents a natural agrotechnology for such regions. This proposal relates to tactics for enhancing bioproductivity in arid regions based on growing algal biomass using local resources of saline water.

To date, microalgae have scarcely been exploited by mankind, either as food or as a source for chemicals. Yet the soaring prices of fossil oil and its anticipated depletion have caused significant increases in the prices of chemicals and have generated interest in the cultivation of chemicals as well as animal feed and human food.

The main advantages of microalgal agriculture are:

(a) Algal cultivation is an efficient biological system for use of solar energy to produce organic matter. Due to near year-round production, with complete ground cover and absence of water limitations, algal cultures are five to ten times more productive than conventional agriculture;

(b) Many species of algae can be induced to produce particularly high concentrations of compounds of commercial interest such as proteins, lipids, starch, chemicals, natural pigments and biopolymers. Indeed, just about any material or chemical that man harvests from the plant world can be obtained from microalgae in much higher concentrations and yields, except lignocellulose (wood and fibers);

(c) The life cycle of most algae is completed within several hours, which makes genetic selection and improvements in the species relatively easy and fast.

(d) For many regions of low bioproductivity throughout the world, perhaps the most important aspect of the cultivation of microalgae relates to the ability of many species to thrive in seawater and/or brackish water, resources which are not suitable for conventional agricultural plants;

(e) An advantage of mass cultivation of microalgal agriculture is that the production system may be fully automated, requiring relatively few operating personnel. This is because algaculture is essentially a continuous, hydraulic system.

Microalgae are still a relatively untapped resource. Selection of species and genetic manipulation to augment the production of desired chemicals, coupled with improved technological processes should create a new and promising agricultural field, particularly suited for hot, arid regions which today support only a meager existence.

Thus, even though the concept of mass production of microalgae to feed a hungry world is very far from realization, it is still valid as a long-range goal. The concept should be expanded to include microalgae for biosynthesis of chemicals and other special products, the emphasis being placed on production based on local resources and skills.

Today, algaculture is still far from being a ready source of inexpensive, mass-produced food and natural products. Experience shows that mass production of microalgae outdoors is a formidable task. Much more must be learned about the biology involved in this biotechnology, and many technological details must be improved. Production procedures have to be simplified, and the average annual yields have to increase several fold before algaculture could become a significant agricultural endeavor. Nevertheless, the promise of cultured algae, particularly as a salt-tolerant crop, seems very real. This is amplified by the growing realization that the deprivation of many hundreds of millions of people in developing areas of the world cannot be correctly and permanently relieved by importing food and materials from the developed countries. This is the consensus of all who are involved in analyzing the problems of hunger and poverty in these regions. The only meaningful solution rests in local development, which would depend on imported knowhow and capital at first, but which would aim at promoting economic independence. In this context, efficient utilization of saline-water for agriculture production is of particular importance, for the resources of sweet water are dwindling, and often have valuable alternative uses. The aim of developing local resources therefore would include in many cases the production of salt-tolerant crops, such as selected species of algae that could be grown for various economic purposes.

BIOLOGICAL PRINCIPLES FOR THE MASS CULTIVATION OF MICROALGAE

The three main environmental factors that govern the production of algal mass are nutrients, temperature, and light.

As summarized by Goldman (1979), algal specific growth rates (μ) in nature act as dependent variables, being governed by a multitude of environmental parameters such as light intensity (I), temperature (T), nutrient concentration (S), pH, etc. The responses to these parameters are distinctly species-specific. Thus,

$$u = f(I, T, S, pH, species, etc.)$$

The specific growth rate is defined as:

$$\mu = \frac{\ln 2}{g} = \frac{1}{X} \cdot \frac{dX}{dt}$$

in which μ is the specific growth rate (t^{-1}), ln 2 is log to the base e, g is the cell generation period (t), X is the biomass concentration (g L^{-1}) and dX/dt is the change in biomass concentration with respect to time [e.g., (g $L^{-1}h^{-1}$)], which expresses the productivity, or output are (Pirt 1975) per unit volume. Algal productivity can be expressed on a per unit area basis by considering that, for a unit volume of culture with area A and depth d, the total production of biomass B per unit time is dB/dt. This latter term can then be divided by the area A to give P, the areal yield:

$$p = \frac{dB}{dt} \cdot \frac{1}{A} = d \cdot \frac{dX}{dt} = \mu Xd$$

At steady state, the turnover of liquid in the culture per unit time (the flow rate D) equals the specific growth rate (μ).

Nutrition

The response of algal growth rates to variations in the environment may be elucidated by looking at the response to each of the environmental limitations to growth. By keeping two factors constant, the effect of the varying factor can be quantified. Thus, when temperature and light intensity are kept constant, the specific growth rate μ depends on some limiting nutrient, assuming all others are available in excess.

For maximal output in outdoor mass culture, it is imperative that all nutrients should be in concentrations that do not limit growth. This is readily obtainable in commercial mass cultures, in which any nutrient deficiency may be detected in time and corrected by frequent monitoring.

Another important requirement is that all nutrients should be in correct balance. This task is more complicated but could be obtained by running a complete analysis of the growth medium on frequent occasions. Thus, unlike the situation in the natural habitats of algae, nutrient limitation has no practical role in algal mass production.

Temperature

Environmental temperature is a factor to which the algal biomass responds continuously. Cell temperature equals the temperature of the culture medium, in contrast with other parameters of the medium, such as the pH. In addition to affecting the rates of cellular reactions, temperature also affects the nature of metabolism, the nutritional requirements, and the composition of biomass.

Over most of the temperature range below the optimum, the temperature coefficent of growth rate corresponds to a Q_{10} of about 2, i.e., a twofold increase in growth rate per 10°C rise in temperature. Usually the growth rate approaches zero at 10° to 25°C below the optimum temperature (Pirt 1975). According to Goldman and Carpenter (1974), the Arrhenius equation, which relates the rates of chemical reactions to temperature, describes very well the relationship between the specific growth rate of algae and the temperature.

The temperature of the culture in the pond is determined by the temperature of the surrounding air, the extent and duration of solar irradiance—most of which is converted to heat while being absorbed in the algal mass—and the relative humidity of the air which governs the extent of evaporative cooling. In addition, the depth and surface of a culture, as well as the materials from which the pond is constructed, are important factors in stabilizing pond temperature. The relative humidity has a most profound effect on the difference between air and pond temperature. In tropical Bangkok, measurement of the daily temperature course indicated that culture temperatures may exceed air temperature by as much as 13°C on sunny days during January or June. Only on cloudy days would the temperature of the air and the culture be the same (Payer et al. 1980). In contrast, results from the author's laboratory which is situated in the arid Negev desert, indicate that without exception, pond daytime temperature is lower by a few degrees than air temperature. Even in ponds covered with 0.2mm thick, transparent polyethylene sheets to increase the temperature in the winter, the temperature of the culture lags behind the air temperature by 6° to 8°C, throughout the diurnal cycle (Richmond 1983).

Light

When nutrients and temperature are not limiting growth in the pond, light availability for the average cell becomes the dominant production factor.

In densely populated mass cultures, the cells are exposed to intermittent radiation which imposes a light-dark cycle to which the average algal cell is continuously exposed. This cycle may be completed in a few seconds or a few scores of seconds, and is a function of the speed of travel of the individual cells back and forth from the upper, illuminated layers of the pond to the lower, darkened ones. The light regime which thus ensues is influenced by the intensity of solar irradiance and depends on the depth of the pond, the extent of turbulence and particularly, on the population density. Thus, the availability of light to each cell in photoautotrophic culture is a function of the intensity and duration of light irradiance as well as the concentration of cells or population density which affect the extent of mutual shading (Tamiya 1957). The latter results from the absorbance of the incident light by the algal cells closest to the illuminated surface, thereby decreasing the amount of irradiance available for the cells bellow. The greater the population density, the higher the extent of mutual shading and the greater the fraction of cells that are not illuminated at a given instant. The population density was found to constitute a major factor in the production of microalgae. The importance of this parameter resides in that under conditions of light limitation of growth, manipulation of the population density represents, in effect, the only practical means by which to modify the amount of light energy available for the individual cell in the culture.

Measuring the effect of the population density on the potential photosynthetic activity (as indicated by O_2 evolution exhibited under standard conditions for photosynthesis) revealed an inverse relationship between the potential specific rate of photosynthesis and the population density in the pond. Thus the higher the density, the lower the potential rate for photosynthesis. This relates to a basic issue in production of photoautotrophic algal mass: At densities of 400 to 500 mg L^{-1} (dry weight), which were found to be optimal for maximal areal output of *Spirulina* biomass, solar irradiation is almost completely absorbed in the upper 3 to 4cm of the culture, leaving some 70 percent of the cells in the pond in complete darkness at any given instant (Richmond et al. 1980). Hence, at the highest areal output and thus peak efficiency of the culture, the individual cells are far from displaying their maximal potential for photosynthesis.

A basic factor which modifies the effects of the population density is mass cultures in mixing. Many observations indicate that a turbulent flow in the pond represents a very important requirement for maximal production *Spirulina*. Mixing has several functions (Richmond and Becker 1986), most important is insuring that a favorable regime of light intermittance be maintained, i.e., short dark intervals between the flashes of solar irradiance. The crucial importance of mixing in affecting the output rate of microalgae is not sufficiently understood at the present. Indeed, maintaining a high turbulent flow rate in the raceway, i.e., 60 to 80cm sec^{-1}, places a significant burden on the investment capital and maintenance costs of *Spirulina* culture. Yet, Richmond and Vonshak (1978) demonstrated that doubling the flow speed in small 1m^2 ponds increased the output of *Spirulina* mass by some 50 percent.

Clearly, the lower the population density, the higher the specific growth rate, as is to be expected in a system which is primarily light-limited. The relative effect of decreasing the population density, and thus of increasing the rate of light utilization per cell, is most pronounced in the summer, when temperature is not growth-limiting, and much less so in the winter, when the major environmental factor limiting the rates of growth and of output is temperature. In summer, on the other hand, light is the dominant limiting factor for growth, and thus the culture responds much more markedly to any change in this major limitation. Indeed, in light-limited growth, a close relationship must exist between the specific growth rate (μ) and cell density (X). Since μ is modified substantially by temperature, this relationship varies greatly throughout the year and, the more severe the temperature limitation on μ, the smaller must be the dependence of μ on X, becoming hardly noticeable in winter. At the same time, the relative response of the culture to "summer conditions" declined as the population density increased, until at relatively very high densities, no response to and no seasonal effect on the specific growth rate was observed. Clearly, in such dense cultures, light limitation due to mutual shading was so extreme that most of the growth rate potential of the algae was limited by light, thereby blocking any potential effect of temperature on growth. Thus, the interrelationship between the effects of temperature and light irradiance is an essential parameter in the production of algae biomass.

An important point to bear in mind is that under artificial-pond conditions, the limitation of growth by either temperature or solar irradiance alone takes place only in its extremes. In practice, the growth rate of photosynthetic microalgae is governed by both temperature and light and at the same time may yet be influenced by nutritional factors. Eppely and Sloan (1966) provided clear evidence that the effects of light and temperature on algal growth rates were interrelated, which was also demonstrated by Vonshak et al. (1982). At any given solar light intensity, elevation of temperature above 12°C in *Spirulina* culture resulted in increased concentration of pond oxygen and, similarly, for each temperature range, any increase in irradiance elevated pond oxygen concentration.

The intricate relationship between light and temperature is demonstrated in a study of Vonshak et al. (1982), in which light and temperature change roles as the major limiting factors for growth and output rate. By following the daily course of temperature and radiation and correlating them with the oxygen concentration in a *Spirulina* pond, the environmental limitations imposed on the culture were sorted out. In winter, peak O_2 in the pond coincided with the peak in daily temperature, and during a typical day in winter, the rate of increases in O_2 evolution in the early morning, up to about 9:00 A.M., was clearly very low, until a rise in temperature became evident in the late morning. In contrast, peak O_2 concentration coincided with the peak of illumination during the summer. Moreover, in summer, when the relatively high temperature in the pond was maintained during the night, the rates of increase in O_2 and in light intensity ran very closely parallel. Clearly, under the temperatures prevailing in the pond in summer, O_2 evolution was mainly controlled by the rate of irradiance.

TECHNICAL CONSIDERATIONS IN MASS CULTURES

The Mode of Cultivation

Mass production of microalgae requires an inexpensive yet reliable enclosure for growing the culture. In practice, the design of these enclosures represents a compromise between the cost of the investment in relation to the expected returns and the desire to establish conditions for the highest possible output rate, i.e., high flow velocity and turbulence, smooth long-lasting lining, and some means of elevating the temperature in the winter.

The basic design presently employed for mass-cultivation consists of an oblong, shallow (a few inches deep) raceway stirred with paddles and lined with some plastic sheet, usually polyvinylchloride (PVC). Commercial pond areas range between 500 to 5000m² (see Figure 5.1). These ponds may be open and exposed to the atmosphere or closed, i.e., covered with a transparent material. Another form of a closed reactor consists of transparent, polyethylene tubes, with a wall thickness of about 0.3mm and a diameter of 5 to 15cm. These tubes are placed on the ground arranged in a form of a raceway, the algal-laden medium being circulated by a proper pump. Alternatively, the tubes may be placed on terraces, on a hillside.

Figure 5.1   A 1000 m² pond under construction by "Ein-Yahav Algae" in the Arava desert, Israel. Note the fiberglass rods to support a polyethelene cover in winter. The lining is of grey P.V.C., 2 mm thick. The width of each channel is 5 meters.

Covering ponds for the production of warm-water algae such as *Spirulina platensis* (optimal temperature 37°C) is mandatory in the winter in many subtropical and moderate regions, when the temperature in an open pond may decline to only a few degrees above the freezing point. At the author's laboratory at Sede-Boker, covering a 100m² pond in the type of polyethylene film used for greenhouses raised the daytime temperature of the medium by 6 to 8 degrees Celsius. (see Figure 5.2). Also, covering the pond prevents radiative cooling of the system at night. Apart from trapping longwave radiation during the day and decreasing heat-loss during the night, closed systems curtail evaporative losses.

In areas where water loss by evaporation far exceeds the gain from rainfall as is typical of the warm sunny regions most suitable for algal production, evaporative losses may be as high as 2500mm per year, the equivalent of some 20 pond-volumes. Clearly, such high evaporation increases the costs of water and pumping but more important, it increases the salinity of the medium, necessitating its replacement when algal growth becomes retarded.

An advantage of closed systems is a reduction in the amount of dirt and insects contaminating the algal product. Closed systems also have some disadvantages. Light penetration is markedly reduced because most of the commercially available materials used for tubing or for covering ponds are not completely transparent. In addition, dust accumulated on the outer

Figure 5.2   A 100 m² Spirulina pond covered by greenhouse polyethelene, operated by the Algal Biotechnology Laboratory at the Blaustein Institute for Desert Research, Ben-Gurion University, Sede Boqer, Israel.

surface of the covers and water condensing on its inner surface contributes to reducing the radiation reaching the culture by some 40 percent. Another obvious disadvantage is that a closed system entails a significant increase in the capital outlay per unit of pond area (by some 15 percent).

Harvesting the Algal Mass

A major difficulty in developing commercial microalgae production is the process of harvesting the biomass, i.e., removing it from the growth medium, where the algal cells grow as a dilute (200 to 500 mg L^{-1}) suspension, and concentrating it by circa two orders of magnitude. Some potential harvesting devices are as follows:

(1) *Centrifugation*—The most direct method for the thorough removal of algal cells from the growth medium is by subjecting the algal-laden medium to centrifugal forces. The self-cleaning plate separator, the nozzle and screw centrifuges effectively concentrate all types of microalgae. However, the high investment cost and energy demand (ca. 1 kWh m^{-3}) make centrifuges impractical for the mass production of inexpensive algal biomass.

(2) *Filtration*—Natural gravity represents another separation method. Comparing a micro-strainer with a vibrating screen, Mohn (1980)

found both machines to be reliable, the energy consumed and the cost of harvesting being a fraction of those of the plate separator centrifuge—0.2 to 0.4 kWh and DM 0.02 to 0.04 per m^3, respectively.

Harvesting by pressure filtration is yet another principle for algal separation. Of the many systems tested by Mohn (1980), the chamber filter press, which is used both in the brewing industry and for dewatering sludge, seemed superior in its very high reliability and low harvesting cost. Another mode of filtration by pressure is provided by vacuum filtration.

Clearly, the low cost filtration-devices are only suitable for fairly large microalgae, such as *Spirulina platensis,* which may grow filaments up to 500 μm long (see Figure 5.3). For smaller organisms, measuring 1 to 5 μ^{-1}m in diameter, such as species of *Chlorella* or *Scenedemus,* harvesting must be carried out either by centrifugation or with the aid of a flocculating agent.

(3) *Flocculation*—Separation may be greatly facilitated by introducing chemicals, such as aluminum sulfate, which induce the single cells to flocculate. However, the algal powder which is obtained after dehydration contains about 20 percent aluminum and therefore this form of separation may have only limited use as a feed, unless the algae are further treated. A system designed to extract the aluminum from the

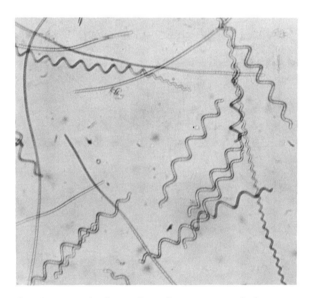

Figure 5.3   Photomicrograph of *Spirulina platensis,* magnified × 160. Note the great morphological diversities between the different strains. (Helicity in *Spirulina* may be lost.) Long filaments are desirable to ease the separation of the biomass from the growth medium. Although the culture is grown outdoors, it is practically monoalgal.

dry matter by acidification and washing is feasible, but, of course, increases the cost of the product. Obviously, if available at low cost, edible flocculants such as obtained as by-products from the sugar refining industry, would be very useful in the production of algal single cell biomass for food or feed.

DEHYDRATION OF THE ALGAL MASS

Dehydration poses a problem of major economic importance, in that it may constitute up to 30 percent of the production cost. The various systems for dehydration differ both in the extent of capital investment and in the energy requirements, and have a marked effect on the food value and the taste of the product, particularly in the case of green algae with a hard cell wall. Pabst (1975) has shown that dehydrating algal mass with a thin-layer drum-dryer yields an excellent product from *Scenedesmus*. Spray-drying was found to be a very suitable method for dehydrating algal mass for use as human food. This method is the most expensive form of dehydration, apart from freeze-drying which may be suitable for the production of special biochemicals and enzymes.

Direct dehydration of algal biomass in the sun is feasible, and is indeed the native's way of preparing dry *Spirulina* along Lake Chad in Africa. Nevertheless, sun-drying is not recommended for preparing an algal product intended for human consumption, for two reasons. A rather unpleasant odor may be associated with sun-drying, due to the slowness of the dehydration process, which enables degradative processes to set in before the drying is complete. In addition, the algal mass must be subjected to a short duration of high heat ($\sim 120°C$) in order to increase the biological value of the product and to be safe for human consumption.

For the production of animal feed, however, sun-drying may be an acceptable solution. In this author's laboratory, fish-feed made of *Spirulina* that had been vacuum dried to 20 percent dry matter, is mixed with different proportions of corn meal and dried in the sun. Dehydration is completed to circa 10 percent water, within one day. The resultant product takes the form of irregularly-shaped pieces of the *Spirulina*/corn-meal mixture, which successfully served as the sole diet for vigorously growing *Tilapia* fish in tanks.

MAINTENANCE OF MASS CULTURE

The relationships between the population density and the output rate of the culture throughout the seasons, has been investigated in great detail in *Spirulina*.

A decline in output rate was always associated with a high population density over 500 to 600mg $I.^{-1}$, stemming apparently from the increase in maintenance energy relative to the overall photosynthetic activity. A decrease in the population density below the optimal point also resulted in a significant decrease in the output rate. This apparently indicates that a high intensity of solar irradiance per unit area cannot be exploited at peak efficiency when the population density is relatively low. An essential point is that maximal output rate was obtained at a relatively high population density, exhibiting specific growth rates which were circa one-half of the maximum.

The most prevalent device used today for creating a flow in shallow, open raceways is the paddle wheel. In a closed system, a suitable pump could be used, the specific type of which should be carefully selected to avoid harmful shearing forces. Clement and Van Landeghem (1970) introduced the principle of air-lift which has not been widely tested.

It should be stressed that slow, essentially laminar flow results in low efficiency of solar energy utilization not only because at any given time most of the culture is exposed to insufficient irradiance, but also because the upper layer of the pond is exposed to a radiation intensity which at best cannot be efficiently utilized, and at worst, as in the case of *Spirulina* strains sensitive to high radiation, causes damages through photoinhibition and photooxidation. For this reason, an abrupt change in cell concentration, as caused by a large dilution, may be harmful.

Successful maintenance of microalgae in an outdoor mass culture requires a constant feedback, i.e., up-to-the-minute information from which to assess the state of the culture. The concentration of dissolved oxygen in the pond was repeatedly found in the author's laboratory, as well as by other workers (Stengel and Reckerman, 1978), to be a most sensitive and reliable parameter from which to assess the relative well-being of the culture. The O_2 concentration which is below saturation at night climbs quickly at sunrise, reaching on a hot and bright sunny day on the early afternoon a value of over 400 percent saturation. The lower the turbulence in the pond, the higher may be the concentration of dissolved O_2.

The concentration of O_2 in the pond relates to two contrasting aspects: When it is increasing rapidly during the day, the culture is judged to be active and well. Yet the rise in O_2 concentrations to extreme values is potentially dangerous. It suppresses the process of photosynthesis and forms a prerequisite for the development of photooxidation, which causes deterioration and could lead to the complete loss of the culture. In contrast, a relatively slow rise in dissolved O_2 which is accompanied with a decline in the maximal concentration of pond O_2 is in itself harmless, but should ring an alarm because it may reflect the onset of deterioration in the culture. Indeed, any unexplainable decline in O_2 concentration indicates some weakness in the culture. In the author's laboratory cultures were saved in time from complete deterioration due to the early warning provided by a definite, albeit initially small, decline in dissolved oxygen.

The optimal pH in an algal culture should be carefully maintained. The pH may be readily controlled by addition of CO_2 or of bicarbonate to compensate for the carbon that is taken up by the algae and results in elevation of the pH. The pH may be also lowered by additions of acid that releases CO_2 from carbonates. In *Chlorella* grown mixotrophically, acetic acid is routinely used for both carbon nutrition and maintenance of pH.

The most crucial challenge in the commercial production of microalgae is to maintain, throughout the year, a monoalgal culture. The basic demand in this respect is to provide growth conditions which will not sway too much from the optimal for the cultured species. Since nutrition deficiencies can be easily controlled in mass cultures, the most important factor that affects species competition is the temperature. In *Spirulina* culture, the further away the temperature declines from the 35° to 37°C optimal for *Spirulina*, the slower the growth rate and the easier for contaminants to take over the culture. When the culture is harvested by filtration, any organisms small enough to pass through the filter, may develop into a serious contaminant. Thus, the best mode of harvesting the algal biomass should answer two criteria: it should completely remove all the biomass during harvesting and it should be such that no cell breakage would take place.

THE NUTRITIVE POTENTIAL OF MICROALGAE AS FOOD AND FEED

As a rule, algal proteins are poorly utilized when intact cells are fed to monogastric animals or humans. The effect of various methods for processing and drying the algae on their digestibility has been rather extensively studied. Cyanobacteria in general and *Spirulina* in particular are unique in that they are highly digestible and thus do not require special processing. According to Becker and Venkataraman (1982), who studied protein digestibility *in vitro* by simulating the intestinal enzyme system pepsin-pancreatin, small differences only were observed between the digestibility of fresh *Spirulina* (82%) and sun-dried and freeze-dried *Spirulina*, which yielded 65 and 70 percent digestibility, respectively. Even smaller differences were observed in a study of de Hernandez and Shimada (1978) who studied the effects of autoclaving, sonification, boiling, and treatment with 2N HCl on the digestibility of *Spirulina*. All of these treatments yielded approximately the same digestibility as fresh *Spirulina*, i.e., 76 percent.

Spirulina was tested in many animal-feeding experiments. The most common and simple method of evaluating proteins by animal feeding tests is the determination of the Protein Efficiency Ratio (PER). Becker et al. (1976) compared the PER of *Scenedesmus* to that of *Spirulina* which were dried in different methods. As expected, the PER values of sun-dried *Spirulina* were higher than those of sun-dried *Scenedesmus*. The PER values for sun-dried *Spirulina* were lower than the PER of drum-dried *Scenedesmus* demonstrating the value of this method of drying.

A common method for nutritional tests of a protein source is depletion-repletion cycle, in which the test animals are first under-fed and then supplied with sufficient quantities of the tested feed. In one experiment reported by Becker and Venkatarman (1982), regeneration of enzyme activity was most in casein diet, but the group fed methionine-fortified *Spirulina* yielded nearly the same results.

Spirulina can be very well used as a supplement of the diet. This is well demonstrated in a study by Narashima et al. (1982). A diet containing 10 percent of protein, provided in equal amounts for algae and barley, have Digestibility Coefficient (DC) and Biological Value (BV) values of 81.1 and 75.5 percent, compared to 82.0 and 71.2 percent that were obtained for these parameters by a diet of barley alone. The hypocholesterolemic effect of diets containing *Spirulina* was compared to casein diets. The total serum cholesterol of a 10 percent casein diet was 256.6 (mg·100 ml^{-1} serum), the free cholesterol being 78.0. The same figures following a diet containing 15 percent *Spirulina* were 220.0 and 53.0, respectively. Also, total liver cholesterol was 48.5 mg 100 g^{-1} fresh liver following a 10 percent casein diet, being only 36.4 in the 15 percent *Spirulina* diet.

Summing up, *Spirulina* was clearly demonstrated as being a satisfactory source of protein for many animals. It is particularly useful as a food supplement and has a cholesterol-lowering effect.

Spirulina *as a Food Supplement for Humans*

Furst (1978) recounts the report of Fray Torbibio de Benavente who reached the Valley of Mexico in 1524 and described the harvest of "tecuitlatl": At a certain time of year, when it is thickest, the natives along the lake of Mexico would use a very fine-meshed net to collect a "fine mud which breeds upon the water." On shore they make on the earth or the sand come very smooth beds, and they cast the harvest down to dry, sufficient to make a cake 3 to 4cm thick, which in a few days reaches the thickness of 2 to 3mm. According to the report, "the Indians eat much of this product and enjoy it well, trading it by all the merchants of the land, as cheese is among us."

In 1963 the French Petroleum Institute became interested in reports of a dried algae cake called "dihe" that was eaten by people living along the shores of Lake Chad in Central Africa. A decade later Jean Leonard, a botanist on a Belgian expedition crossing the Sahara, independently discovered "dihe" and reported on the indigenous techniques used by the Kanenbou tribe for its production (Furst 1978). Among the Kanenbou, dihe is eaten frequently; depending on the season, it is present in seven of ten meals. Direct consumption of the dihe biscuits takes place only for superstitious reasons among pregnant women because of the belief that its dark color will screen the unborn baby from the eyes of sorcerers. In general, dihe is eaten as a constituent of a number of sauces. In a meal, a person eats approximately 10 to 12 g of dihe, which satisfies at most 8 percent of the caloric need and more than 10 percent of the protein requirement. That dihe may represent an "emergency" sort of food may be inferred from the finding that its consumption decreases when the economic conditions, or the local availability, allow consumption of meat or fish. However, during periods of famine, dihe is still consumed extensively (Ciferri 1983).

The nutritive value of *Spirulina* is amplified in that it has a relatively low percentage of nucleic acids (circa 4%), as compared with the high content of nucleic acids in bacteria. Also, it is extremely high in vitamin B12. The mucoproteic membranes that separate the cells are easy to digest, unlike the cellulose cell wall found in many other nutritional algae; it is completely non-toxic, and its lipids are made up of unsaturated fatty acids that do not form cholesterol. This makes *Spirulina* an interesting food item perhaps for persons suffering from coronary illness and obesity, as was suggested by Durand-Chastel (1976).

Spirulina has been tested extensively as a human food staple. Indeed, whole *Spirulina* has been fed to undernourished children and adults (Sautier and Trémoliére 1976) with satisfactory results.

In addition to being exceptionally high in protein, *Spirulina* appears to have the highest vitamin B12 content of any unprocessed plant or animal food, representing a boon for vegetarian diets. Two heaping tablespoons of *Spirulina* (20 gm), provide all the body requirements of vitamins B12 as well as significant quantities of other B-complex vitamines, including 70 percent of the Recommended Daily Allowance (RDA) for vitamin B1 (thiamine), 50 percent of B2 (riboflavin) and 12 percent for B3 (niacin) (Switzer 1980). Also, 10 gm of *Spirulina* contain about 25,000 International Units of vitamin A, representing over 500 percent of the RDA. Other nutritional attributes of *Spirulina* include essential unsaturated fatty acids, the most important of which is gamma-linolenic acid (6,9,12-octadecatrienoic-acid). This acid is synthesized by the algae by direct desaturation of linoleic acid and is primarily located in the mono-, and digalactosyl diglyceride fractions.

The possibility of preparing fermented foods similar to cheese, yogurt, and tofu also offers many exciting new possibilities for *Spirulina*. Also, extraction methods could provide a decolored *Spirulina*, high protein powder suitable for widespread use (Switzer 1980).

The effect of *Spirulina* tables as supplement to a reducing diet on clinical-chemical parameters and the body weight of patients was recently conducted in Germany (Schmülling et al. 1984). The results of this short-term study were that during four weeks the placebo pills were ingested, a statistically non-significant weight loss of 0.7 ± 0.4 Kg was observed. During the four weeks that *Spirulina* tablets were taken up (14 tablets before each meal), body weight dropped significantly by 1.4 ± 0.4 Kg. The researchers concluded that perhaps a faster weight reduction occurred with *Spirulina*. Within a four weeks test phase, no alarming changes occurred in either clinical-chemical, or subjective tests. Long term studies were thus deemed justified.

Venkataraman et al. (1977a) studied the supplementary value of the proteins of *Scenedesmus acutus* compared to rice, ragi *(Eleusine coracana)*, wheat, and peanut proteins. Protein Efficiency Ratios (PER) based on the growth responses of weanling male rats were measured at two levels of algae

(25 and 50% of the total protein) in the cereal-based diets. Diets containing cereal (rice, ragi, and wheat) and *Scenedesmus* proteins in the ratio 2:1 gave significantly higher PER than cereal diets alone. The highest PER was obtained for diets containing algae and rice protein in the ratio of 1:1. *Scenedesmus* protein supplemented ragi and wheat proteins to a greater extent than rice proteins. They also evaluated *Scenedesmus acutus* processed by different methods viz., Drum-Drying (DD), sun-drying (SD) and cooked sun-drying (CSD) for growth responses and histopathological changes in wistar strain albino rats. A casein diet containing 10 percent protein was used as reference and protein levels in the diets containing algae were also maintained at 10 percent or 20 percent. The highest weight gain was observed in 20 percent protein, drum-dried algae, while the lowest weight was recorded with sun-dried material. A similar trend was also observed with the food consumption pattern of the various diets. Severe fatty infiltration was seen in livers of rats fed with SD and CSD algal diets, perhaps because protein from SD and CSD algae was of low availability (Venkataraman et al. 1977b).

Comparative toxicological studies with algae in India, Thailand and Peru were done using the recommended guidelines for chemical composition, analyses for biogenic and non-biogenic toxic substances, biochemical tests, nutritional effects of nucleic acid uptake, sanitary analyses, safety evaluations, clinical studies and acceptability studies. The results demonstrated a high nutritive value of microalgae, and no harmful effect could be detected in any of the tests (Becker and Venkataraman, 1980).

USES OF MICROALGAE

As reviewed by Cohen (1985), microalgae may be used for a great many purposes, in addition to food supplement for humans or animal feed. Lipids represent one interesting group of natural products, many forms of which are found in microalgae. Most prevalent are fatty acids esterified to glycerol, sugars or bases, but many other forms of lipids or lipoid structures, e.g., hydrocarbons, waxes, sterols chlorophylls and carotens, are well known. Several types of polar lipids have been discovered in algae, e.g., chlorosulfo-lipids in *Chyrsophyceae, Xanthophyceae, Chlorophyceae*, and *Cyanobacteria*, or diacyglycerol in *Chlamidomonas, Voluox* and *Dunaliella*. Certain species of microalgae, e.g., *Spirulina*, are rich sources of essential fatty acids such as gamma-linolenic acid, which was reported to have a therapeutic effect on hyperlipidemia and other physiological disorders. Also, *Porphyridum* is a good source for arachidonic acid, a precursor of prostaglandins. Wax esters were reported to accumulate in *Euglena* as well as in *Chromonas*. Likewise, sterols may be found in most algae, *Ochromonas danica* containing the highest (1 percent of the dry weight) concentration. Sterols of industrial potential such as chondrilasterol from *Scenedesmus* or unusual steroids from *Glenodinium*, e.g., linear mono- and diunsaturated C29 and

C31 and branched-chain pentaunsaturated C34, portray the rich list of lipids that may be extracted from a vast array of microalgae (Cohen 1985).

Hydrocarbons are also present in some species, and *Botryoccus braunii* in stationary phase may contain up to 80 percent of hydrocarbons.

An important group of compounds in algae are pigments, particularly cartenoids, chlorophylls, and phycobilins. *Dunaliella* is a particularly rich source of beta-carotene, one strain *(D. bardawil)* may accumulate this carotenoid up to 10 percent of the dry weight when light intensity is high and growth is limited. *Spirulina* is a good source of pure chlorophyll, and preparation based on *Spirulina* chlorophyll was patented as a strong deodorant. In addition, this alga contains relatively large amounts of phycocyanin, and also phycoerythrin. These and other pigments could be well utilized as natural colors for the food, drug and cosmetic industries, replacing the currently used synthetic pigments that are suspected of being carcinogens.

Polysaccharides represent the only group of algal chemicals that are already widely utilized commercially, i.e., Agar, alginic acid, and carrageenan which are extracted from macroalgae. Of the microalgae, *Porphyridium* synthesizes and excretes to the growth medium large amounts of sulfated polysaccharides which resemble carrageenan in their structure and properties. Also, starch is produced by many green algae, and in a termophilic strain of *Chlorella*, starch content rose as high of 50 percent of the total dry weight. Another polysaccharide of potential importance is poly-beta-hydroxybutyric acid, which was reported to reach six percent of the total dry weight of *Spirulina* growing exponentially.

Antibiotics and toxins in microalgae have been reported often. Antibiotic activity in *Chlorella*, as well as in several other microalgae, e.g., *Ochromonas* and *Chlamidomonas*, was ascribed to unidentified fatty acids or their photooxidative products, and an extract of many species of diatoms was reported to have antifungal effects (Cohen 1985).

In summary, it seems evident that all the needs of man in natural products, except fibers and wood, could be obtained from microalgae. It seems safe to assume that the very extensive number of species of microalgae (30,000 or more, most of which have not been so far investigated), holds a promise for many possibilities of economic usage.

THE PROSPECTS FOR INDUSTRIAL ALGACULTURE

The culture of algae for industrial purposes is a novel biotechnology, naturally prompting the question of whether it will ever become an important means of production of food, feeds, and chemicals. I believe there is solid evidence that the utilization of algae for various economic purposes will gradually develop into an important industrial endeavor, particularly in warm, sunny regions, where the degree of salinity in the water available is unsuitable for the production of conventional agricultural crops.

A crucial question in analyzing the future prospects of algaculture concerns the market potential for algal products. No comprehensive answers are available yet, but certain points have become clear: The nutritional value of various algae as animal feeds and as food for humans has been substantiated by hundreds of research studies. In addition, scores of studies have described various therapeutic effects of microalgae. There is a growing list of chemicals that can be extracted from microalgae for commercial purposes. Most important in this respect is that fact that while tens of thousands of algal species have been taxonomically defined, only a small fraction have been surveyed for their possible economic potential. Yet, it seems possible to produce from these microorganisms nearly all the products that are currently obtained from conventional crops. Such crops do not usually produce continuously all year round, and most important, require a supply of sweet water, a resource which is becoming scarce in arid and semi-arid lands all over the world. Being unicellular and having a short life cycle, microalgae in general and cyanobacteria in particular represent a most suitable material for genetic manipulation. Transfer of genes for the synthesis of specific molecules should eventually allow large scale production of many products that are presently obtained, rather inefficiently, from terrestrial plants or from heterotrophic microorganisms cultured in expensive reactors.

The pressing issue in commercial algaculture is not so much the market potential of algae products as it is the cost of their production. The current prices of commonly used animal feeds, i.e., various grains, and of high-protein plants such as soy bean for human consumption, are approximately one tenth the cost of production of algae in the small industrial plants in operation today.

What, then, are the chances for microalgae in the competition with conventional crops for land, water and capital? There are several indications that the cost of production of microalgae, which today confines them to the health-food market, will gradually but consistently decline, in proportion to the continuous expansion of the market. In general, the history of agriculture and industry provides numerous examples for the natural course of development of new fields of endeavor. Repeatedly, be it with rubber trees or wheat, experience has shown that with time, productivity increases and the cost per unit production decreases.

It is almost self-evident that, due to the substantial capital investment needed per unit pond area, the cost of production is greatly dependent on the yield per area. The assumption of a rather high output rate was assumed, and this was a major reason for the relatively low cost calculated for large scale production. In reality to date, only about one half to one third of these outputs have actually been obtained over a long term production period, making the actual cost per unit product two to three times higher than originally expected. Nevertheless, yields greater than 10 Kg m^{-2} per year^{-1} are possible and have been obtained for periods lasting a few weeks. Theoretically, the photosynthetic efficiency can be circa eight percent where the temperature does not limit growth, which implies a tremendous output rate, i.e., ca. 200 tons of dry matter ha^{-1} year^{-1}. However, even a consistent output one third the theoretical maximum will significantly reduce the current cost of production, which ranges between $6 to $20 (US) per Kg of drum- or spray-dried algal powder.

The current low yields of 15 to 30 tons ha^{-1} per year^{-1} that are usually obtained in outdoor mass cultures reflect the present state of ignorance in large-scale production of microalgae. It seems appropriate to compare the present know-how in algaculture with that thousands of years ago at the beginning of agriculture, when the cultivated plant species and the cultivation methods used only reflected man's preliminary selection of species and rudimentary skills in cultivating them. Even a superficial view of the methods and machinery currently used for commercial production of microalgae reveals that the industry is still in the initial phase of trial and error, adapting machines and materials from other industries. Every phase of this biotechnology may be significantly improved.

As long as the commercial aspects of microalgal culture are not recognized, there are no opportunities to relate technically to problems associated with large-scale operation. There is every reason to assume that with the establishment and gradual expansion of a microalgal industry, this biotechnology will become increasingly more specialized and more efficient, resulting in substantial reduction of the cost of production. A breakthrough in commercial algaculture already resulted from the increased demand for some microalgal species such as health foods, which prompted establishment of large-scale algaculture in a few countries. The experience gained in the present production plants will have far-reaching effects on advancing this novel biotechnology. Also, the know-how obtained in large-scale commercial production of health foods will be instrumental in the development of other uses for microalgae, e.g., supplements for human food and various special chemicals. A significant cut in the cost of algal production could be expected when the market further expands, e.g., through demand for special feed supplements for animals, particularly fish and other aquatic organisms, but also for poultry, hogs, and ruminants.

From the standpoint of enhancement of productivity of arid regions, the most important advantage of algaculture which will have a decisive effect on its future prospects is the halotolerance of algal species, thriving in saline water unsuitable for the production of most agricultural crops. When experience and knowhow in this biotechnology become such that production would be greatly simplified and its cost significantly reduced, algaculture in brackish water will have clear economic advantages in many warm arid lands.

REFERENCES

Becker, E. W., L. V. Venkataraman and P. M. Khanum. 1976. Effects of different methods of processing on the protein efficiency ratio of the green alga *Scenedesmus acutus*. *Nutrition Reports International* 14:305–15.

Becker, E. W. and L. V. Venkataraman. 1980. In *Algae Biomass*, eds. G. Shelef and C. J. Soeder. Elsevier/North Holland, Biomedical Press, Amsterdam. Pp. 35–50.

———. 1982. *Biotechnology and exploitation of algae: The Indian approach*. German Agency for Technical Cooperation, Eschborn, FRG:1–216.

Ciferri, O. 1983. *Spirulina*, the edible microorganism. *Microbiological Review* 55:578.

Clement, G. and H. Van Landeghem. 1970. *Brichte der Deutschen Botanischen Gesellschaft* 83 no. 11:559.

Cohen, Z. 1985. Products from algae. In *Algal Mass Culture*, ed. A. Richmond. CRC Press, Boca Raton, Fla. (in press).

de Hernandez, J. T., and A. S. Schimada. 1978. Estudias sobre el valor nutritivo del alga expiculina *(Spirulina maxima)*. *Arch, Latinoam. Nut.* 28:196–207.

Durand-Chastel, H. 1976. The texuitlatl and the aquaculture, F.A.O. Technical Conference on Aquaculture, May 26-June 2nd. Kyoto, Japan.

Eppely, R. W. and P. R. Sloan. 1966. *Physologia Plantarium* 19:47.

Furst, P. T. 1978. *Human Nature*, 60–65.

Goldman, J. C. 1979. Outdoor algal mass cultures II. Photosynthetic yield limitations. *Water Research* 13:119.

Goldman, J. C. and E. J. Carpenter. 1974. A kinetic approach to the effect of temperature on algal growth. *Limnology and Oceanography* 19:756.

Mohn, F. H. 1980. In *Algae Biomass*, eds. G. Shelef and C. J. Soeder. Elsevier/North Holland, Biomedical Press, Amsterdam. Pp. 566–633.

Narashimha, D. L. R., G. S. Venkataraman, S. K. Duggal, and O. Eggum. 1982. Nutritional quality of the blue-green alga *Spirulina plantensis geitler*. *Journal of Science, Food and Agriculture* 33:456–60.

Pabst, W. 1975. In *Proc. I. Symp. Mikrobielle Proteing winnug*. *Verlag Chemie Weinheim*:173–78.

Payer, H. D., Y. Chiemrichak, K. Hasakul, C. Kongpanichkul, L. Kraidej, M. Nguttragul, S. Reungmanipytoon, and P. Buri. 1980. In *Algae Biomass*, eds. G. Shelef and C. J. Soeder. Elsevier/North Holland Medical Press, Amsterdam. Pp. 389–400.

Pirt, J. S. 1975. *Principles of microbe and cell cultivation*. Blackwell Scientific Publications, Oxford.

Richmond, A. 1983. Phototropic microalgae. In *Biotechnology*, Vol. 3, eds. H. J. Rehm and G. Reed. *Verlag Chemie Weinheim*, Pp. 110–43.

Richmond, A. and W. Becker. 1086. Technological aspects—a general outline. In *Algal Mass Culture*, ed. A. Richmond. CRC Press, Boca Raton, Fla.

Richmond, A. and A. Vonshak. 1978. Spirulina culture in Israel. *Archive Fuer Hydrobiologie Supplement, Limnology* 11:274.

Richmond, A., A. Vonshak and S. Malis-Arad. 1980. In *Algae Biomass*, eds. G. Shelef and C. J. Soeder. Elsevier/North Holland Biomedical Press, Amsterdam.

Sautier, C. and J. Trémolière. 1976. Valeur alimentaire des algues *Spirulines* chez l'homme. *Annals de la Nutrition et de l'Alimentation* 30:317–34.

Schmulling, M. et al. 1984. The influence of *Spirulina geitleri* tablets as a supplement to a reducing diet on clinical-chemical parameters and the body weight of obese patients. (personal communication)

Stengel, E. and H. Rickerman. 1978. *Archives of Hydrobiology* 82:263.

Switzer, L. 1980. *Spirulina*. Pfogeus Corporation, Berkeley, Calif.

Tamiya, H. 1957. *Ann. Rev. Plant Physiol.* 8:309.

Venkataraman, L. V., W. E. Becker, P. M. Khanum, and I. A. S. Murthy. 1977a. *Nutrition Reports International* 15:145.

Venkataraman, L. V., W. E. Becker, P. M. Khanum, and K. R. Nathew. 1977b. *Nutrition Reports International* 16:231.

Vonshak, A., A. Abeliovich, S. Boussiba, S. Malis-Arad, and A. Richmond, 1982. Production of *Spirulina* biomass. Effects of environment factors and population density. *Biomass* 2.

PART II

DESERT ANIMALS

SIX

How Do Desert Animals
Get Enough Water?

KENNETH A. NAGY

INTRODUCTION

Deserts are defined primarily on the basis of low precipitation. Water is the resource most noticeably in short supply for desert organisms, especially during the typical periods of seasonal drought. Despite the apparently severe water shortage, animal life in deserts is surprisingly abundant and diverse.

There are many explanations for the success of animals in deserts. These include: (1) the desert is not really as stressful as it appears to humans, (2) desert animals conserve water so well that they do not need much water to survive, (3) desert animals are poor at conserving water, but they are very effective at finding and consuming all the water they need, and (4) desert animals simply avoid the stressful seasons by becoming inactive (torpor, estivation) or by migrating out of the desert. None of these explanations by itself can account for the ability of all desert animals to avoid death by dehydration. In fact, all of these explanations are true to some extent, depending on the species of animal in question (Schmidt-Nielsen 1964).

This chapter has three sections and three purposes. The first section is a brief and nontechnical review of the means desert animals use to maintain water balance, along with some examples to illustrate these points. The focus is on terrestrial vertebrate animals (mammals, birds, reptiles, and amphibians), although some examples of invertebrates are included. The purpose of this section is to illustrate the many ways animals use to get enough water in deserts, so that we might appreciate and perhaps make use of different mechanisms of desert survival. Several recent reviews cover this topic in more detail (Quinton 1979; Gilles 1979; Maloiy 1979).

The second section provides a more detailed examination of the water relations of a representative herbivorous mammal, the jackrabbit (*Lepus californicus deserti*), living in the Mojave Desert in the southwestern United States. Its purpose is to focus on the seasonal challenges to survival that a plant-eating animal faces in a winter-rainfall desert, and to illustrate that some animal species can persist in deserts even when they experience great mortality during droughts.

The last section is an overview of the general patterns of water balance in animals living in a winter-rainfall desert, in relation to their diet. This provides a conceptual model that may be useful for understanding basic survival mechanisms, as well as for defining a typical pattern, against which other patterns may be contrasted to reveal adaptations to desert existence.

BALANCING A WATER BUDGET

Most animals must regulate the amount of water in their bodies within relatively narrow limits to avoid death. Body water is being lost continuously, and it must be replaced more or less continuously. The rates at which water is leaving and entering the body water pool are the critical variables in examining water balance. Although a low rate of water loss is clearly adaptive in deserts, some desert animals have high rates of water loss, but are able to fare quite well because they can achieve high rates of water gain.

Water Loss

The minimum amount of water an animal needs to obtain each day is determined by its minimum daily rate of total water loss. Animals lose water in excretions (feces, urine, salt gland fluid), secretions (sweat glands, mammary glands, defensive secretions) and by evaporation (across skin, respiratory surface, and eyes). Among vertebrate animals, total water loss rates are lowest in some desert animals. Mammals such as kangaroo rats, camels, and desert antelope produce very dry feces, and small desert rodents can produce highly concentrated urine. Several species of desert-dwelling reptiles and birds have salt glands that excrete excess salts in concentrated form, thus conserving water. No birds or reptiles have sweat glands, but some mammals and amphibians do, and these function to help prevent overheating through evaporative cooling. Evaporative water loss usually accounts for about half of the total water loss from vertebrates. About half of this is from the skin and the other half from the respiratory tract. Water evaporation from the wet surface of eyes can be a large proportion of total evaporation when animals have their eyes open. Desert animals typically have lower rates of evaporation from skin and respiratory surfaces than do nondesert animals. The skin of desert animals is often less permeable to water, and desert animals can reduce respiratory water loss in a variety of ways, including: (1) extracting more oxygen from inhaled air (which reduces the volume of air requiring saturation with water vapor in the lungs), (2) cooling exhaled air as it passes out over cool nasal membranes (which causes some vapor to condense and remain in the body), and (3) allowing body temperature to drop (which reduces metabolism and the requirement for oxygen).

These examples of water conservation fall in the categories of physiological and morphological mechanisms. Desert animals also have behavioral mechanisms for reducing daily water losses. An obvious and common example is avoiding the need to use evaporation of water for cooling purposes by selecting microhabitats that do not impose a thermal stress. Less obvious examples include: (1) selection of humid microhabitats, or at least enclosed areas such as burrows, that will become humidified rapidly by evaporated body water, as sites of retreat, (2) selection of the more humid and less windy times of the 24-hour cycle to engage in surface activity outside refuges, (3) keeping eyes closed as long as possible, and (4) selecting a diet that is highly digestible and low in salts, as this reduces the amount of feces and urine (and salt gland secretions) that must be voided each day. There are some animals, such as pack rats (*Neotoma lepida*) that do not have significant physiological or morphological adaptations for water conservation, but they survive and reproduce very successfully in the desert, primarily by behavioral adjustments.

Water Storage

It is theoretically possible for desert animals to enhance their water balance status by storing excess water somewhere in their bodies as a hedge against droughts. However, few animals actually do this. Most desert birds and mammals have normal body water contents, regardless of season, and depots of stored water generally are not found upon autopsy. A few reptiles, such as desert tortoises (*Gopherus agassizi*) may store large amounts of water as dilute urine in their urinary bladders for future reabsorption, as do many desert amphibians. A more commonly observed form of "storage," which I call "negative storage," is the phenomenon of tolerance to dehydration. Many desert amphibians and reptiles can survive large reductions in body water content, up to 50 percent in some species. Unlike these ectothermic vertebrates, desert birds and mammals do not show such a large tolerance to dehydration, although camels and other large, plant-eating mammals can tolerate reabsorption of much water from the large mass of food material in their stomachs.

Water Gain

Animals can gain body water as a result of energy metabolism, by osmotic uptake through skin, by drinking liquid water, by taking up water vapor from the air around them, and by eating moist food. So-called "metabolic water" is formed, along with carbon dioxide and heat, during the oxidation of the energy-yielding components of food (carbohydrates, lipids, and proteins). Metabolic water becomes part of the body water pool, so it must be considered as an avenue of water gain. The rate at which water is formed metabolically is determined by the rate of energy metabolism, which is responsive to aspects of an animal that are usually unrelated to water balance. There is no evidence that any vertebrate increases its metabolic rate, and hence its rate of metabolic water production, in response to water stress. In fact, dehydrated animals usually have depressed metabolic rates. In the simple situation where an animal is neither eating nor drinking, water gain consists essentially of metabolic water production as body substances are oxidized, and water loss is virtually all via evaporation. In dry air, the rate of evaporation exceeds the rate of metabolic water production in all species except the few small desert birds and rodents that have especially low rates of respiratory water loss (due to very cool nasal passages). Thus, most desert vertebrates will dehydrate slowly under these conditions. However, as ambient humidity rises, net evaporation declines, and the body water pool can stay constant or increase in humid air.

Osmotic uptake of liquid water across the skin to any significant degree occurs only in desert amphibians, where it is quite an important component of their water budget. The skin of desert birds, mammals, and reptiles has such a low permeability to water, that osmotic influx of water is generally negligible. When birds, mammals, and reptiles encounter water in the desert, they usually drink it, rather than sit in it, as do amphibians. An Australian lizard, the Thorny Devil (*Moloch horridus*), was once thought to take up water osmotically, because it gained weight while sitting in shallow water. It was subsequently discovered that the water was moving, via capillary action, in fine capillary grooves in the skin leading to the mouth, where the water was being ingested and swallowed.

Some desert birds (doves, sand grouse, quail) and mammals (bighorn sheep, camels) must have water for drinking during drought periods, and they are found only near watering holes during these periods. These animals may be found far from drinking water during times when their plant food is green and succulent, as it provides abundant water. Most species of desert reptiles, many small mammals, and some birds can be found living year-round in areas where permanent sources of drinking water are absent. Many of these animals probably drink during the infrequent occasions when rain water is available, but they most likely live through droughts without drinking any water at all.

Dew is available for drinking in some deserts on some occasions. Periodic advective fogs occur in the Namib desert. Some species of lizards, beetles, and a species of snake drink fog water that condenses on their bodies or on objects in their environment. Larger Namib animals may ingest condensed fog water by licking or eating plants that are wetted during fogs. Dew also occurs frequently in the Negev desert, and animals may use this source of drinking water.

Two other forms of "dew" may be used by some desert animals. Flat rocks on the desert surface can cool quickly at night by radiation to the cold sky. The undersides of these rocks may become cold enough to cause condensation of water vapor in the soil. This water should be available to small burrowing animals, but its use by an animal in the field has not yet been documented. Burrowing, nocturnal, ectothermic animals, such as scorpions and geckos, may make use of another form of dew for drinking. While active on the cool surface of the soil at night, these animals become cooler than their burrows, which are below the surface and stay warm longer. If a cool scorpion enters a warm, humid burrow, water could condense on its body and this could be imbibed. Again, use of this form of drinking water by animals has not been documented in nature.

Water vapor moves by diffusion through permeable membranes, such as skin and respiratory surfaces of animals. Thus, vapor input increases from zero in completely dry air to the maximal value in saturated air. However, water vapor is simultaneously moving through these same membranes from the body water pool into the surrounding air. These water fluxes can be measured by isotopically labeling either the animal's body water or ambient water vapor. Evaporation of water from vertebrate animals nearly always exceeds diffusion of ambient vapor into their bodies, so there is usually a net loss of water across skin, respiratory surfaces, and eyes. However, some small, desert invertebrates are able to gain weight by absorbing vapor from the air faster than they are losing it (Edney 1977). Some of these animals can gain weight in air that has only 50 to 60 percent relative humidity. The mechanism one species uses to accomplish this is to expose a drop of body fluid containing a high concentration of solutes, allow it to take up water vapor according to the difference in water activities between fluid and vapor, then withdraw the fluid back into the body. Other species may expose their rectal pads, which contain water at low activities, and absorb vapor that way. No vertebrate animal is known to accomplish this remarkable feat.

Water in the diet is the main source of water for most desert vertebrates most of the year. The amount of preformed water in different foods ranges from near zero in air-dried seeds lying on the hot soil surface at midday to about 90 percent water in some new, growing leaves, some fleshy fruits, and some tissues of cacti and succulents.

The most remarkable of desert vertebrates, in terms of independence from water supply, are the several species of small rodents and birds that can maintain water balance on a diet of air-dried seeds with no moist food or drinking water. These animals (kangaroo rats, Black-throated Sparrows, Australian hopping mice, gerbils) have very low rates of evaporation and produce very dry feces and extremely concentrated urine. As a result, their minimum water requirements are so low that metabolic water production (which is no higher than any other animal of the same taxon and body mass) can satisfy a large portion of their needs. The remainder comes from preformed water in the seeds. The water content of seeds can vary between zero and perhaps 30 percent depending on the humidity of the air around the seeds. Kangaroo rats require seeds with a minimum of about five percent water in order to achieve water balance. Kangaroo rats forage at night when temperatures are lower and humidities higher than during the day, and they also take seeds that are buried shallowly in the soil where the humidity may be somewhat higher than in the air. These aspects of foraging behavior help insure that the seeds consumed contain adequate amounts of preformed water. Kangaroo rats also have fur-lined cheek pouches which they fill with seeds for later storage in their burrows. It is likely that these stored seeds take up additional water by absorption of vapor in the more humid burrow. Thus, kangaroo rats could make use of soil water and water vapor in burrow air (that either came from the soil or from the animal itself) which would otherwise be unavailable. By selecting moist soil for digging the storage chamber, granivorous desert rodents could enhance their water budget quite a bit. Unfortunately, this possibility has not yet been investigated in nature, to my knowledge.

Insectivorous and carnivorous animals can probably maintain water balance without drinking, if they can consume enough food to maintain energy balance. Live animals are usually 65 to 75 percent water (about two to three grams of water per gram of dry matter), so the water content of the diet of a carnivore is relatively constant. Theirs is not a problem of diet quality, but one of food quantity, and prey availability changes during a typical desert year.

In striking contrast to this situation, the diet quality for herbivores changes dramatically with season, but food availability does not change markedly. The biomass (dry matter) of above-ground plant parts does not vary dramatically with season. Leaves and stems that are green and growing in spring may be brown and dead in summer, but they are still there to be consumed. However, the water content of that dead vegetation may be too low to allow herbivores to maintain water balance while eating it in the absence of drinking water. The relationship between season and water balance in a desert herbivore is examined in more detail in the next section.

THE JACKRABBIT: A DESERT HERBIVORE

Black-tailed jackrabbits *(Lepus californicus deserti)* are medium-sized (two kg) herbivores that live in the deserts of the southwestern United States. In the Mojave Desert, most jackrabbits have access to drinking water only when the winter rains occur. Occasional rains occur during warm seasons, but these are from local thundershowers, and the water often disappears within minutes after hitting the hot soil. Jackrabbits normally do not use burrows, but they will do so during the few hot afternoons each year when air temperatures exceed 43°C. Jackrabbits depend almost exclusively on the water in their diet during the summer, fall, and early winter drought period.

We measured water relations of jackrabbits in the field throughout a year, and determined minimum water and nutrient requirements at different seasons by doing feeding experiments on captive jackrabbits fed the same diet that field animals had at that time of year. Water flux rates in the field were measured by following the washout rate of tritiated water injected into jackrabbits as a tracer of body water kinetics (Nagy et al. 1976; Shoemaker et al. 1976; Costa et al. 1976).

The results (see Figure 6.1) indicated that jackrabbits were obtaining about five times as much water as they needed in spring, when their food plants were lush, succulent and growing rapidly. However, by midsummer, most plants had dried out, and the diet items selected by jackrabbits did not provide enough water to them. Intake rates of energy and nitrogen were still adequate in summer, and wild jackrabbits could have survived on the summer diet if they had access to drinking water. In autumn and early winter, drinking water would not have made up for the low-quality diet (now primarily woody twigs, branches, and bark of shrubs), which was also deficient in digestible energy and nitrogen.

We concluded that jackrabbits are unable to survive during summer and autumn in typical creosote-scrub habitat in the Mojave Desert, because they are unable to obtain enough water (and enough energy and nitrogen later in autumn) from the low-quality diet available to them. Yet, jackrabbits continue to persist year after year in this desert. How do they do it? We suggest that most jackrabbits die during the drought (population studies support

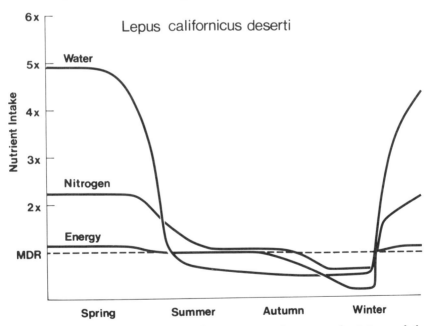

Figure 6.1 Relationship between daily nutrient intake rates and minimum daily requirements (dashed line) for jackrabbits eating natural diets in the field (Mojave Desert) at different seasons. As the summer drought progresses, first the diet ceases to provide adequate water, then in autumn digestible energy and nitrogen fall below minimum requirements before the winter rains begin.

this, indicating annual mortality of 80 to 95 percent). The few who have claimed home ranges that include moister areas where green vegetation persists throughout the year will survive. When winter rains stimulate plant growth, the surviving jackrabbits reproduce rapidly and repopulate the now green and lush desert. Thus, it appears that the key to desert survival for jackrabbits is not so much their physiological, morphological, or behavioral adaptation to water stress, as it is their population dynamics and population distribution. There seem to be many ways to survive in deserts.

It is likely that humans have had two substantial impacts on the jackrabbit population in the Mojave desert. Humans have been pumping water out of the ground there for about a century, and the water table has lowered considerably in the last several decades. This has probably caused many of the natural oases that formerly existed to disappear, thereby reducing the number of places that jackrabbits can survive the droughts. The second impact of humans is their creation of agricultural areas, golf courses, school and park lawns, and home gardens where green vegetation occurs nearly year-round. The commonly observed "roadside effect," where desert plants are green alongside roads at times when plants another 10 meters into the desert are brown (this is due to water run-off and accumulation in soil adjacent to and under paved roads), is another situation resulting from human activities in deserts. Jackrabbits now make use (sometimes heavy use) of these new "oases" during summer and autumn.

PATTERNS IN SEASONAL WATER BALANCE

Several other species of Mojave desert herbivorous and insectivorous verte-brates have been studied throughout an annual cycle (Nagy 1972; Nagy and Medica 1986; Nagy 1983). These results suggest that there are some general patterns of water relations that animals follow in this winter-rainfall desert (see Figure 6.2).

Water input to this desert occurs as rainfall during a brief period in winter (generally November and December). This rain falls from large winter cold fronts from the northwest. In summer and fall, moist tropical air from the southeast and southwest causes predictable rain from thunderstorms in the Sonora, Chihuahua, and Colorado deserts to the south and east of the Mojave Desert, and occasional but unpredictable thunderstorms may occur in the Mojave as well.

Water flux through the plants peaks in spring, as the shrubs produce new leaves and the winter annuals germinate and mature while using the rainwater stored in the soil. Water influx in herbivores also peaks in spring as they feed on the succulent vegetation. As the plants begin dying and drying out in late spring and early summer, the herbivores can maintain high rates of water intake by selectively feeding on vegetation that is still green. Water flux in both plants and herbivores is low in summer and autumn until winter

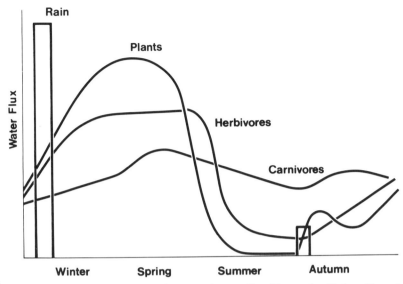

Figure 6.2   Seasonal changes in the rate of water flux (1) into the Mojave Desert as rain, (2) through plants, (3) through herbivores, and (4) through carnivores in the ecosystem.

rains occur, unless the occasional summer thundershower adds water to the system.

Carnivores also have highest water intakes in spring (see Figure 6.2), but their response is somewhat delayed in comparison to herbivores (on whom carnivores feed). Because the diet of carnivores has a relatively constant water content, an increase in water influx rate represents an increase in feeding rate, rather than an increase in diet water content. Thus, the peak in late spring corresponds with greater feeding during the breeding season. Carnivores maintain relatively high water intake rates in summer, and autumn because their diet (herbivores) does not dry out as does the diet of their prey. Thus, carnivores are taking advantage, indirectly, of the adaptations for water balance possessed by their prey. These adaptations allow herbivores to survive longer, which, in effect, aids the carnivores. Some carnivores, such as insectivorous lizards, are able to maintain high rates of water intake through autumn by switching their diet from herbivores that eat moist plant parts to those that are adapted to survive on dry plant matter. Termites, ants and some beetles are examples of primary consumers that can survive on dry diets. Again, the carnivores are taking advantage of desert adaptations possessed by organisms lower in the food chain. It is reasonable to suggest that top carnivores, such as coyotes, may be completely insulated from seasonal water shortages by the water balance adaptations of the organisms in the trophic levels below them, provided that the top carnivores are sufficiently conservative with water to permit them to maintain water balance without drinking.

It seems clear from this analysis that rainfall is a central parameter in the lives of desert animals. The timing of the main rainfall event, whether summer or winter, should have a major influence on the structure of a desert ecosystem. It should be very profitable to make comparisons of these results for the Mojave Desert with results for a summer-rainfall desert such as the Chihuahuan desert in Mexico.

The general patterns of seasonal water relations of herbivores and carnivores in Figure 6.2 may serve as models of "typical" animals. Comparisons of new results for other species with these models should help reveal new adaptations to deserts (if the patterns are different), or strengthen and broaden the applicability of the present models (if the patterns are similar). However, many deserts are characterized by large year-to-year variations as well as large seasonal variations in rainfall. Thus, it is especially important to conduct field measurements for several years to evaluate the long-term challenges and solutions to desert survival.

ACKNOWLEDGMENTS

Preparation of this paper and some of the research reported here was funded by Contract DE-AC03-76-SF00012 from the U.S. Department of Energy to the University of California.

REFERENCES

Costa, W. R., K. A. Nagy, and V. H. Shoemaker. 1976. Observations of the behavior of jackrabbits (Lepus californicus) in the Mojave Desert. Journal of Mammology. 57:399–402.

Edney, E. B. 1977. Water Balance in Land Arthropods. Springer-Verlag, Berlin.

Gilles, R. 1979. Mechanisms of Osmoregulation in Animals. John Wiley & Sons, Chichester.

Maloiy, G. M. O. 1979. Comparative Physiology of Osmoregulation in Animals. Vols. 1 and 2. Academic Press, London.

Nagy, K. A. 1972. Water and electrolyte budgets of a free-living desert lizard, Sauromalus obesus. Journal of Comparative Physiology 79:39–62.

Nagy, K. A. 1983. Ecological energetics. R. B. Huey, E. R. Pianka, and T. W. Schoener. (Eds.). In Lizard Ecology. Harvard University Press, Cambridge. Pp. 24–54.

Nagy, K. A., and P. A. Medica. 1986. Physiological ecology of desert tortoises in southern Nevada. Herpetologica 42:73–92.

Nagy, K. A., V. H. Shoemaker, and W. R. Costa. 1976. Water, electrolyte and nitrogen budgets of jackrabbits (Lepus californicus) in the Mojave Desert. Physiological Zoology 49:351–63.

Quinton, P. M. 1979. Comparative water metabolism in animals: Protozoa to man. In Comparative Animal Nutrition, Vol. 3, ed. M. Rechcigl. S. Karger, Basel. Pp. 100–231.

Schmidt-Nielsen, K. 1964. Desert Animals: Physiological Problems of Heat and Water. Oxford University Press, New York.

Shoemaker, V. H., K. A. Nagy and W. R. Costa. 1976. Energy utilization and temperature regulation by jackrabbits (Lepus californicus) in the Mojave Desert. Physiological Zoology 49:364–75.

SEVEN

Water Balance in Two Negev Desert Phasianids: The Chukar and the Sand Partridge

A. ALLAN DEGEN AND BERRY PINSHOW

ABSTRACT

Two ground-dwelling phasianids, the sand partridge *(Ammoperdix heyi)* and the chukar *(Alectoris chukar)*, are permanent residents of the Negev desert and are sympatric over much of their Negev ranges. The sand partridge, smaller of the two species (body mass 150 to 250 g) inhabits only arid and very arid areas, whereas the chukar (body mass 400 to 600 g) inhabits deserts only at the margins of its broad Palearctic range. Since desert species generally have lower water requirements than species inhabiting mesic and humid environments, we reasoned that sand partridges would have lower water requirements than chukars, and that this might, in part, explain their different geographical distributions. We therefore measured the water balance of these two species.

We found no difference in water turnover rate between chukars and sand partridges, compared allometrically, either under laboratory conditions (60.0 vs 46.7 $ml \cdot kg^{-0.75} \cdot day^{-1}$) with dry food and water available, *ad libitum*, or under free-living conditions (80.1 vs 79.1 $ml \cdot kg^{-0.75} \cdot day^{-1}$). Both species must drink when only dry food is available; however, need not drink when food of high preformed water content is consumed. Water turnover rate, at least in chukars, showed seasonal trends dependent on forage availability (100 vs 266 to 329 $ml \cdot kg^{-1} \cdot day^{-1}$ in the dry season and after winter rains, respectively). There was no apparent difference in water turnover rate between species when water was available *ad libitum*. However, when offered

This is publication No. 57 from the Mitrani Center for Desert Ecology, Jacob Blaustein Institute.

water intermittently, sand partridges lost body mass more slowly than did chukars, and were better able to recover body mass upon drinking. In addition, sand partridges tolerated drinking NaCl solutions with higher concentrations than can chukars. The last two differences may contribute to the ability of sand partridges to inhabit extremely arid deserts where chukars are absent.

INTRODUCTION

In order to survive in deserts, birds must maintain water balance in the face of severe and widely fluctuating environmental conditions. They must adjust to periodic shortages of water and periods of extreme air temperatures, high solar radiation, and low water vapor pressure (Dawson 1984).

Some diurnal birds (e.g., mourning doves, *Zenaidura macroura*, and sand grouse, *Pterocles* spp.) can inhabit deserts by being able to fly great distances daily to obtain water (Dawson 1976), while others (insectivorous and carnivorous species) can inhabit the desert by eating foods high in preformed water and thereby need not drink (Fisher, Lindgren, and Dawson 1972). In addition, nocturnal predators such as owls and nightjars are inactive during the day and eat food high in preformed water. Diurnal granivorous birds, especially weak fliers such as members of the family phasianidae, are most vulnerable to the harsh desert conditions for they lack the above-mentioned attributes. Also, seeds, their principal food during the summer, yield little preformed water at a time when their water requirements for thermoregulation are greatest.

Although some granivorous passerine birds, at least under laboratory conditions, are able to survive and maintain body mass when offered dry food without drinking water, most seed-eating birds must drink (Bartholomew and Cade 1963; Bartholomew 1972; Dawson 1976). Other primarily granivorous birds, however, can meet their water requirements if succulent vegetation and/or insects are added to their diet (Leopold and McCabe 1957; Gullion 1960; Bartholomew and MacMillen 1961).

The subject of this paper is the water balance of two, primarily granivorous, terrestrial phasianids, the chukar *(Alectoris chukar)* and the sand partridge *(Ammoperdix heyi)*, both permanent residents in Israel. The chukar (350 to 600 g body mass) has an extensive natural distribution in the southern and central Palearctic (Cramp and Simmons 1980) and has been successfully introduced into North America and elsewhere (Bohl 1971). Although considered a bird of semi-arid environments (Cramp and Simmons 1980), the chukar occupies mesic and xeric areas as well. For example, in Israel chukars inhabit Mediterranean, montane, steppe, and desert biomes, and occur in a wide variety of natural and agricultural habitats (Dor 1975).

Two subspecies of chukar are found in Israel: *A. c. cypriotes* in the mesic, Mediterranean zone; and the smaller, paler *A. c. sinaica* in arid areas, including the Negev and Sinai deserts (Nissani 1974). Given its wide geographic range and broad habitat affinities, the chukar may serve as an instructive example of an ecological generalist that is behaviorally and physiologically adapted to the desert environment.

By contrast, the sand partridge (150 to 250 g body mass), smaller than the chukar, is wholly restricted to xeric habitats in southwestern Asia and northeastern Africa. In Israel, it occurs in areas in which the average annual precipitation does not exceed 200mm. Its range includes the Negev and Judean deserts and the lower Jordan valley. It is also found in the most extreme desert region of Israel, the Arava (part of Rift Valley), which has an annual precipitation of 50mm or less and a daily average summer maximum air temperature of about 40°C. In comparison with the chukar, the sand partridge can be considered a desert specialist.

The two species are sympatric over much of their desert ranges in Israel within an area approximately bounded by the 200 and 90mm isohyets. Sand partridges, however, are found in extreme arid areas where chukars are absent. Given the difference in their geographical distributions, we reasoned that the two species might differ in their relative water requirements, since desert species generally have lower water requirements than species inhabiting mesic and humid environments. This has been used as a criterion for defining the distribution of some mammalian (Macfarlane and Howard 1972; Nicol 1978) and avian (Thomas 1982) species.

STUDY AREA

The studies reported here were all made around Sede Boqer (30°52′N, 34° 47′E) in the Negev desert highlands, where chukars and sand partridges are sympatric. Bioclimatically, the region is classed as arid, having 250 to 300 "biologically dry" days per year and a precipitation:evaporation ratio of less than 0.2 (UNESCO 1977). Rain occurs during the winter and, at Sede Boqer, averages 90mm per annum, with large annual differences in total precipitation and in its temporal and spatial distribution (Evenari, Shanan, and Tadmor 1982). Relative humidity averages 58 percent, and dew occurs on about 190 nights annually (Zangvil and Druian 1980). Temperatures are highest in August, with a daily mean of 25.3°C, and are lowest in January, with a daily mean of 9.7°C (Desert Meteorology Unit, Jacob Blaustein Institute for Desert Research).

The major period of plant growth is in winter and early spring, i.e., about mid-January to mid-April, and most herbaceous vegetation is dormant by late May. The onset of germination and the growth of annual and perennial plants are linked to the timing of winter rain, and the extent of plant production is largely determined by the amount and distribution of precipitation. Large annual variations in primary production, especially of annual plants, are characteristic of the region (Evenari, Shanan, and Tadmor 1982).

Birds were captured at two sites: Sede Zin, a loess-covered plain, and in Nahal Zin, an adjacent large canyon. Sede Zin supports sparse natural vegetation dominated by scattered shrubs (e.g., *Hammada scoparia, Zygophyllum dumosum, Atriplex halimus, Artemesia herba-alba*) and includes a variety of herbs and geophytes. Cultivated fields of a neighboring agricultural settlement are also present on the plateau. Nahal Zin supports relatively lush natural vegetation in the immediate vicinity of the main river bed and its tributaries, and generally sparse vegetation in the surrounding flood plain and adjacent slopes. Pools of open water are present throughout the year at several locations.

LABORATORY STUDIES

Maintenance of Birds and General Procedures

Birds were maintained in individual wire mesh cages (30 × 20 × 40 cm) in a controlled environment room, with a 12-hour light: 12-hour dark cycle. Air temperature was maintained at 27°C ± 1°C, and relative humidity ranged between 40 and 65 percent. The birds were fed commercial chicken chow that contained 10 to 12 percent water and the remaining dry matter contained 15 to 19 percent protein, 3 percent fat and 6 percent ash. Gross energy content of the chow ranged between 17.7 and 18.0 kJ per g dry matter.

Drinking water, when offered, was supplied in L-shaped drinkers with raised sides that prevented spillage. A similar drinker was placed near the cages to measure evaporation for which we corrected. Excreta and spilled food were collected in a tray under each cage and were separated manually. Birds were acclimated to these conditions for at least 20 days before measurements began.

All measurements were made starting at 9:00 A.M. each day. Birds were weighed daily for 10 days, and daily measurements were made of food and water intakes. The 10-day excreta output for each bird was pooled, and samples of food and excreta were oven dried at 70°C to constant mass and analyzed for energy content with a ballistic bomb calorimeter. Dry matter digestibility was calculated by difference between dry matter content of the chow consumed and excreta produced and averaged 75 percent. Assimilation energy was calculated from the energy content of the dry matter of food consumed and excreta produced and averaged 80 percent.

Total Water Intake: Ad Libitum Conditions

The balance method was used in three experiments to measure total water intake, i.e., drinking water plus preformed and metabolic water (Pinshow, Degen, and Alkon 1983; Degen 1985; Levgoren, Degen, Pinshow and Golan 1986). To estimate metabolic water produced, we assumed equal digestibilities for all food components and that 1 g each of metabolizable protein, fat, and carbohydrate yielded 0.50 g, 1.07 g, and 0.56 g water, respectively (Schmidt-Nielsen 1979).

Total water turnover was estimated (Degen, Pinshow, and Alkon 1982) using tritiated water following Degen, Pinshow, Alkon, and Arnon (1981). Briefly, the procedure was as follows. A 0.2 ml blood sample was taken by rupturing the basilic vein to measure background level radioactivity. The bird was then weighed, and injected intramuscularly with 0.1 mCi per kg body mass of tritiated water. Following at least 45 min for tritiated water equilibration with body fluids, during which time the bird did not have access to either food or water, a second blood sample was taken to measure total body water volume (i.e., tritiated water space). Further blood samples were then taken to estimate rates of water turnover on the basis of the decline in specific activity of tritium with time.

Table 7.1 summarizes results from birds maintained under laboratory conditions with *ad libitum* dry ration and water. Mean body mass for chukars was 400.5 g and for sand partridges was 172.6 g. Dry matter intake scaled to body mass$^{0.75}$ was similar for the two species and averaged 34.5 $g \cdot kg^{-0.75} \cdot day^{-1}$ for chukars and 31.4 $g \cdot kg^{-0.75} \cdot day^{-1}$ for sand partridges. Mass specific total water intake was similar for the two species; scaled to body mass$^{0.75}$ it was similar for the two species in two studies and was lower in sand partridges than in chukars in a third study. For the three studies, water turnover averaged 46.7 $ml \cdot kg^{-0.75} \cdot day^{-1}$ for sand partridges and 60.0 $ml \cdot kg^{-0.75} \cdot day^{-1}$ for chukars. Water drunk was 72 percent of the total water intake for chukars and 67 percent for sand partridges and the ratio of total water intake (ml) to dry matter intake (g) was 1.73 for chukars and 1.49 for sand partridges.

Responses to Water Deprivation

Two studies were made in which responses to water deprivation were measured: (1) birds were offered water *ad libitum* and then abruptly were denied water until they reached 80 percent of their initial body mass

Table 7.1   **Body Mass, Dry Matter Intake (DMI), and Total Water Intake (TWI) in Chukars and Sand Partridges Offered Water and Dry Food, ad libitum, under Laboratory Conditions**

	Sand partridges	Chukars
Body mass (g)	172.6 (14)	400.5 (18)
DMI (g/day)	8.4 (14)	17.5 (13)
$(g \cdot kg^{-0.75} \cdot day^{-1})$	31.4 (14)	34.5 (13)
TWI (ml)	12.5 (14)	30.2 (18)
$(ml \cdot kg^{-0.75} \cdot day^{-1})$	46.7 (14)	60.0 (18)
Water drunk (ml/day)	8.4 (14)	22.4 (13)
Water drunk/TWI (%)	67.2 (14)	71.9 (13)
TWI/DMI	1.5 (14)	1.7 (18)

Note: Values are presented as means; sample size shown in parentheses.
Source: Degen, Pinshow, and Alkon 1982; Degen 1985; and Levgoren, Degen, Pinshow, and Golan 1986.

(Pinshow, Degen, and Alkon 1983); and (2) birds were gradually denied water for lengthening periods of time (Degen 1985). In the second study, water was offered to the birds once daily for 10 days; once every second day for 10 days; once every third day for 15 days; once every fourth day for 20 days; once every fifth day for 25 days; and once every sixth day for 30 days. On the days water was offered, it was available for 30 min.

In both experiments, least-squares linear regression equations were calculated for the natural logarithmic transforms of the percentage of initial body mass as it changed with time (Kleiber 1975) of water deprivation, and daily changes in body mass were expressed as the percentage change in body mass from the previous day using the equation:

$$\% \text{ change/day} = 100 \left[1 - e^{-(\text{slope} \times 2.302)} \right]$$

Ability to recover body mass when water was offered was measured in both studies.

On the first day following abrupt water removal, body mass of sand partridges declined proportionately faster than did that of chukars (4.6% vs 3.0% body mass), and their rate of decline to 80 percent of their initial body mass was also more rapid (2.9% vs 2.0% body mass per day). Of the total body mass loss for chukars (87.1 g), 60.6 percent was water, and of the total body mass loss for sand partridges (36.1 g), 83.8 percent was water. On the first day water was offered, chukars recovered to 92.8 percent of their initial body mass and sand partridges to 94.7 percent. Both species attained 98 percent of their initial body mass in 5 days and returned to their initial body mass in 14 days (see Table 7.2).

Table 7.2   Body Mass (m_b) Changes During Water Deprivation and Recovery in Sand Partridges and Chukars under Laboratory Conditions

	Sand partridges (4)	Chukars (4)	
Water Deprivation			sig.
m_{bi} (g)	164.4 ± 21.2	416.5 ± 46.1	
% m_b loss on first day	4.55 ± 1.86	2.95 ± 0.80	0.03
Daily % m_b loss until 80% m_{bi}	2.87 ± 0.58	1.98 ± 0.26	0.03
Days to reach 80% m_{bi}	7.00 ± 2.45	11.75 ± 1.50	0.03
Recovery			
% m_{bi} on first day of recovery	94.7 ± 5.0	92.8 ± 2.5	ns
Days to reach 95% m_{bi}	3.75 ± 3.77	1.75 ± 0.5	ns
Days to reach 98% m_{bi}[a]	4.33 ± 5.77[a]	5.25 ± 4.03	ns
Final % m_{bi}	99.2 ± 1.7	101.2 ± 1.67	ns

[a]One sand partridge never reached 98% m_{bi} during the experimental recovery period. Birds declined in m_b until 80 percent of their initial body mass (m_{bi}), then recovered with access to water ad libitum.

Note: Values are means ± SD. Differences between means significant (sig.) at level indicated.

Source: Pinshow, Degen, and Alkon 1983.

With gradual water deprivation, rates of body mass loss at 1 to 3 days of water deprivation were higher in chukars (1.5% to 2.8% per day) than in sand partridges (1.3% to 2.2% per day), but were similar at 4 to 6 days of water deprivation (1.2% to 1.3% per day) (see Table 7.3). Sand partridges consistently recovered their original body mass faster than chukars, and the difference between species was significant in the 5 day water deprivation treatment. Upon drinking after 6 days of water deprivation, sand partridges recovered to 99.1 percent of their initial body mass and chukars to 98.1 percent (see Table 7.4).

Responses to Saline Water Intake

Four chukars and four sand partridges were offered drinking water *ad libitum*, containing NaCl in gradually increasing concentrations (Levgoren, Degen, Pinshow, and Golan 1986). The concentration was increased by 0.1M every 10 days from 0.0M (deionized water) to 0.5M NaCl. In a second study, four birds of each species received constant volumes of NaCl solution that were introduced into their crops by intubation. Chukars received 0.26 $ml \cdot kg^{-0.75} \cdot day^{-1}$ and sand partridges 0.18 $ml \cdot kg^{-0.75} \cdot day^{-1}$, corresponding to the volumes of deionized water they drank in the initial experiments. They received 0.2 M, 0.3M and 0.4M NaCl; each solution for 10 days.

Two of four chukars died after 6 days of drinking 0.4M NaCl *ad libitum*, however the four sand partridges survived drinking 0.5M NaCl *ad libitum* for 10 days. Drinking rate in chukars increased with increasing salinity, whereas in sand partridges it progressively decreased. Both species lost body mass when drinking NaCl solutions of 0.3M or greater, but the rate of body mass decline was less in sand partridges than in chukars. Sand partridges drinking 0.3M and 0.4M NaCl lost body mass slower than ones deprived of water (0.22% and 0.70% vs 1.22% body mass per day), whereas chukars drinking 0.3M and 0.4M NaCl lost body mass faster than water-deprived ones (1.75% and 3.62% vs 1.23% body mass per day). Chukars receiving restricted volumes of NaCl solutions lost body mass slower than when allowed to drink the same concentrations *ad libitum*, and at 0.3M lost body mass slower than water-deprived ones (0.65% vs 1.23% body mass per day).

Food intake, dry matter digestibility, fraction of gross energy assimilated, and ash content of excreta decreased with increasing drinking water salinity in both species. However, these responses occurred at lower NaCl concentrations in chukars than in sand partridges.

OUTDOOR STUDIES ON CAGED BIRDS

Chukars were maintained in an outdoor aviary that was partitioned into four similar cages (each 5 × 3 × 2.5m) constructed of chicken wire (Degen, Pinshow, and Shaw 1984). The birds were fed a diet of a 1:1 mixture of chicken chow and whole sorghum seeds (dry ration) with occasional green

Table 7.3 Changes in Body Mass (m_b) during One to Six Days of Water Deprivation

Days of H₂O Deprivation	Sand partridges (6)					Chukars (5)					
	n	slope ($\times 10^{-2}$)	S.E.$_b$ ($\times 10^{-2}$)	r	m_b change (%/day)	n	slope ($\times 10^{-2}$)	S.E.$_b$ ($\times 10^{-2}$)	r	m_b change (%/day)	sig.[a]
1	107	-.949	.039	.92	-2.21	89	-1.193	.087	.83	-2.78	.001
2	89	-.697	.045	.86	-1.62	74	-.792	.056	.86	-1.85	.05
3	119	-.570	.032	.85	-1.32	99	-.662	.046	.82	-1.53	.01
4	149	-.544	.036	.78	-1.26	124	-.553	.036	.81	-1.28	ns
5	179	-.529	.035	.75	-1.22	149	-.530	.031	.82	-1.23	ns
6	209	-.539	.042	.67	-1.25	174	-.550	.035	.80	-1.27	ns

[a] Level of significance between slopes within treatments.

Note: All intercepts were 2.000 and all regressions were significant ($p < 0.001$). Slope = slopes of the regressions; S.E.$_b$ = standard error of the slopes; n = number of observations. Values are derived from linear regressions of log m_b over time of water deprivation.

Source: Degen 1985.

Table 7.5 Body Mass (m_b), Total Body Water (TBW), and Total Water Influx of Chukars on Four Treatment Diets

Cage	Diet	Body mass (g)			Total body water		Total water influx	
		Initial	Day 8	Day 14	(ml)	(% m_b)	(ml day^{-1})	(ml kg^{-1} day^{-1})
I	dry ration + water	428.2 ± 44.4	422.5 ± 42.7	418.3 ± 42.7	284.9 ± 67.6	67.6 ± 0.9ac	30.6 ± 5.8	72.4 ± 7.2a
II	dry ration + greens	432.5 ± 31.0	436.0 ± 19.8	436.2 ± 19.3	285.4 ± 16.4	65.6 ± 1.8ab	21.9 ± 4.6	50.2 ± 9.9b
III	dry ration + greens + water	402.8 ± 42.0	404.9 ± 43.3	405.0 ± 42.4	261.1 ± 36.8	64.4 ± 2.3b	24.1 ± 3.7	59.7 ± 8.8ab
IV	greens	380.4 ± 39.3	323.4 ± 48.1	312.3 ± 34.0	220.5 ± 38.2	68.1 ± 1.9c	32.3 ± 5.4	103.1 ± 20.9c

Note: There were 6 Chukars in each treatment. Values are given as means ± SD. Values in the same column that are followed by different superscripts are significantly different from each other. TBW was calculated on day 8; water influx was measured between days 8 and 14.

Source: Degen, Pinshow, and Shaw 1984.

Table 7.4   Percentage of Initial Body Mass (m_{bi}) in Sand Partridges and Chukars after Drinking

Days of H$_2$O deprivation	Sand partridges (6)	Chukars (5)
1	100.1 ± 0.5	99.8 ± 0.5
2	99.8 ± 0.9	99.8 ± 0.7
3	99.9 ± 1.0	99.5 ± 0.5
4	99.7 ± 1.5	99.3 ± 1.2
5	99.8 ± 1.3	99.2 ± 1.3[a]
6	99.1 ± 2.7	98.7 ± 2.8

[a]Difference between species is significant ($p < 0.05$).

Note: Values are means ± SD.

Source: Degen 1985.

vegetation (greens) and tap water *ad libitum* for at least 6 weeks prior to the study. During the study, greens consisted of alfalfa seedlings and 5 to 10 day old wheat sprouts.

Twenty-four adult chukars were separated into four groups. Each group was offered one of the following diets for 14 days: dry ration + water; dry ration + greens; dry ration + greens + water; and greens only. Each group had access to its diet, *ad libitum*. Birds were weighed at the start of the experiment and on days 8 and 14. Total body water volume on day 8 and total water turnover rate between days 8 and 14 were estimated using tritiated water.

All birds, except those receiving only green vegetation, maintained their body mass throughout the study. Birds offered only greens lost 15 percent of their initial body mass after 8 days and a further 2.9 percent in the following 6 days (see Figure 7.1).

On day 8 of treatment, total body water volume of the birds ranged from 64.4 percent of body mass for birds receiving dry ration + greens + water to 68.1 percent in birds receiving greens only. Water turnover rate between days 8 and 14 of treatment ranged from 50.2 ml·kg^{-1}·day^{-1} for birds receiving dry ration + greens to 103.1 ml·kg^{-1}·day^{-1} for birds receiving greens only. Differences in both total body water volume and water turnover rate among treatments were significant (see Table 7.5).

STUDIES ON FREE-LIVING BIRDS

Seasonal studies on water turnover rate in free-living chukars and sand partridges were made using tritiated water (Alkon, Pinshow, and Degen 1982; Degen, Pinshow and Alkon 1983; Alkon, Degen, Pinshow, and Shaw

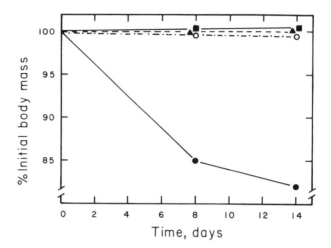

Figure 7.1   Changes in body mass with time, expressed as percent initial body mass, in chukars offered four different diets: dry ration + water (open circles); dry ration + green vegetation (filled squares); dry ration + green vegetation + water (filled triangles); and green vegetation only (filled circles).

1985). Birds were captured with sorghum-baited, wire mesh traps (90 × 90 × 60 cm) having funnel entrances. Captured birds were either processed in the laboratory, a 15 min drive from trapping sites, or in the field. The birds were marked with individually identifiable backtabs (Alkon 1974) and with aluminum and colored plastic leg bands. Total body water volume was estimated for all birds and total water turnover rate for those recaptured.

Water turnover rates remained relatively constant from spring through autumn: approximately 100 $ml \cdot kg^{-1} \cdot day^{-1}$ for chukars and 120 $ml \cdot kg^{-1} \cdot day^{-1}$ for sand partridges. When compared allometrically, there was no difference between species: 80.1 $ml \cdot kg^{-0.75} \cdot day^{-1}$ for chukars and 79.1 $ml \cdot kg^{-0.75} \cdot day^{-1}$ for sand partridges. Immediately after winter rains, water turnover rate in chukars increased significantly to 329 $ml \cdot kg^{-1} \cdot day^{-1}$ in 1981 and 266 $ml \cdot kg^{-1} \cdot day^{-1}$ in 1982. In addition, at the time of rains, their mean total body water volume increased from 65.9 percent to 73.6 percent of body mass in 1980–81 and from 62 percent to 68.3 percent of body mass in 1981–82 (see Table 7.6).

DISCUSSION

Captive Birds

To compare total water intake among birds, Pinshow, Degen, and Alkon (1983) calculated an allometric equation relating total water turnover to body mass for 19 avian species for which measurement conditions were as follows: (1) the birds were supplied with food and tap (or deionized) water *ad libitum*,

Table 7.6   Seasonal Body Mass (m_b), Tritiated Water Space (TOH), and Water Turnover Rates (WTR) in Chukars and Sand Partridges

	Chukars	Sand partridges
Autumn 1980		
*m_b (g)	446.2 ± 51.6 (30)	
TOH space (% m_b)	65.9 ± 2.5 (30)	
#m_b (g)	409.6 ± 38.1 (13)	
WTR (ml · kg^{-1} · day^{-1})	98.7 ± 14.4 (13)	
During rains 1981		
*m_b (g)	420.6 ± 49.3 (11)	
TOH space (% m_b)	73.6 ± 3.8 (11)	
#m_b (g)	414.5 ± 32.6 (4)	
WTR (ml · kg^{-1} · day^{-1})	102.8 ± 4.4 (4)	
Post rains 1981		
*m_b (g)	447.1 ± 54.3 (17)	
TOH space (% m_b)	70.0 ± 1.9 (17)	
#m_b (g)	435.2 ± 42.0 (8)	
WTR (ml · kg^{-1} · day^{-1})	328.5 ± 67.0 (8)	
Summer 1981		
*m_b (g)	460.8 ± 56.0 (40)	176.6 ± 21.4 (42)
TOH space (% m_b)	67.4 ± 2.5 (40)	69.8 ± 4.8 (42)
#m_b (g)	444.5 ± 52.2 (29)	173.1 ± 21.9 (39)
WTR (ml · kg^{-1} · day^{-1})	100.6 ± 19.8 (29)	122.5 ± 31.9 (39)
Before and during rains 1982		
*m_b (g)	456.2 ± 45.0 (10)	
TOH space (% mb)	62.8 ± 5.0 (10)	
# m_b (g)	479.7 ± 64.7 (6)	
WTR (ml · kg^{-1} · day^{-1})	160.9 ± 28.5 (6)	
Post rains 1982		
*m_b (g)	449.0 ± 77.0 (15)	
TOH space (% m_b)	68.3 ± 3.0 (15)	
#m_b (g)	479.3 ± 63.6 (8)	
WTR (ml · kg^{-1} · day^{-1})	266.2 ± 62.9 (8)	
Spring 1983		
*m_b (g)	534.0 ± 66.8 (5)	204.7 ± 9.9 (7)
TOH space (% m_b)	67.3 ± 2.9 (5)	67.6 ± 1.5 (7)
#m_b (g)	498.5 ± 70.2 (4)	202.9 ± 12.6 (5)
WTR (ml · kg^{-1} · day^{-1})	96.0 ± 23.8 (4)	118.4 ± 16.5 (5)

Note: Values are represented as means ± SD; sample size shown in parentheses. * indicates birds that were captured once and in which TOH space was measured. # indicates recaptured birds in which WTR was measured.

Source: Alkon, Pinshow, and Degen 1982; Degen, Pinshow, and Alkon 1983; Alkon, Degen, Pinshow, and Shaw 1985.

and (2) the birds were confined and apparently non-stressed. The calculated regression equation was:

log water turnover rate (ml/day) = 0.745 log body mass (g) + log 0.651

In two studies we found no difference in total water intake between chukars and sand partridges when compared allometrically (Pinshow, Degen, and Alkon 1983; Degen 1985), and in a third study sand partridges had a lower intake than chukars (Levgoren, Degen, Pinshow, and Golan 1986). McNabb (1969) reported no difference in *ad libitum* water intake among caged birds of three new world quail species that inhabit different climatic areas. It appears that wild phasianids have relatively low water turnover rates, averaging 41 percent to 54 percent of the value calculated for their body masses by the above equation (see Table 7.7) and, that comparison of water intake measurements made under nonstressful laboratory conditions might be of limited value in the interspecific comparison of phasianids.

We considered two conflicting possibilities when measuring rates of body mass loss in response to water deprivation. Based on allometric considerations, we expected sand partridges to lose body mass at a relatively faster rate than chukars. However, based on ecological considerations, we expected sand partridges to lose body mass at a relatively slower rate than chukars.

Other studies on water-deprived birds have shown that body mass loss was slowest in xerophilous species, and not necessarily in the largest ones. For example, when deprived of water and offered only dry food, the xerophilous Gambel's quail (*Callipepla gambelii*, body mass = 150 g), and the mesophilous California quail (*Callipepla californicus*, body mass = 150 g), both lost 2.2 percent body mass per day (Bartholomew and MacMillen 1961; McNabb 1969), whereas the mesophilous bobwhite (*Colinus virginianus*, body mass = 180 g), largest of these three phasianids, lost 3.7 percent body mass per day (McNabb 1969).

Contrasting results were found in the responses to water deprivation in sand partridges and chukars. With abrupt water deprivation, sand partridges lost body mass at a faster rate than chukars (Pinshow, Degen, and Alkon 1983). However, when denied water for gradually increasing intervals, sand partridges lost body mass more slowly than did chukars when deprived of water for 1 to 3 days and lost body mass at a similar rate to chukars when deprived of water for 4 to 6 days.

In the former study, birds were abruptly denied water following 60 days of *ad libitum* intake. During these 60 days, the birds had no need to conserve body fluids and their excretory systems were probably ridding the body of excess water. Abrupt deprivation of drinking water may not result in the immediate curtailment of the excretion of water and/or the immediate onset of water-conserving mechanisms. This may result in a period of continued loss of water and body mass, even in the absence of drinking water. In the latter study, sand partridges drank 8.6 ml per day when water was available *ad libitum*, and 3.9 ml per day when available for only 30 minutes daily. Yet,

Table 7.7 Measured and Predicted Water Flux Per Day for Captive Phasianid Birds Offered Food and Water *ad libitum*

	Body mass (g)	Water flux measured (A) (ml)	Water flux predicted[a] (B) (ml)	A/B (%)	Habitat	Reference
Coturnix quail (*Coturnix coturnix*)	111.0	23.5	22.4	105.0	Domestic	Chapman and McFarland 1971
Gambel's quail (*Callipepla gambelii*)	148.8	14.3	27.9	51.3	Xeric	McNabb 1969
California quail (*Callipepla californicus*)	149.4	12.4	28.0	44.4	Mesic, Xeric	McNabb 1969
Sand partridge (*Ammoperdix heyi*)	172.6	12.5	30.2	41.4	Xeric	Present review
Bobwhite (*colinus virginianus*)	180.5	17.3	32.2	53.7	Humid, Mesic	McNabb 1969
Chukar (*Alectoris chukar*)	400.5	30.2	56.6	53.4	Mesic, Xeric	Present review
Domestic fowl (*Gallus domesticus*)	4045.9	268.1	328.6	81.6	Domestic	Chapman and Black 1967 Chapman and Mihai 1972

[a] Using equation for 19 birds:: log water flux (ml/day) = 0.747 log body mass (g) + log 0.664.

Note: Measurements were made either by total water balance or tritiated water.

Source: Pinshow, Degen, and Alkon 1983.

in both cases, the birds gained body mass and presumably met water requirements. This suggests that their *ad libitum* water intake greatly exceeded their requirements and their renal and digestive systems had to void this excess water.

The gradual increase in intervals of water deprivation allowed water conservation mechanisms to respond. The most pronounced difference between the species was in their rates of evaporative water loss. In spite of the difference in body mass between species, mass specific evaporative water loss of chukars was 1.4 times that of sand partridges. Evaporative water loss was 41 percent of the total water loss in sand partridges and 60 percent in chukars. This value for chukars was similar to that found in three other dehydrated phasianid species, but that for sand partridges was 20 percent to 30 percent lower than these species (McNabb 1969).

During dehydration, mean voided fluid osmolality was approximately 600 mOsm/kg in chukars and sand partridges (Thomas, Pinshow, and Degen 1984). Since both species lack functional salt glands (Thomas, Degen, and Pinshow 1982), we expected that these birds drinking NaCl solutions of 0.3M or greater would have a more rapid decline in body mass than water-deprived ones, for they would be forced to use body fluids to excrete excess electrolytes. Indeed, chukars drinking 0.3M and 0.4M NaCl lost body mass faster than water-deprived ones. However, sand partridges drinking these solutions lost body mass more slowly than water-deprived ones.

This may be explained by the different patterns of fluid intake exhibited by chukars and sand partridges. Chukars increased their consumption with increasing NaCl concentrations, a response also found in the song sparrow, *Melospiza melodia,* (Bartholomew and Cade 1963); whereas sand partridges decreased their consumption, as found in the zebra finch, *Phoephila guttata,* and the savannah sparrow, *Passerculus sandwichenesis beldingi* (Poulson and Bartholomew 1962; Skadhauge and Bradshaw 1974). The latter species were more tolerant of NaCl solutions than were the former.

The fact that a decrease in fluid intake of NaCl solutions could be beneficial was also observed in chukars. Chukars administered restricted volumes of 0.3M and 0.4M NaCl lost body mass more slowly than chukars drinking the same solutions *ad libitum.* In addition, the individual chukar with the lowest drinking rate at 0.3M NaCl lost body mass more slowly than the other chukars (1.2% vs at least 1.7% per day), and the two chukars with the highest drinking rates lost body mass fastest, and died after drinking 0.4M NaCl for 6 days.

These observations could be related to one of the modes of electrolyte excretion in birds. Cations are co-precipitated with uric acid and urates which allows a portion of urinary electrolytes to be voided that neither require urinary water nor increase urine osmolality (McNabb and McNabb 1980). As a result, birds ingesting small amounts of salt are able to excrete a large portion of it without excreting additional water, while birds ingesting large quantities of salt have to excrete most of it dissolved in water (obligatory urine).

Free-Living Birds

We observed birds of both species drinking in the wild. Others have reported that chukars concentrate at open water sources during the summer (e.g., Alkon 1974) and that they may be dependent on free water when succulent vegetation is not available (Bump 1953; Christensen 1954; McLean 1955; Harper, Harry, and Bailey 1958). Little information is available on the dependence of sand partridges on free water. Meinertzhagen (1954) reported that sand partridges invariably occur near open water while G. Ilani (personal communication) reported that some populations live in areas devoid of surface water.

Our laboratory studies have shown that both chukars and sand partridges must drink when only dry food is available (Pinshow, Degen, and Alkon 1983; Degen 1985). Outdoor, caged studies have shown that chukars can maintain body mass when green vegetation consisting of young seedlings (80% water) are added to their diet (Degen, Pinshow, and Shaw 1984). This has also been demonstrated for sand partridges under laboratory conditions (our unpublished observations). Chukars receiving only green vegetation in outdoor cages had the highest water turnover rates, however they could not maintain body mass. Their physiological requirements for water were apparently exceeded, but their energy demands could not be met. These birds also had the highest total body water volume:body mass ratio, reflecting a loss of body solids and a decline in the physical condition of the birds.

We observed similar responses in free-living birds. From spring to early winter (before rains), water turnover rates remained relatively constant for the two species and there was no difference between them when compared allometrically. Before the rains, seeds were their principal food. Immediately after the rains, which brought about widespread germination of annuals, water turnover rates increased significantly in chukars. Green vegetation was their principal food during this period (Alkon, Pinshow, and Degen 1982; Alkon, Degen, Pinshow, and Shaw 1984). No measurements during and after the winter rains were made on sand partridges as none were captured.

We concluded that seasonal changes in water turnover rate were a function of the birds' preformed water intake, i.e., high water turnover rate was the unavoidable consequence of a diet consisting primarily of green vegetation. In 1981–82, the water content of chukar crop contents rose from 57 percent in summer/autumn, to 68 percent in early winter (January) and to 82 percent in late winter (February/March). The birds' diets shifted from 64 percent seeds and 4 percent vegetation, to 37 percent seeds and 25 percent vegetation and to 5 percent seeds and 82 percent vegetation, respectively, during these periods (see Figure 7.2). We calculated that the water content of the chukar diet during late winter, 1981, was 87 percent (Alkon, Degen, Pinshow, and Shaw 1985).

Differences in maximum daily water turnover rates between 1981 and 1982 (329 ml/kg vs 266 ml/kg) were interpreted to mean that less green

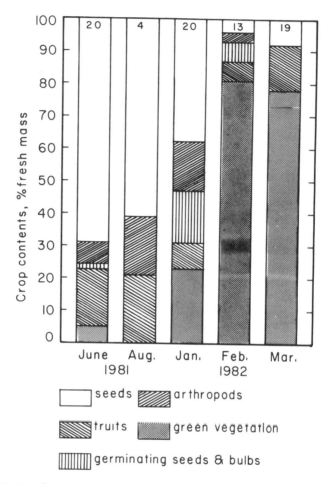

Figure 7.2 Fresh matter components of chukar crop contents during summer (June, August), winter (January, February), and spring (March). Crop contents were separated into items of high (green vegetation, germinating seeds and bulbs, fruits, and arthropods) and low (seeds) moisture content. The numbers of crops analyzed each season are given at the top of each column (Degen, Pinshow, and Shaw 1984).

forage was available relative to seeds and as a result chukars consumed proportionately less vegetation. Indeed, in 1981, there were heavy winter rains and rich development of vegetation. In contrast, in 1982, there was light rainfall and poor development of vegetation. In addition, at the time of winter rains there were significant increases in the total body water:body mass ratio in chukars. This suggested a decline in body condition, as was observed in caged birds offered a diet of greens only, which was probably due to mobilization of fat reserves because of inclement weather during winter and/or due to the birds' inability to consume enough energy when feeding mainly on green vegetation.

Conclusions

(1) There was no difference in water turnover rate between chukars and sand partridges, compared allometrically, either under laboratory conditions with dry food and water available *ad libitum*, or under free-living conditions.

(2) Both species must drink when only dry food is available; however, need not drink when food of high preformed water content is consumed.

(3) Water turnover rates in chukars showed seasonal trends dependent on forage availability.

(4) When offered water intermittently, sand partridges lost body mass more slowly than did chukars, and were better able to recover body mass upon drinking.

(5) Sand partridges can tolerate drinking NaCl solutions with higher concentrations than can chukars.

The last two differences may contribute to the ability of sand partridges to inhabit extremely arid deserts where chukars are absent.

ACKNOWLEDGMENT

The preparation of this review was supported, in part, by a United States–Israel Binational Science Foundation grant (2911/82) to A. Allan Degen.

REFERENCES

Alkon, P. U. 1974. Social behavior in a population of chukar partridge (*Alectoris chukar cypriotes*) in Israel. Ph.D. thesis Cornell University, Ithaca, N.Y.

Alkon, P. U., A. A. Degen, B. Pinshow and P. J. Shaw. 1985. Phenology, diet, and water turnover rates of Negev desert chukars. *Journal of Arid Environments* 9:51–61.

Alkon, P. U., B. Pinshow and A. A. Degen. 1982. Seasonal water turnover rates and body water volumes in desert chukars. *Condor* 84:332–37.

Bartholomew, G. A. 1972. The water economy of seed-eating birds that survive without drinking. *Proceedings of the International Ornithological Congress* 15:237–45.

Bartholomew, G. A., and T. J. Cade. 1963. The water economy of land birds. *Auk* 80:504–39.

Bartholomew, G. A., and R. E. MacMillen. 1961. Water economy of the California quail and its use of sea water. *Auk* 78:504–14.

Bohl, W. H. 1971. The chukar and great partridges. U.S. Fish and Wildlife Service, Foreign Game Leaflet. 24.

Bump, G. 1953. Summary of field work in the Middle East and observations on project activities in the southwest. U.S. Fish and Wildlife Service, Final Report, 1952–53. Foreign Game Introduction Project.

Christenson, G. C. 1954. The chukar partridge in Nevada. Nevada Fish and Game Commission, Biological Bulletin 1.

Cramp, S., and K. E. L. Simmons. 1980. Handbook of the birds of Europe, the Middle East and North Africa. *The Birds of the Western Palearctic, Vol. 2.* Oxford University Press, London.

Dawson, W. R. 1976. Physiological and behavioral adjustments of birds to heat and aridity. *Proceedings of the International Ornithological Congress* 16:455–67.

———. 1984. Physiological studies of desert birds: Present and future considerations. *Journal of Arid Environments* 7:133–55.

Degen, A. A. 1985. Responses to intermittent water intakes in sand partridges and chukars. *Physiological Zoology* 58:1–8.

Degen, A. A., B. Pinshow, and P. U. Alkon. 1982. Water flux in chukar partridges (*Alectoris chukar*) and a comparison with other birds. *Physiological Zoology* 55:64–71.

———. 1983. Summer water turnover rates in free-living chukars and sand partridges in the Negev desert. *Condor* 85:333–37.

Degen, A. A., B. Pinshow, P. U. Alkon, and H. Arnon. 1981. Tritiated water for estimating total body water and water turnover rate in birds. *Journal of Applied Physiology* 51:1183–88.

Degen, A. A., B. Pinshow, and P. J. Shaw. 1984. Must desert chukars (*Alectoris chukar sinaica*) drink water? Water influx and body mass changes in response to dietary water content. *Auk* 101:47–52.

Dor, M. 1975. *Zoological Lexicon, Vertebrata* (in Hebrew). Dvir Tel-Aviv.

Evenari, M., L. Shanan, and N. Tadmor. 1982. *The Negev: The Challenge of the Desert.* 2nd ed. Harvard University Press, Cambridge.

Fisher, C. D., E. Lindgren, and W. R. Dawson. 1972. Drinking patterns and behavior of Australian desert birds in relation to their ecology and abundance. *Condor* 74:111–36.

Gullion, G. W. 1960. The ecology of Gambel's quail in Nevada and the arid southwest. *Ecology* 41:518–36.

Harper, H. T., B. H. Harry, and W. D. Bailey. 1958. The chukar partridge in California. *Calif. Fish and Game* 44:5–50.

Kleiber, M. 1975. *The Fire of Life.* R. E. Krieger Pub. Co., Huntington, NY.

Leopold, A. S., and A. McCabe. 1957. Natural history of the Montezuma quail in Mexico. *Condor* 59:3–26.

Levgoren, M., A. A. Degen, B. Pinshow, and Y. Golan. 1986. Responses to saline drinking water in two desert phasianids, the chukar and the sand partridge. *Physiological Zoology* 59:123–29.

Macfarlane, W. V., and B. Howard. 1972. Comparative water and energy economy of wild and domestic animals. *Symposium, Zoological Society of London* 31:261–96.

McLean, D. L. 1955. California chukar partridge report. Western States Commission Quarterly Report 2(2).

McNabb, F. M. A. 1969. A comparative study of water balance in three species of quail. I. Water turnover in the absence of temperature stress. *Comparative Biochemistry and Physiology* 28:1045–58.

McNabb, F. M. A., and R. A. McNabb. 1980. Physiological chemistry of uric acid: solubility, colloid and ion-binding properties. *Comparative Biochemistry and Physiology* 67A:27–34.

Meinertzhagen, R. 1954. *Birds of Arabia.* Oliver and Boyd, London.

Nicol, S. C. 1978. Rates of water turnover in marsupials and eutherians: a comparative review with new data on the Tasmanian devil. *Australian Journal of Zoology* 26:465–73.

Nissani, R. 1974. Geographic variability of the chukar partridge, *Alectoris chukar* (Gray), and Bergmann's rule. M.Sc. thesis Hebrew University, Jerusalem (in Hebrew).

Pinshow, B., A. A. Degen, and P. U. Alkon. 1983. Water intake, existence energy, and responses to water deprivation in the sand partridge *Ammoperdix heyi* and the chukar *Alectoris chukar:* Two phasianids of the Negev desert. *Physiological Zoology* 56:281–89.

Poulson, T. L., and G. A. Bartholomew. 1962. Salt balance in the savannah sparrow. *Physiological Zoology* 35:109–19.

Schmidt-Nielsen, K. 1979. *Animal Physiology.* Cambridge University Press, Cambridge.

Skadhauge, E., and S. D. Bradshaw. 1974. Saline drinking and cloacal excretion of salt and water in the zebra finch. *American Journal of Physiology* 227:1263–67.

Thomas, D. H. 1982. Physiology of the avian kidney. In *Veterinary nephrology,* ed. W. Hall. Wm. Heinemann Medical Books London.

Thomas, D. H., A. A. Degen, and B. Pinshow. 1982. Do phasianid birds really have functional salt glands? Absence of nasal salt secretion in salt loaded sand partridges and chukars *(Ammoperdix heyi* and *Alectoris chukar sinaica)*. *Physiological Zoology* 55:323–26.

Thomas, D. H., B. Pinshow, and A. A. Degen. 1984. Renal and lower intestinal contributions to the water economy of desert dwelling phasianid birds: Comparison of free-living and captive chukars and sand partridges. *Physiological Zoology* 57:128–36.

UNESCO. 1977. Map of the world distribution of arid regions. *MAB Technical Notes*. 7. Union Typographique, Villeneuve-Saint-Georges.

Zangvil, A., and P. Druian. 1980. Measurements of dew at a desert site in southern Israel. *Geographical Research Forum* 2:26–34.

EIGHT

Moonlighting and Other Insights into the Behavioral Ecology of Negev Porcupines

PHILIP U. ALKON

ABSTRACT

Indian crested porcupines *(Hystrix indica)* are large, nocturnal, herbivorous rodents that excavate belowground plant biomass and also consume a variety of agricultural crops. As a first step in defining their foraging strategies and deriving rational approaches to damage control, we measured year-round temporal and spatial activity patterns in Negev desert porcupines by radio location telemetry. During fall and winter, porcupines optimized surface activity for minimal exposure to moonlight, presumably as an anti-predator behavior. The moon avoidance response disappeared by summer, when activity duration corresponded to total night hours regardless of moon phase. Short summer nights may contain insufficient moonless hours to warrant use of dark periods alone for activity. The foraging time and food intake forgone during bright phases of winter lunar cycles is defined as a predator avoidance cost, and can be expressed in the currencies of optimal foraging models. The northern range limits of the species may be set for foraging time requirements relative to the duration of summer nights. Porcupine home ranges averaged 1.5 km², but differed between "natural" and "agricultural" foragers. Porcupines also remained closer to dens during moonlight periods. Attempts to define porcupine foraging strategies using simple, deterministic models were equivocal. Available data suggest, however, that food intake will be significantly constrained by available foraging time in animals dependent on natural

This is publication No. 55 from the Mitrani Center for Desert Ecology, Jacob Blaustein Institute.

biomass, and by gut capacity for those consuming cultivated potatoes. From patterns of porcupine foraging in crops, we propose artificial lighting and field geometries that minimize edge as two passive means of damage control. In summary, porcupines are excellent subjects for elucidating the foraging ecology of large, generalist herbivores in uncertain desert environments. Future research directions are outlined.

RESEARCH FRAMEWORK

Indian crested porcupines *(Hystrix indica)* (see Figure 8.1) are large ($\bar{x}$ body mass = 14 kg), nocturnal herbivores that are active year-round. In their Negev desert habitats these hystricomorph rodents must contend with overall low levels of plant biomass, and with marked temporal and spatial fluctuations in available food and water. What are the survival strategies of large herbivores in uncertain desert environments? Specifically, how do crested porcupines meet their substantial nutrient and water requirements while faced with large environmental fluctuations on the one hand, and with internal and external constraints on food intake on the other?

These questions comprise the framework of an ongoing project on the

Figure 8.1   An Indian crested porcupine *(Hystrix indica)* in captivity.
This adult male was used in feeding experiments.

behavioral ecology of crested porcupines in the Negev desert highlands. Our ultimate aim is to define the animal's foraging strategies in terms of contemporary ecological optimization theory.

WHY PORCUPINES?

Crested porcupines possess two attributes that enhance their survival in warm deserts. First, in common with many desert mammals, they are nocturnal and thereby avoid the thermoregulatory stresses imposed by daytime desert climates during much of the year. During daytime they den in family groups or clans, using either natural caves or large burrows which they excavate. Second, porcupines consume substantial amounts of below-ground plant biomass, e.g., tubers, bulbs, rhizomes (Gutterman 1982). They thereby exploit a relatively stable food resource for which they have no important competitors.

Because geophytes and hemicryptophytes are prominent in Negev flora (Danin 1983; Evenari 1981), it is likely that porcupines exert a significant influence on vegetation patterns as plant predators (Olsvig-Whittaker et al. 1983). Moreover, in excavating belowground plant storage organs they create soil pockets that are favorable habitats for germination (Gutterman 1982). Resultant soil displacement and microtopographical modifications also influence soil and water regimes in Negev hillside ecosystems (Yair and Shachak 1982). Thus, Negev porcupines may be important regulators of biological and physical ecosystem processes.

Porcupines are also of economic interest as a source of wild meat and, more importantly, as agricultural pests. In Israel, porcupines consume a variety of root and above-ground crops, and gnaw irrigation tubing and the bark of cultivated trees. In fact, they are widely perceived as the most serious agricultural pest among the country's large mammals (Dr. L. Benjamini, pers. comm.). We suspect that they may be especially troublesome in arid zones where irrigation, fertilization and other artificial inputs result in highly productive habitats that contrast sharply with surrounding desert landscapes. Our porcupine work encompasses both natural and agricultural habitats, and thus should yield useful insights on resolving wildlife damage problems in desert agriculture.

APPROACH

Our initial field work aimed at characterizing seasonal patterns of porcupine surface activity and their environmental determinants. In experiments with captive animals we also sought to measure porcupine feeding rates and to estimate their energy and water requirements (Alkon et al. 1986). Because porcupines are nocturnal and wary (a likely reason for the paucity of scientific information on their field behavior), direct visual observation of their activity was not feasible. We therefore employed radiotracking as the principal field study method. Animals were live-captured (Alkon 1984) and equipped with transmitter collars, and their night-long activity patterns were remotely monitored throughout the year at intervals of three to ten nights depending on seasonal variability (Alkon and Saltz 1985a; Saltz and Alkon 1985). Sufficient data to estimate seasonal activity parameters were obtained for eight individuals in the Sede Boqer population. The variables measured were presence or absence of surface activity and location.

SOME RESULTS AND IMPLICATIONS

"Moonlighting"

Many desert rodents restrict surface activity to dark moonless periods, presumably to avoid predators (Rosenzweig 1974). We suspected that porcupines might behave similarly. Indeed, during autumn and winter (defined here as October through March), porcupines scheduled surface activity so as to optimize for minimal exposure to moonlight (see Figure 8.2A) (Saltz and Alkon 1983). On nights beginning with a period of dark (lunar phases 1 to 6), animals left their dens soon after sunset, and they remained active longer as the moon appeared later at night and as its size diminished. During phases with the moon present at sunset (7 to 12), the animals increasingly delayed surface activity as moon duration and size increased. Moon phase also influenced movement patterns. On a year-round basis, porcupines were recorded at significantly shorter distances from dens during moonlit hours than during dark periods (i.e., 438 ± 118mm vs 673 ± 144m) (Saltz and Alkon forthcoming).

Beginning in April, however, the temporal moon-avoidance response waned, and it completely disappeared in all animals by late summer (see Figure 8.2b). In fact, mean surface activity duration increased from 6.7 ± 0.8 hrs in winter to 9.2 ± 1.3 hrs in August and September (Alkon and Saltz 1985b). Activity duration in winter corresponded to all available moonless hours and to about one-half of total night hours (based on civil twilight). In late summer, activity duration corresponded to total night hours or twice that of available moonless hours. Thus porcupine surface activity appears bounded by available dark hours during winter and by total night hours during late summer (Alkon and Saltz forthcoming).

Why do porcupines avoid moonlight? We hypothesize that this is an anti-predator behavior. Porcupines exposed to bright ambient light are more visible and presumably risk a greater probability of detection by nocturnal predators. Anecdotal observations suggest that large cats (e.g., leopards) are efficient porcupine predators (Kingdon 1974), but we have also observed wolves (*Canis lupus pallipes*) chasing porcupines in the study area. Such harassment may in itself be a strong selective force. By forcing prey to forego feeding and to expend considerable energy in escape and defense, predator harassment may result in nutritional deficits among susceptible prey and thereby render them less fit reproductively.

Why then do porcupines risk substantial moonlight exposure in summer? It is conceivable that porcupines have no choice, owing to seasonal limitations in length of night and available moonless hours. At 30° N latitude, duration of night declines from 12.8 hrs in mid-December to 8.9 hrs in mid-June; monthly moonless periods decline from 211 hrs in January to only 143 hrs in July (List 1958). According to this hypothesis insufficient moonless hours are available in late summer to allow porcupines to exploit dark periods alone for surface activity. At some point in late spring or early summer (depending on individual) the animals abandon a moonlight avoidance response altogether and expand activity to include the entire night. It is conceivable that porcupines could optimize temporal activity patterns for some reduction in exposure to moonlight even in late summer, but the marginal benefits may not be worth the effort required for precise tracking of lunar conditions. It is also possible that porcupines actually require more time for foraging during summer owing to depleted food supplies. This hypothesis is consistent with seasonal vegetation dynamics.

Time and Energy Requirements

We have not yet derived detailed activity budgets for field porcupines owing to limitations in present monitoring techniques. Yet feeding tests with captive animals indicate that porcupines must expend substantial time for foraging alone (Alkon and Saltz 1985a). For example, fasted porcupines required about 6 hrs of feeding on freely available potatoes (a favored food) to become satiated. It is likely that the foraging times needed by field animals are even greater. We also estimated the daily maintenance energy requirements of captive animals as 220 kj.kg^{-1}.d^{-1}, or 3080 k;.d^{-1} for an average 14 kg animal (Alkon et al. 1986). This is equivalent to about 1400 g fresh mass of potatoes or of *Erodium hirtum* tubers, a heavily consumed wild forage. Either diet would also satisfy the water requirements of the animals.

How Porcupines Perceive Risk

Optimization analyses are framed in terms of costs and benefits. Many of the costs and benefits associated with various behavioral options are relatively easy to quantify in units of energy or time, the most commonly accepted "currencies" of animal behavior. Predation cost, the probability of sustaining

Figure 8.2 (opposite) Temporal distribution of porcupine surface activity according to moon phase. Shading represents percent of marked porcupines that were out of their dens in 50 minute intervals following sunset. Phases 1 to 6 are during a waning moon (moon is absent at sunset); phases 7 to 12 are during a waxing moon (moon present at sunset). 8.2.a. Winter (October–March) patterns. 8.2.b. Summer (April–September) patterns. (Alkon and Saltz forthcoming).

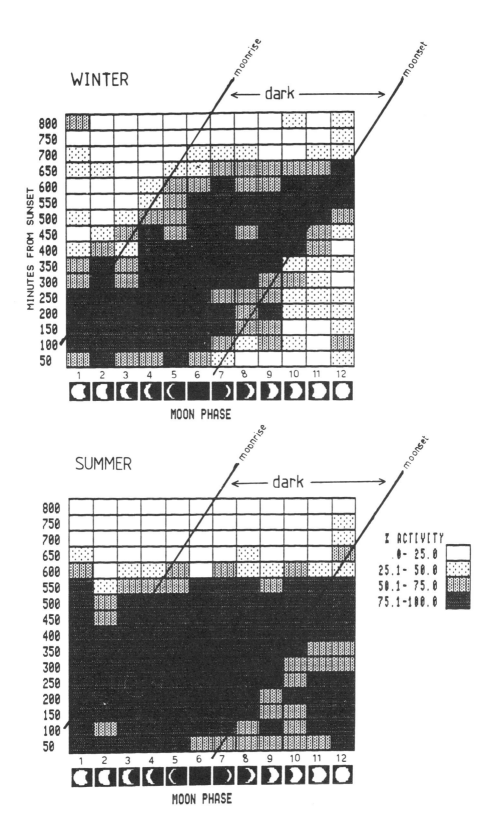

injury or death owing to predation, is a much less tractable variable. Given the technological, budgetary, and manpower constraints on field studies, it is usually impossible to estimate the mortality risks associated with foraging decisions made by free-ranging animals. How then may we incorporate predation risk in quantitative models of animal behavior?

I believe that the winter activity patterns of porcupines offer a revealing clue. Figure 8.3 depicts surface activity during an average winter lunar cycle as percent departures from mean activity duration. Essentially, porcupines display a compensatory pattern of activity, i.e., a reduction in activity during bright moon phases and expanded activity in subsequent dark nights. (The large variability of individual behavior during phases 3, 9, and 10, as reflected by high cv values, suggests that the animals are faced with especially tough decisions during transition phases from bright to dark nights and vice versa). Such a pattern is obviously founded on a wholly predictable environmental fluctuation of appropriate duration, such as the lunar cycle.

Of particular interest is the deficit in activity incurred during bright moonlit nights. This amounts to up to -1.8 ± 0.2 hrs per night (or -24 percent of mean activity duration) during phase 12, and a cumulative deficit of -13.6 ± 2.7 hrs during the consecutive 10-day period encompassed by phases 1, 2, 11 and 12. Moreover, from feeding rates of captive animals and assuming that all activity deficits are equivalent to a loss of foraging, the energy deficit during bright nights is about 5032 kj (on a diet of freely available potatoes), or 6.1 percent of the 10-day maintenance energy requirement of a 14 kg porcupine (Alkon, Kotler, and Saltz forthcoming).

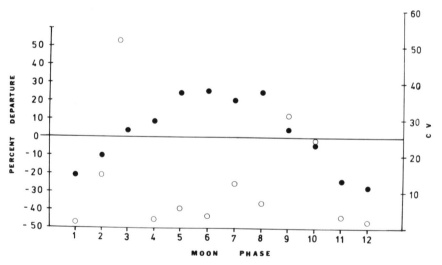

Figure 8.3   Compensatory activity durations of porcupine surface activity during an average winter lunar cycle. Data are percent departures from mean surface activity from six animals. Solid circles are percent departures; open circles are coefficients of variation. Moon phases are as in Figure 8.2. (Alkon and Saltz forthcoming).

We propose that the extent of a benefit forgone (e.g., foraging time or energy intake forfeited) provides a realistic and tractable means of ascribing quantitative values to the "minimal" (nonlethal) costs of predation (Alkon, Kotler, and Saltz forthcoming). In the present example, we conclude that porcupines perceive moon-exposure risk as equivalent to up to 20 percent of their per diem activity time and energy requirement, or about 6 percent of that requirement over a 10-day span. Given that porcupines remain closer to their dens on bright than dark nights, minimal predation costs may also be quantitatively estimated as spatial units or "food patches" not exploited when the moon is present.

On the Limits to Porcupine Distribution

Both field and captive animal data suggest that porcupines need, on the average, at least seven hours of surface activity to meet foraging needs. This implies that *H. indica* should not occur in areas where nights are shorter than seven hours for any appreciable period. To test this hypothesis, we examined a recent range map (Harrison 1972) and found that the most northern population of this widespread Asiatic species is reported in Turkmen S.S.R. near the Caspian Sea. At this latitude (45° N) the duration of night during the summer solstice is 7.1 hours (List 1958). This suggests that the northern latitudinal distribution of the species may, indeed, be determined by temporal surface activity requirements. To exist north of this limit, crested porcupines would either be smaller (and thereby have lower energy and foraging time requirements) or would not be strictly nocturnal. Apparently, neither of these conditions are met.

Food and Other Environmental Influences

It is axiomatic that food density fluctuations influence animal behavior patterns. The presence of agricultural fields having dense food resources available within discrete temporal and spatial bounds, provided a promising "natural" experimental setting for testing foraging responses. Potatoes were especially useful in this regard: They are heavily consumed by porcupines, are available in immense quantities during early and mid-winter, and then largely "disappear" by January or February following harvest. We also assumed that seasonal changes in the availability of geophytes and other natural forage corresponded to climatic regime and general phenology, i.e., peak abundances in early spring and declining thereafter.

Initially we compared rather gross behavioral parameters (e.g., total activity duration; incidence in agricultural fields) with the presence and absence of potatoes, and found no consistent responses for the sample population (Alkon and Saltz 1985a). However, detailed analysis of home ranges and movement patterns were more revealing (Saltz and Alkon forthcoming). First, we discovered that individuals had rather characteristic home ranges, some of which included agricultural fields and others of which comprised natural habitats. Thus, the study population consisted of two rather distinct components, i.e., "agricultural" porcupines and "natural" porcupines. Moreover, this dichotomy was a function of the dens with which the animals were associated and thus appears to be learned. In fact, in instances where animals shifted dens, they also adopted the foraging areas of their new den mates. We also found that agricultural porcupines had smaller (0.9 ± 0.3 km² vs 1.4 ± 0.4 km², under moonless conditions) and more seasonally stable home ranges, with fewer irregular movements, than animals dependent on natural forage. In general, porcupines appear conservative in spatial aspects of their behavior such that home ranges are defined in terms of long-term (annual) needs. The differences in home range sizes among population components do, however, suggest a strong influence of food density on movement and dispersion patterns. Moreover, we suspect that porcupines exhibit short-term "fine-grained" shifts in the exploitation of specific food patches within their home ranges.

Our data also sufficed to test other environmental influences. We found that ambient temperature (over a range of near-ground temperatures of −0.2°C to 26.2°C) has no infuence on activity duration, but that rainfall curtailed surface activity to four hours or less regardless of moon phase (Alkon and Saltz 1985a).

Some Hints on Foraging Strategies

In contemporary ecological parlance, porcupines appear to generally behave as "energy maximizers" rather than "time minimizers" (Krebs, Huston, and Charnov 1978). That is, they spend as much time surface-active (and presumably foraging) as possible given the constraints on their activity. It is conceivable, however, that their foraging goals do not fit either of these simple categories, and that foraging strategies change in accordance with fluctuations in environmental conditions and the animals' requirements. For example, minimal water demands and tolerances to plant defensive compounds (known to be present in geophytes and other potential foods) may constrain diet choice and food intake. Simple optimization models also present conceptual difficulties in separating goals from constraints (Krebs et al. 1978), as may be especially crucial in dealing with winter moon-avoidance behavior. In fact, our initial comparisons of porcupine temporal activity patterns with predictions of simple deterministic optimal foraging models (Rosenzweig 1974; Schoener 1983) suggest that more complex and dynamic solutions are needed to explain porcupine behavior.

We do have some basis, however, for predicting the animals' foraging patterns according to food type. Specifically, we predict that porcupines foraging on unharvested potatoes (a plentiful food source available in large packages) will move quickly to the potato fields; expend little time or energy in finding and uncovering potatoes; and then feed intensively for about one hour until they consume 500 g fresh mass of potatoes (i.e., their estimated stomach capacity) (Alkon and Saltz 1985a). Feeding rates will decline thereafter as a function of the passage of injesta, and the animals will have substantial time between feeding bouts for other activities (e.g., resting, searching for better potatoes, defending territories, guarding against predators). The major constraint on food intake is gut capacity, and the animals will incur the largest costs and risks in moving to and from the fields. By contrast, porcupines foraging on wild geophytes (small, scattered food packages) will invest substantial time and energy in finding and excavating food, but relatively little time in feeding. The animals will forage continuously and will have little time for other activities. They are unlikely to fill their stomachs, and the major constraint on their food intake will be the time available for foraging. They will incur relatively uniform costs and risks throughout the duration of surface activity.

DAMAGE AND MANAGEMENT

To measure porcupine foraging patterns and estimate damages, we systematically counted digs in sample potato fields at Kibbutz Sede Boqer (Alkon and Saltz 1985c). Early season digs for immature tubers were deep and extensive, and often resulted in the destruction of entire plants. As potatoes increased in size (and in profitability), digging rates rose, but individual tubers were closer to the surface, and excavations resulted in less vegetative and root damage. We estimate that porcupines caused a maximal destruction of 0.6 percent of the crop during the 100-day potato season, equivalent to a profit loss of $1200 for the 40 ha of potatoes cultivated at Sede Boqer. This level of damage would not appear to warrant a substantial investment in intensive damage control.

As long-lived animals with low reproductive rates (first breeding at > one yr. of age, 112-day gestation) that invest heavily in rearing a few offspring (two to three young per litter) (Weir 1974), porcupines should be susceptible to population control strategies based on elimination of breeding individuals (Stenseth and Hansson 1981). However, the methods currently employed for population control (trapping and spotlight-shooting at night) are inefficient and man-power intensive. Den destruction is also practiced occasionally, but this requires precise information on home ranges and den locations of problem individuals. Trapping and shooting are also apt to be nonselective.

As an alternative approach we propose damage control by crop protection rather than by population reduction. Our studies suggest two promising techniques based on known patterns of porcupine behavior (Alkon and Saltz 1985a, c). First, we observed that porcupine diggings were almost entirely restricted to the three outermost furrows of potato fields (the animals appear reluctant to penetrate dense vegetation). This suggests that the vulnerability of a crop is a function of the extent of field periphery. We therefore propose that adjustments in field geometry that reduce edge (e.g., square instead of rectangular configurations; single large fields instead of smaller disjunct fields) will lessen proportional crop vulnerability. Second, moonlight avoidance by porcupines suggests that light may be an effective barrier, at least for winter crops. This hypothesis was confirmed by field observations, which revealed that the density of digs was significantly less along margins of potato fields that were closest to existing artificial lighting (e.g., perimeter lights of the Kibbutz). We therefore propose low-intensity illumination (sufficient to create shadows) as a crop-protection method. This approach could take advantage of already existing artificial lighting, and may not need to be implemented during bright moonlit phases of lunar cycles.

FUTURE PLANS

Our work thus far has elucidated some basic features of porcupine activity patterns and the animals' food requirements. This information is a basis for the next phase of the project: analyzing porcupine foraging strategies and developing quantitative models of the animals' foraging behavior. To do this we plan to obtain detailed field information on porcupine activity budgets (including time spent foraging), diet composition, and the seasonal availability and nutritional value of all principal foods. Using tests with captive animals, we also intend to define minimal water requirements, measure responses to plant toxins, and estimate intake rates and digestibilities of all principal foods. Field studies will employ habitats and time periods that offer maximum contrasts in environmental conditions. We will use current simple foraging models, but anticipate that dynamic and stochastic solutions may be required to understand and predict porcupine foraging behavior. We hope to test hypotheses on ecologically acceptable means for controlling porcupine damage in agricultural arid zones. We also intend to develop acoustical biotelemetry technique for remotely monitoring the detailed behavior of porcupines by computer-aided analysis of sounds produced by free-ranging animals equipped with microphone transmitters (Alkon and Cohen 1986).

ACKNOWLEDGMENTS

This research benefited from the assistance of several colleagues at the Blaustein Institute for Desert Research, and from students at Ben-Gurion University and the Sede Boqer Environmental High School. I especially wish to thank David Saltz, a graduate student in the Environmental Biology Program at Hebrew University during the study, for his substantial contributions. Kibbutz Sede Boqer and the Israel Nature Reserves Authority gave invaluable cooperation, and funding support was provided by the Israel Academy of Sciences. The manuscript was prepared by Sally Alkon.

I gratefully recognize the help of Professor Michael Evenari, for his wise counsel, encouragement, and support in my new career as a desert ecologist.

REFERENCES

Alkon, P. U. 1984. Chemical restraint of Indian crested porcupines *(Hystrix indica)*. *Mammalia* 48:150–52.

———. 1985a. Cultivated potatoes and the nutritional ecology of crested porcupines *(Hystrix indica)* in a desert biome. *Journal of Applied Ecology* 22:727–37.

———. 1985b. Investigating the field behavior of crested porcupines *(Hystrix indica)*. In *Nocturnal Mammals: Techniques for Study*, ed. R. P. Brooks. School of Forest Resources, Research Paper No. 48. Pennsylvania State University, University Park. pp. 19–28.

———. 1985c. Patterns of crested porcupine *(Hystrix indica)* damage to cultivated potatoes. *Agriculture, Ecosystems and Environment* 14:171–83.

———. Temporal activity patterns of Indian crested porcupines *(Hystrix indica)*: environmental influences and ecological implications (forthcoming).

Alkon, P. U., and A. Cohen. 1986. Acoustical biotelemetry for wildlife research: a preliminary test and prospects. *Wildlife Society Bulletin* 14:193–96.

Alkon, P. U., A. A. Degen, A. Cohen, and H. Pollak. 1986. Seasonal water intakes and energy requirements of Indian crested porcupines *(Hystrix indica)* in captivity. *Journal of Mammalogy* 67:333–42.

Alkon, P. U., B. P. Kotler, and D. Saltz. Predation costs of a foraging herbivore (forthcoming).

Danin, A. 1983. *Desert Vegetation of Israel and Sinai*. Cana Publishing House, Jerusalem.

Evenari, M. 1981. "Ecology of the Negev desert, a critical review". In *Developments in Arid Zone Ecology and Environmental Quality*, ed. H. Shuval. Balaban I. S. S., Philadelphia. pp. 1–33.

Gutterman, Y. 1982. Observations on the feeding habits of the Indian crested porcupine *(Hystrix indica)* and the distribution of some hemicryptophytes and geophytes in the Negev desert highlands. *Journal of Arid Environments* 5:261–68.

Harrison, D. L. 1972. *The Mammals of Arabia*. Vol. 3. Ernest Benn, London.

Kingdon, J. 1974. *East African Mammals: An Evolutionary Atlas*. Academic Press, London.

Krebs, J. R., A. I. Houston, and E. L. Charnov. 1978. Some recent developments in optimal foraging. In *Behavioral Ecology*, eds. A. C. Kamil and T. D. Sargent. Blackwell Scientific Publications, Oxford. pp. 3–8.

List, R. J. 1958. *Smithsonian Meteorological Tables*, 6th ed. Smithsonian Institution, Washington, D.C.

Olsvig-Whittaker, L., M. Shachak, and A. Yair. 1983. Vegetation patterns related to environmental factors in a Negev desert watershed. *Vegetatio* 54:153–56.

Rosenzweig, M. L. 1974. On the optimal aboveground activity of bannertail kangaroo rats. *Journal of Mammalogy* 55:193–99.

Saltz, D., and P. U. Alkon, 1983. Autumn and winter activity patterns of crested porcupines in the Negev highlands. Abstract. *Israel Journal of Zoology* 32:163.

———. 1985. A simple, computer-aided method for estimating radio location error. *Journal of Wildlife Management* 49:664–68.

———. Spatial activity patterns of Indian crested porcupines in a desert biome (forthcoming).

Schoener, T. W. 1983. Simple models of feeding territory size: a reconciliation. *American Naturalist* 121:608–29.

Stenseth, N. C., and L. Hannson. 1981. The importance of population dynamics in heterogeneous landscapes: management of vertebrate pests and some other animals. *Agro-Ecosystems* 7:187–211.

Weir, B. T. 1974. Reproductive characteristics of Hystricomorph rodents. In *The Biology of Hystricomorph Rodents*, eds. I. W. Rolands and B. J. Weir. Academic Press, London. pp. 265–301.

Yair, A. and M. Shachak. 1982. A case study of energy, water, and soil flow chains in an arid ecosystem. *Oecologia* 54:389–97.

PART III

DESERT ECOLOGY
IN THEORY
AND FIELD STUDY

NINE

The Stability of the Negev Desert Ecosystems: Why and How to Investigate It

URIEL N. SAFRIEL

ABSTRACT

The research approach required for responsible prediction of ecosystems' responses to disturbances depends much on whether ecosystems function as intrinsically interacting units or if they are merely the sum of autoecologies of their populations; and on whether ecosystems possess 'static' or 'time-varying' stability properties. Of all ecosystems, it is in deserts that most species seem to depend heavily not on other species, but on a single, common, climatic factor which is highly unstable. If it is proven that autoecological knowledge alone is inadequate for the prediction of desert responses to disturbances, the ecosystem-as-a-functional-unit approach for studying responses to perturbations should prevail universally.

It is proposed to express the state of the desert ecosystem by several of its major functional processes, and to measure fluctuations in the rates of these processes, relative to the variability in the desert's climatic states. Desert ecosystems may not have a single stable state, against which their stability properties can be judged. Yet, desert ecosystems need not be permanently unstable, and should not constantly track environmental vicissitudes. Rather, it is proposed to examine whether desert ecosystems possess multiple stable states, which differ in their stability properties.

It is suggested that a consistent relation between the (large) number of climatic states and the (much smaller) number of ecosystem-stable states may exist. It is also proposed that the effect of conventional

This is publication No. 49 of the Mitrani Center for Desert Ecology, Jacob Blaustein Institute.

anthropogenic stressors is analogous, or simulates, the effect of extreme natural desert climatic states. Therefore, desert ecosystems may respond to any given conventional anthropogenic stressor by attaining one of their natural multiple stable states.

The Negev desert of Israel has several merits for studying ecosystems' responses to stressors, and the issue of a desert ecosystem's stability should be approached through coordinated, interdisciplinary, integrated research, in several sites set aside for intensive long-term research near the Sede Boqer Campus of the Blaustein Institute for Desert Research.

WHY STUDY DESERT ECOSYSTEMS?

After more than a decade of a national and an international scientific endeavor (e.g., IBP and MAB), the ability to predict ecosystems' responses to man-induced disturbances remains a major challenge to both basic and applied ecologists (Barrett & Rosenberg 1981). At the basic level, the selection of the correct research approach, with prospects of yielding a reasonable prediction of ecosystems' response to anthropogenic disturbances, depends much on two rather controversial issues related to the notions of ecosystem and stability. One basic question is whether ecosystems can be viewed as arbitrarily bound parts of nature, or if they constitute intricate networks for strong interactions and regulatory feedbacks between their populations and abiotic factors, consistent in space and time (the "ecosystem hypothesis," Noy-Meir 1980). Another question is whether these interactions and feedbacks are able to induce the system to maintain consistent stability properties (Botkin & Sobel 1975). At the applied level, the power to predict an ecosystem's response to man-induced disturbances or at least to forecast the short-term effects, is (or should be) expected from the scientific community by both the administration and the general public (Paine 1981; Cooper 1982).

Deserts are particularly suitable for the study of ecosystems' responses to disturbances. At the level of basic research, they provide an interesting test of the 'ecosystem hypothesis' and its associated stability implications. An alternative hypothesis is that the dynamics of each population is determined mainly by its independent reaction to the physical environment; hence, the 'ecosystem' is no more than the sum of autoecologies of all its species (the "autoecological hypothesis" (Noy-Meir 1980). This can best be evaluated in environments where interactions between species may prove to be negligible in comparison with the overwhelming effect is felt of the extremely unstable weather-dependent availability of a single, universally-limiting factor such as water in deserts.

At the level of applied research, desert environments are exciting because of their dual reaction to anthropogenic effects. In developed countries deserts withdraw, as a result of expansion and redeployment of human populations and industries, driven by economic and "environmentalist" pressures; whereas in developing countries non-desert environments become 'desertified'.

At the level of research feasibility, the desert environment lends itself smoothly for studying the problem in question. The densities of populations are usually relatively low, hence the tracking of their dynamics is manageable. Since the dominant plants are not very large in size, and usually well-spaced, plant community structure and functioning can be adequately measured and experimented with. Simulations of natural disturbances can be easily performed. What is most remarkable about desert ecosystem research is that the abiotic driving of the whole system can be functionally condensed and adequately expressed by a single, clearly defined, routinely monitored and easily followed variable: precipitation. This is unlike other ecosystems (e.g., the Northern Hardwood Forest, see Borman and Likens 1979) since in deserts water functions not just as a controller of nutrient availability and an agent in soil erosion, but as a major controller of energy fixation and transfer, and as a universal limiting resource. Finally, space for experimental manipulations and long-term measurements, relatively free of interferences and trespassing, is still amply available in deserts.

In the following, it is proposed that desert ecosystem research may prove particularly appealing, because the within- and between-years variance of its environmental variables is so great, that responses to conventional anthropogenic interventions may be found within the range of its response to the naturally prevailing spectrum of disturbances.

ARE THERE NATURAL DISTURBANCES IN DESERT ECOSYSTEMS?

What is actually a disturbance? It is an unusual exogenous agent having (Allen 1984, Patten et al. 1984) the potential of interfering with what is regarded as the normal functioning of the ecosystem. It is thus detrimental to that system (Auerbach 1981) though not necessarily to all its components (Allen 1984). Its origin may be foreign to the natural environment or it could be natural but applied at an "excessive level" (Barrett et al. 1976). Since the term "disturbance" has a wide usage, it may be replaced by "stressor", which will be restricted to "disturbing" agents, in the ecosystem context. Ecosystems affected by disturbances or by stressors become perturbed, or stressed. The response of an ecosystem to an applied stressor can be quantified by several measures: Its *resistance* (Webster et al. 1975) to displacement from its normal state, as expressed by the magnitude of that displacement; the length of the *time-delay* before any displacement occurs (Vitousek et al. 1981); and, provided displacement has occurred, its *"resilience,"* or the rate and characteristics of processes of recovery (Webster et al. 1975).

Are the above definitions useful when applied to desert ecosystems? Are desert ecosystems ever in equilibrium, even though natural stressors exist there, to which they can exhibit resistance or resilience?

Since the single climatic variable that so forcefully drives desert ecosystems is fluctuating in an extremely vigorous and erratic manner, the concepts of natural stressor and the resistance, time-delay and resilience components of ecosystems' stability defined by the system's normal state may not be operational in deserts. Alternatively, because averages of desert climatic variables of one year never duplicate those of the preceding year, desert ecosystems may normally be far from equilibrium. Hence, their stressors are neither unusual nor detrimental, but constantly shape their structure in a dynamic manner (DeAngelis et al. 1984).

PERMANENT INSTABILITY OR MULTIPLE STABLE STATES?

Could it be that the number of desert ecosystem states converge upon the number of climatic states? Namely, resistance and resilience may be negligible; and desert ecosystems are never at equilibrium, but simply track the climatic vagaries. This description may be formulated as a null hypothesis which is rather analogous to the previously discussed "autoecological hypothesis." The hypothesis to be tested against it, is that though the number of desert climatic states may be infinitely large, the number of states acquired by a desert ecosystem is finite, and much smaller (though still larger than the number of equilibrium states typical of non-desert ecosystems). Thus, it is proposed that desert ecosystems do not stay in a single stable equilibrium point from which they can or cannot be displaced by a stressor; they naturally wander between several, fixed stable points.

The relationships between the number of climatic states and the number of desert ecosystem states or stable points depends on the properties of the system's components of stability; namely, on the size of the set, or segment of climatic states to which an ecosystem at a given state will either resist or will be amply resilient. This multiple-stable-states hypothesis is in accord with the "ecosystem hypothesis." The ability to predict the number of ecosystem-stable states associated with every possible number of desert climatic states is theoretically challenging (Patten et al, 1984).

ANTHROPOGENIC STRESSES AND THE NATURAL MULTIPLE STABLE STATES OF DESERTS

The multiple-stable-states hypothesis generates a proposition of an applied value. Coping with common anthropogenic stresses may often be beyond many non-desert ecosystems' resistance and resilience properties. Hence, a prediction of ecosystems' fates following such stresses is rather risky, since under these circumstances the behavior of stressed ecosystems may be entirely novel. If, however, the number of desert climatic states is enormous, and among them the occurrence of extremes is erratic but not uncommon, and the 'natural' responses result in a large but still limited number of desert-ecosystem states, then most anthropogenic stressors may be analogous to and simulate a certain extreme climatic state (e.g., a discharge of a certain chemical through an industrial effluent eradicates a population of only one species, that is also the only one to be eradicated, given a certain reduction in rainfall). Hence, the responses of a desert ecosystem to anthropogenic stressors may produce states that are within the range of stable states produced by responses to the naturally occurring climatic states. Thus, the prediction of a desert ecosystem's response to anthropogenic stressors may merely constitute a process of the correct selection from an array of already familiar responses. The only difference between the effect of an anthropogenic stressor and a naturally occurring one is that the former may persist much longer; hence the predicted ecosystem response may prevail for periods much longer than those lasting naturally.

STATIC OR TIME-VARYING STABILITY?

In the preceding discussion stability is described in terms of the ecosystem's tendency to return to an equilibrium state, *at rest*, after being perturbed. In an extensive literature review, Connell and Sousa (1983) were unable to reveal a clear evidence for the occurrence of multiple stable states in natural ecosystems. Botkin and Sobel (1975) suggested that all kinds of "static" stability may only rarely apply to natural ecosystems, due to three different, but complementary, processes. First, many ecosystems go through local successional events, during which time-periods an equilibrium state is not achieved. Second, in several ecosystem types, long-lived dominant organisms exist, whose life-times span over centuries, during which periods regional or even global climatic-change events occur. Hence, even if a given climatic-climax has been achieved, within centuries these ecosystems are still unable to attain equilibrium. Third, even within "ecological time" (as opposed to "evolutionary time") evolutionary progression may interfere with the attainment of stability, through a steady appearance of innovative adaptations.

The question therefore arises whether desert ecosystems can not achieve a "static" equilibrium state, due not to tracking the short-term desert climatic fluctuations (the previously discussed null hypothesis), but due to their successional dynamics, and the high longevities and genetic plasticity that some of their functionally dominant species may possess. Even if this is the case, desert ecosystems are not constantly unstable; but instead of having "static" stability properties, their persistence wanders within stochastically defined bounds (Connell and Sousa 1983), and they possess the features of time-varying stability, as defined by Botkin and Sobel (1975).

Time-varying stability has two major properties. First, time-varying *persistence*, which is the moderation in the size of fluctuations in the ecosystem-state, measured by the distance from a given state-point (which is not necessarily a "static" stable point), within which ecosystem states may

wander. Second, *recurrence*, which is the repetition of a previously occupied state, measured by the certainty at which a state becomes close to a
point already occupied by it in the past. Ecosystems may then have
recurrent states, as well as non-recurrent, i.e., transient states. The ecosystem time-varying stability increases with the decrease in the distances
between states and with the increase in the ratio of recurrent to transient
states that typify it.

Perturbation of a time-varying ecosystem then means an induced change
in the system's persistence and recurrence properties; the system may
become less stable through attaining a state that wanders within a greater
distance from a given initial state, and through causing some recurrent states
to become transient.

STABILITY PROPERTIES AND THE
PULSE-AND-RESERVE PATTERNS OF DESERT
FUNCTIONING

Implicit in both the multiple-stable-states hypothesis and the time-varying
stability hypothesis is the assumption that desert ecosystems possess a
measurable degree of stability. It was claimed (Noy-Meir 1974) that desert
ecosystems have low resistance: Their populations respond intimately to
climatic fluctuations. But these population fluctuations show consistent
relationship with climatic fluctuations, and are well-bounded. The non-
resistant desert ecosystem acquires its resilience property through the
prevalence of the "pulse and reserve" pattern of its structure and function
(Noy-Meir 1973): An erratic environmental event triggers a pulse of production; this production is rapidly lost, but a substantial amount drains to a
storage sink, serving as a source and memory for the next pulse. Thus,
fluctuations along desert trophic webs are damped due to delays and storage
of surplus unpredictable resources, which become less accessible but more
reliable (Shmida et al. 1986). To conclude, the fast reaction to the changing
environmental states, coupled with the backing of the memory reserve,
provide the desert ecosystem with high resilience or recurrence (Evenari
1981), which may result in consistent relations between the number of
environmental states and the lower, consistent number of stable ecosystem
states.

STABILITY AND OPPORTUNISTIC MIGRATIONS AND
DIETS; PLANT SECONDARY COMPOUNDS; AND DEW

Several observed or implied phenomena may contribute to the resilience of
desert ecosystems. When the climatic temporal variability is coupled with
opportunistic migration abilities in consumers, and with colonization abilities in producers, the desert spatial heterogeneity may provide refuges, and

reduce biotic oscillations (Noy-Meir 1974; Shmida et al. 1986). Many herbivores and predators exhibit dietary flexibility and opportunism, which may contribute to stability too (Noy-Meir 1974). Nutrients (especially nitrogen compounds) may be relatively low in deserts. The nutrient storage may be depleted by the production pulse of ephemeral plants (Noy-Meir 1974), such that in several subsequent years, regardless of their climatic states, producers will be nutrient-limited, and the ecosystem may remain unchanged until most litter-bound nutrients are recycled.

It is also conceivable that desert consumer populations are largely controlled by plant food quality. Nutrient-low plants may inhibit reproduction of desert herbivores, thus limiting the fluctuations in populations of long-lived consumers. Or, stressed plants may produce fewer secondary compounds than normal, which results in increased herbivory; in better years herbivory will be suppressed due to ample doses of secondary compounds in plants (Rhoades 1979). The possible net result is that combined plant-herbivore biomass would remain stable throughout a sizable portion of time. Finally, dew, which is a reliable water source in some deserts (Evenari 1981a), may comprise a stabilizing agent, especially where the algae and lichen trophic webs are cardinal to the system's functioning.

STABILITY AND ANTHROPOGENIC STRESS

The proposed relationship between the reaction of the desert ecosystem to natural perturbation and its reaction to anthropogenic stress is entirely speculative at this stage. Boesch and Rosenberg (1981) showed that the wide physiological tolerance of marine benthic species living in unstable environments extends to common marine anthropogenic stresses. Hutchinson (1984) demonstrated that arctic ecosystems (which in several respects are similar to desert ecosystems) exhibit adaptations to natural stressors that act as preadaptations to a significant number of anthropogenic stressors; and Noy-Meir (1974a) suggested that preadapted resilience towards man-induced catastrophes is more likely to be found in deserts than in other ecosystems.

THE LONG-TERM, INTEGRATED, INTERDISCIPLINARY RESEARCH APPROACH

The elucidation of a desert ecosystem's type of stability, (multiple stable states, time-varying stability, or simple environmental tracking), requires long-term research. In 1977, a committee convened by the United States National Science Foundation to consider ecological research needs, concluded that

> Ecology requires long-term studies. They are indispensable and must be initiated. All ecosystems are in a process of long-term change . . . at present, few

research strategies allow us to separate long-term cyclic from unidirectional changes; or anthropogenically-induced changes from natural ones. This and other central ecological issues make clear the need for long-term quantitative data sets, which have irreplaceable theoretical and applied utility [USNSF 1977].

The committee recognized "that long-term measurements serve not only to test hypotheses, but have been the source of new and important questions," but urged that such programs should be based on "a central issue or a hypothesis, to test or to guide the collection of data." They also noted that some long-term studies "with vaguer initial rationales seem to have made possible the identification of important issues which can be missed in too highly structured projects" (USNSF 1977).

Whereas the central issue is the stability properties of ecosystems in general and their applied implications, stability of desert ecosystems cannot be adequately addressed as long as existing gaps in the knowledge of desert ecology remain unbridged: In understanding litter decomposition and nutrient recycling in relation to desert precipitation and production pulses; in comprehension of primary production and water budgets at the community level; in appreciation of the role of nutritional quality and of plant secondary compounds in foraging and life-history tactics; and in the knowledge of the extent of genetic variability within populations under varying regimes of desert environmental conditions. The required approach to these studies is a system approach, executed through a concentrated effort of an interdisciplinary integrated research by a team of experts, each one approaching the central issue from his own angle of expertise, but all collaborating through a coordination of the research plans and efforts and through a free exchange of ideas and data.

WHY STUDY DESERT STABILITY IN THE NEGEV?

The United States National Science Foundation committee on long-term ecological measurements convened also in 1978 and defined criteria for site selection for such long-term ecological studies. Following these recommendations, it is proposed to establish, in the near future, several sites for intensive research and long-term measurements for a combined, interdisciplinary, and integrated research into the stability properties of ecosystems in the Negev Desesrt of Israel.

The committee recommended (USNSF 1978) as follows:

1. "A site should lie in a transition zone for the major variable under investigation, so that changes will be readily and rapidly apparent." In the Negev there is a wide north-south transect of ca. 100km, along which a gradient from 300 to 50mm annual precipitation exists;

2. "The sites should include relatively natural ecosystems, as well as those impacted by man." The Negev desert exhibits an array of different land

uses persisting through different time intervals, during varying lengths of time before the present. Nowadays, in spite of the Negev's proximity to the heavily populated Mediterranean region of Israel, there are still extensive areas virtually unaffected by man;

3. "The area should be such that it is possible to construct an adequate hydrological budget, which is prerequisite to constructing accurate chemical budgets of nutrients or toxins." In the Negev there are extensive areas with the required rock basins, and an experience in constructing their hydrological budgets already exists (Yair et al. 1980);

4. A site should be where "a substantial record of past study and research in the area" exists. Detailed climatological, geological and soil maps for the Negev are available, and a recent bibliography on the Negev's scientific literature in biology alone (Safriel 1986) has more than 200 entries;

5. It is highly desirable that there are "good facilities in close proximity to the sites, together with an active program of study and research by qualified scientists". The Mitrani Center for Desert Ecology, part of the Blaustein Institute for Desert Research, is located at about the center of the Negev, right on the 100mm isohyet, and had already produced a significant amount of ecological research in its immediate, as well as more remote, desert environments (Safriel 1984).

WHAT SHOULD BE MEASURED?

What should be measured at the proposed intensive long-term research sites in order to assess the desert-ecosystem's stability properties? Obviously, it is impractical to define the ecosystem's 'state' by values of all components of the system's structure, and by rates of all its processes. This is also not required; it is intuitively felt that a system's state can be characterized by a relatively small number of key-functions and that structural details of two different points in time need not be all identical in order to produce a single functional state that prevails during these two points in time. Thus, Amir (1983) proposed to measure the system's productivity as an indicator for its functioning, and in this way enable the quantification of ecological impacts of anthropogenic stressors. Lugo and McCormick (1981) suggested to obtain a measure of response to stress not just by monitoring changes in energy flows, but also by following the loss of specific pathways, and the acceleration of repair processes; and Likens et al. (1977) and Vitousek et al. (1981) actually measured processes within the nitrogen cycle of a forest ecosystem. Both groups pointed at the linkage of the processes with components of ecosystem responses to perturbations, and suggested ways by which these processes might interact to produce an overall ecosystem response.

Vitousek et al. (1981) concluded that the dynamics of a mobile nutrient is a convenient measure of ecosystem reponse to disturbance, because these dynamics "sensitively reflect the functional state of the ecosystem," and they constitute "system-level process with direct consequences to the regrowth of the ecosystem" after stress. Finally, nutrient dynamics are directly measurable, within a short time scale. These postulates may be equally valid for desert ecosystems, where water should be viewed as a mobilizable, though not fully recycled, nutrient.

OUTLINES FOR A RESEARCH PROTOCOL

The initial stage of research is the identification of those ecosystem components which are most sensitive to climatic changes—those that exhibit the highest between-years weather-associated variance. Subsequent research efforts should concentrate on these components.

It may prove practical to identify these components rapidly in transition zones—boundaries between ecosystems, where the sensitivity of the components might be greater than in core areas. The components to be screened are functional groups of species, critical linkages, and storages (e.g. soil water and nutrients), that may buffer species and linkage responses and should be studied for a minimal period of at least one complete turnover (Connell and Sousa 1983).

Long-term measurements of the undisturbed ecosystem should go hand-in-hand with experimental manipulations in the field and in the laboratory. Field manipulations should range from simulations of actual precipitation, through landscape management leading to run-off alterations, to artificial enrichment and depletion of nutrient and food resources, thus simulating actual events following weather changes.

Laboratory work should concentrate on physiological mechanisms involved in populations' responses to climatic changes, and their associated outcomes. Also, an assessment of the degree of genetic variability and plasticity of key-species is required for the prediction of community responses, and this may be acquired through an isozyme electrophoretic analysis, reciprocal transplantation of individuals, and heritability experiments.

Mathematical modelling of processes and interactions should closely follow the research throughout its entire course; this will guarantee orderly bookkeeping of the enormous body of accumulated data, will provide insight into the obtained results, and will furnish guidance and intelligent steering for future activities.

To conclude, if the ecologists' claim to be able to provide "ecological" consultancy is to be taken seriously, they should get into the rather tedious, but potentially exciting venture of integrated, interdisciplinary, long-term research business. The critical issue is that of ecosystem stability; deserts in general, and the Negev desert of Israel in particular offer unique opportunities for tackling this issue, thus leading towards a construction of a powerful tool for predicting ecosystems' responses to man-induced perturbations.

ACKNOWLEDGEMENTS

Thanks are due to Dr. M. Shachak, for discussions and comments.

REFERENCES

Allen, T. F. H. 1984. The abuse of the concept "disturbance": A scaling problem. *Bulletin of the Ecological Society of America* 65: 54.

Amir, S. 1983. Quantifying ecological impacts: On using productivity and standing crop as indicators for the measurements of ecosystem functioning. Ecosystem Research Center, Cornell University.

Auerbach, S. I. 1981. Ecosystem response to stress: A review of concepts and approaches. In *Stress Effects on Natural Ecosystems*, ed. G. W. Barrett and K. Rosenberg. John Wiley & Sons, New York. Pp. 29–41.

Barrett, G. W., G. M. van Dyne, and E. P. Odum. 1976. Stress ecology. *Bioscience* 26: 192–94.

Barrett, G. W., and R. Rosenberg, eds. 1981. *Stress Effects on Natural Ecosystems*. John Wiley & Sons, New York.

Boesch, D. F., and R. Rosenberg. 1981. Response to stress in marine benthic communities. In *Stress Effects on Natural Ecosystems*, ed. G. W. Barrett and K. Rosenberg. John Wiley & Sons, New York.

Borman, F. H., and G. E. Likens. 1979. *Patterns and Processes in a Forested Ecosystem*. Springer-Verlag, New York.

Botkin, D. B. and M. J. Sobel. 1975. Stability in time-varying ecosystems. *American Naturalist* 109: 625–46.

Connell, J. H. and W. P. Sousa. 1983. On the evidence needed to judge ecological stability or persistence. *American Naturalist* 121: 789–824.

Cooper, A. W. 1982. Why doesn't anyone listen to ecologists—and what can ESA do about it? *Bulletin of the Ecological Society of America* 63: 348–56.

De Angelis, D. L., W. M. Post, and R. V. O'Neil. 1984. Ecological modeling and disturbance evaluation. *Bulletin of the Ecological Society of America* 65: 54.

Evenari, M. 1981. Synthesis. In *Arid Land Ecosystems: Structure, Functioning and Management*, vol. 2, ed. D. W. Goodall and R. A. Perry. Cambridge University Press, Cambridge. Pp. 555–91.

————. 1981a. Ecology of the Negev desert, a critical review of our knowledge. In *Development in Arid Zone Ecology and Environmental Quality*, ed. H. Shuval. Balaban ISS, Philadelphia, Pp. 1–33.

Hutchinson, T. C. 1984. Common responses of terrestrial ecosystems to natural and anthropogenic stress: Emphasis on boreal and arctic systems. *Bulletin of the Ecological Society of America*. 65: 110.

Likens, G. E., F. H. Borman, R. S. Pierce, J. S. Eaton, and N. M. Johnson. 1977. *Biogeochemistry of a Forested Ecosystem*. Springer-Verlag, New York.

Lugo, A. E., and J. F. McCormick. 1981a. Influence of environmental stressors upon energy flow in a natural terrestrial ecosystem. In *Stress Effects on Natural Ecosystems*, ed. G. W. Barrett and K. Rosenberg. John Wiley & Sons, New York. Pp. 79–102.

National Science Foundation. 1977. *Report of conference on long-term ecological measurements*. Division of Environmental Biology.

National Science Foundation. 1978. *A pilot program for long-term observations and study of ecosystems in the United States*. Division of Environmental Biology.

Noy-Meir, I. 1973. Desert ecosystems: Environment and producers. *Annual Review of Ecology and Systematics*. 4: 25–51.

————. 1974. Desert Ecosystems: Higher trophic levels. *Annual Review of Ecology and Systematics* 5: 195–214.

————. 1974a. Stability in arid ecosystems and the effects of man on it. *Proceedings of the 1st International Congress of Ecology.* The Hague. Pp. 220–26.

————. 1980. Structure and function of desert ecosystems. *Israel Journal of Botany* 28: 1–19.

Paine, R. T. 1981. Truth in ecology. *Bulletin of the Ecological Society of America* 62: 256–58.

Patten, B. C., J. Gerritsen, and J. P. Schubauer. 1984. State space system theory of ecological disturbance. *Bulletin of the Ecological Society of America* 65: 54.

Rhoades, D. F. 1979. Evolution of plant chemical defense against herbivores. In *Herbivores: Their Interactions with Secondary Plant Metabolites,* ed. G. A. Rosental and D. H. Janzen. Academic Press, New York, Pp. 4–54.

Safriel, U. N. 1984. The Marco and Louise Mitrani Center for Desert Ecology. Goals, structure, achievements and future plans and needs. *The Mitrani Center for Desert Ecology.* Sede Boqer.

————. 1986. A generation of Desert biological research in Israel: A selective bibliography 1961–1985. *The Blaustein International Center for Desert Studies.* Sede Boqer.

Shmida, A., M. Evenari, and I. Noy-Meir. 1986. Hot desert ecosystems: An integrated view. In *Hot Desert Ecosystems,* ed. M. Evenari, I. Noy-Meir, and D. W. Goodall. Elsevier/North Holland, Amsterdam. Pp. 372–387.

Vitousek, P. M., W. A. Reiners, J. M. Melillo, C. C. Grier, and J. R. Gosz. 1981. Nitrogen cycling and loss following forest perturbation: The components of response. In *Stress Effects on Natural Ecosystems,* ed. G. W. Barrett and K. Rosenberg. John Wiley & Sons, New York. Pp. 115–27.

Webster, J. R., J. B. Waide, and B. C. Patten. 1975. Nutrient cycling and the stability of ecosystems. In *Mineral Cycling in Southeastern Ecosystems,* ed. F. G. Howell, J. B. Gentry, and M. H. Smith. ERDA Symposium series CONF-740513. National Technical Information Service, Springfield, Va. Pp. 1–27.

Yair, A., D. Sharon, and H. Lavee. 1980. Trends in run off and erosion processes over an arid limestone hillside, northern Negev, Israel. *Hydrol. Sci. Bull.* 25: 243–55.

TEN

Studies in Watershed Ecology of an Arid Area

AARON YAIR AND MOSHE SHACHAK

ABSTRACT

This chapter reviews the approach adopted and results obtained in the study of an arid ecosystem. The research was conducted at the Sede Boqer experimental site where data have been collected since 1972. The research project focused on two main aspects:

(1) A systematic study, within a limited area (11,325m^2) of the temporal and spatial variability in rainfall, run-off, soil moisture, soil properties, distribution of plant communities, burrowing and digging activities of animals, soil erosion and sediment transport.
(2) A study of the interrelationship among the above variables, stressing feedback processes between abiotic and biotic aspects.

The validity of the conclusions, based on data collected in a small area and over a short period of time, was checked for both space and time. The extrapolation to a larger scale was based on the comparison of the study area with an area located 40km north of the experimental area and whose surface properties and rainfall regime differ from those prevailing at Sede Boqer. The extrapolation, through time, included the analysis of variables indicative of the soil moisture regime at various time scales up to thousands of years.

Last, the possible application of results obtained for increasing productivity in an arid area is briefly discussed, together with various theoretical implications for our understanding of the desert environment.

This is publication no. 58 from the Mitrani Center for Desert Ecology, Jacob Blaustein Institute for Desert Research.

INTRODUCTION

Experimental Scales of Ecosystem Studies

The majority of experimental ecosystem studies were conducted with the site approach (Caswell 1976; Innis 1978; Kremer et al. 1978; Nixon and Oviatt 1973; Steele 1974; Wiegert 1975) or with the watershed approach (Coats et al. 1976; Gosz 1975; Johnson and Swank 1973; Likens et al. 1977). In the site approach, the area selected represents larger areas, the inference being that ecosystem properties do not vary significantly as a function of experimental scale. If so, flow values of different scales can be combined into one ecosystem model (Goodall 1974; Noy-Meir 1973, 1981; Woodmansee 1978). The site approach raises two main problems. First, the criteria for boundary selection of the study area is often not clearly defined in ecosystem terms. The boundaries of the site may vary within the same study area in accordance with the specific topic under investigation, e.g., the study of plant communities may be based on units covering a few m², while the study of animal populations may extend over many km². Second, the boundaries of the site selected are often arbitrary with respect to the water flow regime, which according to the research at Hubbard Brook (Likens et al. 1977) exercises a strong control, via the movement of nutrients, on the ecosystem. If the idea that the hydrological cycle exercises a strong influence on the ecosystem is accepted, then the site approach becomes more problematic. Many detailed hydrological studies, carried out in humid as well as in arid areas, indicate spatial and temporal nonuniformity in waterflow in very small watersheds (Betson and Marius 1969; Dunne and Black 1970; Dunne et al. 1975; Yair and Lavee 1982). This nonuniformity is not random and can be defined in the field. Clearly, if the site approach disregards such important natural boundaries the ability to extrapolate from a small site to larger areas is lost.

The strong linkage between nutrient flow and the hydrologic cycle led to the selection of the watershed divide as a convenient boundary for the area over which ecosystem properties can be studied (Likens et al. 1977). In contrast to the site approach, the watershed approach has a well defined experimental scale. However, the watershed approach has not solved the problem that smaller units within the watershed may have different flow values (water, nutrients, soil, etc.) than the total watershed. Such a situation is especially characteristic of those areas where frequent spatial and temporal discontinuities in waterflow may occur within the watershed. For such areas, an extension of the watershed approach is needed which will provide an experimental framework for the study of units smaller than a watershed. These could then be combined to explain processes and flow values of the whole watershed.

The arid ecosystem research study initiated in 1972 in the northern Negev included three aspects.

Small-Scale Study of Water Resources Distribution

This study was based on two assumptions. The first was that the spatial distribution of water resources exercises, even at the smallest scale, a strong influence on the ecosystem. The second assumption was that the spatial and temporal distribution of water resources vary greatly over short distances within small watersheds. This led to the idea that water resources should be studied over units smaller than the whole watershed. As hillslopes cover up to 95 percent of the area of small watersheds, the study of water resources focused on hillslopes rather than channel flow processes. For this purpose a densely instrumented site was installed where the hydrological response of surface units (which differ in their surface properties) to spatial and temporal variations in rainfall, was studied.

The Effect of Water Resources Distribution on Ecosystem Properties

In this section an attempt is made to answer the question: How does the assumed nonuniform distribution of water resources affect the organization of the ecosystem considered? Variables characteristic of the population, community, and ecosystem levels were analyzed. In addition, the validity of the conclusions, based on hydrological data collected over a short monitoring period, were checked for longer periods. This was done by the analysis of the spatial distribution of perennial shrubs and soil forming processes. In addition, the validity of the conclusions was tested for a large scale by comparing the Sede Boqer watershed with an area located 40km to the north, whose surface properties and rainfall conditions differ from those of the Sede Boqer experimental site.

Studies of Feedback Processes

Preliminary observations (Yair 1974) drew attention to the role that should be attributed to the burrowing and digging activity of desert animals on soil erosion. Consequently, the influence of the spatial distribution of water resources on the abundance of biological activity and the effect of this activity on soil erosion processes, soil desalination, and decomposition were included in the study.

Study Area

The study area is located in the Northern Negev Desert (see Figure 10.1). Rainfall is limited to the winter months (October to April). Average annual rainfall, based on a record of 32 years, is 93mm with extreme values of 34mm to 167mm. The number of rain days varies from 15 to 42, and only a few rains yield more than 20mm per day. Mean monthly temperatures vary from 9° C

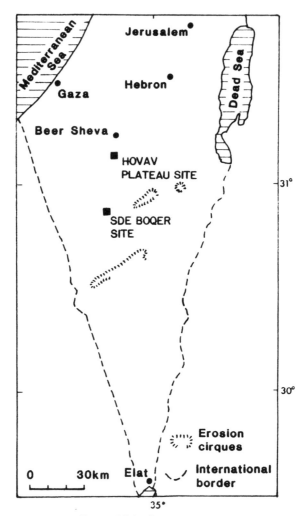

Figure 10.1   Location map

in January to 25° C in August. Average daily relative humidity attains 60 to 70 percent in winter and 40 to 50 percent in summer.

The experimental site, covering an area of 11,325m², is limited to one half of a first order drainage basin extending on one side of the channel (see Figure 10.2). The relative relief for any given slope is less than 22m. Geologically the study area is composed of three formations. The Drorim formation outcrops at the lower part of the site. Rock strata are thin and densely jointed. The upper part of the slopes carved in this formation are rocky and the lower part is covered by an extensive stony colluvial serozem soil. The Shivta formation overlies the Drorim formation and thus occurs in the middle slope. In is a massive crystalline limestone that forms a stepped topography. Bedrock is exposed over most of the area (see Figure 10.3). Soil material is found in rock crevices and at the base of bedrock steps. The Netser formation overlies the Shivta formation and thus occurs on the upper slope. It resembles the Drorim formation in its structural properties, but the soil cover is very patchy and shallow.

From the point of view of spatial distribution of rock and soil covered areas, the experimental site can be subdivided into two main parts; the rocky part that extends over the Netser, Shivta, and upper part of the Drorim formations and the soil covered area which extends over the lower part of the Drorim formation (see Figure 10.2).

WATER RESOURCES DISTRIBUTION

In the present study, special attention was accorded to the spatial and temporal variations in rainfall and run-off, which determine the amount of water infiltrating into the soil at any given location.

Rainfall Properties

Spatial distribution of rainfall

Studies on the spatial distribution of rainfall over limited areas show differences, for a given rainstorm, of ten to 70 percent (Cappus 1958; Sharon 1970; Shanan 1976; Sharon 1980).

To obtain the detailed distribution of rainfall, a very dense network of 19 raingauges was established. The gauges were installed in three lines (see Figure 10.2) along the base of the hillslope; at mid-slope and along the local divide of the watershed. The gauges were installed 30cm above the ground with their orifices parallel to the local sloping ground (Yair et al. 1978; Sharon 1980). In this way, each raingauge constitutes a representative sample of the ground surface with respect to local aspect and slope inclination. In addition, two rainfall recorders were installed, one on the ridge and the second near the channel (see Figure 10.2). Raingauge observations were made shortly after each storm. Wind speed and direction were measured for several years at 3.5m above the ground by a Woelfle recorder located at the top of the hill.

The typical spatial distribution of the actual rainfall amount reaching the ground surface is presented in Figure 10.4. The distribution is systematically nonuniform, with a fixed pattern. Rainfall is usually higher on Northwest-facing portions of the hillside, facing the wind direction. It decreased as the aspect changed on the north or west. The detailed analysis of the nonuniform rainfall distribution has been given by Sharon (1980) who explains it by the geometric relationships between the direction and inclination of incoming rainfall and varying local aspect and slope inclination.

Considering that rainfall duration is uniform over the small study area, differences in rainfall amounts actually reflect differences in rain intensity

A. Meteorological instrumentation

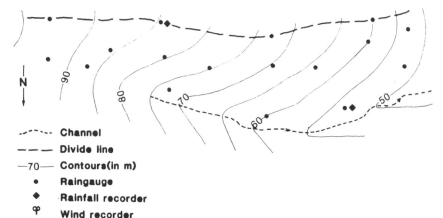

- ·-·-· Channel
- ─ ─ ─ Divide line
- ─70─ Contours(in m)
- • Raingauge
- ◆ Rainfall recorder
- φ Wind recorder

B. Runoff and erosion plots

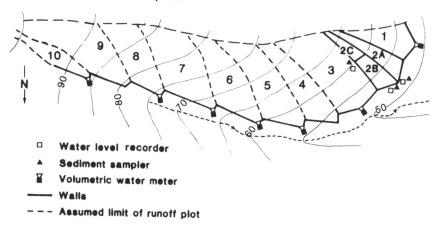

- □ Water level recorder
- ▲ Sediment sampler
- ☒ Volumetric water meter
- ─── Walls
- ─ ─ ─ Assumed limit of runoff plot

C. Lithology and surface properties

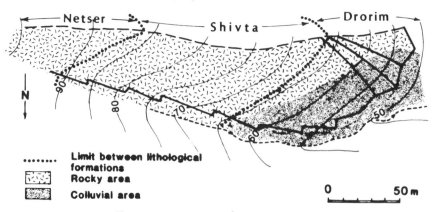

- ········ Limit between lithological formations
- Rocky area
- Colluvial area

0   50 m

Figure 10.2   Layout of experimental site

Figure 10.3   Shivta formation rocky slope

and may thus entail nonuniform spatial generation in run-off. Assuming uniform surface properties one would expect higher run-off where rainfall amount and intensity are high and low run-off where they are low.

Temporal variations

Most rainstorms in the area are frontal rains. They are low to medium intensity rainfalls, lasting several hours or few days, and are of relatively longer duration than convective storms (Yair and Lavee 1985).

Most studies dealing with rainfall-run-off relationships are based on the response of a watershed to whole rainstorms. A rainstorm is usually defined as a wet spell which may last for one or more days. Two consecutive wet spells are separated by a time interval of no less than one day without precipitation. This definition of a wet spell, suitable for humid areas, is inappropriate for arid areas where most rainstorms often last just a few hours. Furthermore, it neglects the temporal variations during the wet spell. A detailed analysis of this aspect of the Sede Boqer site shows that all frontal rainfalls actually consist of several separate showers, often of short duration, each totalling a few mm (Yair and Lavee 1985). Consecutive showers are separated by time intervals of from a few minutes to more than an hour, during which the topsoil can drain and dry. Furthermore, the resulting run-off events are brief and intermittent.

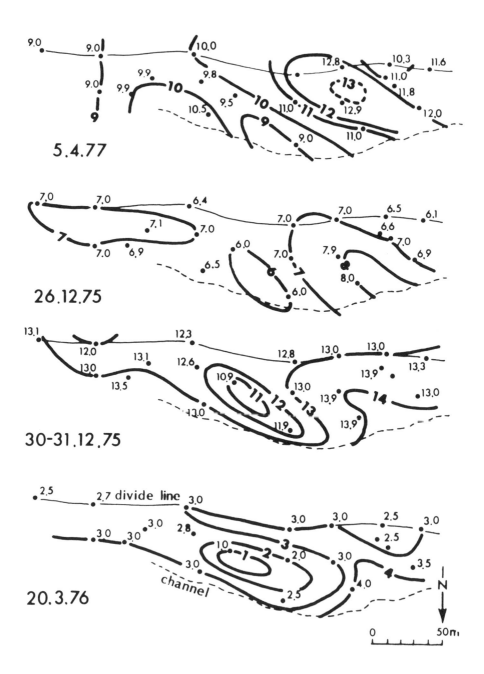

Figure 10.4   The characteristic rainfall distribution at the Sede Boqer
experimental site

Runoff Properties

Influence of surface properties

Arid areas belong to the morphogenetic zone of the globe where physical weathering predominates over chemical processes. The resulting landscape is often rugged and characterized by the subdivision of the slopes into two distinct units. The upper slope is characterized by extensive bedrock outcrops with a patchy and shallow soil cover. The lower slope has a contiguous soil cover composed of unconsolidated material of varying particle size composition. This soil mantle is derived from particles eroded from the upper slope which were deposited at the lower part. The extent of the rocky slope section increases with decreasing average annual rainfall while the extent and thickness of the soil cover increases towards the more humid areas.

The analysis of the rainfall-run-off relationships as controlled by surface units included the following:

(a) Sprinkling experiments, under controlled rainfall conditions, for the establishment of the infiltration curves characteristic of the rocky and soil-covered slope units.

(b) Lateral variations in run-off response to natural rainstorms within the experimental site as a function of surface properties.

(c) The degree of flow continuity along a slope whose upper part is rocky and lower part is covered by a soil mantle.

Infiltration

The assumed basic difference in the infiltration capacity between bedrock and soil covered areas was checked experimentally using a rainfall simulator which can accurately reproduce the characteristics of natural rainstorms (Morin et al. 1970). The infiltration tests were conducted with an intensity of 26mm/hr and for a duration of 10 to 60 minutes until reaching the minimum infiltration value. According to Kutiel (1978) rainstorms with an intensity equal to or greater than 26 mm/hr represent 6 to 7 percent of the precipitation in the area and have an average annual cumulative duration of only about 15 minutes. During any single rainstorm the intensity used for the sprinkling experiment can therefore be expected to last for a few minutes only. The results of the sprinkling experiments are presented in Figure 10.5. The infiltration curves obtained indicate that the infiltration capacity of the bedrock surface is always lower than that of the colluvial slope. The initial infiltration capacity of the colluvium is 41mm/hr and it remained quite high until the end of the experiment. A similar high infiltration rate was obtained by Morin and Jarosch (1977) for loess soils in the northwestern Negev. These researchers used the same equipment as in the present study but their infiltration test was performed with a much higher rain intensity, 56mm/hr.

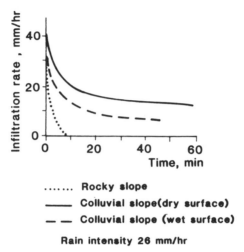

.... Rocky slope

———— Colluvial slope(dry surface)

— — Colluvial slope (wet surface)

Rain intensity 26 mm/hr

Figure 10.5   Infiltration characteristics of bedrock and soil covered areas

To summarize, the threshold amount of rainfall necessary to generate run-off on rocky slopes is low. Data obtained at the Sede Boqer experimental site show that it is on the order of 1 to 3mm. Over the soil-covered area, the threshold value is higher; 3 to 5mm. As the frequency of daily rainfall events exceeding 3mm is much lower than that of less than 3mm (see Figure 10.6), the frequency as well as the magnitude of run-off events can be expected to be much higher on rocky than on soil-covered slopes.

Spatial variations in runoff

The study of the spatial variations in run-off was initially based on ten contiguous plots draining parallel strips of the entire experimental site. Low walls constructed at the base of the slopes directed run-off water to collectors which were emptied through volumetric water meters (see Figure 10.2).

Figure 10.7 presents the characteristic lateral variation in run-off generation for a storm of 12.9mm to 16.6mm. Run-off generation is nonuniform and no relationship can be observed between rainfall amount, intensity, and run-off yield. In fact plot seven, located within the area of minimum rainfall, generated the highest run-off per unit area, whereas plots 1 to 3, located within the area of maximum rainfall, generated the lowest run-off. The results obtained cannot be explained either by the length of the slopes or by the difference in their slope gradient (see Table 10.1). On the basis of previous works (Yair 1974; Yair and Lavee 1976) the following explanation was advanced: The whole of plot 7 extends over the rocky area of the Shivta formation, where extensive outcrops of smooth bare bedrock surfaces occur (see Figure 10.2). Due to the low porosity of the crystalline limestone being low, the infiltration rate and losses are reduced, entailing high run-off yields. A different situation exists over plots 1 to 3. The whole of plot 1 and most of

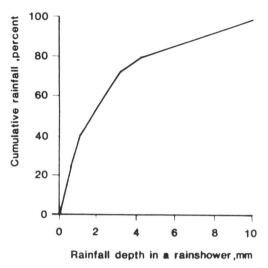

Figure 10.6   Frequency and magnitude of rainshowers at Sede Boqer
experimental site (1975–1979)

Plot no.	10	9	8	7	6	5	4	3	2	1
Rainfall,mm	14.5	14.7	14.3	13.5	13.3	14.7	15.4	15.5	15.5	16.5
Runoff, mm	0.8	0.9	1.9	2.9	1.7	1.8	0.5	0.5	0.5	0.5

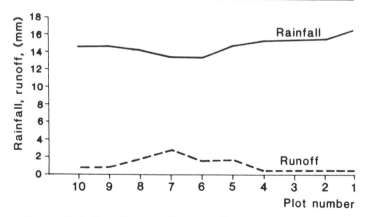

Figure 10.7   Rainfall—run-off relationship, lateral variation

Table 10.1   Rainfall year 1972–1973, run-off & sediment data

Plot no.	Area (m²)	% of total drained area	Slope length (m)	Slope angle(%)	% of total runoff	Sediment removed (g per 100m²)	% of total sediment
	Surface properties				Runoff & sediment data		
1	590	5.2	55	27	4.3	220	1.7
2	870	7.7	63	27.5	3.6	132	1.5
3	1830	16.2	68	28.5	9.1	169	4.0
4	1025	9.1	72	29	9.6	no data	no data
5	1230	10.9	72	29.5	13.5	235	3.7
6	1250	11.0	70	25	9.7	333	5.4
7	1520	13.4	70	24	21.4	2168	42.3
8	1050	9.3	63	26	12.1	1653	22.3
9	1440	12.7	75	17.5	12.8	928	17.2
10	510	4.5	76	11.5	3.9	302	2.0

plots 2 and 3 extend over the Drorim formation characterized by densely jointed bedrock and contiguous colluvial soil at the lower slope section. Infiltration capacities of the unconsolidated colluvial material are much higher than those of the smooth bedrock outcrops entailing the low run-off yields.

Data presented so far lead to the idea that under the climatic conditions prevailing in the area, run-off generation is mainly controlled by the ratio of rocky surface to soil-covered surface. High run-off can be expected where this ratio is high while low run-off is to be expected where this ratio is low.

Flow discontinuity along a slope

The spatial distribution pattern of bedrock and soil-covered areas immediately raises an important hydrological and ecological problem. How much of the run-off generated over the upper rocky slope section is absorbed on its way downslope by the soil-covered unit whose absorption capacity is high? Or in other terms, what is the effect of the high absorption belt (that forms the lower part of the slope) on the run-off contribution of the upper slope to storm channel run-off?

The study of the degree of run-off continuity along a slope, subdivided into two units, was conducted in two different ways: Sprinkling experiments and natural rainfall events.

Sprinkling Experiments

Three sprinkling experiments were carried out at the same time on three consecutive days, on plot 2A (see Figure 10.2). This plot extends over a slope section whose upper part is rocky and lower part colluvial. The experiments were performed at the following rain intensities and durations:

First run, 15mm/hr for a duration of 30 min; second run, 30mm/hr for a duration of 30 min; third run, 60mm/hr for a duration of 15 min. At each run the time interval between the start of rainfall and that of run-off was noted at various parts of the sprinkled area. Parallel to that, flow lines were mapped by using dyes of different colors. A comparison of the different rain intensities and durations in this experiment with those of natural rainstorms (Kutiel 1978) shows that the experiments were performed at high to very high intensities with unusually rare durations. The accumulated rainfall for the first two runs was 22.5mm, representing approximately 25 percent of the average annual rainfall.

The pattern of flow lines mapped during the sprinkling experiments is presented in Figure 10.8. At the first run, conducted under dry surface conditions, run-off started within the upper rocky slope section four minutes after the onset of rainfall and was continuous thereafter until the end of the run. All run-off generated within the rocky area infiltrated into the soil on reaching the colluvial slope section. Within the latter section a trickle of water, unrelated to the run-off generated upslope, was observed towards the end of the run in a place where a patch of bedrock exists (see Figure 10.8). A similar trend was observed on the second run and only on the third run was there an integrated flow along the whole slope.

Natural Rainfall Events

In order to check the degree of flow continuity along a slope under natural rainfall conditions, plot number 2 was subdivided into three subplots (see Figure 10.9). One subplot (A) extends from the divide to the slope base and covers the two surface units; and two subplots (B and C) are adjoining short ones, each of which drains a rocky- or a soil-covered unit. Each of the subplots was equipped with a stage recorder. This allows for the analysis of the hydrographs obtained simultaneously at all subplots and the analysis of run-off contribution from the upper to the lower slope under various rainfall conditions.

The results of the sprinkling experiment are corroborated by data obtained under natural rainfall conditions. Figure 10.9 presents the characteristic hydrographs obtained during a storm of 18mm in eight hours. The storm consisted of several showers that caused separate flow events. Subplot 2C, with the smallest but rockiest area, generated more individual flows than each of the larger adjoining subplots, 2A and 2B, and more run-off per unit area than the other subplots together. Data obtained indicate that most and possibly all run-off generated upslope was absorbed on its way down-

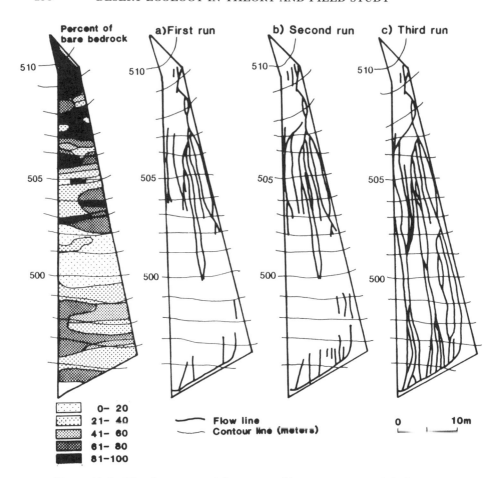

Figure 10.8   Flow lines mapped during sprinkling experiments, Subplot 2A

slope on reaching the colluvium. Similar discontinuities in the run-off process along a slope whose lower part is colluvial were also recorded on rainstorms of higher intensities and duration than those displayed in Figure 10.9 (Yair and Danin 1980; Yair and Lavee 1985) as well as over a longer period (Yair 1983).

Run-off discontinuity along the contact belt and the bedrock-colluvial slope was explained so far by the difference in the infiltration capacity of those two distinct surface units. However, as can be seen in Figure 10.9, the process can be greatly enhanced by the temporal variations during a storm. An important characteristic, neglected in most rainfall studies, is that most rainfalls in the area actually consist of several separate showers, often of short duration, each one totalling rainfall of a few millimeters. Under the above conditions, the depth of the water layer at each of the showers can be expected to be quite shallow. Considering the roughness of the stony

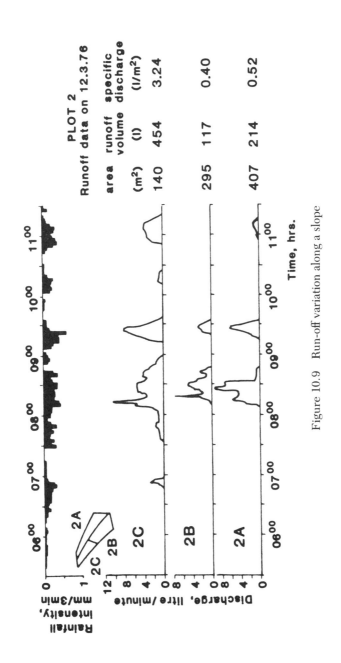

Figure 10.9 Run-off variation along a slope

environment, flow velocities are low. Needless to say, the combination of low flow velocities with short duration flow occurrence leads to the result that run-off generated upslope does not have enough time to reach the slope base before rainfall cessation.

Run-off data obtained at the sprinkling experiment and more than 100 individual flows recorded at the Sede Boqer experimental site during the past decade show that a continuous flow along a slope 60m long can be expected to occur in only about 5 percent of the rainstorms in the area (Yair and Lavee 1985) thus representing rather extreme conditions.

Soil Moisture Distribution

The hydrological findings led to the hypothesis that the lower part of the colluvial slope should display drier conditions than its upper part.

The soil moisture regime along a slope was studied following major rainstorms and over a whole year. Figure 10.10 shows the characteristic variation of soil moisture along a whole slope following a rainstorm of 23mm. The cumulative rainfall amount since the beginning of the rainfall season was 35.6mm. Data analysis shows that the slope is subdivided into two distinct sections; the stepped rocky slope and the colluvial slope. The best soil moisture regime is found at the massive rocky limestone, and at the upper colluvium.

High run-off generated over the extensive bedrock surfaces is collected by the limited soil strips at the base of rocky steps, as well as by the rock crevices and bedding planes filled with soil material.

No systematic downslope increases in soil moisture content could be observed at the surface within the rocky slope section (Figure 10.10). This is due to the fact that the rocky and soil strips are arranged in parallel bands whose width is not constant, varying mainly with the geological structure of the bedrock. In other words, the bedrock/soil ratio may vary within the rocky slope thus entailing spatial variability in soil moisture.

The highest soil moisture is encountered in the rock crevices. This results from a combination of higher water input from the rocky surfaces with a limited volume of soil material filling those crevices. Furthermore evaporation losses from the soil found along the bedding planes are seriously reduced as this soil is not exposed to direct solar radiation, being covered by a rock block whose thermal conductivity is low. The absorption and water-holding capacity of this soil is further increased by its relatively high content of clay particles, probably derived by local enhanced weathering processes related to its good soil moisture regime (Yair and De Ploey 1979).

A more systematic variation in soil moisture is observed along the colluvial slope. High soil moisture, similar to that observed on the rocky slope, was obtained at the upper part of the colluvium, wherefrom soil moisture content decreases downslope. The slope base clearly displays the worst soil moisture regime at the surface and especially at depth (Figure 10.10).

A. At surface level–at 20 stations along a slope

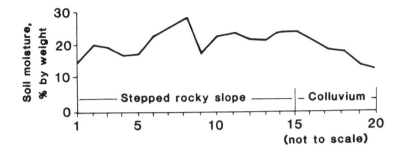

B. Soil strips & lower colluvium   C. Joint & bedding plane

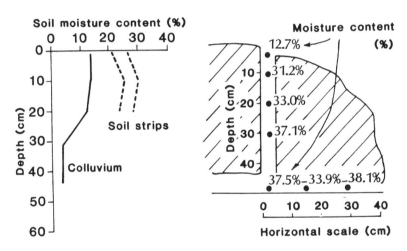

Figure 10.10   Soil moisture content of various microenvironments

WATER RESOURCES AND ECOSYSTEM FUNCTIONING

Data analysis presented so far refer to short term hydrological events collected over a decade. A legitimate question one would ask is how the ecosystem responds to the frequent discontinuity observed in the waterflow along arid slopes? In other words do the short term events exercise a long-lasting influence on the population, community, and ecosystem levels of organization. The relationship between the short-term hydrological events and the long-term ecosystem properties were studied at different time scales ranging from the annual scale to thousands of years. In addition, the effect of water resources distribution on the population, community, and ecosystem levels were investigated.

In the following section, the relationship among water resources distribution, population dynamics, community structure, and soil forming processes is analyzed.

Time Scales

Short time scale

The abundance of the burrowing isopod, *H. reaumuri*, could demonstrate short-term interaction with water resources distribution (Yair and Shachak 1982). Isopods are annual organisms that can survive in the arid environment only in those places where soil moisture content at a depth of 40 to 50cm is higher than 6 percent at the end of the summer. The spatial distribution of their burrows can thus be considered as representative of the soil moisture regime over an annual time scale.

The study of the spatial distribution of the burrowing activity of isopods is based on a grid system which consists of 24 rows parallel to the rock strata. Once a year, at the end of the summer, the distribution of isopod burrows was mapped. The distribution for the period, 1973–82, is presented in Figure 10.11. This distribution is spatially nonuniform. The highest abundance is concentrated within the massive limestone of the Shivta formation and upper colluvium. Lower densities are found at the Netser and Drorim formations and especially at the lower part of the colluvial slope. Such a pattern fits with the spatial distribution of soil moisture. The high biological activity in the Shivta formation is related to the favorable microenvironments represented by the rock fissures of the massive limestone. The low density at the Netser outcrops is related to the fact that the patchy and shallow soil dries quickly. In the case of the Drorim formation, its upper part, which is rocky, displays a soil moisture regime quite similar to that of the Shivta formation. However its lower part, which is covered by a colluvial mantle, displays the lowest density.

The meso time scale

Plant species identified in the study area (Yair and Danin 1980) range from Mediterranean to Saharo-Arabian species. The age of shrubs in the Negev is assumed to vary from tens of years to a few hundred (Fahn et al. 1963). The spatial distribution of perennial shrubs is thus indicative of the prevailing soil moisture regime over a relatively long period.

A detailed analysis of plant species and species diversity within plot 2 is presented in Table 10.2. Data analysis shows that the rocky slope (subplot 2C) with a relatively high concentration of water resources is characterized by high values for the numbers of species, species diversity, and percentage of Mediterranean species. The colluvial slope (subplot 2B), with a low concentration of water resources, displays relatively low values for the above variables, and the highest percentage of Saharo-Arabian species. Of special

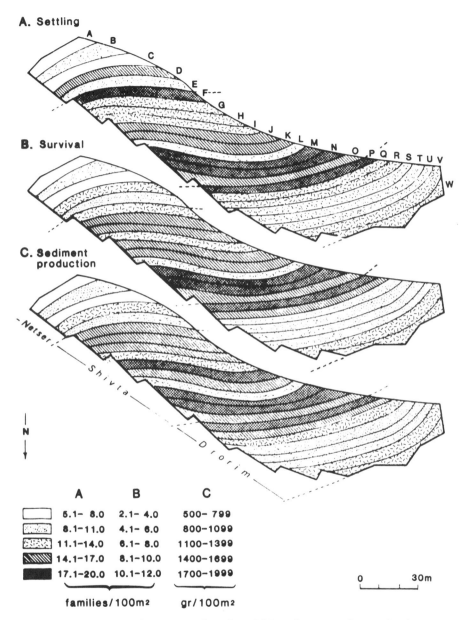

A. Settling

B. Survival

C. Sediment production

	A	B	C
	5.1- 8.0	2.1- 4.0	500- 799
	8.1-11.0	4.1- 6.0	800-1099
	11.1-14.0	6.1- 8.0	1100-1399
	14.1-17.0	8.1-10.0	1400-1699
	17.1-20.0	10.1-12.0	1700-1999

families/100m²   gr/100m²

0   30m

Figure 10.11   Settling, survival, and available sediment production by the
Isopods, *Hemilepistus reaumuri* (1973–1982)

Table 10.2   Floristic parameters, Sede Boqer

Site	H	S	M	SA
Subplot 2A	1,742	18	22.2	33.3
Subplot 2B	1,643	16	12.5	37.5
Subplot 2C	2,239	19	31.6	26.3
Top of colluvium	1,810	19	26.3	31.6
Base of colluvium	1,591	14	7.1	42.9

H – species diversity calculated by the Shannon–Wiener equation:

S – number of semishrub species

M – percentage of species belonging to the Mediterranean, Mediterranean–Irano–Turanian chorotypes:

SA – percentage of species belonging to the Saharo–Arabian chorotype.
(After Yair & Danin, 1980)

interest is the contrast that exists between the upper and lower colluvium. The latter displays the driest conditions encountered along the slope, with only 7 percent Mediterranean species, but 43 percent Saharo-Arabian species.

Long time scale.

Soil-forming processes are strongly influenced by the amount of water available for weathering and leaching. In an arid area, where water availability is limited, the development of well-differentiated profiles can be expected to be extremely slow. A time lapse of thousands of years is required for the formation of a complete profile subdivided into distinct diagnostic soil horizons. The study of soil properties along a colluvial slope can thus be indicative of the hydric conditions prevailing along the colluvium at the recent geological time scale.

In order to study the variation in soil properties along the colluvium, a trench starting at the upper part of the colluvium was dug, for a distance of 20m, down to the bedrock (see Figure 10.12). Detailed soil profiles were studied at the upper, middle, and lower part of the colluvium (Wieder et al. 1985). The conclusions, pertaining to the purpose of this chapter are as follows:

1. Vertical and lateral soil differentiation in the colluvium, as expressed by vertical and lateral distribution of secondary carbonates, gypsum, and salts indicate a downslope decrease in leaching intensity.

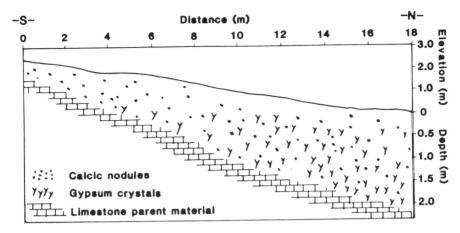

Figure 10.12   Occurrence of calcic nodules and gypsum along the colluvial slope
section

2. The highest leaching intensity occurs at the upper part of the colluvium where soils characteristic of wetter areas ($\approx$250mm) appear. The
   B horizon has well-developed secondary carbonate nodules, but no
   gypsum. Salinity as expressed by electrical conductivity is low throughout the whole profile, being lower than 3mmho/cm at a depth of about
   80cm.

3. The least leaching intensity is displayed by the lower part of the
   colluvial segment. A gypsic horizon occurs close to the surface, at a
   depth of 25 to 30cm. Salinity is high reaching 20mmho/cm at a depth of
   45cm. It is worthwhile noting that a gypsic horizon at such a depth was
   found in a nearby loessial plain (Dan et al. 1973) where run-off
   contribution is assumed to be negligible. Gypsum amount and salinity
   increase with depth where gypsum layers are mixed with calcic layers.
   The upper gypsic horizon is assumed to reflect the zonal character of
   the profile, whereas the lower gypsic and calcic horizons probably
   reflect the cumulative growth of the colluvium at a geological time
   scale.

Levels of Organization

Most ecological studies are carried out on three levels of organization:
population; communities; and ecosystem (Krebs 1978). In our study, the
question emerges of the effect of water resources distribution on each level
of organization. The effects of water resources on mortality, dispersal, site
selection, and habitat distribution were the population level problems
selected (Shachak and Yair 1984). Species richness, species diversity, species
geobotanical origin, and species distribution along environmental gradients
were the community level variables studied. Trophic relationships, i.e.,

animal predation on plants, were selected to represent the effect of water resource distribution on the ecosystem level.

Population

The desert isopod, *H. reaumuri*, is suitable for the population level studies because:

1) It is possible to identify and determine almost all colonization sites in the field.

2) It is possible to determine, by direct observations in the field, whether the sites selected for colonization were safe sites (survival and mortality rate).

3) Each individual completes its life cycle in only two burrows; (a) the burrow in which it hatched and matured (May through February); (b) the burrow in which pair formation and reproduction occurred (February through May).

4) Population density determination is relatively easy.

5) The main factor in site suitability is soil moisture. If the burrowing site does not provide at least six percent soil moisture all summer then the inhabitants perish (Shachak 1980; Coenen-Stass 1981).

Figure 10.13 shows the long-term average mortality and habitat distribution of *H. reaumuri* on the hillslope. It can be seen that for an organism like *H. reaumuri*, population level variables are related to water resource

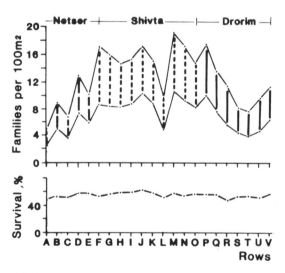

Figure 10.13   Long-term average abundance of *Hemilepistus reaumuri* (1973–1982)

concentration; in rows F to P, with high concentrations of run-off, colonization, survival, and isopod densities were relatively high. In contrast, in rows A to E and D to V, in which additional run-off is low, the above population variables are respectively low (Shachak and Yair 1984).

Community

Three strip transects, from the water divide to the channel, each 100 contiguous 0.5 × 1m² quadrats were sampled at the Sede Boqer site. Presence of all vascular plants were recorded. Data were subjected to detrended correspondence analysis (Hill 1979; Hill and Gauch 1980). Quantitative data and detailed analysis can be found in Olsvig-Whittaker et al., 1983. Qualitative summary of the relationship among surface properties, water resources, and vascular plant community patterns is given in Table 10.3.

The results suggest that the strength of apparent vegetation responses to water regime is strongly affected by the life forms of plant species involved. Geophytes (Zohary 1962) are restricted to relatively mesic locations of Shivta and upper colluvium. Shrubs that exploit deeper soil for moisture than other species predominate in the upper colluvium and Shivta, where moisture resources are available throughout the long dry season. Annuals and hemicryptophytes seem at a disadvantage in sites of interaction between geophytes and shrubs. Hence, their species richness is relatively high in sites with low soil moisture availability.

Trophic relationship

One of the prominent energy flow pathways in the Negev Desert is the conversion of solar radiation into organic matter by geophytes and hemicry-

---

Table 10.3   The relationship among surface properties, water resources and plant community (after Olsvig, Whittaker, et al. 1983)

	Species richness			
Annuals	high	low	low	low
Hemicryptophytes	high	high	low	low
Geophytes	low	high	high	low
Shrubs	low	high	high	high
Spatial heterogeneity (pattern diversity)	low	high	intermediate	intermediate
Animal activity	low	intermediate–high: concentrated in Shivta	intermediate	low

ptophytes. During the dry season, energy is stored in underground organs. This energy is available for porcupine, *Hystrix indica*, predation. However, in order to consume this available energy the porcupines have to search for the underground storage organs and dig them up (Yair and Shachak 1982). Site selection for digging is highly-developed in porcupines and the probability of empty digging is low. Therefore, the spatial and temporal distribution of porcupine diggings is a good indicator of geophytes-porcupine energy flow processes.

The long-term spatial variation in the energy flow indexed by the porcupine digging intensities is summarized in Figure 10.14. It is clear that energy flow rates are nonuniformly distributed on the hillslope. High and low rates

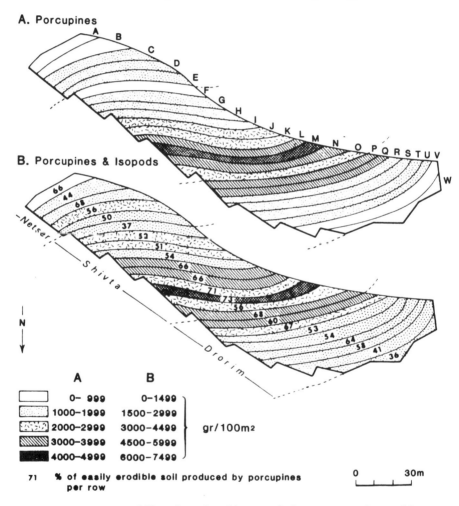

Figure 10.14   Erodible soil produced by animals (porcupines and isopods)
(Average for the period 1973–1979)

of energy flow in the geophyte-porcupine food chain are correlated with water resources in the site.

In conclusion, all ecological variables considered indicative of different time scales and levels of organization show that the arid hillslope ecosystem is highly controlled by the characteristics of the short-term hydrological processes prevailing in the area. In addition, the results suggest that in arid areas, processes related to population, community, and ecosystem levels are explainable and to some degree predictable if water resource distribution processes are known.

ECOLOGICAL FEEDBACKS—BIOTIC ABIOTIC INTERACTIONS

Consumers and Ecosystem Processes

In our research program we explored the possibilities of feedback processes on the hillslope. Our main objective was to determine whether water resources ecosystem relationships are "one way" processes or if the biotic elements exert some control on the water resources distribution. The effect of consumers on resources distribution was selected because it was possible to determine quantitatively their effects on the system. Kitchell et al. (1979) terminology is used to analyse the consumers effect on hillside ecosystem processes.

In a recent paper, Kitchell et al. (1979) synthesized consumer's effects on ecosystem level processes into two general categories: translocation and transformation. Translocation implies "redistribution of materials when mobile consumers across subsystem boundaries." Transformation means altering particle size distribution or changing surface/volume ratios of particles in the ecosystem.

In Sede Boqer we studied the effects of two species of animals *Hemilepistus reaumuri* and *Hystrix indica* on soil erosion and desalination which are mainly translocation processes. *Hemilepistus reaumuri* also controls organic decomposition processes which combine translocation and transformation.

For feeding and burrowing, the isopods consume large quantities of soil at a depth of 40 to 50cm. The soil consumed is defecated and deposited in piles on the topsoil (Shachak 1980). Porcupines participate in soil translocation processes by disturbance of soil surface structure. This disturbance is a byproduct of their foraging for underground storage organs of plants. We termed the piles of soil produced by animals' activity *easily erodable soil* (Yair and Shachak 1982). Three ecosystem processes are associated with the production of easily erodable soil: soil erosion, soil desalination and organic matter decomposition.

Soil Erosion

Studies on soil erosion usually neglect the effect of the biological factor on soil erosion. This approach is expressed by the fact that this factor is missing from the formulae used for the prediction of soil erosion that are based on the interaction between the physical properties of two sets of factors: (1) rainfall and run-off energy; (2) soil erodibility as related to soil texture, aggregate size, etc. However, detailed field observations conducted at the Sede Boqer experimental site drew attention to the intense digging and burrowing activity by desert animals (i.e., porcupines and isopods) and the possible effect on soil erosion. Porcupines seeking bulbs for food break the soil crust which otherwise, due to its mechanical properties and biological cover of soil lichens and algae, inhibits soil erosion. Thus, fine soil particles with loose aggregates are made available for transport by shallow flows. Similarly, burrowing by isopods deliver small faeces which disintegrate easily under the impact of raindrops (Yair 1974). Following these observations, measurements were made of the amounts of available sediment produced through biological activity (see Figure 10.14). These amounts were compared to the amounts of soil actually eroded from the experimental site (see Table 10.4).

A strikingly nonuniform sediment contribution by the slopes was obtained. The three plots, numbered 7 to 9, supplied 88 percent of the total

Table 10.4 Comparison of the amounts of soil actually eroded in the storm of 24.11.72 (18mm rainfall) with the amounts of easily erodible soil prepared by biological activity

Plot	Surface properties			Sediment		
	Area (m2)	Slope length (m)	Slope gradient (%)	B Easily erodible soil (g/m2)	I Actually eroded soil (g/m2)	I/B
1	590	55	27.0	10.6	No data	
2	890	63	27.5	20.7	2.5	0.12
3	1,830	68	28.5	42.1	5.3	0.13
4	1,025	72	29.0	61.6	9.2	0.15
5	1,230	72	29.5	43.6	4.2	0.10
6	1,250	70	25.0	90.3	13.7	0.15
7	1,520	70	24.0	84.2	133.5	1.59
8	1,050	63	26.0	57.0	80.6	1.41
9	1,440	75	17.5	22.4	39.4	1.76
10	510	76	11.5	22.1	9.9	0.45

amount of sediment delivered by the drained area. The sediment contribution by the other plots, which cover altogether 64.6 percent of the surface, amounted to only 12 percent, and varied from 0.5 percent to 4.3 percent for individual plots.

Such differences in the supply of sediment are far beyond the differences recorded in the run-off yields of the plots and in their topographic properties such as plot area, length of slope and mean slope gradient (Yair 1974). A comparison between the spatial distribution of easily erodible soil (see Figure 10.14) and the pattern of soil erosion (see Table 10.4) shows a great similarity and suggests the existence of a link between the two patterns. The accelerated erosion observed on plot 7, which extends wholly over the Shivta formation, and on plots 8 and 9, whose lower parts are on the same formation, can be explained as follows: In the Shivta formation extensive rock outcrops generate per unit area a relatively high run-off coefficient. Run-off, moving orthogonally to the rock terraces, gains in energy at the base of the terraces where run-off hits the disaggregated, loose and easy to remove soil prepared by the activity of the isopods and porcupines. Under such conditions the ratio of actually eroded soil amount (I) to the amount prepared through biological activity (B) is higher than one, indicating that probably most of the latter amount was removed in addition to soil of nonbiotic origin.

In the Drorim and Netzer outcrops erosion processes are less intense. This can be explained by the combination of the following factors characteristic of both formations: (1) the amounts of easily erodible soil are limited; (2) rock outcrops are densely jointed, less extensive and less contiguous, generating less run-off per unit area; (3) surface roughness is high. Flow velocity may therefore be expected to be slow and of limited erosive power. Under such conditions, the ratio I/B is very low, indicating that most of the easily erodible soil was not removed from the area and was probably integrated into the colluvial part of plots 2 to 6.

A question emerges, how does biological activity control water resource distribution in the study area? In a rocky desert, soil moisture regime is mainly a function of the ratio of bare bedrock to soil cover. By increasing soil erosion, animal activity maintains or increases the extent of bare bedrock outcrops which allow water concentration and thus, the formation of moist microenvironments. Without this activity, as eolian loess continues to be deposited in the area, one would expect a gradual covering of the bedrock surfaces by the eolian deposits. Such a cover would limit run-off generation and determine a gradual increase in environmental aridity.

Soil Desalination

Airborne salts which have accumulated as a result of low precipitation and high evaporation rates (Evenari et al. 1983) are the main sources of salts in the Negev Desert. Since leaching rate is not sufficient to remove salts to a great depth, they accumulate at a shallow depth within the soil profile. If the salts are not removed, a gradual salination of the desert soil can be expected. One process of soil desalination is accomplished by the burrowing activity of isopods. *Hemilepistus reaumuri* consume large quantities of soil up to a depth of 40 to 50cm, where salts tend to accumulate. This saline soil is then deposited on the topsoil in the form of faeces and is available for removal by surface run-off water. Figure 10.15 shows that the concentration of soluble salts in run-off water is higher on the rocky plot, 2C, where the abundance of isopods is high, than on the colluvial plot, 4A, where biological activity is low. This difference can be explained by the fact that most of the sediment

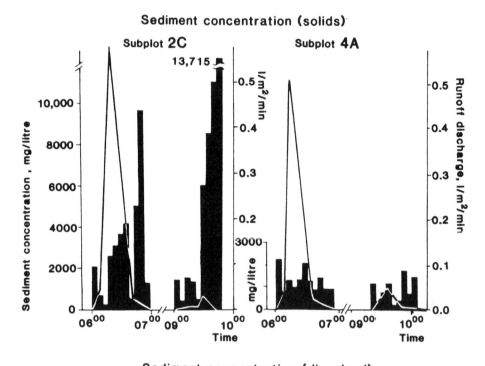

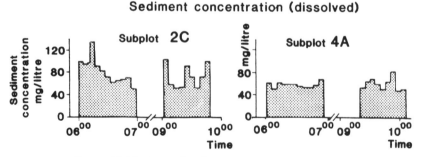

Figure 10.15   Ion and sediment concentration in run-off water, storm of 26.12.1980

eroded from the rocky plot is derived from the isopods' faeces which are more saline than the crusted topsoil (see Table 10.5).

The regulatory effect of the activity of isopods on desalination processes results in a feedback mechanism. Over the rocky slopes the increased processes of soil erosion and soil desalination seem to be helpful in maintaining a favorable environment characterized by a higher water availability for plants due to low salt and high moisture content in the soil. However, most of the salts removed from the upper rocky slope are often deposited, due to the discontinuous waterflow, within the colluvial slope section, where a gradual process of soil salination takes place.

Organic Decomposition

Studies by Orshan and Diskin (1969) showed that vegetation in the Negev is characteristically biseasonal. A short period of intensive growth is seen in the spring, followed by a rather prolonged reduction period during the summer when the net production is negative, and a buildup of dead organic matter is produced. From our field observations in the Negev, it appears that most of the primary production is transferred to the standing dead and the non-green surface dead. High feeding activity of *H. reaumuri* at the end of May and June, when the new generation begins above ground feeding, coincides with a change of live green plant tissues to standing dead and soil surface dead tissues.

Table 10.5 Soluble Ion concentrations (mg/100gr soil) of Hemilepistus reaumuri faecal material and topsoil, Sede Boqer

Ion	Massive limestone		Stony colluvial soil	
	Isopods' feaces $\bar{x}$	topsoil $\bar{x}$	Isopods' feaces $\bar{x}$	topsoil $\bar{x}$
Ca^{+2}	143.74	2.81	89.06	3.97
Na^{+}	0.15	0.06	0.63	0.06
K^{+}	0.08	0.04	0.07	0.01
Mg^{+2}	1.40	0.40	0.75	0.49
SO_4^{-2}	220.31	4.13	104.35	4.52
Cl^{-}	20.81	1.00	25.42	1.54
HCO_3^{-}	36.56	3.40	35.26	3.75

Isopods feed on both standing and surface dead materials, thus it seems that they function mainly in the transference of standing and surface dead plant materials to the soil (Shachak et al. 1976).

By ingesting organic matter and inorganic soil particles, *H. reaumuri* alter the structure of the decomposition substrate by forming a special microenvironment. In this way their activity may directly influence the rate of decomposition by microbes. If the decomposition rate determines nutrient availability in the desert ecosystem, the activity of the desert isopod *H. reaumuri* may affect the rate of primary production. Similar results were obtained by Kozlovskaja and Striganova (1977) for *H. cristatus* in South Turkmenia, USSR.

In conclusion, there is some evidence that soil erosion, soil desalination, and organic decomposition, controlled by animal activity, affect water resources distribution. However, water resources-animal activity feedback is site dependent. In areas with huge concentrations of water resources, positive feedback is prominent, i.e., soil erosion, soil desalination and organic decomposition rates are high and the end product is an increase in water resources concentration. In areas with low concentration of water resources the rates of these processes are too low to induce the positive feedbacks.

REGIONAL SCALE OF ECOSYSTEM FUNCTIONING

Surface Properties—Aridity Relationships

Any study of ecosystem properties conducted in great detail at a small experimental scale has to answer the questions concerning the validity of the conclusions (derived from the small scale study) to larger areas. In other words, how far can we extrapolate from data obtained at the Sede Boqer experimental site to regional aspects of the Negev Desert.

The hypothesis that ecosystem properties in the study area are controlled by the bedrock/soil ratio leads to the idea that the covering of a rocky slope by a soil layer should result in increased environmental aridity. The possibility to check this hypothesis is, fortunately, provided by the natural conditions prevailing in the northern Negev. Loess material of eolian origin started to penetrate in great amounts into the Negev some 80,000 years ago (Horowitz 1979; Goldberg 1981). The loess was deposited directly over rocky hillslopes devoid of any contiguous soil cover. Thus, before loess penetration the whole area covered by the present study had similar surface properties, i.e., steep rocky slopes with a shallow and patchy soil cover. However, loess deposition was not uniform over the whole area. The loess cover is especially extensive in the northern part of the Negev (see Figure 10.16) where average rainfall is 150 to 250mm. The typical topography is that of rolling plains with gentle slopes. Loess thickness may reach up to 12m (Bruins and Yaalon 1979). In the southern part of the area the Negev Highlands, where

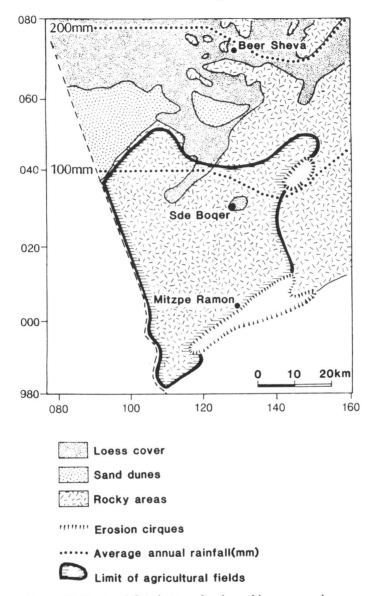

Loess cover

Sand dunes

Rocky areas

'''''''' Erosion cirques

•••••• Average annual rainfall(mm)

Limit of agricultural fields

Figure 10.16   Areal distribution of rocky and loess covered areas

average annual rainfall is 75 to 100mm, the loess cover is more limited. A contiguous loess cover is characteristic here of the bottom of the main valleys but is absent over the hillslopes. This area is characterized by a rugged topography of deeply incised plateau with extensive steep rocky slopes. Bare bedrock may form 50 to 80 percent of the slope surface where the soil cover is shallow and patchy.

In order to check the hypothesis that the ratio of bare bedrock/soil cover controls the degree of environmental aridity in a desert arid area, the southern rocky area with 75 to 100mm average annual rainfall was compared with the northern, loess-covered area, where annual rainfall is 150 to 200mm.

Two different approaches were adopted. The first, the small scale approach, based on a detailed comparative study of two selected slopes that represent the rocky and the loess-covered areas. This study included the analysis of soil properties, soil moisture, properties of the vegetal cover, and some aspects of animal species diversity and abundance. The second approach, the large scale approach, deals with aspects indicative of environmental differences observed and controlled by the regional scale such as the spatial distribution of human activity and drainage network characteristics.

Comparative Study of Slopes

The study compares two north-facing slopes, one located near the Sede Boqer experimental site and the second is the Hovav Plateau area (see Figure 10.1). Both slopes are subdivided into an upper rocky and a lower colluvial unit. The rocky slope at Sede Boqer is composed of the Shivta massive limestone that forms a stepped topography. Bare bedrock is exposed over 60 to 80 percent of the surface (see Figure 10.3). The colluvial mantle at the slope base is stony. The rocky slope at the Hovav Plateau is composed of flinty chalk very densely jointed. The rock weathers into cobbles and gravels imbedded in a quite contiguous thin loess veneer. The colluvium is stoneless (see Figure 10.17) and richer in sand content than that of Sede Boqer.

Figure 10.17   Hovav plateau: stoneless loess cover at lower elevations

The detailed analysis of data collected is beyond the scope of this chapter. Thus only the most important results relevant to the purpose of this chapter are presented.

Soil moisture

The characteristic trends of soil moisture distribution following a major rainstorm and by the end of the summer are presented in Table 10.6. It appears that water availability is higher at the southern than at the northern site. Of special interest is the fact that soil moisture content by the end of the long hot summer is below the wilting point at the Hovav Plateau but above this point at Sede Boqer. This difference in soil moisture is expressed by the fact that less than .1 percent Mediterranean species were found at the Hovav Plateau area (Kadmon 1984), whereas, at Sede Boqer Mediterranean species represented up to 30 percent (Yair and Danin 1980).

Soil properties

Figure 10.18 presents the data collected for the colluvial slope section where two pits were dug in each of the studied slopes, one at the top of the colluvium and the second at its base. Data analysis leads to the following two main points:

—Both colluvial slopes show that leaching processes are more pronounced at the upper than at the lower part of the colluvium.

—All variables presented, indicative of leaching intensity, show that southern Sede Boqer soils are more leached than northern Hovav Plateau soils.

Animal activity

Some aspects of animal activity are presented in Table 10.7. Data obtained display a higher aridity for the northern, wetter area. Of special interest is the data concerning the snail species. Species diversity of snails is higher at Sede Boqer than at the Hovav Plateau. Furthermore, three out of the five snail species identified at Sede Boqer are of Mediterranean origin, whereas

Table 10.6   Sede Boqer vs. Ramat Hovav—soil moisture of colluvial slope section (After Karnieli & Kadmon)

	Sde Boqer	Ramat Hovav
Average soil moisture after a major rainstorm	20%	11%
Maximum soil moisture	34%	15%
Average soil moisture during summer	7%	3%

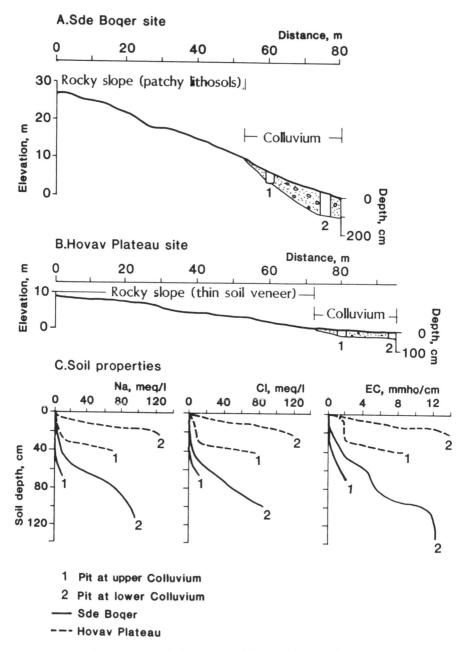

Figure 10.18   Sede Boqer and Ramat Hovav, soil properties

Table 10.7.   Sede Boqer and Ramat Hovav

Animal abundance (per 100m2)

Species	Index	Sde Boqer	Ramat Hovav
1. H. reaumuri	families	25	1
2. Hystrix indica	diggings	30	0.2
3. T. seetzenii	individuals	260	6
4. S. zonata	individuals	20	20

Snail species richness

	Sde Boqer	Ramat Hovav
1. Euchondrus albulus	+	
2. E. desertorum	+	
3. Sphincterochila zonata	+	+
4. S. prophetarum	+	
5. Trochoidea seetzenii	+	+
6. Granopupa granum	+	

those identified at the northern site, especially *Sphincterochila zonata* are indicative of the driest conditions for snails.

Regional Aspects

Ancient agricultural systems

Extensive abandoned agricultural systems (see Figure 10.19) have been found in the Negev Desert. According to archaeological findings (Aharoni et al. 1960) some of the fields are more than 2500 years old. All researchers agree that the existence of the sedentary agriculture in a desert area was made possible by ingenious water-harvesting techniques designed to collect overland flow from slopes adjoining the fields (Evenari et al. 1983; Kedar 1967, 1975; Yair 1983). The examination of the distribution of ancient farms compiled by Kedar (1967) reveals that most of the cultivated area is confined to the rocky Negev Highlands (see Figure 10.16) whereas no vestiges of ancient run-off farms can be observed within the northern loessial plains. The same pattern is encountered for the distribution of cisterns that represent an integral part of ancient agricultural systems. Some of the cisterns are located at a slight elevation above the main channel and were fed by floodwater. Many cisterns are found on the slopes where they were fed by conduits collecting hillslope run-off. All cisterns were carved by man in soft

Figure 10.19   View of an ancient farm

chalky formations. These formations outcrop in the Negev Highlands as well as in the margins of the northern loess plains. However, despite the occurrence of soft chalk, and relatively high rainfall, very few cisterns are found in the northern area whereas hundreds of them were identified in the rocky highlands. The explanation proposed for the regional distribution of ancient fields and cisterns is directly related to the bare bedrock/soil cover ratio. According to Kedar (1967) and Evenari et al. (1983) the ratio of catchment area to cultivated area is about 20:1. From the hydrological data presented it appears that run-off-generating areas extend mainly over steep rocky slopes devoid of contiguous soil cover. Under these conditions, only a dissected area with narrow valleys and rocky slopes could offer a suitable combination for run-off farming in the desert. This combination does exist in the Negev Highlands where the density of small narrow and steep valleys is high. The opposite situation exists in the loessial flat or rolling plains extending south of Beer Sheva. Here most of the area is covered by a contiguous soil with a high absorption capacity. Run-off generation is limited preventing the possibility of developing sedentary agriculture based on water harvesting.

Drainage network characteristics

A detailed quantitative analysis of the drainage networks in the two areas is beyond the scope of the present paper. Our attention focuses on the effect of .

loess penetration on the pre-loessic drainage network. Loess penetration resulted, due to the decrease in run-off, in a drastic decrease of the transporting capacity of the preexisting drainage networks. Channels that before loess penetration were able to transport coarse to very coarse pebbles (Enzel 1984) started to deposit fine silty and sandy particles whose transportation energy is much lower than that of the coarse pebbles. The deposition rate of the fine-grained material was so rapid that whole valleys were completely buried under the loess cover (see Figure 10.20). The burial of the former drainage network resulted in some places in its complete disorganization. Lakes, where gypsum up to 2mm thick was deposited, were recently recognized in the area (Enzel 1984). One of these lakes formed in the vicinity of the Hovav Plateau, at an elevation of 340m across the Sekher Valley. This valley is one of the major rivers draining the northern Negev. Its drainage area from its upper reaches to the lake is about 150km². The very existence of the lake, dated to ± 10,000 years ago, indicates that at that time the Sekher Valley ended in a swampy area being unable to make its way westward to the Mediterranean Sea as it obviously did before loess penetration.

In conclusion, the study of some ecosystem properties at the local and regional scale confirm the hypothesis advanced that within the arid area, studied ecosystem properties are not directly controlled by the average annual rainfall but rather by the run-off amount. In areas of low run-off, water infiltrates to a shallow depth. Almost all of this water is lost afterwards

Figure 10.20   Old channel buried by loess material

by evaporation. Such a process leads to low soil moisture content especially during the summer and the leaching of salts is low. The combination of low moisture and high salinity creates an arid environment. In areas of high run-off, water is able to infiltrate to great depths. Salts are leached to relatively great depths where soil moisture at the end of the summer remains relatively high, allowing for high productivity per unit area.

APPLICATION: HILLSLOPE
MINICATCHMENT TECHNIQUE

Run-Off Farming

Plant ecologists usually relate productivity to average annual rainfall. The trends displayed in Figure 10.21 represent average values and can be considered as correct on a global scale, i.e., when the whole of the arid zone

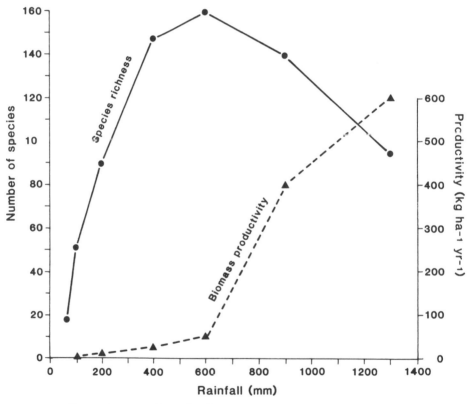

Figure 10.21   Relationship between annual rainfall and productivity
(after Shmida et al., in press)

is compared with more mesic areas. Such an approach is probably valid in areas where run-off generation is negligible and rainfall is the only source of water input into the soil. This approach could be misleading in those areas where pronounced spatial differences in infiltration rates and run-off generation result in the redistribution of water resources. The concentration of run-off water from a large contributing area into a small adjoining area allows for a deep wetting of the soil beyond that allowed by the direct rainfall. The deeply infiltrated water is an efficient agent in the evacuation of salts from the soil profile and, most important, in the creation of a water reservoir at a depth beyond that influenced by evaporation. The deeply infiltrated water is thus available for plants, during the hot season, resulting in a local increased productivity. This fact was known to farmers living in the Negev Desert who long ago practiced sophisticated techniques for run-off harvesting and water storage, in an area with less than 100mm annual rainfall. Agriculture was based on small whole watersheds where the hillslopes were used as run-off contributing areas and the loess-covered valley floors as cultivated fields (Kedar 1975; Evenari et al. 1983; Yair 1983). Run-off collected from the hillslopes was directed into the fields by conduits several hundred meters long. The ratio of the catchment area to the cultivated area varies from 17:1 to 30:1, the average being 20:1. Hydrological considerations (Evenari et al. 1983; show that each cultivated unit in the valley would be expected to receive, in a normal rainfall year, an amount of water equivalent to a rainfall of 200 to 300mm in addition to 100mm of direct rainfall. It should be noted that similar run-off farming is still practiced in the small valleys of the rocky mountains of Santa Catherina in Sinai where average annual rainfall is estimated to be only 75mm.

The same approach, concentration of water resources from a large into a small contributing area, is practiced on gentle alluvial loess plains. Each tree planted has its own, closed, catchment area. Such a technique was used by Evenari and his team at the Avdat and Mashash farms in the northern Negev. Most catchments had an area of 250 to 500m^2, with some smaller or larger.

Common to all agricultural systems in arid areas is that they are composed of four distinct components; water harvesting, water transportation, water storage, and water utilization by plants. A question emerges: Is it possible to improve previous techniques in order to increase productivity in the desert? Or what can be done to improve the efficiency of each of the four components listed above? The answer to the above questions should take the following into consideration.

1. Is run-off farming as practiced by the Nabatean farmers and renovated at the Avdat farm the most efficient way to collect run-off in the desert? The same question applies to the microcatchment technique where run-off water is collected from flat stoneless loessial plains.

2. Is there a way to minimize water losses by shortening or eliminating the long water conduits where infiltration losses may be important?

3. Irrigation of the cultivated fields is done by flooding. Is there a way to decrease water losses due to evaporation from the flooded fields?

4. Cultivation so far has been limited to valley floors and loessial plains where slopes are gentle and soil thickness exceeds 100cm. Is there a possibility of extending the area used to some parts of the steep rocky slopes which are usually regarded as useless due to their shallow and stony soil?

The Hillslope Minicatchment

The hypothesis

The run-off-harvesting agriculture and its positive effect on productivity result from the direct intervention of man, who by building hundreds of kilometers of water conduits and hundreds of dams across the valley floors changed the natural environment by concentrating water, thus increasing the depth of water infiltration.

Our studies indicate that the upper colluvium receives, in addition to the direct rainfall, an amount of run-off equivalent to 200 to 300mm and altogether 300 to 400mm. In other words, the amount of water that infiltrates into the upper colluvium, without man's intervention, is similar to that received by the cultivated valley fields whose water supply comes through water conduits from remote areas. The discovery of the "wet belt" on the upper colluvium where the efficiency of water concentration, water storage, and biomass production are relatively high led to the hypothesis that the fertility of this belt could be further increased. For this purpose water collectors, called "hillslope minicatchments" (HMC) were dug across the slope at the upper colluvium (see Figure 10.22).

To test the hypothesis that the simple and cheap technique of the hillslope minicatchments allows an increase in productivity, trees were planted in the minicatchments. The experimental grove aims to test the possibility of increasing the productivity of the "wet belt" from the level of shrub cover to the level of supporting trees.

Experimental design

An east-facing slope was selected for the proposed study. Furrows for water collection were dug across the upper part of the colluvium down to a distance of 16m from the upper margin of the rocky slope. Trees were planted in November, 1982 and January, 1983. The trees that survived the first long summer (ten months) were provided with one of two types of water-collectors in the fall of 1983.

—Small furrows with a water capacity of 100 to 600 liters—average capacity of 300 liters (small HMC).

Figure 10.22   View of a hillslope minicatchment

—Large furrows with a water capacity of 500 to 2500 liters, the average being 1500 liters (large HMC). The large furrows were reinforced on their downslope side by a stone cover (see Figure 10.22).

The length of the rocky contributing slopes varied from 32m to 85m with an average of 59m. The contributing area varied from 100m² to 800m² with a mean of 265m².

Five tree species were selected for planting. Two species, *Pistacia atlantica* and *Ceratonia siliqua* were selected because they are a component of the Negev Highland vegetation. Two other species were introduced, *Prosopis juliflora*, which is a new world species of arid and semi-arid zones, and *Callitris verrucosa* a xeric Australian species. The fifth species selected was *Pinus halepensis*, the most abundant species planted in the rocky Mediterranean zone of Israel. This species was planted in order to compare biomass production in the Negev desert when utilizing the HMC water-management technique with Mediterranean zone production.

Preliminary results

The purpose of this section is to compare the hillslope minicatchment water technology to previous methods of run-off harvesting applied to the northern Negev. The discussion includes aspects of water-harvesting, water storage and biomass production. The study has been too short to allow drawing final conclusions, especially as regards the last aspect. Data and ideas presented should be considered preliminary and subject to further confirmation.

WATER HARVESTING   Tables 10.8 and 10.9 display the degree of efficient transformation of rainfall into run-off by areas which differ in their surface properties. The data on the hillslope minicatchments were collected from rocky slopes at the Sede Boqer experimental site. The Avdat farm collects its water from rocky, stony, and soil-covered areas, and the loess microcatchments from alluvial, stoneless areas in the Mashash farm.

Analysis of Table 10.8 leads to the following main points: The rocky slopes represent the area which is most responsive to rainfall in terms of frequency as well as magnitude of run-off. The lowest annual run-off coefficient is higher at Sede Boqer than at Avdat. This means that the hillslope minicatchments can get a substantial amount of run-off water, even in drought years. This is not the case at the Avdat farm where in some years, run-off contribution could be negligible. Furthermore, most of the run-off at the small Avdat watersheds was provided by a limited number of high flows that explain the relatively high average annual run-off coefficient. Between these floods, run-off input is limited. For example, only a single flow occurred during a period of two years between December 1961 and December 1963 (Evanari et al. 1983). In other words, the temporal distribution of water input is better in the hillslope minicatchments than at the Avdat cultivated valley fields. Table 10.9 displays the same trends as in Table 10.8. Data for the loess minicatchments were collected at the Mashash farm (Evenari et al. 1984), located about 30km north of Sede Boqer, where annual rainfall is always higher than at Sede Boqer. Despite this difference in rainfall, run-off frequency and yield are relatively low being in the same order of magnitude as those obtained at the Avdat farm. In other words, the loess minicatchments seem to be the less efficient surface for water harvesting in the northern Negev.

WATER STORAGE   Table 10.10 displays soil moisture data for the Avdat cultivated fields and the hillslope minicatchments. Data analysis leads to the following points:

—At the Avdat farm, wetting depth during rainfall years with total rainfall below average is limited to about 90cm. Soil moisture at this depth is about 7 percent, decreasing with depth. Deeper wetting is obtained only during very wet years when soil moisture increases gradually with depth reaching the figure of 11 percent at a depth of 2m.

—Despite the low run-off coefficient recorded at Sede Boqer in 1983–84 wetting depth in the hillslope minicatchment is similar to that observed in wet years at Avdat, and higher than wetting depth during dry and normal years in the farm area. Furthermore, soil moisture at a depth of 2m is as high as that observed in the valley fields during the wet years.

Table 10.8 Hydrological data: Avdat farm and Sede Boqer experimental site.

Location	Drained area	Average # of flows per year	Lowest # of flows per year	Annual runoff coefficient			Period	Annual rainfall
				min	mean	max		
*Sde Boqer three rocky slopes	0.0168 ha x=168 m²	9.3	5	6.5	13.9	57	1975–1979	min 53 max 86 $\bar{x}$ = 71
*Avdat seven small watersheds	1–7 ha. x=4.3 ha.	6.6	1	1.1	8.8	13.1	1960–1967	min 29 max 165 $\bar{x}$ = 88
*Avdat large watershed	345 ha.	3.8	1	0.2	2.4	8.5	1960–1967	"

* Yair, A., 1983:Lavee, H., 1982.

* Evenari, M., et al, 1983.

Table 10.9 Hydrological data: hillslope minicatchment and loess microcatchment (1982–1984)

Year	Hillslope minicatchment			Loess microcatchment*		
	Rain (mm)	♦of flows	Runoff (mm)	Rain (mm)	♦ of flows	Runoff (mm)
1982–83	136	21	27	170	4	7.8
1983–84	72	5	6.5	84.5	1	2.0

* Evenari, et. al., 1984

WATER UTILIZATION   As previously explained, the goal of the tree planting experiment is to determine the maximum production capabilities of the "wet belt" using the hillslope minicatchment technique. As the trees at present are juveniles, we are not yet capable of figuring out maximum production. Only after the trees mature will we be able to know the efficiency of this system of converting water into biomass. However, from our study, we found that for establishment and growth of juvenile trees, a minicatchment with a volume of at least 1,500 liters should be constructed. In addition, with the minicatchment technique the juvenile trees can survive a drought year without adding water.

Trees are long-lived, therefore, we will follow their phenology, growth, and production for many years. Then we will know if the minicatchment is capable of storing water from a good rain year for tree usage during drought years. We will also track the fluctuations in biomass production to determine the relationship among rainfall, run-off, and primary production.

IMPLICATIONS

This study supports the approach adopted by the Hubbard Brook (HB) research team, i.e., that ecosystem properties are strongly controlled by the hydrologic cycle. This approach led the HB research group to adopt a whole watershed for the study of ecosystem properties. The present study shows that in areas characterized by frequent spatial and temporal discontinuities in the water flow regime, over short distances, an extension of the watershed approach is needed. This extension leads to the subdivision of the watershed into small units that have different flow values (water, nutrients, soil, etc.) than the total watershed. If this subdivision is done in a systematic-deterministic way, based on the hydrologic regime then flow values of adjoining units could be combined to explain processes and flow values of the whole watershed.

Table 10.10   Soil moisture (% by weight) at the end of the dry season at cultivated valley fields & hillslope minicatchment

Year	Rainfall (mm)	Depth (cm)			
		0-30	60-90	120-150	180-210
A. Cultivated fields (Avdat) *					
1960-61	57	5.9	6.8	5.8	5.0
1962-63	29	3.9	4.1	4.2	4.2
1963-64	165	4.0	7.2	9.1	11.0
1964-65	153	4.2	7.3	9.3	10.8
1965-66	91	3.9	7.7	6.1	5.7
1966-67	69	3.6	7.3	5.5	6.3
B. Hillslope minicatchment					
1983-84	72	4.6	6.1	8.5	12.5

* Evenari et. al., 1968

Researchers in different disciplines (Shmida et al. 1986, Dan and Yaalon 1982) tend to assume that an increase in rainfall results in a more productive environment and better soil leaching. The present study shows that within the Negev Desert, where average annual rainfall varies from 75 to 200mm this assumption is not valid. The reason is that water availability in a desert area is more influenced by the ability of the surface to efficiently transform rainfall into run-off than by the amount of direct rainfall. This study draws attention to the important role that should be attributed to massive bedrock outcrops in improving the desert environment and to the negative role of contiguous soil cover on the same environment. Soil cover increases the ecological aridity of an area, while massive bedrock, by its positive effect on water concentration, can more than compensate for a deficit of 100mm average annual rainfall in an area where rainfall is scarce and limited. An immediate outcome of the above is that one of the possibilities to improve an arid area is to increase soil erosion in those areas where hard massive bedrock is buried under a soil cover. By uncovering the bedrock, whose run-off efficiency is high, more water is made available to the environment.

The ecosystem described has northern and southern limits which need to be identified. A positive relationship between average annual rainfall and wetting depth can be expected north of the Ramat Hovav area. Southwards, with decreasing average annual rainfall, the frequency and probably the magnitude of run-off events decreases, limiting the effect of water concentration. This effect is well expressed along valley bottoms but less over the hillslopes that are often completely devoid of any vegetation. More should be done to define the limits of the ecosystem described.

Data obtained draw attention to the role that should be attributed to the biological activity of desert animals in a rocky desert. This activity seems to exercise some control over the physical environment through increased rates of soil erosion and soil desalination. However, the degree to which feedback mechanisms exist depends on the physical environment. The feedback process identified within the rocky Negev Highlands, where soil moisture is high, appears to be less significant in the Ramat Hovav loess ecosystem where soil moisture is low.

Data obtained lead to the idea that a revision of the classification of the degree of aridity of a given area is needed. Aridity indices do exist (De Martonne 1927; Thorntwaite 1948; Meigs 1953; Budyko 1974) but all of them consider only meteorological variables such as temperature, rainfall, evaporation, etc. These climatic indices, suitable for climatic classification on a global scale, fail to identify pronounced ecological differences over short distances within the arid climatic belt. An improvement of the existing climatic indices can be obtained by adding variables indicative of the influence of surface properties to the climatic variables.

ACKNOWLEDGMENTS

The interdisciplinary work reported here would have been impossible without the help of many colleagues, scientists, and technicians who participated in the research project at various stages. Prof. D. Sharon and Dr. H. Lavee of the Hebrew University of Jerusalem took part in the hydrometeorological study. Part of this study was carried out by Dr. M. Shachak while he was on sabbatical leave at The Ecosystems Research Center of Cornell University, Ithaca, N.Y. It was published as publication ERC-031 of the Ecosystems Research Center (ERC), and was supported in part by the U.S. Environmental Protection Agency, Cooperative Agreement No. CR807856. Warm thanks are accorded to Mr. E. Milo and Dr. Z. Ofer for their help with the fieldwork and data collection; to Mrs. S. Rozin for the laboratory analysis; to Mr. S. Brand for his help with the computer work and to Mrs. T. Sofer of the Department of Geography of the Hebrew University of Jerusalem for drawing the illustrations.

REFERENCES

Aharoni, Y., M. Evanari, L. Shanan, and N. H. Tadmor. 1960. The ancient desert agriculture of the Negev. *Israel Explor. Jour.* 10: 23–36, 97–111.
Betson, R. P. and J. B. Marius. 1969. Source areas of storm run-off. *Water Resources Research* 5: 574–82.

Bruins, H. J. and D. H. Yaalon. 1979. Stratigraphy of the Netivot section in the desert loess of the Negev (Israel). *Acta Geologica Academiae Scientiarum Hungaricae* 22 (1–4): 161–69.

Budyko, M. I. 1974. *Climate and Life*. Ed. D. H. Miller. New York: Academic Press.

Cappus, P. 1958. Repartition des precipitatious sur un bassin versant de faible superficie. IAHS 43: 515–28.

Caswell, H. 1976. The validation problem. In *Systems Analysis and Simulation in Ecology*, Vol. 4. Ed. B. C. Petten. Academic Press, New York. Pp. 313–25.

Coats, R. N., R. L. Leonard and C. R. Goldman. 1976. Nitrogen uptake and release in a forested watershed, Lake Tahoe Basin, California. *Ecology* 57: 995–1004.

Coenen-Stass, D. 1981. Some aspects of the water balance of two desert woodlice. *Hemilepistus aphganicus* and *H. reaumuri*. *Comparative Biochemistry and Physiology* 70A: 405–19.

Dan, J. R. Moshe, and N. Alperovitch. 1973. The soils of Sede Zin. *Israel Journal of Earth Science* 22: 211–27.

Dan, J. and D. H. Yaalon. 1982. Automorphic saline soils in Israel. Catena Suppl. 1: 103–15.

Danin, A. 1972. Mediterranean elements in rocks of the Negev and Sinai deserts. *Notes Roy. Bot. Gard. Edinburgh* 31: 437–40.

De Martonne, E., 1927. Regions of interior drainage basin. *Geo. Rev.* 17: 397–14.

Dunne, T. 1978. Field studies of hillslope flow processes. *Hillslope Hydrology*, ed. M. J. Kirkby. New York: John Wiley & Sons: pp. 227–90.

Dunne, T. and R. D. Black. 1970. Partial area contribution to storm runoff in a small New England watershed. *Water Resources Research* 6: 1269–1311.

Dunne, T., T. R. Moore, and C. H. Taylor. 1975. Recognition and prediction of runoff producing zones in humid regions. *Hydrological Sciences Bulletin* 20: 305–27.

Enzel, Y. 1984. The geomorphology of the lower Sekher watershed. M. Sc. thesis, Hebrew University, Jerusalem.

Evenari, M., L. Shanan, and N. H. Tadmor. 1968. Runoff farming in the Negev Desert of Israel. *Report no. IX*. Dept. of Botany. Hebrew University, Jerusalem.

————. 1983. The Negev: The Challenge of a Desert. Harvard University Press, Cambridge.

Evenari, M., A. Rogel, D. Massig., and U. Nessler. 1984. Runoff farming in the Negev Desert of Israel. *Report no. VIII*. Dept. of Botany Hebrew University, Jerusalem.

Fahn, A., N. Wachs., and C. Ginzburg. 1963. Dendrochronological studies in the Negev. *Israel Explor. Jour.* 13: 291–99.

Goldberg, P. 1981. Late quaternary stratigraphy of Israel: an ecletic view. *C.N.R.S. colloque no. 598*. Lyon: Prehistoric du Levant. Pp. 55–66.

Goodall, D. W. 1974. Problems of scale and detail in ecological modelling. *Journal of Environmental Management* 2: 149–57.

Gosz, J. R. 1975. Nutrient budgets for undisturbed ecosystems along an elevational gradient in New Mexico. In *Mineral Cycling in Southeastern Ecosystems*, eds. F. G. Howell, J. B. Gentry, and M. H. Smith. U.S. Energy Research and Development Administration. Pp. 780–99.

Hewlett, J. H., and A. R. Hibert. 1967. Factors affecting the response of small watersheds to precipitation in humid areas. In *Proc. of Inter. Symp. of Forest Hydrology*, eds. W. E. Soffer and H. W. Lull. Pp. 275–90.

Hill, M. O. 1979. DECORANA—A FORTRAN program for detrended correspondence analysis and reciprocal averaging. *Selection of Ecology and Systematics*. Cornell University, Ithaca, N.Y.

Hill, M. O. and H. G. Gauch. 1980. Detrended correspondance analysis, an improved ordination technique. *Vegetatio* 42: 47–58.

Horowitz, A. 1979. The *Quarternary of Israel*. Academic Press, N.Y.

Innis, G. S. 1978. Grassland simulation model. *Ecological Studies*, vol. 26. Springer-Verlag, New York.

Johnson, P. L. and W. T. Swank. 1973. Studies of cation budgets in the Southern Appalachians on four experimental watersheds with contrasting vegetation. *Ecology* 54: 70–80.

Kadmon, R. 1984. Spatial variations in vegetation and environmental factors along arid slopes in the Hovav Plateau area. M. Sc. thesis, Hebrew University, Jerusalem.

Karnieli, A. 1982. Spatial variation of soil moisture regime over arid hillslopes. M. Sc. thesis, Hebrew University, Jerusalem (in Hebrew).

Kedar, Y. 1967. The Ancient Agriculture in the Negev. Bialik Foundation, Jerusalem (in Hebrew).

————. 1975. Water and soil from the Negev: Some ancient achievements in the Central Negev. *Geographical Journal* 123: 179–87.

Kirkby, M. J. and R. J. Chorley 1967. Throughflow, overland flow and erosion. *Bull. Inter. Assoc. Sci. Hydrol.* 12: 5–21.

Kitchell, J. R., R. V. O'Neill, D. Webb, W. Gallepp, S. M. Bartell, J. F. Koonce, and B. V. Ausmus. 1979. Consumer regulation of nutrient cycling. *Bioscience* 29: 28–34.

Kozlovskaja, L. S., and B. R. Striganova. 1977. Food digestion and assimilation in desert woodlice and their relations to soil microflora. In *Soil Organisms as a Component of Ecosystems*, eds. U. Lohm and T. Persson. *Proc. 6th Intern. Coll. Zool. Ecological Bulletin*, Stockholm. Pp. 240–45.

Krebs, C. J. 1978. *Ecology: The Experimental Analysis of Distribution and Abundance*. Harper & Row, N.Y.

Kremer, J. N. and S. W. Nixon. 1978. *A Coastal Marine Ecosystem: Simulation and Analysis*. Springer-Verlag, N.Y.

Kutiel, H. 1978. The distribution of rain intensities in Israel. M. Sc. thesis, Hebrew University, Jerusalem (in Hebrew).

Likens, G. E., F. H. Borman, R. S. Pierce, J. S. Eaton, and N. M. Johnson. 1977. *Biogeochemistry of a Forested Ecosystem*. Springer-Verlag, N.Y.

Meigs, P. 1953. World distribution of arid and semi-arid homoclimates. *Arid Zone Research* 1: 203–19 (UNESCO, Paris).

Morin, J., C. B. Cluff, and W. K. Powers. 1970. Realistic rainfall simulation for field testing. *Trans. of the Amer. Geophys. Union* 51(4): 292.

Morin, J. and H. S. Jarosch. 1977. Rainfall—runoff analysis for bare soils. Pamphlet no. 164, The Volcanic Center, Division of Scientific Publications, Beit Dagan, Israel.

Nixon, S. W. and C. A. Oviatt. 1973. Ecology of a New England salt marsh. *Ecological Monographs* 43: 463–98.

Noy-Meir, E. 1973. Desert ecosystems: Environment and producers. *Ann. Rev. of Ecol. and Syst.* 5: 195–213.

————. 1981. Spatial effects in modelling of arid ecosystems. In *Arid Land Ecosystems; Structure, Functioning, and Management, Vol. 2*, eds. D. W. Goodall and R. A. Perry. Cambridge University Press, Cambridge.

Olsvig-Whittaker, L., M. Shachak, and A. Yair. 1983. Vegetation patterns related to environmental factors in a Negev Desert watershed. *Vegetatio* 54: 153–65.

Orshan, G. and S. Diskin. 1969. Seasonal changes in productivity under desert conditions. In *Functioning of Terrestrial Ecosystems at the Primary Production Level*, ed. F. E. Eckart. Copenhagen: UNESCO. Pp. 131–42.

Shachak, M. 1980. Energy allocation and life history strategy of the desert isopod, *Hemilepistus reaumuri*. *Oecologia* 45: 404–13.

Shachak, M., E. A. Chapman, and Y. Steinberger. 1976. Feeding, energy flow, and soil turnover in the desert isopod, *Hemilepistus reaumuri*. Oecologia 24: 57–69.

Shachak, M. and A. Yair. 1984. Population dynamics and the role of *Hemilepistus reaumuri* in a desert ecosystem. In *The Biology of Terrestrial Isopods*, eds. S. L. Sutton and D. M. Holdich. Oxford Science Publications, Oxford. Pp. 295–314.

Shanan, L. 1976. Rainfall-runoff relationships in small watersheds in the Avdat region of the Negev Desert Highlands. Ph. D. thesis, Hebrew University, Jerusalem.

Sharon, D. 1970. Areal patterns of rainfall in a small watershed. Symp. on Results of Research on Representative and Experimental Basins. *IAHS Publ.* 96: 3–11.

————. 1980. The distribution of hydrologically effective rainfall incident on sloping ground. *Journal of Hydrology* 46: 165–88.

Shmida, A., M. Evenari, and I. Noy-Meir. 1986. Hot desert ecosystems: An integrated view. In *Hot Desert Ecosystems*, eds. M. Evenari, I Noy-Meir, and D. W. Goodall. Elsevier/North Holland, Amsterdam, pp. 379–88.

Steele, J. H. 1974. *The structure of marine ecosystems*. Harvard University Press.

Thornthwaite, C. W. 1948. An approach towards a rational classification of climate. *Geog. Rev.* 38: 55–94.

Wieder, M., A. Yair, and A. Arzi. 1985. Catenary soil relationships on arid hillslopes. *Catena* Suppl. 6: 41–57.

Wiegert, R. G. 1975. Simulation models of ecosystems. *Annual Review of Ecology and Systematics* 6: 311–38.

Woodmansee, R. G. 1978. Critique and analysis of the grassland ecosystem model ELM 73. In *Grassland and Simulation Model*, ed. G. S. Innis. Springer-Verlag, N.Y.

Yaalon, D. H. and J. Dan. 1974. Accumulation and distribution of loess derived deposits in the semi desert fringe areas of Israel. *Zeitsch. fuer Geomorphol. N.F.* 20: 91–105.

Yair, A. 1974. Sources of runoff and sediment supplied by the slopes of a first order drainage basin in an arid environment. Abhandlungen der Akademe der Wissenshaften in Gottingen. Mathematish-Physikalische Klasse, III. *Folge* 29: 403–17.

———. 1983. Hillslope hydrology, water harvesting and real distribution of some ancient agricultural systems in the Northern Negev Desert. *Journal of Arid Environments* 6: 283–301.

Yair, A. and A. Danin. 1980. Spatial variations in vegetation as related to the soil moisture regime over an arid limestone hillside, Northern Negev, Israel. *Oecologia* 47: 83–88.

Yair, A. and J. De Ploey. 1979. Field observations and laboratory experiments concerning the creep process of rock blocks in an arid environment. *Catena* 6: 245–58.

Yair, A. and H. Lavee. 1976. Runoff generative process and runoff yield from talus mantled slopes. *Earth Sur. Process* 1: 235–47.

———. 1982. Application of the concept of partial area contribution to small arid watersheds. In *Rainfall-Runoff Relationships*, ed. P. V. Singh. *Water Res. Publ.* 335–50.

———. 1985. Runoff generation in arid and semi-arid zones. In *Hydrological Forecasting*, eds. M. G. Anderson and T. P. Burt. John Wiley & Sons, N.Y. Pp. 183–220.

Yair, A. and M. Shachak. 1982. A case study of energy, water and soil flow chains in an arid ecosystem. Oecologia 54: 389–97.

Yair, A., D. Sharon, and H. Lavee. 1978. An instrumented watershed for the study of partial area contribution of runoff in the arid zone. *Zeitsch. fuer Geom. Supp.* 29: 71–82.

ELEVEN

Additive and Synergistic Nature of Multiple Stresses in the Stability of Desert Ecosystems

ARTHUR WALLACE

ABSTRACT

Desert ecosystems are characterized by a number of harsh abiotic conditions, such as heat, drought, wind, salt, occasional floods, high-lime or sandy soil. These combined, sometimes with intense animal activity, make for the fragile ecosystems so easily subject to further desertification. When man-made stresses are further superimposed upon these stresses, results can be devastating because of the additive nature of the stresses. Several sets of biological studies have indicated that growth promoters and growth inhibitors tend to be additive and synergistic in their interactions. Although it appears most likely that the stresses faced by desert biota are also additive and synergistic, persons involved with reclamation, preservation, and revegetation of deserts would benefit from definitive experiments that demonstrate the additive and synergistic interactive nature of multiple stresses in deserts.

INTRODUCTION

Desertification, defined as human-induced barrenness of the land, is caused by man-made stresses superimposed upon many natural stresses. The impoverishing effects of desertification can be counteracted, however, by minimizing the effects of stresses or eliminating their causes. The research we are doing addresses both destructive and recovery aspects of desertification.

First, we are testing an hypothesis that desertification occurs as the result

The Laboratory of Biomedical and Environmental Sciences is operated for the U.S. Department of Energy by the University of California under contract no. DE-AC03-76-SF00012.

of a multiplicity of natural and man-made stresses that act in an additive manner or, in some cases, in a synergistic manner to produce severe consequences. Second, we are endeavoring to demonstrate feasible options to counteract the impoverishing effects of desertification by avoiding man-made stresses and lessening the natural stresses. Quantitative measurements are being obtained to develop a theory of interacting forces in deserts. This line of investigation can do much to focus efforts on critical problems as the world endeavors to combat desertification.

The hypothesis we are testing suggests that arid ecosystems with stresses already caused by high temperatures, prolonged drought, low soil organic matter with resulting poor soil physical conditions, and other unfavorable conditions can poorly tolerate the addition of man-made stresses. The hypothesis predicts that desertification is an inevitable consequence of unwisely disturbing desert land. However, it also predicts that desertification can be avoided or minimized if the impacts of man-made stresses are corrected. Understanding the stresses and how they interact are the key to success in that area.

LITERATURE REVIEW

The processes resulting in deterioration of the productivity of land in arid areas are generally identifiable, but there is considerable confusion as to why and when desertification occurs. The potential for the tragedy of desertification in the United States is real, since nearly one-fourth of the land mass of the 48 contiguous states is properly classified as arid (Walton 1969; Dregne 1970, 1979; U.S. Dept. Int. 1980).

It is gradually being understood that multiple stresses cause additive and synergistic effects in many, if not all, situations in biology. Examples are different types of herbicides used simultaneously, two or three or more trace elements contaminating simultaneously, several mineral nutrient deficiencies occurring at once, and both deficiency and toxicity present within the system (Berry and Wallace 1981; Colby 1968a; Putnam and Penner 1974; Wallace and Romney 1977, 1980; Wallace et al. 1980b, 1981). When an additive effect occurs for two different stresses (A and B), the combined effect is $A \times B$ (Colby 1968b). If A depresses 20 percent and B depresses 20 percent, the combined effect is $0.8 \times 0.8 = 0.64$ or 36 percent depression. It can readily be seen that several such stresses could become lethal to a system if all were additive. Favorable factors to biological productivity can also be additive or synergistic in their effect (Wallace and Berry 1983; Wallace 1984). This is to be expected as the opposite of stresses and is a key to overcoming desertification.

Arid lands are constantly subjected to severe natural stresses. Heat, drought, and windstorms are continuously imposed on natural ecosystems as well as on agricultural lands. Wild animals—mammals and especially anthropods—can be severe stresses, particularly when other stresses are operating

(Wallace et al. 1980a). Under arid conditions there are other limiting factors which are not conducive to optimal biological development; some can even result in hostile conditions. These include shallow soil, soil with very low quantities of soil organic matter, coarse soil with low water and nutrient-holding capacities, low nutrient supplies of such essential elements as phosphorus, zinc and others, and excess concentrations of salt or boron which are expressions of the high alkalinity of young soils undergoing chemical degradation.

In addition to these natural stresses, other stresses have been imposed by man. For example, air pollution now spreads over large arrid areas. Acid rain on occasion is a product of such air pollution, and some stress to biota is experienced, even though the calcareous soil naturally present can buffer the acid. Irrigation often adds stresses while alleviating drought stress. Without adequate drainage, for example, irrigation can increase the salinity of soil or it can add excess levels of the trace element boron.

Plowed land in arid regions can be excessively subjected to erosion with severe losses of scarce fertile soil. Continued tillage of arid soils can cause them to lose what little soil organic matter they contain, resulting in poor physical conditions and low fertility. Crop cultivation depletes arid soil of certain nutrients. If there is no understanding of the plant nutrition involved, a desertification can result, not necessarily as a result of that deficiency alone, but as a result of its being added to other stresses which can become synergistic at that point.

It is well known that when desert lands are disturbed or when natural vegetation is destroyed, the land will remain bare and in a state that will permit only growth of seasonal, annual plant species with no return to the original shrub condition, even after many decades or hundreds of years. The effect is truly further desertification of a desert. The stresses impinging on the system will not permit natural shrub restoration to occur within a practical time frame. Manipulation by man, however, can reverse the process, but at restoration costs which may be prohibitively expensive.

EXPERIMENTAL WORK

Field Studies

Adjusting the levels of some stresses in the field, such as in the Northern Mojave Desert at the Nevada Test Site, is relatively easy. For example, water and nutrient stress can be lessened by shrub population thinning, water stress can be lessened by nitrogen fertilization, small and large mammal stress or vegetation can be eliminated with special types of fencing (Hunter et al. 1980), salt stress can be increased by adding salt, soil structure stress can be decreased with polymer soil amendments, anthropod stress may be minimized by sprays. Natural year-to-year variations can provide heat and drought stresses (Wallace et al. 1980b), so that studies be meaningful, they are being made with relatively large plots and carried on for a reasonably long number of years—at least five. Measurements are simple to minimize costs, but accurate enough to go into prediction equations (Romney et al. 1973).

Laboratory Studies

With desert plants in large containers, various combinations and levels of water, soil structure, salt, nutrients, simulated grazing, and air pollution, single and multiple stresses and antistresses are produced with the effects being monitored as growth and survival.

REFERENCES

Berry, W. L., and A. Wallace. 1981. Toxicity: The concept and relationship to the dose response curve. *Journal Plant Nutrition* 3:13–19.

Colby, S. R. 1968a. Calculating synergistic and antagonistic responses in herbicide combinations. *Weed Science* 15:20–22.

———. 1968b. Comparison of two methods for testing herbicidal synergism. *Weed Science Society America* Abstract, 13.

Dregne, H. E. 1970. *Arid Lands in Transition*. American Association for the Advancement of Science, Baltimore, Md.

———. 1979. Technological limitations to arid zone development Pp. 23–29. *Advances in Desert and Arid Land Technology and Development* Vol. 1, eds. A. Bishay and W. C. McGinnies. Harwood Academic Publishers, New York.

Hunter, R. B., A. Wallace, and E. M. Romney. 1980. Fencing enhances shrub survival and growth for Mojave Desert revegetation. *Great Masin Naturalist* Memoirs 4:212–15.

Putnam, A. R., and D. Penner. 1974. Pesticide interaction in higher plants. *Residue Reviews* 50:73–106.

Romney, E. M., A. Wallace, and R. B. Hunter. 1978. Plant response to nitrogen fertilization in the Northern Mojave Desert and its relationship to water manipulation, p. 232–43. In *Nitrogen in Desert Ecosystems*. Dowden, Hutchinson and Ross, Stroudsburg, Penn.

Romney, E. M., et al. 1973. Some characteristics of soil and perennial vegetation in Northern Mojave Desert areas of the Nevada test site. *UCLA Report* 12–916.

Tolba, M. K. 1979. What could be done to combat desertification, pp. 5–22. In *Advances in Desert and Arid Land Technology and Development* Vol. 1, eds. A. Bishay and W. C. McGinnies. Harwood Academic Publishers, New York.

U. S. Department of Interior. 1980. Desertification in the U. S.: Status and issues. *Working Review Draft*.

Wallace, A. 1984. The next agricultural revolution. *Communications Soil Science and Plant Analysis* 15:191–97.

Wallace, A., and W. L. Berry. 1983. Possible effects when two deficient essential elements are applied simultaneously. *Journal of Plant Nutrition* 6:1013–16.

Wallace, A., and E. M. Romney. 1977. Synergistic trace metal effects in plants. *Communications in Soil Science and Plant Analysis* 8:699–707.

———. 1980. Some problems in the study of simultaneous multiple nutrient deficiencies in plants. *Journal Plant Nutrition* 1:213–20.

Wallace, A., E. M. Romney, and G. V. Alexander. 1981. Multiple trace element toxicities in plants. *Journal of Plant Nutrition* 3:257–63.

Wallace, A., E. M. Romney, and R. B. Hunter. 1980a. The challenge of a desert: Revegetation of disturbed desert lands. *Great Basin Naturalist Memoirs* 4:216–25.

Wallace, A., E. M. Romney, J. Kinnear, and G. V. Alexander. 1980b. Single and multiple trace metal excess effects on three different plant species. *Journal of Plant Nutrition* 2:11–23.

Walton, K. 1969. *The Arid Zones*. Aldine Publishing Co., Chicago, Ill.

TWELVE

Mapping Desert Alluvial Deposits from Satellite Imagery

P. M. MERIFIELD

ABSTRACT

In most of the world's deserts, alluvial deposits and geomorphic surfaces have not been mapped sufficiently for land use planning and engineering/environmental purposes. Satellite imagery is particularly well suited for mapping desert regions. Multispectral data in the visible and near-infrared region of the spectrum from Landsats one through five enable discrimination on the basis of surface composition. The ability to separate discrete units is improved by spectral band ratioing and combining bands and ratios into color composite images. Older alluvial fan materials of different clast size that are coated with desert varnish cannot be separated when utilizing Landsat images alone. Synthetic aperture radar data from the unmanned Seasat and the manned Shuttle missions, on the other hand, provide information on surface roughness. Gradations in coarseness from smooth desert pavement to bouldery debris flows can be recognized in radar imagery. In order to utilize the complementary effects of Landsat and Seasat data, the images can be digitally coregistered and displayed in a single image. A synergistic effect enables many more units to be mapped than from either Landsat or radar data alone.

The penetration of several meters of sand in arid regions by the spaceborne synthetic aperture radar has recently been demonstrated. The ability to image buried features has wide application in geologic exploration, geomorphology and archaeology. The development of the thermal infrared multispectral scanner, which detects mineralogical differences better than visible or near-infrared sensors, and improved computer image processing techniques, promise further improvements in mapping arid regions.

INTRODUCTION

Satellite imagery is particularly well suited for mapping desert surfaces. Being generally free of clouds, arid regions are amenable to imaging in the visible and infrared regions of the spectrum, and in the absence of masking vegetation, earth materials are well-exposed. Alluvial deposits cover vast areas of the world's deserts. In the Mojave Desert of California, for example, alluvial deposits blanket the intermontane basins and make up fully 50 percent of the land surface. With few exceptions, these deposits have not been mapped sufficiently for land use planning and engineering/environmental applications. Knowledge of the distribution and composition of alluvial deposits is important; it is, for example, pertinent to unraveling Quaternary stratigraphy, deciphering Quaternary climates, and improving our understanding of the origin of desert varnish and desert pavement.

For practical reasons, the deserts are being viewed with more and more interest for siting and routing of engineered facilities, as well as new agricultural and urban development. Much of the world's future growth will probably occur by expansion into arid lands. Knowledge of the distribution and nature of Quaternary alluvial deposits is fundamental to developing such regions. A number of potential energy technologies have been proposed as especially suited for desert regions. In southern California, new electric generating plants (coal-fired, wind turbine, solar thermal, geothermal, and solar ponds) are planned for the desert to supplant oil- and gas-burning plants now located along the coastline. Additional roadways, pipelines, and transmission corridors will accompany development. Some alluvial deposits (sand, gravel, clay) will be sought for construction materials; others may constitute hazards (windblown sands, expansive clays, soils subject to hydro-compaction). The mapping of alluvial deposits in arid lands has many practical applications, among them:

- To delineate soils with agricultural potential
- To target areas for ground water exploration
- To date stable geomorphic surfaces for determining fault activity
- To site engineered facilities, e.g., power plants
- To route transmission lines, pipelines, and highway corridors
- To explore for minerals (placer and lode)
- To identify construction materials
- To allocate land use by responsible agencies (delineating areas of critical environmental concern, recreational areas, etc.)
- To characterize playas (dry lakes) as potential waste disposal sites.

Whether a playa (dry lake, salt pan) is suitable for use as a disposal site for hazardous wastes will depend on its hydrogeological setting and the engineering properties (primarily permeability) of its sediments.

Alluvial deposits may be in themselves valuable mineral deposits (glass sands, placers, mineral salts and clays in playas) as well as indicators of mineralization in the source rocks from which they are derived. In some places Quaternary alluvial deposits are important aquifers which contain vast untapped ground water resources. Satellite imagery is proving to be an efficient means of mapping these deposits on a reconnaissance scale (1:250,000 with Landsat 1 to 3 data); larger-scale mapping is feasible with Landsat 4 and 5 data and radar imagery from the Seasat and Shuttle missions.

LANDSAT MISSIONS

Landsat 1, launched in 1972, was the first of five satellites placed in near-circular, sun-synchronous orbits for earth resources applications. Landsats 1, 2, and 3 carried two sensors, a return-beam vidicon (RBV) and a multispectral scanner (MSS). The MSS, which has proven the more useful of the two as a mapping tool, gathers light reflected from the earth by means of a mirror oscillating through 11.56° normal to the orbital path. At an altitude of 918km the scan of the mirror produces a swath-width on the earth's surface of 185km. Owing to the 80° inclination of the orbit, most of the earth can be imaged every 18 days, with a ground resolution of 80m. Reflected light is detected in four spectral bands, two in the visible and two in the near infrared regions of the spectrum, 0.5 to 0.6µm (Band 4), 0.6 to 0.7µm (Band 5), 0.7 to 0.8µm (Band 6), and 0.8 to 1.1µm (Band 7). A fifth band on Landsat 3 operated in the thermal infrared region (10 to 12.5µm). The data are transmitted directly to ground receiving stations or recorded on magnetic tape for later transmission.

Experience with the first three Landsats provided the impetus for the development of an improved sensor known as the thematic mapper (TM) with improved spatial resolution, spectral separation and radiometric accuracy. The TM was carried aboard Landsat 4, launched in July 1982, and Landsat 5, launched in March 1984, into a sun-synchronous, near-polar orbits at altitudes of about 705km. This lower orbit provided repetitive coverage of every point on the earth at 16-day intervals and a maximum ground resolution of 30m. The TM operates in seven spectral bands in the visible, near-infrared and thermal infrared regions. The bands were selected especially for vegetation monitoring with the exception of Band 7, which was chosen for geologic applications. The band designations, spectral ranges, and designated applications are as follows (US Geological Survey 1982):

Band 1 (0.45–0.52µm) Designed for water body penetration, making it useful for coastal water mapping. Also useful for differentiating soil from vegetation, and deciduous from coniferous flora.

Band 2 (0.52–0.60µm) Designed to measure visible green reflectance peak of vegetation for vigor assessment.

Band 3 (0.63–0.69µm) A chlorophyll absorption band important for vegetation discrimination.

Band 4 (0.76–0.90µm) Useful for determining biomass content and delineating water bodies.

Band 5 (1.55–1.75µm) Indicates vegetation moisture content and soil moisture. Also useful for differentiating snow from clouds.

Band 6 (10.40–12.50µm) A thermal infrared band of use in vegetation stress analysis, soil moisture discrimination, and thermal mapping.

Band 7 (2.08–2.35µm) A band selected for its potential for discriminating rock types and for hydrothermal mapping.

Landsats 4 and 5 communicate with the new Tracking and Data Relay Satellites (TDRS), relaying data on earth in near real-time and eliminating the need for onboard tape recordings, which proved to have limited lifetimes on previous missions.

SEASAT AND SHUTTLE MISSIONS

The Seasat spacecraft, launched in 1978, was designed for gathering oceanographic data. One of the five instruments carried onboard was a synthetic aperture radar (SAR). In this system, pulsed electromagnetic radiation in the microwave region is transmitted by an antenna to the ground. Energy reflected from surface features returns to a receiving antenna and is converted to an image. The transmitting antenna was oriented such that a 100km ground swath was covered with a median incidence angle of 20° from the vertical from the nearly circular 800km-high orbit with an inclination of 108 degrees. The SAR operates in the L-band (23.4cm wavelength) microwave region of the spectrum, a region providing good penetration of atmospheric water (clouds and rain) and good suppression of vegetation (Sabins 1978). Ground resolution for the imaging system was about 25m. Extensive ground coverage of the United States was achieved during the mission, even though it lasted only 95 days owing to a failure of the electrical system.

   The manned space shuttle Columbia, launched in 1981, carried a scientific payload consisting of several remote-sensing experiments, including a side-looking synthetic aperture radar with a median look direction of 50 degrees from the vertical. The shuttle orbited at an altitude of 262km and an inclination of 38 degrees. As with Seasat, the Shuttle Imaging Radar (SIR-A) on Columbia operated in the L-band region of the spectrum (23cm wavelength) and covered a ground swath 50km wide.

MAPPING ALLUVIAL DEPOSITS FROM SATELLITE DATA

Landsat Imagery

Landsat data enable discrimination between materials of different surface composition by means of their spectral reflectances, i.e., brightness in black and white images and hue in color composite images. On the basis of relative brightness or hue in conjunction with morphology and association with other land features, alluvial deposits can be differentiated if not identified. Vast regions can be mapped at reconnaissance scales with a minimum of field work necessary to positively identify the mapped units. With training the interpreter gains confidence in identification. Aeolian sand can generally be identified, for example, because it is among the brightest objects in the image. Playas can be identified by their central location in the bolson and their change in appearance as a function of moisture content. But in the visible and near infrared regions of the spectrum, only limonitic (hydrous iron oxide) materials and vegetation can be identified directly from their spectral characteristics alone (Kahle 1982).

The identification of limonitic materials and vegetation is greatly facilitiated by the spectral band ratioing of MSS data. The brightness levels in ratio images are obtained by dividing the intensity of one wavelength band by that of another on a pixel-by-pixel basis. The imaged object appears comparatively dark if the ratio is less than one and bright if greater than one. Vegetation appears dark in the ratio of the red to the green bands because the spectral reflectance of green, leafy vegetation is less in the red band than the green band, while the reverse is true for most earth materials.

The 5/4 ratio is also useful for highlighting hydrous iron oxides, because the spectral reflectance curve falls off steeply toward the blue end of the visible spectrum for limonitic materials, as shown in the following example (Merifield et al. 1975). Figure 12.1 compares the Landsat Band 4 image and the 5/4 ratio image centered in the foothills of the Tehachapi Mountains northwest of the town of Rosamond in the western Mojave Desert. Alluvial fans of different ages are much more easily separated on the ratio image (see Figure 12.1b). Of particular interest is the general correlation between the gray levels and the age and elevation of the alluvial materials. The older, more dissected surfaces are brighter, and the younger fans are darker. This relation is explained by the relative abundance of hydrous iron oxides. The more mature surfaces possess well-developed soils, which are red-brown because of the presence of hydrous iron oxides. The youthful materials, occupying the active fans and washes, have had no soil development and contain no hydrous iron oxide alteration products. The technique is restricted to areas where mature soils are exposed at the surface. In the eastern Mojave Desert, mature red-brown soils are obscured by varnished desert pavements.

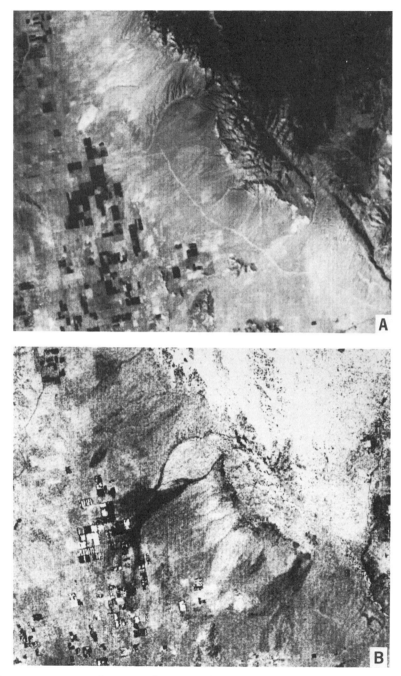

Figure 12.1   A. Landsat 1, Band 4. B. Landsat 1, ratio of Band 5 to Band 4. Images are centered 23 km southwest of Mojave, California. Width of images is 30 km.

Radar Imagery

It has been recognized for some time that synthetic aperture radar (SAR) is effective in discriminating desert alluvial materials. The dominant factor in determining the amplitude of the return and, thus, the brightness of the image is surface roughness (Reeves et al. 1975). If the roughness is at a scale much less than the radar wavelength (less than about $1/10$ the wavelength), the surface will appear smooth and no energy will be scattered back to the receiver, thus creating a dark image. If the roughness is at a scale equal to or greater than the radar wavelength, the surface will act as a diffuse reflector and produce a bright image. Surfaces with intermediate roughness will produce shades of gray on the image. The 23cm wavelength of the Seasat and SIR-A radars is ideal for discriminating desert alluvial deposits, whose grain size falls within the gray scale range.

MacDonald and Waite (1973) applied side-looking airborne radar to mapping alluvium in arid regions; they utilized Ka-band radar (0.86cm wavelength) to distinguish older from younger alluvium in north-central Nevada. Shaber et al. (1976) made a more extensive study of alluvial as well as evaporite deposits in Death Valley, California, using airborne L-band radar. Sugiura and Sabins (1980) differentiated six units on airborne SAR imagery of a 2000-km² area in the Bristol Lake region of the Mojave Desert, and sand dunes in radar imagery have been studied extensively by Blom and Elachi (1981).

Realizing the contribution of both Landsat images in providing spectral reflectance information in the visible and near-infrared regions and roughness information in the microwave region, Daily et al. (1979) combined Landsat data with side-looking airborne radar data in a single image by registering the images on a pixel-by-pixel basis. They concluded from the study that a "dramatic synergistic effect" was achieved by combining visible and near-infrared Landsat data with radar data. Subtle differences in the alluvial fan and evaporite deposits on the playas were revealed, and a nearly complete separation of the Quaternary units was achieved.

STUDIES IN THE EASTERN MOJAVE DESERT

The eastern Mojave Desert is characterized by lofty mountain ranges exposing a great variety of rock types that shed detritus into huge interior drainage basins. Rainfall is less than 10cm per year in the basins; vegetation, which belongs to the Creosote Bush scrub climax plant community, generally covers less than 10 percent of the surface.

Fringing the mountain ranges, which shed primarily metamorphic or volcanic rocks, are desert pavements, geomorphic surfaces which have received considerable attention in the literature on desert research. The term "desert pavement" as used here refers to a comparatively smooth surface layer of stones a few centimeters thick above a soil which generally contains stones dispersed through it. The surface is easily trafficable, not unlike a cobblestone street. In the Old World deserts, smooth pavements are termed *reg* or *serir*, to distinguish them from untrafficable rocky or boulder-strewn surfaces called *hamada* (Mabbutt 1977).

Pavements of the eastern Mojave Desert occur on the higher portions of alluvial fans, possess a moderate- to well-developed coat of desert varnish, and are comparatively unvegetated. Vegetation, commonly mesquite, is concentrated in the active washes that traverse, and often deeply incise, the pavements.

Pavements owe their origin to complex, imperfectly understood processes, including deflation, wash erosion, upward displacement of stones, and surface weathering (Cooke 1970; Mabbutt 1977). Pavements may form initially in a relatively short time (Hunt and Mabey 1966) and henceforth provide a protective coat of armor for the underlying soil. Nevertheless they continue to evolve over thousands of years. Larger clasts disintegrate by spalling or cleaving along inherent planes of weakness, aided by salt-weathering and clay-wedging among other chemical weathering processes (Cooke 1970; Mabbutt 1977; Peterson 1980). The resulting flakes and slabs are redistributed by rainwash and creep to form a densely packed mosaic. Pavements are composed of rock fragments comparatively resistant to weathering, primarily from metamorphic and volcanic source areas. The evolutionary changes mentioned above cause pavements to become smoother with age. Other parameters, such as differences in source rock, chemical processes and climate, may also influence smoothness.

Recent work with K/Ar-dated flows in the Cima volcanic field in the Mojave Desert has revealed that over time (> 0.75 m.y.) the soil profile becomes plugged by the accumulation of pedogenic clay and calcium carbonate, which reduces infiltration. This process leads to increased run-off which strips the pavement and underlying silt horizon, exposing a rubblized petrocalcic horizon (Dohrenwend et al. 1984).

In the arid climate of the eastern Mojave Desert, rock surfaces exposed for long periods acquire a coat of desert varnish (Engel and Sharp 1958). Thus, stable outcrops of bedrock, as well as stable pavement surfaces, develop uniform dark brown to black colors on exposed surfaces. Visible coats of varnish require 3000 to 5000 years to form (Hayden 1976); the presence or absence of varnish, therefore, is useful for distinguishing early from later Holocene surfaces. Desert varnish consists primarily of clay minerals, but the characteristic color stems from the manganese oxide mineral birnessite and from hematite (Potter and Rossman 1977, 1979). The varnish is believed to form by the accretion of materials external to the host rocks and derived from wind-blown dust and run-off, with biogenic processes playing an important role in its formation (Dorn and Oberlander 1981, 1982).

Desert pavements are easily disrupted by vehicular traffic. Still plainly visible in the eastern Mojave Desert are the vehicle tracks of General George Patton's training exercises during World War II. These and the random tracks of off-road vehicles will scar pavements for centuries. The effects of vehicular use on pavements are twofold: (1) light traffic strips an area of pavement and vegetation, exposing the soft silt layer to erosion by wind and water; (2) heavy traffic compacts the silt layer, reducing wind erosion but promoting run-off and thus rill erosion (Wilshire and Nakata 1976). It is important to map pavements, some bearing magnificent intaglios constructed by prehistoric man, so they can be circumvented by planners of utility corridors and placed off-limits to recreation vehicles.

Desert surface materials covered with a coat of desert varnish are indistinguishable in Landsat imagery as well as small-scale photography, regardless of differences in composition or texture (sand, cobbles, boulders). Figure 12.2 compares Landsat and Seasat images of an area on the southwest flank of the Chocolate Mountains south of the Salton Sea in southeastern California. The Algodones sand dunes can be identified in the lower portion of the Landsat image, and older fan material (darker) is readily separated from younger alluvium (lighter). Figure 12.3 is a generalized interpretation of the Landsat scene. The stippled areas (both fine and coarse stipple) were interpreted to belong to a single unit. Field checks in a test area straddling Highway 78 showed this unit to be smooth desert pavement (Figure 12.4) with fragments averaging 0.5 to 2.5cm. Subsequently obtained Seasat SAR imagery showed several areas producing a bright image (see Figure 12.1b) suggesting a surface roughness at a scale near the radar wavelength or greater. As shown in Figure 12.5, the surface of these bright areas is strewn with boulders up to 38cm. The Seasat SAR imagery, therefore, provides a dimension in mapping desert alluvial deposits and geomorphic surfaces not provided by visible and near-infrared sensors. In particular varnished surfaces, indistinguishable in the visible and near-infrared regions of the spectrum, can be separated on the basis of surface fragment size, pebbles, cobbles, boulders, etc.

Because of the digital format of the Landsat and Seasat data, the two can be combined into a single image. Digital registration of the Landsat 3 MSS and Seasat SAR data of an area near Vidal Junction (see Figure 12.6) was accomplished using algorithms developed at the Image Processing Laboratory of the Jet Propulsion Laboratory (Merifield et al. 1984). The process involved identification of common tie points (in this case 118) between the two scenes and subsequently rotating and distorting the Seasat "slave" component to fit the "master" Landsat Band 7 image. Only one-fourth of the Seasat SAR pixels were used in order to degrade the Seasat image to about the same resolution as the Landsat scenes.

A color composite image was subsequently generated by projecting the Seasat scene with a blue filter, Landsat Band 7 with a green filter and Landsat Band 4 with a red filter. Surfaces rough to the Seasat SAR show up bright blue and unvarnished alluvial deposits appear in various shades of brown. Alluvial units were mapped on an overlay of a print of the coregistered image enlarged to a scale near 1:250,000. The Seasat component produced a sharp contrast between rugged bedrock outcrops and smoother

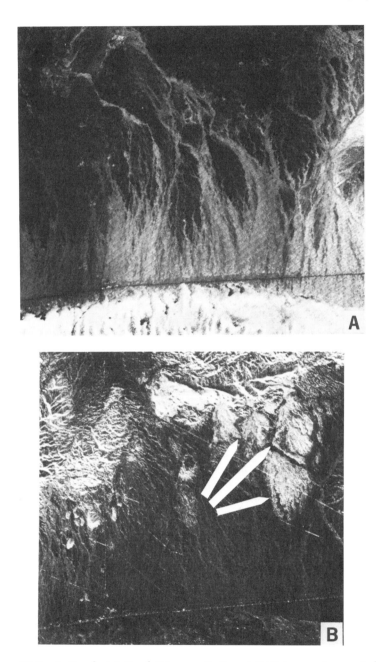

Figure 12.2   A. Landsat 3 Band 7 image. B. Seasat SAR image. Arrows indicate bright areas (heavily stippled areas in Figure 12.3). Images centered about 15 km east of Glamis, southwestern Chocolate Mountains, California. Distance left to right across images about 30 km.

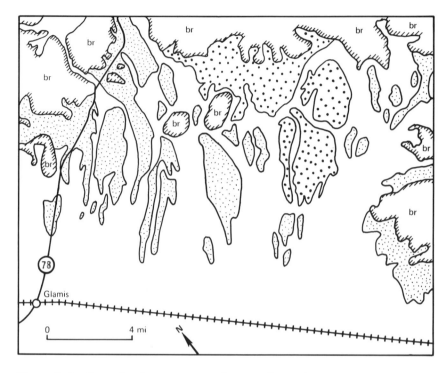

Figure 12.3   Generalized interpretation from Landsat and Seasat images, southwest Chocolate Mountains.
br—bedrock; light stipple—desert pavement; heavy stipple—boulder-strewn surface; blank—younger alluvium.

piedmont surfaces, enabling bedrock-alluvium contacts to be readily delineated. Twenty-four separate units were separated on the coregistered image of the test area where a previous interpretation of a computer-enhanced Landsat 3 color composite (Bands 4, 5, and 7) had produced only six units.

At location A in Figure 12.6 is a bouldery alluvial deposit of probable debris-flow origin shown on the ground in Figure 12.7. The extreme roughness of this surface results in a bright blue image. The distal end of the deposit at B is less rough (see Figure 12.8), and hence the intensity of the blue radar component in the coregistered image (see Figure 12.6) is less. Because the surfaces at both locations are coated with desert varnish, they cannot be distinguished on Landsat images alone. Smooth, varnished pavement surfaces, such as at C (see Figure 12.6) lack the blue radar component; this surface is shown in Figure 12.9. Active dune sand (see Figure 12.10) produces a bright image, such as at D, owing to the predominance of quartz, which is highly reflective, in Bands 4 and 7. Intermediate shades of yellow-brown manifest alluvial mixtures of quartz sand with fragments of darker colored minerals and rock fragments.

Full resolution Seasat SAR data can be coregistered with Landsat 4 TM

Figure 12.4   Desert pavement adjacent to Highway 78,
southwestern Chocolate Mountains, California.

Figure 12.5   Boulder-strewn surface producing bright areas in Figure 12.2b
(heavily stippled areas in Figure 12.3).

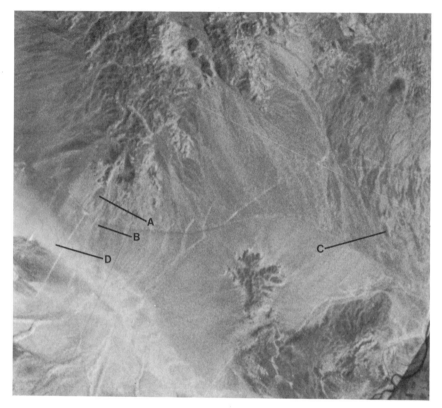

Figure 12.6   Coregistered Landsat MSS/Seasat SAR image. Landsat Band 4 projected in red, Landsat Band 7 projected in green, and Seasat projected in blue. The Seasat component does not cover the extreme lower right corner near the Colorado River. Image is centered 18 km west of Vidal Junction in eastern California. Distance from left to right across image is about 45 km.

data, both of which have about the same resolution. The greater spatial resolution enables finer discrimination of surficial units. The seven spectral bands, moreover, allow a much finer differentiation of units with compositional variations. Unvarnished alluvial fans derived from different source rocks (volcanic, granitic, metamorphic) can readily be distinguished. Work currently in progress suggests that the mapping can be accomplished at scales as large as 1:62,500.

Data from the space shuttle Columbia SIR-A experiment can be used in the same way as the Seasat SAR data. A number of areas of the world were covered that were not imaged by Seasat, including some remarkable images of southern Egypt. So surprising were these images of the eastern Sahara Desert that at first the investigators believed they must be of another area (Elachi 1983). Radar waves are strongly attenuated by moist soil, but theoretically they should penetrate several meters of dry sand, although this

Figure 12.7 Varnished bouldery fan deposit of probable debris-flow origin, location A in Figure 12.6.

Figure 12.8 Varnished cobble-boulder fan deposit of probable debris-flow origin, location B in Figure 12.6.

is by far the most dramatic demonstration of this phenomenon in the natural setting.

The images of southern Egypt revealed drainage systems that had never been observed on aerial photographs or Landsat images. Field checking indicated that in places the images appeared bright where they should have appeared dark because they were smooth sand surfaces that should act as specular reflectors to the radar. When holes 0.8 to 2.5m were excavated in these bright areas, limestone was encountered. Thus the radar was penetrating the sand layer and reflecting off the limestone. All deserts are not as dry as the eastern Sahara, where it rains only once every 50 years. But it has recently been demonstrated that at least intermittently soil conditions are sufficiently dry in the Mojave Desert to permit subsurface radar penetration. Igneous dikes, buried as deep as two meters beneath alluvium, were detected on Seasat SAR imagery (see Figure 12.11) about 70km north of Palm Springs in the western Mojave Desert (Blom et al. 1984).

About 10 percent of the earth's surface is believed to be dry enough to obtain some subsurface radar penetration. Other arid regions in China, South Africa, and Peru, as well as the American deserts, will be imaged on future shuttle flights, and it is planned to bury reflectors at various depths to determine more accurately the penetrating ability of the radar waves (Elachi 1983).

CONCLUSION

Satellite imagery had already proven its worth in mapping desert surfaces and elucidating desert processes. But the exciting results of the SIR-A experiment further attested to the value of satellite-borne radar in desert studies. The ability to penetrate several meters of sand portends many significant applications for radar imagery. The detection of bedrock features otherwise obscured from surface detection will be valuable in mineral exploration as well as geomorphic studies. The site selection and evaluation for engineered structures would also benefit from the ability to determine the depth to bedrock and locate buried faults. Certainly ground-penetrating radar studies would significantly aid in the search for archaeological sites in arid regions.

Another instrument for desert studies showing significant promise is the thermal infrared multispectral scanner (TIMS). This sensor detects thermal radiation emitted from the earth's surface in the 8 to 13μm wavelength region. In this portion of the spectrum silicates, the principal components of rocks and soils, have diagnostic spectral emission features. With this instrument the identification of earth materials on the basis of their mineral composition becomes a real possibility. Airborne TIMS imagery of Death Valley, California has shown that alluvial fans with compositional differences related to the source rocks from which they were derived can be readily distinguished (Kahle and Goetz 1983). Refined versions of TIMS, carried

Figure 12.9   Varnished desert pavement, location C in Figure 12.6.

Figure 12.10   Dune sand, location D in Figure 12.6.

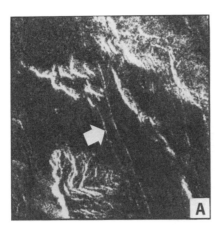 

Figure 12.11   A. Seasat SAR image. Arrow locates one of several buried dikes. Upper right corner is at about 34°30′ N, 116°30′ W. Distance from left to right across image is about 7 km. B. Aerial photograph of a portion of area shown in (A). Arrow indicates approximate location of dike in (B). (Courtesy of R. B. Blom, Jet Propulsion Laboratory, Pasadena, California.)

onboard spacecraft, will add yet another new dimension to studies of arid surfaces when used in conjunction with visible and radar sensors.

In fact, using advanced image processing techniques, data from a wide variety of sources, in addition to remote sensor data, can be combined and displayed in a single image. The data need only be in digital format and registered to a single geographic base. It may be useful, for example, to combine topographic or geophysical data with remote sensor data. This ability to combine a multiplicity of data on the computer greatly increases the amount of information in an image. A number of computer processing techniques are also available to aid the user. Classification schemes, for example, select areas with similar image characteristics, and thus delineate "mappable" units. Many image-processing techniques are becoming available for small computers, which means that in time they will be available at relatively low cost.

ACKNOWLEDGMENTS

Studies in the eastern Mojave Desert have been conducted in collaboration with graduate students Rick Hazen and William Yang. The author is indebted to Diane Evans of the Jet Propulsion Laboratory, Pasadena, California, for her assistance in generating the coregistered image (Figure 12.6). Image processing was accomplished at the Image Processing Laboratory of the Jet Propulsion Laboratory. A portion of the work being conducted has been supported by the Non-renewable Resources Office of the National Aeronautics and Space Administration.

REFERENCES

Blom, R. B., R. E. Crippen, and C. Elachi. 1984. Detection of subsurface features in Seasat radar images of Means Valley, Mojave Desert, California. *Geology* 12: 346–49.

Blom, R. B. and C. Elachi. 1981. Spaceborne and airborne imaging radar observations of sand dunes. *Journal of Geophysical Research* 86: 3061–3073.

Cooke, R. U. 1970. Stone pavements in deserts. *Association of American Geographers Annals* 60: 560–77.

Daily, M. I., T. Farr, C. Elachi, and G. Schaber. 1979. Geologic interpretation from composited radar and Landsat imagery. *Photogrammetric Engineering and Remote Sensing* 45, (8): 1109–1116.

Dohrenwend, J. C., L. D. McFadden, B. D. Turrin, and S. G. Wells. 1984. K-Ar dating of Cima volcanic field, eastern Mojave desert, California: late Cenozoic volcanic history and landscape evolution, *Geology* 12: 163–167.

Dorn, R. I. and T. M. Oberlander. 1982. Rock varnish. *Progress in Physical Geography* 6 (3): 317–67.

Dorn, R. I. and T. M. Oberlander. 1981. Rock varnish origin, characteristics and usage. *Zeitschrift für Geomorphologie* Neue Folge 25 (4): 420–36.

Elachi, C. 1983. Seeing under the Sahara: spaceborne imaging radar. *Engineering and Science*, September, California Institute of Technology.

Engel, C. G. and Sharp. R. P. 1958. Chemical data on desert varnish, *Geological Society of America Bulletin* 69 (5): 487–518.

Hayden, J. D. 1976. Pre-altithermal archaeology in the Sierra Pinacati, Sonora, Mexico. *American Antiquity* 41: 274–89.

Hunt, C. B. and D. R. Mabey. 1966. Stratigraphy and Structure, Death Valley, California. *U.S. Geological Survey Professional Paper* 494–A.

Kahle, A. B. 1982. Spectral remote sensing of rocks in arid lands. *Symposium on Remote Sensing of Environment, First Thematic Conference: Remote Sensing of Arid and Semi-Arid Lands, Cairo, Egypt*. January, p. 279–95.

Kahle, A. B. and A. F. H. Goetz. 1983. Mineralogic information from a new airborne thermal infrared multispectral scanner. *Science* 24–27.

Mabbutt, J. A. 1977. *Desert Landforms*. The MIT Press, Cambridge, Mass.

MacDonald, H. C. and W. P. Waite. 1973. Imaging radars provide texture and roughness parameters in semi-arid environments. *Modern Geology* 4: 145–158.

Merifield, P. M., D. L. Lamar, and J. V. Lamar. 1975. Enhancement of geologic features near Mojave, California, by spectral band ratioing of Landsat MSS data. *Proceedings of the Tenth International Symposium, Remote Sensing of Environment*, pp. 1067–1075.

Merifield, P. M., R. S. Hazen, and D. L. Evans. 1984. Descrimination of desert surface materials for engineering/environmental geology applications utilizing coregistered Landsat MSS and Seasat SAR data. *Proceedings of the International Symposium on Remote Sensing of Environment, Third Thematic Conference*, "Remote Sensing for Exploration Geology," Colorado Springs, Colorado, pp. 487–96.

Peterson, G. L. 1980. "Broken rocks in the desert environment". *In Geology and Mineral Wealth of the California Desert, Dibblee Volume*, D. L. Fife and A. R. Brown, eds. South Coast Geological Society, Santa Ana, Calif., pp. 403–408.

Potter, R. M. and G. R. Rossman. 1979. The manganese and iron oxide mineralogy of desert varnish. *Chemical Geology* 25: 79–94.

Potter, R. M. and G. R. Rossman. 1977. Desert varnish: The importance of clay minerals. *Science* 196: 1146–1448.

Reeves, R. G., A. Anson, and D. Landen, eds. 1975. *Manual of Remote Sensing*. American Society of Photogrammetry, Falls Church, Va.

Sabins, F. F., Jr. 1978. *Remote Sensing, Principles and Interpretation*. W. H. Freeman and Company, San Francisco, Calif.

Schaber, G. G., G. L. Berlin, and W. E. Brown, Jr. 1976. Variations in surface roughness within Death Valley, California: Geologic evaluation of 25-cm wavelength radar images. *Geological Society America Bulletin* 87: 29–41.

Sugiura, R., and F. Sabins. 1980. The evaluation of 3-cm wavelength radar for mapping surface deposits in the Bristol Lake/Granite Mountain area, Mojave Desert, California. In *Radar Geology: An Assessment*. Report of the Radar Geology Workshop, Snowmass, Colorado, 1979, pp. 439–456.

U.S. Geological Survey. 1982. *Landsat Data Users Notes, Issue 23*, July 1982, Eros Data Center, Sious Falls, South Dakota, pp. 1–16.

Webb, R. H., and H. G. Wilshire. 1983. *Environmental Effects of Off-road Vehicles*. Springer-Verlag, Inc., New York.

Wilshire, H. G. and J. K. Nakata. 1976. Off-road vehicle effects on California's Mojave desert. *California Geology* 29: 123–132.

THIRTEEN

Climatic Change, Hydrology, and Water Management in Arid Lands

JOHN A. DRACUP

Climate is a literary specialty and no untrained hand can turn out a good article on it.

Mark Twain

During the past several years many climatologists have noted a significant increase in the variability of the weather (CIA 1974; Fritz 1977; Schneider 1977a; Wallis 1977b). It is now apparent that the years 1956–71 constituted an abnormally stable period in terms of temperature and precipitation fluctuations, and that the disastrous worldwide weather conditions of 1972 heralded the end of that era. As Mitchell (1977) states, "It appears that we're returning to normalcy, and that means greater variability in the weather than we're used to."

Although mankind has built large-scale water supply systems, such as the State Water Project in California, in order to supply current and projected future demands, the possibility of a sudden severe climatic change hangs like the sword of Damocles over arid lands throughout the world. Water systems are built under the single assumption that the means and standard deviations of the annual streamflows will remain stationary. Some United States water agencies assume that not only will the climate remain constant throughout the 50- to 100-year life of the project but that, in fact, the annual streamflows will be repeated in exactly the same sequence as has occurred during the past 50 to 100 years! An examination of current hydrologic planning procedures reveals a tendency to deny the potential for climatic change.

A classic example of neglecting climatic change occurred with the case of the Colorado River in the arid southwestern United States. The Colorado River Compact resulted in splitting the river between the Upper and Lower Basin states. But due to a reliance on a short and unusually above-normal hydrologic record, more water was allocated than the long-term record indicated was available (Dracup 1977; Hundley 1975).

In order for hydrologists and water managers to analyze these problems, certain key questions must be considered:

1. What events cause these climatic changes, and to what extent can they be predicted?

2. What is the range of potential climate changes that might occur within the next 50 to 100 years?

3. Can these potential climatic changes be translated into a range of hydrologic variables, such as precipitation, potential evapotranspiration, and surface water run-off?

4. How can water resource managers and planning agents change their methodologies to account for these new ranges of hydrologic variables?

The above questions are examined in terms of climatic forecasts using the examples of El Nino and the Southern Oscillation, and the reported carbon dioxide increases in the atmosphere. Next, the current state of the art and the potential for future climatic forecasts are examined. Finally, the translation of these potential climatic changes into hydrologic variables and the resulting changes in the management of water systems are presented.

CLIMATE CHANGE AND EL NINO

In January of any given year, a southward-moving ocean current brings warm water to the usually cold coasts of Ecuador and Peru. Local fishermen have named this current El Nino, partly due to its proximity to Christmas Day and partly due to the rich bounty of flora and fauna contained within it. Scientists, however, have limited the El Nino designation to significant events that only occur when the elevation of sea surface temperature (SST) at at least three of five coastal stations located between 5°S and 12°S exceeds one standard deviation for four or more consecutive months (Cane 1983).

Scientists also have proposed a coupling between El Nino and the Southern Oscillation (ENSO). The Southern Oscillation is a fluctuation in atmospheric pressure at sea level, oscillating between the southeast Pacific subtropical high and a region of low pressure extending across the Indian Ocean from northern Australia to Africa (Rasmusson and Wallace 1983).

The existence of the Southern Oscillation has been known since 1924, and El Nino events have been documented as early as 1726. El Nino events occur about once every four years, with the interval varying between two and ten years. Cane (1983) states:

> There are enough similarities among the different events to justify a common name, and a conceptually useful picture of the typical El Nino has emerged. Nevertheless, no two events are precisely alike with regard to amplitude, time of onset, spatial characteristics, or biological consequences, and aficionados have been known to compare different events in a manner reminiscent of oenologists discussing vintage years.

Of interest to hydrologists is the coupling between the atmosphere and the ocean and the resulting changes in precipitation and thus surface water run-off. Of special importance was the 1982–83 El Nino, which had dramatic rises in SST and sea levels along the South American coast and throughout the equatorial eastern Pacific. Other characteristics of this event were an abrupt swing of the Southern Oscillation, sea-level pressure drops between Tahiti and Darwin, and surface wind shifts along the equator from easterlies to westerlies.

The worldwide results became well known:

1. Extremely heavy precipitation in the equatorial central Pacific.

2. Severe, record droughts in Indonesia, eastern Australia, southern India, Sri Lanka, and southern African nations.

3. Prolonged, heavy precipitation in Ecuador and northwestern Peru, producing record events several months in advance of the normal wet season.

The westerly wind anomalies caused a southward displacement of the normal jet stream crossing the United States. The results were high winds, severe storms, and flooding in California and the Gulf states, and heavy snows in the mountains of the Southwest. Even so, correlations between California rainfall and the ENSO phenomenon are not well established. Extensive research into the oceanographic-meteorological-hydrological linkages is still in the planning stage.

CLIMATE CHANGE AND CO_2

Measurements of carbon dioxide (CO_2) in the atmosphere indicate changes from 317 parts per million (ppm) in 1958 to 344 ppm in 1984. This increase of 8 percent in 26 years projects to a doubling of pre-industrial concentrations by 2050. Since CO_2 is transparent to incoming solar energy but absorbs heat radiated back from the earth, the result is a warming of the lower atmosphere and potential changes in the earth's climatic system. This has been called the "greenhouse effect." Various researchers using global mathematical models have determined that an average global warming of 1.5° to 4.5°C will result. Other trace gases such as oxides of nitrogen, carbon tetrachloride, ozone, chlorofluorocarbons, and methane are also estimated to have a combined greenhouse effect of at least half again as much as that of CO_2.

CLIMATIC FORECASTS

For a forecast to be useful to a planner, it must contain three basic components: time, location, and magnitude. In the case of a climatic change, a useful forecast would require a determination of the duration of the climatic change, its areal extent, and its magnitude in terms of deviation from normal precipitation, temperature, and/or streamflow. Wallis (1977b) states that climatic change forecasts would need to be specified by area and be accurate over the 50- to 100-year life of a water resource system, plus an additional 10 to 30 years that are needed to plan and build the system.

It is unfortunate that such an ability to forecast climatic change does not currently exist, nor is one expected to appear in the near future (Schneider and Temkin 1977). Nevertheless, there is some empiric and dynamic evidence that some part of climatic fluctuations for seasonal and longer periods is potentially predictable (Leith 1982). The hydrologist is required to turn to a statistical analysis of existing data, to formulate specific scenarios of climate change, and to then determine the appropriate hydrologic and water management requirements.

CLIMATIC CHANGE AND HYDROLOGIC VARIABLES

The rainfall run-off process is highly complex in that it is nonlinear, time-variant, and has its governing parameters distributed throughout the watershed. Parameters affecting run-off include soil moisture, vegetation, geologic structure, and geographic features. Small changes in precipitation can result in large changes in water storages and run-off. Four recent studies have investigated the impact on streamflow of climatic changes of precipitation, temperature, and evapotranspiration.

Nemec and Schaake (1982) studied twelve climate-related scenarios to determine the impact of changes in precipitation ($\pm$ 10 percent and $\pm$ 25 percent) and potential evapotranspiration (+ 12 percent and $\pm$ 4 percent) on streamflow run-off, reservoir yield, and reservoir storage requirements. Three basins, two in the United States and one in Africa, were studied using the well-known Sacramento Soil Moisture Accounting Model and the National Weather Service River Forecast System Model.

The studies indicated that in an arid region (Pease River, Texas) a 10 percent decrease in precipitation and a 4 percent increase in potential evapotranspiration resulted in a 50 percent decrease in run-off and a 180 percent increase in required reservoir storage to produce the same guaranteed yield.

Klemes (1983) conducted a critical statistical significance study of Nemec's and Schaake's (1982) research. He found that due to the short timespan of historical hydrologic records (typically 20 years), there are considerable limitations on the usefulness of modeling the hydrologic impact of climate change. This is because the sampling errors in the data, combined with the sampling uncertainty during future operations, are on the same order of magnitude as the changes ascribed to climate.

A quote from Klemes's conclusions is noteworthy:

Even if the direction of the climate change were certain (which it is not), there would be very little the water planner could do in addition to what he has to do

anyway—i.e., to take into account a possibility that the future can be hydrologically considerably different from the past. The practical consequence for the
planner is to be cautious and refrain from pushing the development of the present
resources to the limit. In other words, the time-honored engineering practice of
keeping a safety margin as a hedge against uncertainty is even more commend-
able from the perspective of climate change than it is without it.

Revelle and Waggoner (1983) also have studied the impact of increases in
temperature and decreases in precipitation on run-off for U.S. drainage
basins with annual precipitations ranging from 200 to 700mm/yr. The
weighted mean annual temperatures were determined by dividing the sum
of the products of average monthly temperature and precipitation by the
mean annual precipitation. Their results indicated that, for a weighted
average initial temperature of 10°C and an initial precipitation of 400mm/yr,
a 2°C increase in temperature will result in a 30 percent decrease in run-off.
Similar decreases in run-off were found for a 10 percent reduction in
precipitation.

Similarly, Stockton and Boggess (1979) found that a 2°C warming and a 10
percent reduction in precipitation would have significant impact on seven
water regions in the southwestern United States.

CLIMATIC CHANGE: WATER RESOURCE PLANNING AND MANAGEMENT

Water resource managers may believe that planning for climatic change
represents a new and untried planning process. These same planners have
faced similar problems in the analysis of hydrologic droughts. Scenarios
associated with severe, sustained droughts or deep, sustained droughts
(Kneese and Bonem 1983) have recently been considered in the planning
process.

Furthermore, problems associated with droughts may be similar to the
problems associated with climatic change. Consider the following impacts of
hydrologic droughts:

1. Available water supply for domestic, municipal, commercial, industrial, and agricultural uses are reduced due to lower than normal
   streamflows, reduced reservoir storage, and depleted ground water
   reserves.

2. Reservoir discharges and hydraulic heads are diminished, causing a
   reduction in the amount of generated hydroelectric power.

3. Diminished soil moisture content, coupled with insufficient available
   water for irrigation purposes, has drastic effects on the agricultural
   sector (especially in agricultural-based economies) and hence may
   affect the price of food on a national or even global scale.

4. Low flows contribute to the degradation of water quality in streams and

lakes due to insufficient quantities of water to flush and dilute contaminants.

5. Diminished water quality and quantity threaten the habitat of innumerable species of fish and wildlife.

6. Dry, parched conditions significantly increase the hazard of fires and cause areas with insufficient vegetation cover to become vulnerable to the eroding forces of wind and rain, which in turn leads to desertification.

As a less tangible effect of droughts, citizens are faced with the potentially stress-producing mandate to conserve water. "When required to cut back on the use of water because of a shortage, many people feel a level of concern. Doing with less, and certainly doing without often produces anxiety" (Buchanan and Gilbert 1977).

Droughts not only affect a wide spectrum of social concerns, but they are also indiscriminant in terms of geography, climate, and political boundary. That is, each and every region will experience conditions of below normal rainfall and run-off at some time. "Hydrologists can pragmatically report on recorded data which show that almost every year, some area of our country experiences the conditions which constitute a drought" (ibid.).

Reconstructed tree-ring analysis indicates that the lowest ten-year average flow occurring in the Colorado River was 9.7 million acre-feet ($12,000 \times 10^6 m^3$) in 1584–93 (Stockton 1977). Planning today to mitigate the impacts of such a severe, sustained drought would result in the development of useful emergency scenarios.

Significant existing literature in the statistical analysis of droughts may lead the way in the analysis of climatic change (Dracup 1980). Matalas and Fiering (1977) have introduced and defined the terms "robustness" and "resilience" in the context of water resource designs. A robust design is one which performs reasonably well under a variety of possible climates. The resilience of an existing water resource system is its capability to withstand the shock of a severe drought without failure of the system. This resilience can be enhanced by changes in the institutional, legal, and economic structure of the region. Other investigators have developed themes concerning demand management as compared to supply management. Demand management has come to mean changes in water resource systems, such as:

1. The introduction of a pricing structure based on the marginal costs of new water systems rather than long-term, average costs.

2. Legal and institutional changes which would, for example, allow the selling of water by individual farmers to the highest bidder, who presumably would impute a higher value to the resource.

3. The introduction and enforcement of water conservation measures in municipal, industrial, and agricultural sectors and the expanded use of waste-water reclamation.

Demand management can be contrasted with supply management, which implies the meeting of current and projected demands for water with expanded storage and conveyance facilities. This supply management approach implies that the economic analyses are limited to a traditional benefit-cost study where the discounted net benefits are greater than the discounted costs. Furthermore, a supply management approach implies an adherence to the existing legal and institutional structure.

Schneider and Londer (1984), state that:

> It may take a decade or two to plan, finance, and build mechanisms to provide adequate water for the coming generation, but present calculations of future needs are usually based on the assumption that there will be no long-term changes in climate . . . If in twenty years it becomes clear that significantly decreased average precipitation or increased evaporation might occur in some regions, it will then be too late to be prepared unless present water supply planning recognizes that the climate of the future could well be significantly different from today's, and we respond now by building larger margins of safety in either supply or demand requirements to meet that contingency.

In other words, long-term planning of water resource systems should take into account both natural climatic variability (e.g., droughts and floods) and the probability of a significant major change in climate patterns. This latter consideration has been typically neglected by water resource planners.

Again quoting from Schneider and Londer (1984):

> Even with the many uncertainties plainly admitted, climatologists still know enough now to state responsibly that significant changes in climatic trends are possible—perhaps even likely—but that the regional details cannot be given at present with anything but intuitive probabilities. This suggests that increased flexibility in water-supply planning is needed to enhance our ability to cope with plausible climatic trends. . . .
>
> . . . The bottom line can be stated simply: we should be careful not to get overly dependent on a single . . . limited source of water in a region, particularly if the source is nonrenewable or the supply projections are based on average sunlight, wind, evaporation, and precipitation records, especially those spanning mere human memory. Moreover, it is comparably risky to have all future supply planning based on any single scenario for future demand . . . Rather, planning should be based on the differing costs and consequences of different policies, given a set of scenarios that span the range of plausible future climatic, economic, and demographic trends. As we improve our ability to forecast the economy, demography, or the climate, preferred scenarios can be identified, probabilities assigned to each, and plans altered to meet changing conditions or projections. Since flexibility—particularly too much of it—can be expensive, it is important to be as quantitative as possible in estimates of future fluctuations and trends in supply and demand.

CONCLUSIONS

Hydrologists and water resource planners are increasingly aware of the potential impacts of long-term climatic variation, but the paucity of reliable, long-term data, along with a complacency resulting from recent climatic calms, has resulted in narrow planning approaches. Hare (1982) aptly states:

> Hydrology is in many ways a subset of the larger body of knowledge called climatology. Yet its professionals, concerned almost wholly with water management, have developed their skills with only a weak and intermittent contact with the atmospheric scientists. Management demands a broader perspective.

The challenge, therefore, is in both research and education, with combined research and multidisciplinary programs in hydrology and meteorology leading the way.

REFERENCES

Buchanan, T. J., and B. K. Gilbert. 1977. The Drought: A pervasive problem. *Water Spectrum* 9 (3): 6–12.

Cane, M. A. 1983. Oceanographic events during El Nino. *Science* 222 (462a): 1189–95.

Central Intelligency Agency. 1974. A study of climatological research as it pertains to intelligence problems. Office of Research and Development, CIA. Washington, D.C. August.

Dracup, J. A. 1977. Impact on the Colorado River Basin and Southwest water supply. *In Climate, Climatic Change, and Water Supply*. National Research Council, National Academy Press Washington, D.C. Chap. 8.

Dracup, J. A., K. S. Lee, and E. G. Paulson, Jr. 1980. On the statistical characteristics of drought events. *Water Resources Research* 16 (2): 289–96. April.

Fritz, H. C. *Cited in:* "Drought: Is Stable Climate at an End?" *Los Angeles Times*. May 7, 1977: 1, 20, 21.

Hare, F. K. 1982. The Great Ideas Today. *Encyclopedia Britannica*.

Hundley, N., Jr. 1975. *Water and the West*. University of California Press, Los Angeles.

Klemes, V. 1983. Climatic change and the planning of water resource systems. *Sixth Canadian Hydrotechnical Conference, Ottawa, Ont*. 1: 485–500.

Kneese, A. V. and G. Bonem. 1983. Hypothetical shocks to water allocation institutions in the Colorado Basin. Presented at the Colorado River Working Symposium: Management Options for the Future. Sante Fe, NM. May 23–26.

Leith, C. E. 1982. *Report of the WMO/ICSU Study Conference on physical basis for climate prediction on seasonal, annual, and decadal time scales*. World Climate Research Programme. Leningrad. September.

Matalas, N. C., and M. B. Fiering. 1977. Water Resource Systems Planning. In *Climate, Climatic Change, and Water Supply*. National Research Council National Academy Press, Washington, D.C. Chapter 6.

Mitchell, J. M. *Cited in:* "Drought: Is Stable Climate at an End?" *Los Angeles Times*. May 7, 1977: 1, 20, 21.

Nemec, J., and J. Schaake. 1982. Sensitivity of water resource systems to climate variation. *Hydrological Sciences Journal* 27 (3) Sept.: 327–43.

Rasmusson, E. M., and J. M. Wallace. 1983. Meteorological aspects of the El Nino/Southern Oscillation. *Science* 222 (4629) 16 Dec.: 1195–1202.

Revelle, R. R., and P. E. Waggoner. 1983. Effects of a carbon dioxide–induced climate change on water supplies in the western United States. In *Changing Climate*. Report of the Carbon Dioxide Assessment Committee, National Research Council. National Academy Press Washington, D.C.

Schneider, S. H. 1977. What climatologists can say to planners. *Proceedings of the symposium on living with climatic change, Phase II*. Reston, Virginia, November 9–11. 1976, Pp. 45–56.

Schneider, S. H., and R. Londer. 1984. *Coevaluation of Climate and Life*. Sierra Club Books, San Francisco.

Schneider, S. H., and R. L. Temkin. 1977. A Water supply and future climate. *In Climate,*

Climatic Change, and Water Supply. National Research Council. National Academy Press, Washington, D.C. Chapter 1.

Stockton, C. W. 1977. Interpretation of past climatic variability from Paleoenvironmental indicators. *In Climate, Climatic Change, and Water Supply*. Chapter 2.

Stockton, C. W., and W. R. Boggess. 1979. *Geohydrological implications of climate change on water resource development*. U.S. Army Coastal Engineering Research Center, Ft. Belvoir, Va.

Turco, R. P., O. B. Toon, T. P. Ackerman, J. B. Pollack, and Carl Sagan. 1983. Nuclear winter: Global consequences of multiple nuclear explosions. *Science* 222 (4630) 23 Dec.: 1283–92.

Wallis, J. R. 1977a. Climate, Climatic Change, and Water Supply. *AGU Trans.*, 58 (11): 1012–24.

Wallis, J. R., 1977b. Overview and Recommendations. *In Climate, Climatic Change, and Water Supply*. National Research Council, National Academy Press, Washington, D.C.

PART IV

GEOLOGY AND WATER RESOURCES

FOURTEEN

Rhythmic Couplets: Sedimentology and Prediction of Reservoir Design Periods in Semiarid Areas

JONATHAN B. LARONNE

ABSTRACT

Storm event–generated rhythmic couplets exist in various lacustrine environments, including reservoirs, and may comprise many strata previously identified as varves. Event-couplets are similar to varves in their textural and structural patterns. Both form due to deposition of turbidity currents and slow diffusion of a sediment-laden jet entering a standing body of water.

Yatir Reservoir deposits are also event-generated couplets. Stratigraphic correlation among couplets offers an opportunity to determine historic event sedimentation rates in this semiarid area. Once completed, the five-stage proposed methodology becomes a tool to predict sediment yield and reservoir design period.

INTRODUCTION

Sediment yield is evaluated to assess reservoir sedimentation rates. Soil erosion, which in the usual connotation (Kirkby and Morgan 1980) is equal to sediment yield less channel erosion and channel storage (the latter expressed by the delivery ratio of the drainage basin), is determined to assess soil loss from agricultural land. Both sediment yield and soil loss are measured by geomorphologists to evaluate landscape denudation rates. Sediment yield (the load of sediment per unit time) involves erosion, transportation, and temporary storage of sediment. Therefore, it is the output of a complex system involving interrelationships between climatic, pedologic, geologic, and geomorphic processes (Laronne and Mosley 1982). This chapter deals exclusively with sediment yield, because this is the output that interests the planner and engineer in determining the rate of reservoir filling or its design period (i.e., its economic life length).

The determination of sediment yield is accomplished currently by four basically different methods (ARS 1975). First is the measurement of bedload and suspended load, which together form the solid sediment. Measurement of these dissimilar mechanisms of transport requires separate measurement techniques. The suspended load is measured at one or preferably several "point" depths in verticals of a given channel cross-section. The suspended sediment discharge is equal to the product of the average cross-sectional concentration and water discharge. Several such cross-sectional measurements during a given time-span are accumulated by rating curve procedures to determine the total suspended load for the given time interval or flow event. These available interpolation and extrapolation techniques to predict and even to postdict suspended sediment loads are neither as precise nor as accurate as commonly believed (Walling and Webb 1981). Moreover, measurement of suspended sediment concentration in several locations within a cross-section is tedious, time-consuming, expensive, and therefore available only for large rivers. Reasonable estimates may also be made by using data from automatic suspended sediment samplers. Such data are almost unavailable in cold and hot desert areas, although much progress has been attained in the last decade (Walling and Kleo 1979); and they are non-existent in the extreme desert environment (except e.g., Schick 1977).

The measurement of bedload discharge by most direct and indirect means is both imprecise and inaccurate (Hubbell 1964), because most samplers vary the velocity distribution near the channel bed and thereby affect bedload rate. A trap installation (Leopold and Emmett 1977) and a vortex tube (Hayward 1979) have 100 percent trapping efficiencies but are very expensive. A recently developed pressure pillow slot trap (Reid et al. 1980) is very promising, as is the Helley-Smith (1971) sampler (see also Emmett 1980).

Sediment yield from small, usually first-order basins can be evaluated by synthesizing erosion data from plot studies using artificial and natural precipitation. Because plot studies are very time-consuming, several plot-based mathematical models are currently in use. The outdated but best known and most widely used model is the universal soil loss equation or USLE (Wischmeir and Smith 1965). Although seemingly intricate and involving the evaluation of several parameters that affect rate of erosion, the use of the equation requires the determination of factors, such as soil erodibility, that are not easily assessed and that are known to be much more complex than envisioned in this equation.

The USLE has been used in conjunction with estimates of sediment delivery ratios to predict sediment yield (Williams and Berndt 1972; Renfro

1975). One basic problem with the USLE, that of generalizing variable, small plot results to an entire area, as well as the use of the delivery ratio, which is a parameter that requires collection of much data and is itself rather difficult to determine accurately (Roehl 1962), is that it must be carefully applied to every new region. A reasonable mistake in one factor of the USLE may result in a large deviation between predicted and actual sediment yields.

The third, less common method to predict sediment yield is the use of climatic-based regional relationships (e.g., Langbein and Schumm 1958). These relationships may also consider land-use variability (Dunne 1979), but they commonly apply only to large areas for which a considerably good sediment yield data base is available.

Other, much less common methods are available to evaluate sediment yield (Laronne and Mosley 1982). Still, reservoir sediment deposition surveys are the most reliable among the currently available techniques because all the bedload and most of the suspended load are trapped in the reservoir.

RESERVOIR SEDIMENTATION

Reservoir sedimentation surveys have been in extensive use to determine rates of reservoir filling. Reservoir sedimentation was reviewed by Wiebe and Drennan (1973); surveys were reviewed as a planning tool by Pemberton (1980).

Sedimentation rate is not equivalent to sediment yield, but to sediment yield less the suspended sediment discharged from the reservoir spillway. Because the average hydraulic residence time in a reservoir increases with increase in reservoir capacity, it is expected that the discharge of the suspended sediment out of a reservoir would be inversely related to its capacity. Using a similar reasoning, Brune (1953) suggested that trapping efficiency, the portion of the sediment yield that remains in a reservoir, is directly related to the capacity/(flow volume) ratio. For ratios larger than unity, the efficiency is larger than 95 percent and often larger than 98 percent. A ratio of 0.1 commonly corresponds to an efficiency of 80 to 95 percent.

Sedimentation surveys are very time-consuming. Therefore, Jolly's (1982) proposed methodology to "accurately" calculate sediment yield from reservoir deposition volumes is not economically feasible in arid areas. Moreover, his black-box empirical approach is not based on the actual flow event that delivers sediment (particularly in ephemeral flow situations) but, rather, on sediment deposition rates that would not be expected to predict long-term rates accurately.

In addition to areal photography, the surveys are usually undertaken by soundings in predetermined ranges, or by adding a width-adjustment

method (Pemberton 1980). Dry reservoir beds are topographically resur-
veyed every few years. These surveys are used to determine the dead
storage volume and the remaining useful quantity of live storage. To predict
reservoir sedimentation, commonly by allocating 100 years of sediment
storage, existing surveys are analyzed for regional reservoir deposition
patterns, from which a dimensionless capacity-elevation diagram is constructed (Pemberton 1980).

Existing surveys have demonstrated that many reservoir deposits are
distributed in three Gilbert-type delta depositional environments: an upper,
topset aggrading, backwater-zone region; a rather short and steeper foreset
bedding region; and a very flat region where bottomset sediments are
horizontally laminated.

Kikkawa (1980) has modeled the rate and spatial distribution of deltalike
reservoir sediments by considering bed and suspended loads entering the
water body, incoming flow character, initial reservoir topography, and the
movement of turbidity currents. A more recent model (Soares et al. 1981)
has been successfully applied to predict the long-term sediment volume and
its spatial distribution in the John Martin Reservoir, Colorado. The model,
basically similar to Kikkawa's (1980), incorporates two parts. The first is a
stochastic analysis of reservoir inflows and deterministic releases, whereby
the cumulative deposition of sediment is shown to be an additive process
defined on a finite Markov chain. The second, deterministic part is a
numerical analysis of the mass and momentum equations, and it is applied to
a season or to an entire year. The stochastic part is based on flow data that
are used to generate synthetic streamflows as input: model calibration is
based on paired flow volume and sediment concentration data. Therefore,
such a mathematical approach is impractical for arid areas where accurate,
long-term data are usually not available in the planning stage of a reservoir.

Reservoir sedimentation surveys have been suggested as excellent data
banks to be used for calculating sediment yield and related drainage basin
historic events (Oldfield 1977). O'Sullivan et al. (1982) developed a method
by which annual laminated sediments with marker horizons were used to
calculate historic sedimentation rates. McHenri and Ritchie (1981) dated
Wisconsin lake sediments and Texas playa deposits by determining Cs-137
concentrations. This technique would also enable the determination of
sedimentation rates for the given dated sediments.

That reservoir deposits also contain laminated, varvelike sediments has
been demonstrated by Wood (1947), Murray-Rust (1972), Christiansson
(1979), and Laronne (1983). Unlike the common annual lake varves, these
studies prove that reservoir varvelike laminae are often deposited by single
flow events. Individual deposit volumes may be used to predict reservoir
sedimentation more accurately than multievent, annual deposits. Therefore,
and because lacustrine varves are very similar to varvelike reservoir (and
lacustrine) rhythmic deposits, a sedimentologic analysis of varves and varve
formation precedes the description of flow event–generated deposits.

RHYTHMIC COUPLETS: VARVES

Rhythmic couplets are individual units of rhythmic deposits with no temporal connotation. Because varves are annual deposits, they have been used to date late Pleistocene and Holocene events. That they are, indeed, annual deposits has been shown by agreement with radioactive dating (Antevs 1957), as well as by other, less accurate methods.

Couplet Distribution

Varves have been extensively described in the northeastern United States and nearby Canada, as well as in northern and central Europe (De Geer 1912; Ludlam 1979), but also in Alaska (Gustavson 1975). Their geologic age ranges from Triassic through Pleistocene, to the Recent. They have been identified under a wide range of lake water depths (a few metres to 406m), and they occur in freshwater, coastal lagoon, and tidal lake environments. Varves are found in lakes of oligotrophic to eutrophic productivity in monomictic (one thermal stratification period), dimictic, and meromictic (lower layer stabilized by chemical stratification) conditions. Under these stratification conditions a thermocline separates an upper, warmer, epilimnion layer from a lower, colder hypolimnion.

Couplet Sedimentologic Character

Classically (De Geer, 1912), varves have been described as comprised of two distinct units (light/dark) interpreted as a lower "summer" layer of coarser sediments deposited by turbidity currents and a darker, clay and organic-rich "winter" layer deposited from suspension. Such a subdivision has been shown to be inaccurate. Three genetically dissimilar parts have been described by Agterberg and Banerjee (1969), who agreed that the lighter silt ("summer") layer is a turbidity current deposit, its thickness decreasing from source (see also Ashley 1975). The clay "winter" layer is, in fact, subdivided to (a) a lower unit of mainly fine silt and coarse clay deposited after stagnation of the turbidity current, and (b) an upper unit of graded clay, representing slow deposition of fine suspended sediment from the entire lake water column. Considering that fines are distally deposited contemporaneous with proximal accumulation of coarser sediments, Ashley (1975) concluded that time lines would parallel the couplet boundaries. But with an increase of distance from the source, the silt/clay (summer/winter) boundary would gradually move closer to the basal couplet boundary.

   Ashley's (1975) description of varves is highlighted by a large number of studied cores and particularly by her excellent microscopic study of given couplets. Subdividing a given couplet with a razor blade, Ashley (1983 personal communication) was able to study not only the structural character of various parts of a couplet, but also their texture. She concluded:

1. The sediments are rhythmic throughout the entire area, in both lake and delta deposits.

2. Couplet thickness is greatest near deltas and in depressions, and clay thickness is much less variable than silt thickness.

3. Clay size is constant everywhere whereas silt size varies and it is positively skewed and better-sorted than the negatively skewed clay.

4. All clay layers are graded, which implies freshwater deposition without considerable flocculation. Silts are multi-micro-graded when fine-textured, and cross-laminated when coarser and thicker. A complete couplet is not a graded bed or lamina, but consists of texturally distinct layers which together represent an annual deposit, although "it is not the result of one sedimentation pulse."

Gustavson (1975) also described a few varves in detail. His findings are in agreement with those of Ashley (1975) that a couplet is a complex sedimentary unit. Unlike Ashley's three-group couplet classification, Gustavson distinguished only two varve types: proximal and distal. The proximal varve is comprised of thick, ripple drift, fine sand overlain by draped laminations of silt and clay. The distal couplet consists of normal and reverse-graded flat fine sand and silt beds grading upward into clay. Ashley (1975) observed cross-laminations in thicker and coarser silt. This strengthens Gustavson's (1975) conclusion that the distal couplet facies is a lateral equivalent of proximal couplets, and the proximal ones are lateral equivalents of coarser prodelta deposits. Shaw (1975) demonstrated that rhythmic couplets constitute as much as one-third of the total thickness of a proglacial delta.

Mechanism of Couplet Formation

De Geer (1912) suggested that varve sedimentation was controlled by the occurrence of turbidity currents. These gravity currents owe their origin to the density contrast between lake and stream water arising from the higher concentration of suspended sediment (rather than temperature or solute concentration) of stream water. Kuenen (1951) demonstrated that turbidity currents can occur in freshwater bodies, and also maintained that flocculation of fines in salt water would cause varve thickness and variability to depend almost entirely on sediment supply and therefore on flow discharge.

Ashley (1975) hypothesized that channel flow supplied largely by precipitation would transport considerably less sediment than the debris-rich meltwater. Thus, the main varve-forming mechanism was concluded to be turbidity currents developed by spring/summer meltwater. In addition, stratification of lake water also appears to be essential for varve formation. Unless sediment discharge is temporally (i.e., seasonally) discontinuous and unless it enters a stratified water body, other depositional features (such as chaotic sedimentation or completely graded sediments) are maintained (Sturm, 1979).

Stratification of ponded water is essential for two reasons. First, slow sedimentation beneath the thermocline is protected from wind-driven water turbulence. Also, anaerobic conditions often occur in conjunction with chemical or thermal stratification, and anoxia limits the activity of benthic organisms that would otherwise bioturbate the sediment. Bioturbation would also be decreased if the settled sediment is of firm (clay) consistency or if sedimentation rate exceeds rate of destruction by organisms. Note that the amount of kinetic energy transmitted from the wind to the lake is directly proportional to its area and fetch, and it is inversely proportional to the amount of protection offered by the topography and vegetation surrounding the lake (Ludlam 1979). Thus, it may be deduced that reduced turbulence and resultant couplet formation are favored in well-protected small lakes and reservoirs.

Other mechanisms favoring couplet formation include rising productivity that leads to large diatom or other algal blooms that are often a cause of rhythmic sedimentation. A rise in temperature may lead to calcite precipitation, thereby diluting the clay deposits with light-colored sediments. Another thermal effect may lead to hypolimnitic anoxia and deposition of associated iron oxide rich laminae (Ludlam 1979).

Turbidity currents are almost unanimously considered to be the main couplet-forming mechanism. Such currents are variable in temporal, longitudinal, and vertical extent. Depending on solute concentration and temperature stratifications of lake water, the entering turbidity current may be a denser underflow (hyperpycnal), an equally dense interflow (homopycnal), or else a lighter hypopycnal surface flow.

Sediment deposition from turbidity currents has been analyzed in terms of the diffusion of a free axial jet in a standing water body, although some experts agree that most assumptions may be gross oversimplifications (Thakur and Mackey 1973; Church and Gilbert 1975). Extent of jet-mixing is inversely proportional to the density contrast between the two fluids. This contrast is decreased as sediment is deposited, and mixing continues at a faster rate until the jet flow is completely dissipated. Thereafter, only clay settles until it is distributed by wind-induced turbulence or by an additional flow.

EVENT-GENERATED RHYTHMIC COUPLETS

Lambert and Hsu (1979) proved that rhythmic couplets of Lake Walensee, Switzerland, which had previously been considered varves, are in fact varvelike event-generated rhythmites. The direct proof relies on three different but linked arguments.

Stumpf (1916, in Lambert and Hsu 1979) installed a sediment trap in the Walensee at a depth of 120m, and recovered it 364 days later on May 9th, 1912. The trap had accumulated a 9mm thick deposit that contained five distinctly colored rhythmic couplets. The precise description of these layers, particularly their color succession, permitted recognition of the rhythmic couplets. Other undisturbed cores showed 171 rhythmic couplets during a 66-year period, an average of 2.6 couplets/yr.

A different labeling method was based on the historic diversion of the Linth River into the lake in 1811, which resulted in the deposition of gray, coarse-grade sands over reddish brown lacustrine muds. The number of couplets in 16 cores between 1811 and 1971 ranged between 300 and 360, or an average deposition rate of ca. 2.1 couplets/yr. The determination of the 1811 datum facilitated recognition of the 1944 catastrophic flood deposits by using an average sedimentation rate. On average, 2.3 couplets/yr had been deposited since 1944.

The foregoing results clearly established that varvelike sediments in certain lakes and reservoirs are probably deposited by specific channel flow events. This conclusion is strengthened by bottom current meter data. Hyperpycnal (underflow) inflow occurred six times in the Walensee (during half a year), reaching velocity maxima of 0.5m/sec with an average velocity of about 0.3m/sec. As the flow arrived 1.5 hr immediately after peak Linth River flow passed the lowest river station, there is no doubt that the currents were induced by a specific flow event.

An additional proof of couplet-event layers was succinctly described by Wood (1947). Construction of the Arkport flood control dam in the Susquehanna watershed, New York, ended in November 1939. No ponding of water occurred during dam construction. Two distinct water stage maxima and an additional, third estimated maximum combined to deposit three distinct couplets during the spring of 1940. Wood (1947) noted that "the deposits consist of ten cm of fine sand, overlain by one to three cm of silt and clay, followed by a layer of sand one cm thick, a layer of silt and clay two cms, a layer of sand one-half cm and a layer of silt and clay three cms."

Event-generated rhythmic couplets were also described and photographed by Christiansson (1979). These were identified in pits dug in Imagi Reservoir, in central Tanzania. In this semiarid grazing terrain (mean annual rainfull—528mm) with run-off totaling 3 to 17 percent of the rainfall, mean annual specific sediment yield is 900 tonnes per square km per yr, and the reservoir is estimated to fill within 120 to 130 years after its construction.

Murray-Rust (1972) studied reservoir sedimentation in Kisongo Reservoir, northern Tanzania, a more humid region (ca. 900mm mean annual rainfall). He also described and photographed event rhythmic couplets. In addition, he attempted to correlate nine couplets deposited during one hydrologic year.

A comparison between Kisongo and Imagi reservoirs is interesting. The specific sediment yield into the Kisongo area was 714 tonnes per square km per yr during nine years, and 1024 tonnes per square km per yr during the following two years. Thus, the specific sediment yield in the Kisongo and Imagi areas is very similar. The original capacity of both reservoirs was identical (about 121,000 cubic m, or 98 ac-ft), but capacity decreased by 41 percent within eleven years of Kisongo's operation. The Kisongo reservoir filled faster because its contributing area is 9.3 square km, as opposed to 1.4 square km draining into Imagi reservoir. Hence, the Kisongo experience is an example of misjudgment in planning.

The Yatir Reservoir

The Yatir Reservoir (coordinates 1484.0802) is located in the southern Hebron Mountains, 25km from Beer Sheva. Its earth dam was completed in the autumn of 1968, thereby concentrating run-off from a 13 square km drainage basin. Although the uppermost part of the basin is forested, most of it is barren and gullied and is used by the Bedouin for goat-grazing. The valleys are filled with loess; soil thickness decreases toward the divides.

The dam failed on April 14th, 1971, after a 70mm/24 hr storm swept through the basin (Figure 14.1). Two gullies subsequently entrenched into the reservoir deposits to a maximum depth of 3m. The entrenchment enabled a visual, direct observation of the stratigraphy of these deposits.

Figure 14.2 depicts a stratigraphic section 100m upchannel from the dam. This is the location where the narrow valley widens to form the reservoir. Total thickness is 2.31m (within three years), with 41 clearly identifiable fine sand or overlying silt/clay units. The thick clayey unit numbered 40 represents the cessation of sediment deposition after the 20th flow event, because each two units in this section are, in fact, a couplet. The thick sandy unit overlying layer 40 represents the sediments deposited by the flow event that caused the failure of the dam.

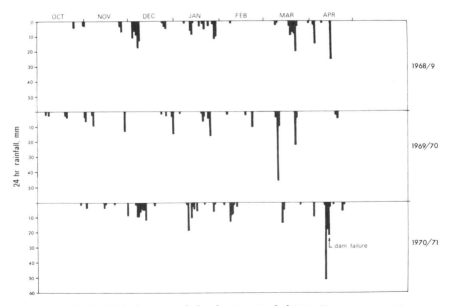

Figure 14.1   24-hr hyetograph for the 3-yr Nachal Yatir Reservoir operation period. The record was collected in the Yatir Forest, ca. 3 km from the reservoir.

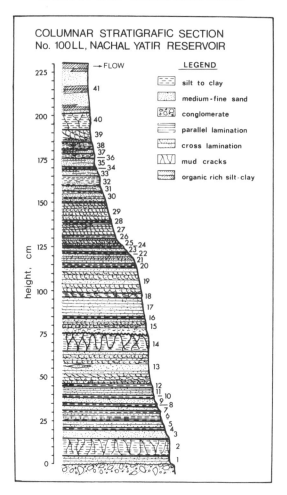

Figure 14.2 Nachal Yatir reservoir couplets (each couplet equivalent to two successive numbered units). This type-section outcrops 100 m upchannel from the dam in the left bank of the southern gully.

Figure 14.1 is a mean daily hyetograph for the three years during which the Yatir Reservoir was in operation. Average annual precipitation for this period was 249mm, and ranged between 219mm (1969–70) to 294mm during the following year. Many individual storms occurred in this period, but it is worth noting that only 20 storms were large (more than 10mm/day). This number of storms fits well the 21 major-event record depicted in Figure 14.2. Note the rhythmic nature of fine sand regularly overlain by silt/clay. The sand/silt boundary is not distinct as this zone is commonly graded. Individual couplet thickness varies from 2.5cm (units 23 and 24) to 29cm (units 13 and 14). The upper, finer unit of each couplet is comprised of clay-rich graded and draped laminations. The lower unit is at some locations

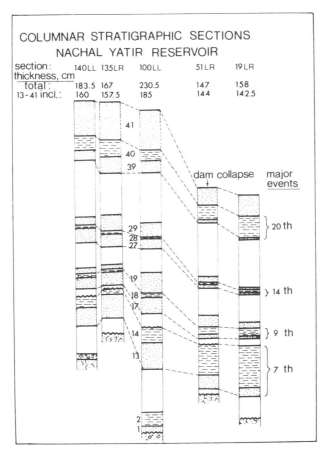

Figure 14.3 Stratigraphic correlation between four marker couplets representing the 7th, 9th, 14th and 20th flow event deposits. Note the delta-like depositional architecture.

medium sand, but more commonly it is comprised of fine sand. The sand is either thinly laminated, in which case it is multigraded (so-called microvarves), or else it is cross-laminated with ripple drift laminations.

The upper contact of every couplet is sharp and contains distinct mud cracks almost undisturbed by organisms or by plant roots. Most couplets conformably overlie lower couplets (e.g., the 40/41 boundary in Figure 14.2), although some boundaries are disconformities (e.g., the 14/15 boundary in Figure 14.2). These latter were created by slow-moving water that eroded miniature channels about 5mm deep, while initially filling the reservoir. Lenses of coarser sediment are also present, but they are only common in upchannel sections.

Four additional outcrops were carefully described (Figure 14.3). Note that the reservoir deposits overlie an unstructured loess or else a well-cemented conglomerate. The sediments deposited by the last impounded flow are clearly identifiable. Other marker horizons were also used to correlate the couplets. Visual continuity could be observed in many locations. The reservoir depositional model, expressed by the thickness of units 13 to 41 inclusive, is essentially a simple Gilbert-type delta. An upper region (sections 140 and 135, Figure 14.3) contains mainly traction load and is 1.6m thick. The lower region is comprised of bottomset laminae dominated by the accumulation of fine suspended sediment (sections 51 and 19, Figure 14.3) with a smaller average thickness. Section 100 is intermediate in terms of texture but comprises the thickest accumulation.

METHODOLOGY TO DETERMINE EVENT SEDIMENTATION RATES

The occurrence of event-generated rhythmic couplets in lakes and reservoirs may be used accurately and feasibly to determine sedimentation rates. In particular, this method could be useful to predict reservoir design periods in desert areas where sediment transport data are not available.

Predicting sedimentation rates for a particular reservoir or for a given basin involves five stages:

1. Locate a nearby reservoir for which good water level observations are available. Correct these observations for incoming sediment and their gradual consolidation after completing stage 4.

2. Core, or if possible dig pits, in the reservoir deposits and identify event couplets as demonstrated in Figure 14.4.

3. Correlate as many couplets as feasible from a net diagram. Determine each couplet volume by multiplying its thickness by its cross-sectional and longitudinal dimensions.

4. Couplet weights are equal to the product of their volume and their specific weight. Determination of the original specific weight is also ultimately required in order to determine rates of consolidation. This may be achieved by regressing specific weights of similar couplet unit samples (i.e., parts of couplets) against their depths beneath the bed of the existing reservoir. Lara and Pemberton (1965) suggested a different empirical solution. Otherwise, consolidation theory (e.g., Lamb and Whitman 1969; Scheidegger 1975) may be used. It should be noted that evaluation of consolidation rates is critical for clay-rich reservoir sediments.

5. Regress known sediment loads with peak discharge, flow volume, and other selected variables, particularly with a sediment availability factor (e.g., Moore 1984). Determine the best event-based prediction equation. Finally, use the historic event rates to determine the probability

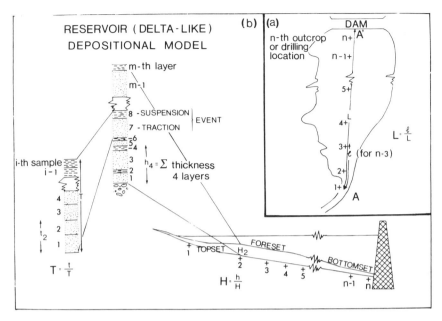

Figure 14.4   Map of a hypothetical reservoir, outlining longitudinal core dimension-less locations (14.4a). Several cores from the periphery would also be required. The section (14.4b) demonstrates the delta. A dimensionless couplet thickness (H) may be used to determine initial couplet specific weight, and a dimensionless couplet portion (T) designates relative time during an event.

distribution function of sedimentation rates in a manner similar to that suggested by Kochel et al. (1982).

CONCLUSIONS

Reservoir deposition rates may be evaluated by synthesizing costly suspended sediment concentration and bedload measurements. The use of USLE type or climatic equations results in large inaccuracies. Other methods are highly specialized.

Two additional methods are based on reservoir sedimentation. The first relies on several resurveys of a given reservoir. The derived sedimentation rates are based on a calculating procedure that averages the effects of small, medium and large events. Although the derived rates are correct for the entire surveyed period, individual future flow events, particularly large ones, will cause underestimation (e.g., see the example of Church and Gilbert 1975).

The delivery of sediment is a complex, spatially variable deterministic and stochastic process. Therefore, event-based sedimentation rates are assumed to offer better long-term estimates of reservoir design periods, particularly in arid areas where channel processes are invariably ephemeral. Sediment supply is, however, also determined by inter-event conditions.

Varves are readily identifiable in several depositional environments. Identification of varvelike rhythmic couplets deposited by individual flow events appears to be simplified in medium and small arid land reservoirs where bioturbation is minimal. Therefore, the proposed and presently-being-tested prediction technique will hopefully prove to be accurate, precise and economically feasible.

ACKNOWLEDGMENTS

André Lambert reviewed the manuscript. Lazar Sharona drafted the figures. Lee helped in the field. Avi Stern helped with the preparation of the manuscript. Funds for this study were granted by The Ben Gurion University.

REFERENCES

Agterberg, F. P. and I. Banerjee. 1969. Stochastic model for the deposition of varves in glacial Lake Barlow-Ojbway, Ontario, Canada. *Can. Jour. of Earth Science*. 6: 625–52.

Antevs, E. 1957. Geological tests of varve and radiocarbon chronologies. *Jour. of Geology*. 65: 129–48.

ARS (Agricultural Research Service). 1975. Present and prospective technology for predicting sediment yields and sources. U.S. Department of Agriculture. Agr. Res. Serv. Rpt. ARS-S—40.

Ashley, G. M. 1975. Rhythmic sedimentation in glacial Lake Hitchcock, Massachusetts Connecticut. In *Glaciofluvial and Glaciolacustrine Sedimentation*, eds. A. V. Jopling and B. C. McDonald. Soc. Econ. Paleontol. and Mineral Pub. 23. Pp. 304–20.

———. 1979. Sedimentology of a tidal lake: Pitt Lake, British Columbia, Canada. In *Moraines and Varves: Genesis, Classification*, ed. C. Schluchter. Balkema, Rotterdam. Pp. 327–45.

Banerjee, I. and B. C. McDonald 1975. Nature of esker sedimentation in *Glaciofluvial and Glaciolacustrine Sedimentation*. A. V. Jopling and B. C. McDonald. Soc. Econ. Paleontol. and Mineral Pub. 23. Pp. 132–54.

Brune, G. M. 1953. Trap efficiency of reservoirs. *Am. Geophys. Union Trans*. 34(3): 407–18.

Christiansson, C. 1979. Imagi Dam—A case study of soil erosion, reservoir sedimentation and water supply at Dodoma, central Tanzania. *Geogr. Annlr*. 61A(3–4): 113–45.

Church, M. and R. Gilbert. 1975. Proglacial fluvial and lacustrine environments. In *Glaciofluvial and Glaciolacustrine Sedimentation*, ed. A. V. Jopling and B. C. McDonald. Soc. of Econ. Paleontol. and Mineral. Pub. 23. Pp. 22–84.

De Geer, G. 1912. A geochronology of the last 12,000 years. Int. Geol. Cong. 1910. *Compte Rendu* 11: 241–53.

Dunne, T. 1979. Sediment yield and land use in tropical catchments. *Jour. of Hydrol*. 42: 281–300.

Emmett, W. W. 1980. A field calibration of the sediment trapping characteristics of the Helley-Smith bedload sampler. U.S. Geol. Survey Prof. Paper 1139.

Gustavson, T. C. 1975. Sedimentation and physical limnology in proglacial Malaspina Lake, southern Alaska. In *Glaciofluvial and Glaciolacustrine Sedimentation*, eds. A. V. Jopling and G. McDonald. Soc. of Econ. Paleontol. and Mineral. Pub. 23, Pp. 249–63.

Hayward, J. A. 1979. Mountain stream sediments. In *The New Zealand Experience*, ed. D. L. Murray and P. Ackroyd. The New Zealand Hydrol. Soc. Pp. 193–212.

Helley, E. J. and W. Smith. 1971. Development and calibration of a pressure-difference bedload sampler. U.S. Geol. Survey Open File Rpt.

Hubbell, D. W. 1964. Apparatus and techniques for measuring bedload: U.S. Geol. Survey Water Supply Paper 1748.

Jolly, J. P. 1982. A proposed method for accurately calculating sediment yield from reservoir deposition volumes. Int'l Assoc. Hydrol. Sci. Pub. 137. Developments in the Explanation and Prediction of Erosion and Sediment Yield. Proc. Exeter Symp. 153–61.

Kikkawa, H. 1980. Reservoir Sedimentation. In Application of Stochastic Processes in Sediment Transport, Eds. H. W. Shen and H. Kikkawa. Water Res. Pub. Littleton, Colo: Chapter 14.

Kirkby, M. J., and R. P. C. Morgan, eds. 1980. Soil Erosion. Wiley Intersci., New York.

Kochel, R. C., V. R. Baker and P. C. Patton. 1982. Paleohydrology of southwestern Texas. Water Res. Res. 18(4): 1165–83.

Kuenen, P. H. 1951. Mechanics of varve formation and the action of turbidity currents. Geol. Foren. Forh. Stockholm 73: 69–84.

Lamb, T. W. and R. V. Whitman. 1969. Consolidation Theory. In Soil Mechanics, eds. Lamb and Whitman. John Wiley & Sons, New York.

Lambert, A. M., and K. J. Hsu. 1979. Varve-like sediments of the Walensee, Switzerland. In Moraines and Varves: Genesis, Classification, ed. Ch. Schluchter. Balkema, Rotterdam. Pp. 287–84.

Langbein, W. B. and S. A. Schumm. 1958. Yield of sediment in relation to mean annual precipitation. Am. Geophys. Union Trans. 39: 1076–84.

Lara, J. M. and E. L. Pemberton. 1965. Initial unit weight of deposited sediments. Proc. of the Federal Inter-Agency Sed. Conf. U.S. Dept. of Agriculture, Misc. Pub. 970. Pp. 818–45.

Laronne, J. B. 1983. Evaluation of event sediment yields based on reservoir sedimentation. Proc. Int'l Geogr. Union (abstracts and program). Commission on Field Experim. in Geomorph. Bucharest

Laronne, J. B., and M. P. Mosley, eds. 1982. Erosion and Sediment Yield. Benchmark Papers in Geol. Series no. 63. Hutchinson and Ross, Stroudsburg, Pa.

Leopold, L. B., and W. W. Emmett. 1977. 1976 bedload measurements, East Fork River, Wyoming. Nat'l Acad. Sci. (U.S.A.) Proc. 74: 2644–48.

Ludlam, S. D. 1979. Rhythmite deposition in lakes of the northeastern United States. In Moraines and Varves: Genesis, Classification, ed. Ch. Schluchter. Balkema, Rotterdam. Pp. 295–302.

McHenri, J. R. and J. C. Ritchie. 1981. Dating recent sediments in impoundments. In Symp. on Surface Water Impoundments, ed. H. G. Stefan. Am. Soc. Civ. Eng., New York. Pp. 1279–89.

Moore, R. J., 1984, A dynamic model of basin sediment yield. Water Res. Res. 20(1): 89–103.

Murray-Rust, D. H. 1972. Soil erosion and reservoir sedimentation in a grazing area west of Arusha, northern Tanzania. Geogr. Annlr. 54A (3–4):325–43.

Oldfield, F. 1977. Lakes and their drainage basins as units of sediment-based ecological study. Progr. Phys. Geogr. 1: 461–504.

O'Sullivan, P. E., M. A. Coard, and D. A. Pickering. 1982. The use of laminated sediments in the estimation and calibration of erosion rates. Int'l Assoc. Hydrol. Sci. Pub. 137. Developments in the Explanation and Prediction of Erosion and Sediment Yield. Proc. Exeter Symp. Pp. 385–96.

Pemberton, E. L. 1980. Survey and prediction of sedimentation in reservoirs. In Application of Stochastic Processes in Sediment Transport, eds. H. W. Shen and H. Kikkawa. Water Res. Pub., Littleton, Colo. Chap. 5.

Reid, I., J. T. Layman, and L. E. Frostick. 1980. The continuous measurement of bedload discharge. Jour. of Hydraul. Res. 18: 243–49.

Renfro, G. W. 1975. Use of erosion equation and sediment delivery ratios for predicting sediment yields. USDA, Agricultural Research Serv. Rpt. ARS-S-40: 33–45.

Roehl, J. W. 1962. Sediment source areas, delivery ratios, and influencing morphological factors. Int'l Assoc. Sci. Hydrol. Pub. 59: 202–13.

Scheidegger, A. E. 1975. Consolidation. In Physical Aspects of Natural Catastrophes. Elsevier. North Holland. Chap. 6.

Schick, A. P. T. 1977. A tentative sediment budget for an extremely arid watershed in the southern Negev. In Geomorphology in arid regions, ed. D. O. Doehring. Proc. 8th Annual Geomorph. Symp., SUNY, Binghamton. Pp. 139–63.

Shaw, John. 1975. Sedimentary successions in Pleistocene ice-marginal lakes. In *Glaciofluvial and Glaciolacustrine Sedimentation*, ed. Jopling and McDonald. Soc. Econ. Paleont. and Miner. Pub. 23. Pp. 281–303.

Soares, E. F., T. E. Unny, and W. C. Lennox. 1981. Long term prediction of sediment storage in reservoirs. Am. Soc. Civ. Eng. Spec. Conf. *Water Forum 81*. Pp. 141–48.

Sturm, M. 1979. Origin and composition of clastic varves. In *Moraines and Varves: Genesis, Classification*, ed. Schluchter. Balkema, Rotterdam. Pp. 281–85.

Thakur, T. R. and D. K. Mackey. 1973. Delta processes. In *Fluvial Processes and Sedimentation*. Proc. Hydrolog. Symp. Nat'l Research Council, Canada. Pp. 509–30.

Walling, D. E. and A. H. A. Kleo. 1979. Sediment yields of rivers in areas of low precipitation: A global view. Int'l Assoc. Hydrol. Sci. In *The Hydrology of Areas of Low Precipitation* (Proc. Canberra Symp.). Pub. 128 479–93.

Walling, D. E., and B. W. Webb. 1981. The reliability of suspended sediment load data. Int'l Assoc. Hydrol. Sci. *Erosion and Sediment Transport* (Proc. of the Florence Symp.). Publ. 133. Pp. 177–94.

Wiebe, K., and L. Drennan. 1973. Sedimentation in reservoirs. In *Fluvial Processes and Sedimentation* (Edmonton Symp.). Nat'l Research Council, Canada. Pp. 539–61.

Williams, J. R. and H. D. Berndt. 1972. Sediment yield computed with universal equation. *Jour. Hydraul. Div.*, Am. Soc. Civ. Eng. Proc. HY12. 2087–98.

Wischmeir, W. H. and D. O. Smith. 1965. Predicting rainfall erosion losses from cropland east of the Rocky Mountains. USDA Agricultural Handbook 28.

Wood, A. E. 1947. Multiple banding of sediments deposited during a single season. *Am. Jour. Sci.* 245(5): 304–13.

FIFTEEN

The Meteorology of Desertification

MORTON G. WURTELE

ABSTRACT

This chapter is intended as a brief introduction for nonspecialists to current thinking on the problem of the atmospheric processes that contribute to extension of the desert margin, and to those processes that might be exploited by man to reverse desertification. Some background is provided on the typical climate of the type of desert under discussion, and some common misconceptions are corrected.

A recent global simulation is described, which yields spectacularly altered rainfall regimes in response to surface property changes. Other simulations with qualitatively similar results are referred to.

Quantitative research on desertification reversal is assessed as in a relatively primitive state of development. Two schemes for reversal are mentioned, and the theoretical support for them is described.

INTRODUCTION

The subject of desertification, or desertization, is not a new one; the periods of drought experienced in the Sahel during the late 1960s and early 1970s gave an immediacy to the subject that led to intensified research, international conferences, and United Nations studies. An excellent review of the interdisciplinary research and conclusions on desertification at this time is contained in the volume by that title, edited by M. H. Glantz (1977). This work represents a watershed on the subject, not because of the introduction of so many new ideas and hypotheses during the years since its publication, but because the techniques involved have become numerical modeling for theory, and sophisticated satellite instrumentation for observation. It is the intention of this chapter to give a brief review of the current status of the subject, comprehensible to a nonspecialist audience. Full references are provided for those wishing to pursue any aspect described. We shall include discussions both of the process of desertification, and of the possibilities for man-made reversal of this process.

Some Elementary Considerations

We must first note a simple common misperception: that deserts exist because there is too little water in the air. An interesting example of this fallacy is given by MacDonald (1962), who reports a plan to increase precipitation in Arizona by creating a huge lake along its southern border. Although some high-latitude deserts, such as the Gobi, are associated with an absolute scarcity of water, most of the deserts that are the subject of this article extend right to the seacoast, as does indeed the Arizona desert, in Mexico, and to a degree, in Southern California. The amount of water per unit volume of air (the absolute humidity) can be larger than that in rainy climates. In some cases, even the relative humidity (the ratio of the amount of water vapor present to the amount the air is capable of holding as vapor) can be climatologically high. A seacoast desert, such as the Atacama in Peru and Chile, may have seasons characterized by damp and foggy climate, but no rainfall.

Another way of appreciating what MacDonald called the "evaporation-precipitation fallacy" is as follows. When water vapor condenses in the air to form a cloud, only a small portion of the vapor becomes liquid. For example, in a typical stratus cloud at, say, 20°C, there will be a liquid water content of some one-half gram per cubic meter. But the air will still contain in vapor form about 32 times this quantity of water. A 10-km high cumulonimbus cloud, containing an average of one gram of liquid water per cubic meter, contains enough liquid for just one centimeter of rain. In order for the cloud to produce more rainfall, it is necessary that a circulation be created such that moist air is continually supplied to the cloud, so that the condensation and precipitation is a continuous process. In the same way, we shall see that an extensive desert is the result of an atmospheric circulation on a large scale, and the problem is a fluid dynamic one, and hence very complex. This is the reason why the problem has been referred to the large sophisticated numerical models of atmospheric flow. It is also the reason why any attempt to reverse the desertification process will be difficult and uncertain.

SCALES OF ATMOSPHERIC MOTION

To understand theories of desertification and suggestions for its reversal, it is essential to understand the concept of scale in atmospheric motions. The largest spatial scale of an atmospheric phenomenon is the atmospheric tide, much like the oceanic tide, but correlated with sun time rather than lunar time. The pressure wave moves round the earth with a maximum at 10 A.M. and 10 P.M., local time, and thus its scale is half the circumference of the earth. Extratropical cyclones are distributed around the globe at intervals averaging about 5000 km. These are examples of what is called the macro scale. The meso, or middle, scale characterizes such phenomena as the sea breeze, which normally extends about 100 km from the coastline, with, obviously, a diurnal period. The thunderstorm is of the order of five to ten km in extent, and may, under favorable circumstances give birth to a tornado of one to two kilometers breadth. Below this scale, are a variety of more or less "unorganized" atmospheric flows, all called microscale. Suffice it to say that in order to make an energy balance of the surface layer, it is necessary to field instruments with response time less than one second. Figure 15.1 shows these scales diagrammatically.

SCALES OF ATMOSPHERIC MOTIONS

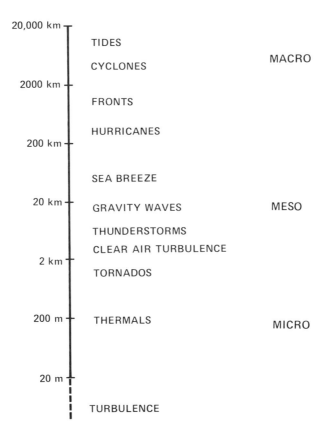

Figure 15.1   The horizontal scale of various atmospheric phenomena.
Note that the scale is logarithmic, and extends over six orders of magnitude.

THE SUBTROPICAL CLIMATE

We shall now see what relevance the atmospheric motion scales have to our problem as desertification. (We are concerned with the subtropical deserts, as remarked above, not the polar deserts.) As a prototype subtropical climate, we may take that of the southwestern United States and northwestern Mexico. This is sometimes called the Mediterranean climate, dominated in summer (in both hemispheres) by the great subtropical high pressure cell that extends over all oceans of the globe, but serves with greatest effectiveness of the eastern end of these oceans (in both hemispheres) and west continental coasts. In these high pressure cells, the air is sinking and spreading out at the surface, flowing in a clockwise circulation from high to low pressure. This is a steady, persistent pattern, and during its sway the land and sea alike are rainless. Figures 15.2 and 15.3 show the mean pressure and flow patterns for July in the eastern Pacific.

The sinking air in the high pressure cell warms by compression. It caps a layer of air, the marine layer, in contact with the relatively cool ocean, to form an inversion, a layer of air in which the temperature increases with height, in contrast to the layers above and below. (It is this inversion that so aggravates the air pollution problem in such climates, but that is not our concern.) The inversion weakens during the day as the surface air warms, and strengthens at night as it cools. Regions characterized by this climate will be summer-dry and receive their rainfall only in winter, when the high pressure cell has retreated toward the equator, and cyclones may invade from the west. If the summer climate seems to be increasingly dominant during the years, desertification is taking place.

It is obvious that we are talking of weather patterns of the macroscale, the scale of the oceans themselves. Man did not create this pattern, nor can he alter it. It is the delicate balance at the periphery, where the duration of the rain season may be more or less long, that anthropogenic factors may possibly come into play.

By these limitations we have greatly restricted our area of relevant concern. Yet even so, the lives and well-being of millions of humans are involved. A discussion of the physics of the interaction of the air with the surface of the earth will bring us one step closer to the theories of desertification.

PROPERTIES OF THE EARTH SURFACE THAT ARE INTERACTIVE WITH THE ATMOSPHERE

The subtropical climate extends over both ocean and land. It follows that, despite the superficial contradiction, an area of the ocean surface can be a desert, in the sense of low rainfall (Thompson 1977). Here we are concerned only with near-desert land areas inhabited by humans.

The following four properties of the land surface affect the atmosphere above it.

1. Albedo
    Visible
    Infrared
2. Moisture and Evapotranspiration
    Water Surfaces
    Soil Moisture
    Vegetation
3. Roughness
    Land: Terrain and Vegetation
    Water: Waves
4. Heat Capacity

The albedo is the reflectivity of the surface, both to visible and to infrared radiation. An albedo of 1.0 means that all incident radiation is reflected, and therefore is the highest possible albedo. To give an idea of typical values, the albedo of a snow surface may be 0.9; of a sandy beach, 0.3; of a grassland, 0.2; and of a forest, 0.15.

The second property involves the availability of moisture to evaporate into the atmosphere. The presence of water surfaces (lakes, rivers, swamps, etc.); the density and character of the vegetative growth; the type of soil (porous or impervious); all these factors are important in determining the possible evaporation of moisture into the air.

The third property is the roughness of the surface. A given flow speed over a snow surface, over a forest, or over a mountain range will create increasing intensities of turbulence and local circulations, which in turn will contribute increasingly to the formation of convective, and possibly precipitating, clouds.

Fourth is the heat capacity of the surface, that is, its ability to absorb radiation with minimum temperature change. A grassy lawn absorbs more radiation than a sandy beach but with less increase in temperature, and so is said to have greater heat capacity than the beach. The albedo and the heat capacity together determine the temperature of a surface exposed to solar radiation, and this temperature is related to the convection engendered.

Although these properties are simply described and understood, it is not so easy to quantify some of them, such as the rate of evaporation from various surfaces. Many atmospheric models omit or grossly oversimplify them. To begin with, they are interactive and not constant. Increasing the moisture content of a surface in general decreases the albedo and increases the heat capacity. It follows that there is feedback from the atmosphere to the terrestrial properties. For example, if, as has been suggested, the albedo of the surface is a factor in the generation of rainfall, it must also be the case that rainfall affects the albedo. This complex feedback relationship has not been incorporated in most of the models that have been used in desertification research.

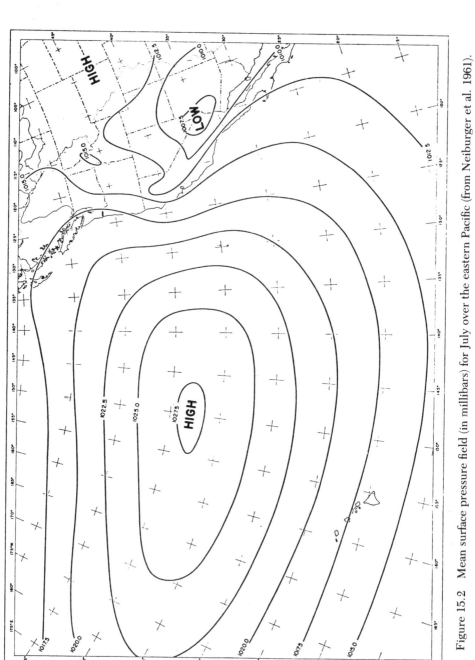

Figure 15.2   Mean surface pressure field (in millibars) for July over the eastern Pacific (from Neiburger et al. 1961).

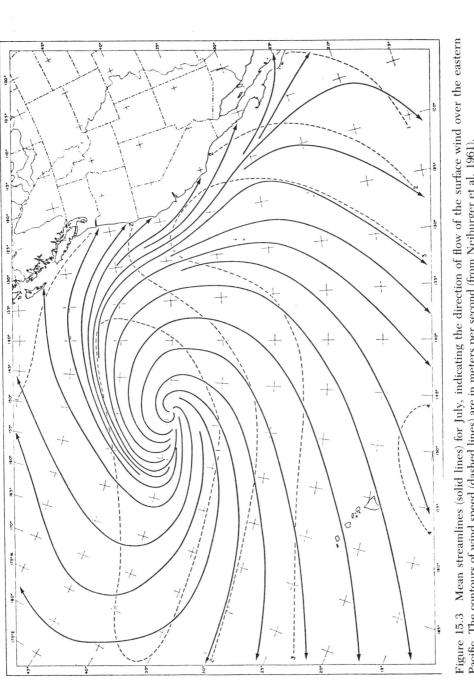

Figure 15.3 Mean streamlines (solid lines) for July, indicating the direction of flow of the surface wind over the eastern Pacific. The contours of wind speed (dashed lines) are in meters per second (from Neiburger et al. 1961).

HYPOTHESES ADVANCED CONCERNING
DESERTIFICATION AND ITS REVERSAL

We are now in a position to state and examine the explanations that have been tendered for the advance and recession of the desert margin, specifically with regard to changes in both directions that may result from human activity, inadvertent or deliberately planned. It should be understood that the discussion, despite its topicality and the controversy surrounding it, has been conducted in the terms of science. Each explanation has been put forward as a hypothesis, and quantitatively tested to the extent that resources and ingenuity permitted. We shall survey this testing for the following hypotheses:

A) Macro-meso scale
   i) Increase in albedo produces descending motion and decreases rainfall. Positive feedback.
   ii) Decrease in landsurface moisture reduces evaporation and decreases rainfall. Positive feedback.

B) Mesoscale
   i) Isolated heat and/or moisture sources on a spatial scale of hundreds of kilometers produce precipitation enhancing circulations.

These physical hypotheses are by no means of recent date. They are documented in contributions by Glantz (1977), although it is probably impossible to identify their true origin. What is unique about the results to be discussed below is that they derive from attempts to test the hypotheses by subjecting them to models incorporating the governing physical laws. Much of the literature under review is naturally rather technical, and therefore the discussion below will be greatly simplified. Even so, the results and conclusions can be accurately formulated.

This phase of desertification research can be said to begin with the study by Charney (1975), suggesting that an increase in the albedo of a marginal desert area would, in reflecting more solar radiation to space, reduce the heat conveyed by convection to the mid-troposphere. This relative cooling would in turn result in sinking motion, reduced cloudiness and rainfall, and decreased vegetation and increased albedo. This positive feedback mechanism was supported by Charney's mathematical analysis of the dynamic equations. Otterman (1974) published a dramatic satellite image of the sharp contrast between the cultivated Negev and uncultivated Sinai, estimating an average albedo over the spectral range 0.5–1.1 µm as more than 40 percent higher for the Sinai than for the Negev.

It was soon realized that the matter was not so simple. It is clear a priori that when surface moisture is taken into account, the heat absorbed in evapotranspiration tends to compensate for the lower albedo in producing an atmospheric surface temperature. Idso (1976), for example, presented evidence that the interface temperature rises with albedo.

At this time, the global circulation models (GCM) were brought to bear on the problem. It should be understood that any computer simulation by a GCM is a significant scientific project in itself. The models represent one or two decades of development and testing. A simulation requires extensive preparation and scores of hours of computer time on the largest mainframes. To date, numerical experiments related to desertification have been conducted by NASA Goddard Institute of Space Sciences and Goddard Space Flight Center; by NOAA Geophysical Fluid Dynamics Laboratory; by the British Meteorological Office; by the National Center for Atmospheric Research; and by the UCLA Department of Atmospheric Sciences. A comprehensive review and interpretation of the results of the period 1977–81 is provided by Mintz (1981). It will be instructive to observe the trend of these experiments and to look at the latest of them in some detail.

In the early experiments of Charney et al. (1977), it was already evident that, as indicated by Idso (1976), the role of surface moisture in the heat and water balance is at least as great as that of surface albedo, and the two physical processes are strongly interactive. Since then, a number of experiments have been carried out with surface moisture and/or surface albedo variable. Perhaps the most spectacular results are those of Suarez and Arakwa (personal communication) with the UCLA GCM. This experiment included two simulations of July global climate: i) the most realistic simulation of which the model is capable (the "control run"); and ii) a simulation (the "dry run") differing from the control run only in permitting no evapotranspiration from any land surface.

Figure 15.4 displays the startling contrast in the precipitation field. The control field is a reasonable approximation to a normal July: monsoonal rain on the Northern Hemispheric continents, dry west coasts, and dry subtropical deserts. (In fact, a result of a simulation so close to nature represents the successful culmination of years of intensive model development.) In the dry run, on the other hand, the large precipitation areas over the land surfaces have disappeared or moved offshore: from the eastern United States, from the Amazon Basin, from Equatorial Africa, and from much of northern India. The virtual disappearance of continental precipitation is a most spectacular result, and is not duplicated in the other simulations reviewed by Mintz (1981). Yet there is general agreement among model results and modelers that the presence or absence of soil moisture has great impact upon the precipitation climate of the earth. The possibility of positive feedback from an initial perturbation of soil condition remains a live consideration as a factor in desertification.

The reason that we are not in a position to come to more firm and confident conclusions on this question is now evident. The global simulations have demonstrated without question that the interaction of the atmosphere with the earth's surface is of greater importance in the determination of climate than had been previously realized, and that this interaction is inadequately represented in our models. In particular, the biosphere-atmosphere coupling has been only very crudely represented. A serious

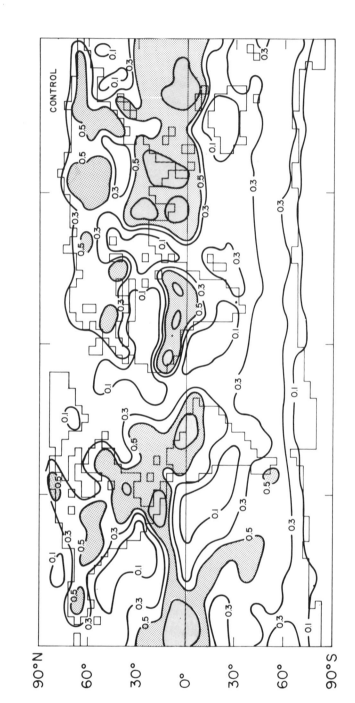

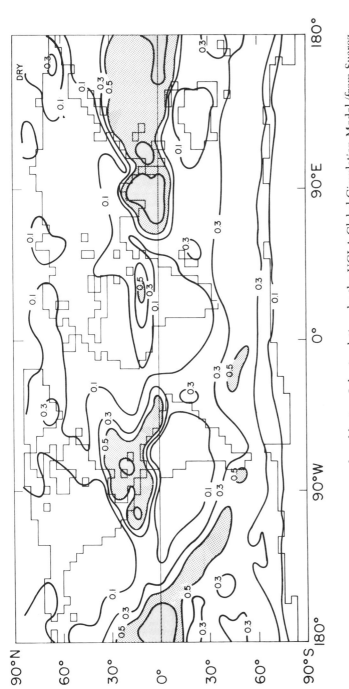

Figure 15.4   Precipitation patterns produced by two July simulations by the UCLA Global Circulation Model (from Suarez and Arakawa personal communication). Top: The "control run," with best model estimate of surface-atmosphere interaction processes. This is a (successful) best attempt to simulate global July rainfall. Bottom: The "dry run," under identical conditions as the "control run," except with evaporation completely suppressed from all land surfaces.

attempt to model the biosphere in the global circulation is now underway. Sellers et al. (1986) include two layers of vegetation, the canopy and the ground cover. Either or both may be absent or present at any given place and time. This vegetation and the associated root systems are allowed to affect the solar and infrared radiative transfer, the drainage and storage of precipitation, transfer of momentum, heat, and water vapor from and to atmosphere and biospheres. Such a model of the biosphere, called "simple" by the authors, would add significantly to the complexity of global circulation modeling; the biosphere has seven prognostic variables. But it is clear that this is the price that we may have to pay for a reasonably secure answer to the problem of desertification, and many other climate problems.

CAN DESERTIFICATION BE REVERSED?

It is obvious that if by reversal we mean by human agency, any intervention on a macroscale is impracticable. Yet a number of serious suggestions for meso-scale modifications of the landscape could conceivably prove cost-effective. As in the case of hypotheses concerning desertification, the conceptions are not new; and it is the attempt at quantitative verification of the hypotheses that will concern us here.

It has long been understood that a local heat source on the earth's surface causes rising air by convection, a phenomenon with some dynamic similarity to the forced rising motion as air flows over mountainous terrain. If the air is not too dry—and we have noted above that desert air is not necessarily low in absolute humidity—showery rainfall may result. This situation was examined by Black and Tarmy (1963), who suggested that strips of earth of length 30 to 125 km, oriented perpendicular to the North African desert coastline, be coated with an asphalt of especially low albedo. They then calculated the "thermal equivalent mountain" and applied a known theory to assess the effect of the air's being forced to flow over this "mountain." The process of convection, leading to precipitation, is much better understood, and even simulated numerical, than was the case in 1963; but the proposal of Black and Tarmy has not been vigorously followed by more recent studies, probably because of the adverse environmental consequences implicit in the asphalting. However, it has been generally accepted that an alternation of high and low albedo areas—produced by any means—could in some circumstances increase convective rainfall.

The environmental modification currently regarded as the most promising for desertification reversal, as well as being beneficial in itself, is the planting and irrigation of strips of vegetation, of the order of 20 km in width and 100 km apart. These would affect the radiative transfer in the same way as (although to a lesser degree than) the asphalt; but more importantly, perhaps, they would also alter the moisture balance, increasing evapotranspiration and humidity, and better retaining soil moisture. Further, the kinematic disturbance of airflow by the vegetative mass would intensify atmospheric turbulence and so contribute to the onset of convection.

These and similar qualitative considerations have been been frequently advanced; a discussion is given by Glantz (1977). Supporting evidence has been adduced (e.g., Schickedanz 1976) from the significant increase in rainfall over irrigated and cultivated areas compared with nonirrigated surroundings. Further, the vegetation planted may be selected to be of especial economic or environmental value. Johnson and Hinman (1980) and Hinman (1984) cite a variety of commercially viable crops appropriate for this particular arid land use.

A preliminary physical/dynamic analysis of a vegetation-strip model has been carried out by Anthes (1984) in somewhat more detail than was done by Black and Tarmy (see figure 15.5). Anthes applies an extremely simplified linear perturbation theory to obtain a preliminary determination of the relationships between the assignable parameters—distance between vegetative strips and width of strips—with magnitude of temperature perturbation, depth of the perturbed layer, and vertical velocity induced by the perturbation. Anthes concludes that if the bands are spaced 50 to 100 km apart, they will achieve maximum effectiveness in initiating convection of the magnitude required for cumulus precipitation. Such conclusions are admittedly highly tentative, and this phase of the research has only begun.

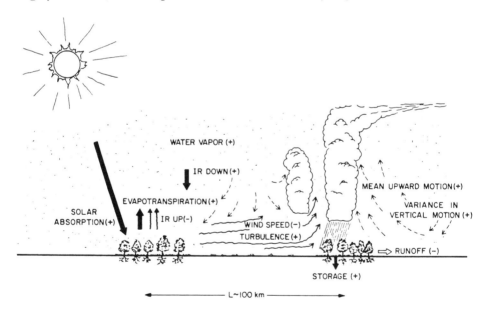

Figure 15.5   Schematic of proposal to enhance precipitation over arid lands by planting of rows of vegetation (from Anthes 1984).

CONCLUSIONS

In approaching the problem of desertification, meteorologists began by asking a deceptively simple question. Is it possible that anthropogenic alterations of the environment could produce significant climatic changes in a biogeophysical positive feedback reaction pattern? The development and use of models increasingly capable of representing atmospheric processes has resulted in an affirmative consensus answer to this question. Together with other studies, e.g., the El Niño phenomenon, desertification research has highlighted the very great importance of earth-atmosphere interactions, in radiative, heat, moisture, and momentum exchanges, and in so doing has made us aware that these interface physical processes are not adequately represented in current models. Thus although most model simulations have indicated positive feedback to changes in albedo and evapotranspiration, quantitative agreement among the models has not been achieved. Some much more detailed models of atmosphere-biosphere interaction are in preparation (e.g., Sellers et al. 1986), and the results of these will indicate how much further the global models will have to be developed in this respect to yield reliable quantitative results.

Insofar as desertification reversal is concerned, it is fair to say that research is only beginning. Some promising suggestions, notably the planting and irrigation of strips of vegetation, have been quantitatively examined in terms of linear dynamics, and the results seem encouraging, in the sense of predicting a (desirable) positive feedback. Nevertheless, much more extensive mesoscale modeling will be required before the results can serve as a guide for a costly pilot field experiment.

Finally, a most important lesson is to be learned from desertification research: Full understanding of the deserts and their extension and reversal will be attained only through the interdisciplinary collaboration of specialists in meteorology, hydrology, ecology, biology, and geology.

REFERENCES

Anthes, R. A. 1984. Enhancement of convective precipitation by mesoscale variations in vegetative covering in semi-arid regions. *Journal of Applied Climatology and Meteorology* 23: 541–554.

Berkofsky, L. 1976. The effects of variable surface albedo on the atmospheric circulation in desert regions. *Journal of Applied Meteorology* 15: 1139–1144.

———. 1979. Desertification, in *McGraw-Hill Yearbook Science and Technology*.

Black, J. F., and B. L. Tarmy. 1963. The use of asphalt coatings to increase rainfall. *Journal of Applied Meteorology* 2: 557–564.

Charney, J. G. 1974. Dynamics of desert and drought in the Sahel. *Quarterly Journal of the Royal Meteorological Society* 101: 193–202.

Charney, J. G., W. J. Quirk, S. H. Chow, and J. Kornfield. 1977. A comparative study of the effects of albedo change on drought in semi-arid regions. *Journal of the Atmospheric Sciences* 34: 1366–1385.

Charney, J. G., P. H. Stone, and W. J. Quirk. 1975. Drought in the Sahara: a biogeophysical feedback mechanism. *Science* 187: 434–35.

Glantz, M. H., ed. 1977. *Desertification*. Westview Press: Boulder, Colo.

Hinman. C. W. 1984. New crops for arid lands. *Science* 225: 1455–1448.

Idso, S. B. 1976. A note on some recently proposed mechanisms of genesis of deserts. *Quarterly Journal of the Royal Meteorological Society* 103: 369–70.

Johnson, J. D., and C. W. Hinman. 1980. Oils and rubber from arid land plants. *Science* 208: 460–64.

MacDonald, J. E. 1962. The evaporation-precipitation fallacy. *Weather* 17: 168–77.

Mintz, Y. 1981. The sensitivity of numerically simulated climates to land-surface boundary conditions, in *J.S.C. Study Conference on Land-Surface Processes in Atmospheric General Circulation Models*, Greenbelt, MD.

Neiburger, M., D. S. Johnson, and C. W. Chien. 1961. *Studies of the structure of the atmosphere over the eastern Pacific ocean in summer*. University of California Press.

Otterman, J. 1974. Baring high-albedo soils by overgrazing: a hypothesized desertification mechanism. *Science* 186: 531–33.

————. 1981. Satellite and field studies of man's impact on the surface in arid regions. *Tellus* 33: 68–77.

Sagan, C., O. B. Toon, and J. B. Pollock. 1979. Anthropogenic albedo changes and the earth's climate. *Science* 206: 1363–1368.

Schickendanz, P. T. 1976. *Effects of irrigation on precipitation in the Great Plains*, Final Report, NSF, RANN, Illinois State Water Survey.

Sellars, P. J., Y. Mintz, Y. C. Sud, and A. Dalcher. 1986. A simple biosphere model use within general circulation models. *Journal of the Atmospheric Sciences* 43:505–31.

Shukla, J., and Y. Mintz. 1982. Influence of land-surface evapotranspiration on the earth's climate. *Science* 215: 1498–1501.

Suarez, M., and A. Arakawa. 1985. Unpublished manuscript.

Sud, Y. C., and M. J. Fennessy. 1982. An observational evapotranspiration function for general circulation models. *Atmosphere-Ocean* 20: 301–16.

Thompson, J. D. 1977. Ocean deserts and ocean oases, in *Desertification*, M. H. Glantz, ed., 103–140.

Walker, J., and P. R. Rowntree. 1977. The effect of soil moisture on circulation and rainfall in a tropical model. *Quarterly Journal of the Royal Meteorological Society* 103: 29–46.

Wetzel, P. J., D. Atlas, and R. H. Woodward. 1984. Determining soil moisture from geosynchronous satellite infrared data: a feasibility study. *Journal of Climatology and Applied Meteorology* 23: 375–91.

SIXTEEN

On the Problem of Soil Moisture Determination from Meteorological Data Allowing for Vegetation Effect

LEV N. GUTMAN AND GEORGE GUTMAN

INTRODUCTION

Information on soil moisture and temperature at the surface and at different depths is of interest in numerous fields of human activity, such as building underground structures (water pipes, sewage, electric and other cables), road building, military mobility (for example, road trafficability for tanks). In agriculture and agrometeorology, this information is often necessary. For semiarid and arid zones, such information becomes especially important.

A great deal of technical difficulty and expense is usually involved in conducting special soil moisture and temperature measurements. It is therefore very tempting to have a model available that would allow the computation of soil moisture and temperature from routine meteorological observations for many regions of the globe. Moreover, such a model would permit the prediction of soil moisture and temperature using the meteorological forecast.

Various difficulties are involved in the construction of a model. These include inhomogeneities of the land surface and of the soil at various depths, lack of information on physical parameters, and presence of different urban constructions and artificial covers (such as concrete), as well as natural vegetation cover. Since vegetation can significantly influence the heat and moisture transfer between the earth's surface and the atmosphere, and since most of the land surface of the globe is covered by vegetation, it is desirable to include the vegetation effect in a model that simulates the heat and moisture transfer at the land surface.

The object of this chapter is to construct a model for an operational soil moisture and temperature computation from meteorological data, taking

into account the effect of the vegetation cover, which hereafter will be referred to as a canopy. To avoid the other difficulties mentioned above, we
assume that the soil is homogeneous and the land surface is horizontal and
free of urban constructions.

To our knowledge, there are no publications devoted even to such a simplified problem, although there are many papers in which soil moisture
and/or soil temperature computations have been carried out. These works
have been directed at the investigation of soil physics or to a methodology
of numerical solution (Havercamp et al. 1977; Dane and Mathis 1981). In
these papers, the boundary conditions at the surface are mostly simplified;
for example, evaporation from the surface is assumed constant and known.
Such assumptions are not adequate for our problem. In some of the papers
an attempt is made to couple the soil part of the problem with a rather
primitive atmospheric model, assuming bare soil, with attention directed at
processes in the soil (Camilio et al. 1983; Schieldge et al. 1982). These works
have allowed us to arrive at the important conclusion that, in principle,
computation of soil moisture and temperature is possible with the accuracy
sufficient for many purposes.

Another group of papers is devoted to meteorological and climatological
problems in which the soil moisture and temperature play an auxiliary role.
In the majority of these works the soil part of the problem is either highly
simplified (Deardorff 1978), or cumbersome calculations and the lack of
necessary data make it very difficult to estimate reliably the accuracy with
which soil moisture is determined (McCumber 1980). In this group of papers,
we refer only to those in which attempts to allow for the vegetational cover
effect have been made. Obviously, canopy models accessible for inclusion
into complex models containing soil and atmospheric parts must be sufficiently simple with respect to mathematics. Nevertheless, there have been
attempts to construct rather complicated two-level, or even multilevel, biosphere models for inclusion into general circulation models of the atmosphere
(Mintz et al. 1983). Deardorff (1978) has suggested a single-level canopy
model, sufficiently simple with respect to mathematics and at the same time
rather comprehensive with respect to physics. The model is based on moisture and heat balance equations for the vegetation layer and for the surface
of the earth and on some empirical relationships. Deardorff's model has
already been employed by some authors (McCumber 1980, Dickinson et
al. 1981). In this chapter we also use Deardorff's model while introducing
minor modifications for its improvement.

Unlike Deardorff and the authors mentioned above, we have made some
preliminary analytical transformations in an attempt to simplify the solution
of the vegetational part of the problem. This chapter includes only the
physical and mathematical formulation of the problem and its method of
solution, and will include the following symbols:

a   anemometer level height
b_T empirical value dependent on type (textural class) of soil only

c   volumetric heat capacity of soil
c_f heat or moisture transfer coefficient for the foliage element
c_{Hg} heat and moisture transfer coefficient applicable to bare soil
c_{Ho} heat and moisture transfer coefficient applicable to soil under a canopy
c_{Hh} heat and moisture transfer coefficient applicable to the top of a dense
             canopy
c_p specific heat of air at constant pressure
D_θ moisture diffusivity of soil
D_T thermal moisture diffusivity of soil
E   evaporation rate, if E>0, or condensation rate, if E<0
E_{tr} transpiration rate (per unit soil surface area)
g   gravity acceleration
h   thickness of the vegetation layer
H   sensible heat flux, positive upward
i,j   depth and time indices
K   hydraulic conductivity of soil
L   latent heat of vaporization
L_r length of roots per unit soil volume
N   number of levels in soil
P   precipitation rate
Q   soil heat flux density, positive downward
q   specific humidity
q_s saturated humidity
r   fraction of potential evaporation rate from foliage
r_a atmospheric resistance
r_c resistance coefficient dependent upon plant type
r_s generalized stomatal resistance
R   surface run-off
R_L downward directed longwave radiative flux
R_S downward directed shortwave radiative flux
R_{Smax} maximum value of R_S
R_w gas constant for water vapor
Ri_B bulk Richardson number
t   time
T   temperature
u   wind speed
W   flux density of soil water transfer, positive downwards
z   vertical coordinate positive downwards (depth in soil)
z_b lower boundary of the solution domain
z_r depth of root zone

Greek
α_f foliage albedo
α_g ground surface albedo
$\Delta z, \Delta t$ depth and time increments
θ volumetric moisture content
θ_d residual water content

θ_{dew} mass of liquid water retained by foliage per unit horizontal area
$\theta_{d\text{max}}$ maximum value of θ_{dew}, beyond which runoff to soil occurs
$\theta_{r\text{min}}$ minimum value of θ in the root zone
θ_s value of θ at saturation
θ_{wilt} wilting point value of θ
ρ density of water
ρ_a density of air
λ thermal conductivity of soil
ψ soil moisture potential
σ Stefan-Boltzman constant
σ_c cloud fraction
σ_f foliage shielding factor of ground from shortwave radiation (area average)
ε_f foliage emissivity
ε_g ground surface emissivity

Subscripts
a reference "anemometer level" height
f foliage surface
g value at the ground surface
af mean value within a canopy
h value at the top of the canopy
s value for saturated soil
b value at the lower boundary in soil

FORMULATION OF THE PROBLEM

We will consider the problem of diurnal moisture and temperature variations in the upper thermally active soil layer, which we assume to be non-swelling. In addition, we assume that we know the values of the wind, temperature, pressure, humidity, precipitation, and direct radiation at the shelter level at all times and that we have all the necessary information about the physical parameters of the soil and the canopy. We imply that there is a layer of air between the shelter and the canopy.

To describe the heat and moisture transfer in the soil, we employ a system of subsurface hydrology equations for unsaturated vapor-liquid flow (Philip 1957; Baver et al. 1972). We assume that nothing depends on the horizontal coordinates and that the ground surface is horizontal. The soil moisture equations will be supplemented by the water extraction term (Molz 1981), which parameterizes the moisture removal from the soil by the roots of the plants.

As a result, the soil-moisture equations are reduced to the following one-dimensional, non-stationary system of partial differential equations:

$$\frac{\partial \theta}{\partial t} = -\frac{\partial}{\partial z}(W/\rho) - S \tag{1}$$

$$c \frac{\partial T}{\partial t} = - \frac{\partial Q}{\partial z} \tag{2}$$

where

$$W/\rho = - D_\theta \frac{\partial \theta}{\partial z} + K - D_T \frac{\partial T}{\partial z} \tag{3}$$

$$Q = - \lambda \frac{\partial T}{\partial z} \tag{4}$$

In these equations the z axis and fluxes are positive downward.

Unlike Philip (1957), eq. (4) does not take into account the transfer of latent heat by vapor movement induced by the moisture gradient. The possibility of omitting this effect can be shown by elementary estimation. The fact is that the thermal vapor diffusivity coefficient becomes extremely small for soil moisture values observed in nature (see e.g., Fig. 2 in Philip 1957).

Neglecting the effect of hysteresis, one can consider parameters c, D_θ, D_T, K, λ and also θ as unique functions of ψ and of the textural class or type of the soil, whereas parameters ρ, θ_s, θ_d depend only on the textural class of the soil. Following Clapp and Hornberger 1978; Nakshabandi and Konke 1965; Farouki 1981; Sellers 1965, we set

$$c = c_s(1 - \theta_s - \theta), \quad \psi = \psi_s(\theta_s/\theta)^{b_T}, \quad K = K_s(\theta/\theta_s)^{2b_T + 3}$$
$$D_\theta = (-\psi_s)b_T K_s \theta_s^{-1}(\theta/\theta_s)^{b_T + 2} \tag{5}$$
$$\lambda = 2.57 \cdot 10^{-4} + 0.062(-\psi)^{-1.04} \quad (\text{cal sec}^{-1}\,\text{cm}^{-1}\,{}^\circ\text{C}^{-1})$$

The expression for λ approximates quite accurately the experimental data plotted in Fig. 4 from Nakshabandi and Konke, 1965. The values θ_s, c_s, ψ_s, K_s and b_T for different soils are given in Table 2 from Clapp and Hornberger, 1978.

To parameterize the soil moisture removal by roots, we adopted an expression for S, suggested recently by Moltz (1981) (see also Iskander, 1981).

$$S = L_r(z)KE_{tr}/\int_0^{z_r} L_r(z)Kdz \tag{6}$$

assuming that $L_r(z)$ and z_r are known.

We now proceed to the formulation of boundary and initial conditions of the problem.

Since the ground surface is assumed to be horizontal, one can, with slight simplification, consider that surface run-off occurs only if the precipitation water does not have time to infiltrate into the soil and to evaporate from the ground surface, which becomes saturated instantly:

$$\left.\begin{array}{l} \text{either } \theta = \theta_s \text{ and } R > 0 \\[1em] \text{or} \quad \theta \leq \theta_s \text{ and } R = 0 \end{array}\right\} \quad \text{at } z = 0 \tag{7}$$

where

$$R = P_g - E_g - W_g \tag{8}$$

$$P_g = \begin{cases} (1 - \sigma_f)P & \text{if } \theta_{dew} < \theta_{dmax} \\ P & \text{if } \theta_{dew} = \theta_{dmax} \end{cases} \tag{9}$$

(7) is actually an upper boundary condition for the soil moisture. (8) is the surface moisture balance equation. (9) allows for the retention of part of the precipitation by the foliage. As an upper boundary condition for the soil temperature, we shall use the ground surface heat balance equation.

$$Q = (1 - \sigma_f) \left[(1 - \alpha_g)R_s + \varepsilon_g R_L\right] - \varepsilon_2 T_g^4 + \sigma_f \varepsilon_1 T_f^4 - H_g - LE_g \tag{10}$$

where

$$\left.\begin{aligned} R_L &= \left[\sigma_c + 1.21(1 - \sigma_c)q_a^{0.08}\right]\sigma T_a^4 \\ \alpha_g &= \begin{cases} 0.31 - 0.34\theta_g/\theta_s & \theta_g < 0.50\theta_s \\ 0.14 & \theta_g \geq 0.50\theta_s \end{cases} \\ \varepsilon_1 &= \varepsilon_f \varepsilon_g \sigma/(\varepsilon_f + \varepsilon_g - \varepsilon_f \varepsilon_g) \\ \varepsilon_2 &= (1 - \sigma_f)\sigma\varepsilon_g + \varepsilon_1\sigma_f \end{aligned}\right\} \tag{11}$$

We assume that R_s is known from observations for all time. It is also possible to use astronomical formulas for R_s, as in McCumber (1980).

Equation (10) contains additional terms, which take into account the effect of the canopy. If $\sigma_f = 0$, eq. (10) becomes the well-known ground surface heat balance equation for the bare soil.

Equations which have to parameterize the influence of the canopy and meteorological conditions on the heat and moisture transfer between the atmosphere and the ground are:

1. Canopy energy balance equation

$$\sigma_f (1 - \alpha_f)R_s + \varepsilon_f R_L + \varepsilon_1 T_g^4 - \varepsilon_3 T_f^4 = H_f + LE_f \tag{12}$$

where:

$$\left.\begin{aligned} \varepsilon_3 &= \varepsilon_1 + \sigma\varepsilon_f \\ H_g &= \rho_a c_p C_{Hg} u_{af}(T_g - T_{af}) \\ H_f &= \sigma_f \rho_a c_p c_u(T_f - T_{af}) \\ E_g &= \rho_a C_{Hg} u_{af}(q_g - q_{af}) \\ E_f &= \sigma_f \rho_a c_u(q_f - q_{af}) \end{aligned}\right\} \tag{13}$$

$$\left.\begin{aligned} c_{Hg} &= (1 - \sigma_f)c_{Ho} + \sigma_f c_{Hh} \\ u_{af} &= (1 - \sigma_f + 0.83\sigma_f c_{Hh}^{1/2})u_a \\ c_u &= 7 \cdot 10^{-2}(u_{af} + 0.3 \text{ m/sec}) \end{aligned}\right\} \tag{14}$$

2. The relationship between the moisture characteristics at the foliage surface and the in-canopy air humidity

$$q_f - q_{af} = r \left[q_s(T_f) - q_{af}\right] \tag{15}$$

where:

$$r = 1 - \delta_c \frac{1 - \zeta^{2/3}}{1 + \xi} \quad (\zeta = \frac{\theta_{dew}}{\theta_{dmax}}) \tag{16}$$

$$\delta_c = \begin{cases} 0, \text{ if there is condensation onto the foliage surface } q_{af} > q_s(T_f) \\ 1, \text{ if there is evaporation from the foliage surface } q_{af} \leq q_s(T_f) \end{cases} \tag{17}$$

$$\xi = \frac{r_f}{r_s} = \frac{1}{r_c c_f u_{af}} \left[\frac{R_{smax}}{R_s + 0.3 R_{smax}} + \left(\frac{\theta_{wilt}}{\theta_{rm}}\right)^2 \right]^{-1} \tag{18}$$

$$q_s(T) = 0.38 \cdot 10^{-2} \exp\left(17.269 \frac{T - 273.16}{T - 35.86}\right) \tag{19}$$

This empirical formula is actually one possible version of the well-known Clausius-Clapeyron equation.

3. The conservation equation for θ_{dew}:

$$\frac{d\zeta}{dt} = \frac{1}{\theta_{dmax}} \left[\sigma_f P - (E_f - E_{tr})\right] \qquad (0 \leq \zeta \leq 1) \tag{20}$$

where

$$E_{tr} = \sigma_c \xi \left(1 - \zeta^{2/3}\right) E_f / r \left(1 + \xi\right) \tag{21}$$

4. Continuity conditions of the heat and water vapor fluxes at the top of the canopy layer

$$H_h = H_g + H_f \quad E_h = E_g + E_f \tag{22}$$

where

$$\left.\begin{array}{l} H_h = \rho_a c_p c_{Hh} u_a (T_h - T_a) \\ E_h = \rho_a c_{Hh} u_a (q_h - q_a) \end{array}\right\} \tag{23}$$

We denote:

$$\begin{array}{l} T_h = (1 - \sigma_f) T_g + \sigma_f T_{af} \\ q_h = (1 - \sigma_f) q_g + \sigma_f q_{af} \end{array} \tag{24}$$

The last two relationships are constructed in accordance with the simplest linear interpolation along σ_f, also suggested in Deardorff (1978).

5. Continuity condition for q at the ground surface

$$q_g = q_s(T_g) \exp(g \psi_g / R_w T_g) \tag{25}$$

6. Semiempirical relationship for c_{Hh} (see [8]):

$$c_{Hh} = \begin{cases} 4.2 \cdot 10^{-3}[1 + 24.5(-4.2 \cdot 10^{-3} Ri_B)^{1/2}] & \text{if } Ri_B < 0 \\ 4.2 \cdot 10^{-3}/(1 + 11.5 Ri_B) & \text{if } Ri_B \geq 0 \end{cases} \tag{26}$$

where

$$Ri_B = \frac{g(a - \sigma_f h)}{u_a^2 + u_c^2} (1 - \frac{T_h}{T_a})$$

$$u_c = \begin{cases} 0.1 \text{m/sec if } T_h < T_a \\ \\ 1.1 \text{m/sec if } T_h \geqslant T_a \end{cases}$$

These relationships imply that a thin, surface layer exists between the canopy and the anemometer level.

For the formulation of the lower boundary conditions of θ and T, we assume that at a certain depth (usually about 1–2 m), diurnal variations of θ and T can be neglected. We consider two cases: the soil below that depth is dry; and the soil below that depth is saturated (water table):

Thus, the lower boundary conditions for θ and T are

$$\left. \begin{array}{l} \theta = \theta_d = \text{const (dry soil)} \\ \text{or} \\ \theta = \theta_s = \text{const (saturated soil)} \\ T = T_b = \text{const} \end{array} \right\} \quad \text{at } z = z_b, \qquad (27)$$

The values θ_d, θ_s, T_b and z_b, are assumed to be known from climatic and edaphic data.

To close the problem, one needs to formulate the initial conditions.

We assume that, at a given moment of time θ and T are given functions of z:

$$\theta = \theta_o(z) \quad T = T_o(z) \quad (0 < z < z_b) \quad \text{at } t = 0 \qquad (28)$$

Equation (20) also requires an initial condition for ζ. Evidently it is difficult to obtain information concerning liquid water on the foliage. Therefore we set

$$\zeta = 0 \text{ at } t = 0 \qquad (29)$$

assuming that our computation starts at the moment when all the water retained by the foliage after the last rain has evaporated.

SOLUTION OF THE PROBLEM

First we introduce a finite-difference time grid $t_j = j\Delta t$, $\phi_j = \phi (z,t_j)$, $j = 1,2, \ldots$, where ϕ is any function or parameter of the problem (including those which are independent of z).

To clarify the explanation of the computation scheme, we shall assume that ϕ_{j-1} are known. We then describe the iterations involved in advancing to the next time step. This procedure will then be used to continue for all j. For brevity we shall omit the index when it is j. This notation permits us to regard equations (12)–(19), (21)–(24), as written for the moment t_j.

Equation (20) can be approximated by the following finite-difference form

$$\frac{\zeta - \zeta_{j-1}}{\Delta t} = \frac{1}{\theta_{d\max}} (\sigma_f P + E_{tr} - E_f) \quad (0 \leqslant \zeta \leqslant 1) \qquad (30)$$

This implicit scheme is chosen in order to refer dependent variables in (30) to the moment t_j, as in equations (12)–(19), (21)–(24).

Considering the crudeness of equation (20), the first order approximation of the time derivative in (30) appears to be sufficient.

Let us assume temporarily that T_g and θ_g (i.e., $(T_g)_j$ and $(\theta_g)_j$) are known. Then, as one can show, (12)–(19), (21)–(24) together with (30) is a closed algebraic system from which wect radiation at the shelter level at all times and that we have all the necessary information about the physical parameters of shall find T_f in the following way.

First, substituting (13), (23) and (24) into (22) and making some simple transformations, we obtain

$$q_{af} = a_a q_a + a_f q_f + a_g q_g \tag{31}$$

$$T_{af} = a_a T_a + a_f T_f + a_g T_g \tag{32}$$

where

$$\left.\begin{aligned}
a_a &= c_{Hh} u_a / \left[c_{Hg} u_{af} + \sigma_f(c_u + c_{Hh} u_a) \right] \\
a_f &= \sigma_f c_u / \left[c_{Hg} u_{af} + \sigma_f(c_u + c_{Hh} u_a) \right] \\
a_g &= 1 - a_a - a_f
\end{aligned}\right\} \tag{33}$$

In the right hand sides of (31) and (32) all quantities with the exception of q_f and T_f, are known. Indeed q_a and T_a are known from observations, T_g and q_g are known, as a consequence of our assumption and eq. (25) respectively.

Concerning a_a, a_g and a_f, we note the following. In Deardoff (1978) it was assumed that c_{Hh} is a known constant. We calculate c_{Hh} from (26), but in (26) we shall use $(T_h)_{j-1}$. Then a_a, a_f and a_g can be calculated with the aid of (33). It should be noted that (31) and (32) are similar to relationships suggested in Deardorff (1978), where a_a, a_f and a_g were assumed to be given functions of σ_f alone. Equations (15) and (31) can be solved for q_f and q_{af}. Substituting q_f and q_{af} obtained in this way, into the expression for E_f from (13), we get

$$E_f = \left[q_s(T_f) - q_{ag} \right] r \sigma_f a_E / (1 - a_f + r a_f) \tag{34}$$

where

$$q_{ag} = (a_a q_a + a_g q_g)/(1 - a_f), \quad a_E = \rho_a c_u(1 - a_f) \tag{35}$$

Note, that $0 \leqslant r \leqslant 1$ and $0 \leqslant a_f \leqslant 1$. Therefore the sign of E_f depends only on the sign of the difference in the brackets in (34).

Substituting (34) into (12) yields an equation, which links T_f with r.

$$F(T_f, r) = \frac{r}{1 - a_f + r a_f} \left[q_s(T_f) - q_{ag} \right] - b(T_f) = 0 \tag{36}$$

where

$$b(T_f) = \frac{c_p}{L}(T_{ag} - T_f) + \frac{1}{L a_E} (R_E - \varepsilon_3 T_f^4) \tag{37}$$

in which

$$R_E = (1 - \alpha_f)R_s + \varepsilon_f R_L + \varepsilon_1 T_g{}^4 \tag{38}$$

$$T_{ag} = (a_a T_a + a_g T_g)/(1 - a_f) \tag{39}$$

The expressions $F(T_f, r)$ and $b(T_f)$ can be treated as given functions of their arguments.

From (34) and (36) we obtain

$$E_f = \sigma_f a_E b(T_f) \tag{40}$$

In this formula, unlike (34), the explicit dependence E_f on r is absent. Combining (13), (31), (35) and (40), we derive:

$$q_f = q_{ag} + b(T_f), \quad q_{af} = q_{ag} + a_f b(T_f) \tag{41}$$

Recalling the expression for E_f: (13), (34) and (40), one can understand from (41) why the differences $q_s(T_f) - q_f$, $q_s(T_f) - q_{af}$ and $q_s(T_f) - q_{ag}$ always have the same signs.

Thus, from (34) and (36) it follows that the sign of $b(T_f)$ determines whether condensation or evaporation is occurring at the foliage:

$$\left. \begin{array}{l} \text{If } b(T_f) < 0 - \text{condensation} \\ \text{If } b(T_f) > 0 - \text{evaporation} \end{array} \right\} \tag{42}$$

On account of (16) and (17) in the case of condensation, T_f can be found from equation (36) in which $r = 1$.

According to (17) and (21), $E_{tr} = 0$ in this case. Therefore, in the case of condensation (30) is reduced to

$$\zeta = \zeta_{j-1} + (\sigma_f P - E_f)\Delta t/\theta_{d\max} \tag{43}$$

In the case of evaporation from the foliage, an equation for T_f can be obtained by excluding r and ζ from (16), (30) and (36).

Indeed, in this case, solving (16) and (36) for ζ and r respectively, and allowing for (41), we express ζ and r in terms of T_f:

$$\zeta(T_f) = \left[(\xi + 1)r(T_f) - \xi \right]^{3/2} \tag{44}$$

$$r(T_f) = (1 - a_f)b(T_f)/[q_s(T_f) - q_{af}] \tag{45}$$

Substituting (40), (44) and (45) into (21) yields an expression for the transpiration rate

$$E_{tr} = \sigma_f a_E \xi[q_s(T_f) - q_f]/(1 - a_f) \tag{46}$$

which accompanies evaporation from the foliage.

If we substitute (40), (44) and (46) into (30), we arrive at an algebraic transcendental equation for T_f in the evaporation case

$$\zeta(T_f) - AF \left(T_f, \frac{\xi}{1 + \xi} \right) - B = 0 \tag{47}$$

where the functions ζ and F are specified by (44) and (36) respectively and

$$A = \Delta t \cdot \rho_a c_u \sigma_f (1 - a_f + \xi)/\theta_{dmax} \tag{48}$$

$$B = \zeta_{j-1} + \Delta t \cdot \sigma_f P/\theta_{dmax}$$

Equation (36) at r = 1, as well as at $r = \dfrac{\xi}{1 + \xi}$, is solved numerically by the Newton-Raphson method (Grove, 1966). Equation (47) is solved using the so-called "rule of false position" (Grove, 1966).

As a result of (42), (44), (45) and (47), one can find T_f and determine whether condensation or evaporation at the foliage is occurring at the moment t_j. Details are given in Appendix A.

Once we obtain T_f, then using (13), (32), (37), (40), (41), (43)–(46), we can calculate the quantities:

$$\zeta, \ r, \ q_f, \ q_{af}, \ T_{af}, \ E_g, \ E_f \text{ and } E_{tr} \tag{49}$$

which are necessary for the computation of the soil temperature T(z,t) and moisture θ(z,t).

Eliminating W/ρ and Q from (1)–(4) yields

$$c \frac{\partial T}{\partial t} = \frac{\partial}{\partial z} \lambda \frac{\partial T}{\partial z} \tag{50}$$

$$\frac{\partial \theta}{\partial t} = \frac{\partial}{\partial z} D_\theta \frac{\partial \theta}{\partial z} - \frac{\partial K}{\partial z} + \frac{\partial}{\partial z} D_T \frac{\partial T}{\partial z} - S \tag{51}$$

Note that in these equations, the time indices have not yet been introduced.

Let us consider the soil temperature eq. (50). Sophocleous (1979) solved the temperature equation in a more general form (including the moisture influence term). His estimates indicated that the dependence of the soil temperature on the soil moisture field is weak.

This fact justified the use of the simplified eq. (4) and also shows that changes of the parameters c and λ with θ only slightly affect T. This is reasonable because the changes of c and λ have to be mutually compensated to a certain extent.

The variables (49) depend on θ_g only through the soil moisture potential ψ_g, which appears in (25). It is easy to show that the exponential factor in (25) is close to unity, if the soil is even slightly wet.

However, in the case of extremely dry soil, the value of θ_g is very small. Therefore, in both cases the effect of θ_g on the values (49) is insignificant.

Thus, taking into account the weak dependence of the soil temperature field on the soil moisture, we shall use $(\theta_g)_{j-1}$ instead of $(\theta_g)_j$ for solving equation (50).

To transform (10) into a convenient linear boundary condition for T, we shall use the fact that the numerical procedure for solving equation (50) contains a certain iterative process.

Let us turn to an approximate relationship

$$T_g^4 = 4 \left(T_g^{(n-1)} \right)^3 T_g - 3 \left(T_g^{(n-1)} \right)^4 \tag{52}$$

which is valid when the temperature difference between two consecutive iterations is relatively small.

In (52) $T_g^{(n-1)}$ is taken from the $(n-1)$th iteration. In analogy with the time indices, hereafter the iterative index in brackets will be omitted whenever it is (n) (i.e., referring to the n-th iteration). For example in (52), T_g means $(T_g)_j^{(n)}$.

Substituting (13) and (52) into (10), we arrive at a linear boundary condition for T at the ground surface:

$$-\lambda \frac{\partial T}{\partial z} + \nu T = \mu \qquad \text{at} \qquad z = 0 \tag{53}$$

where

$$\begin{aligned}
\nu &= \rho_a c_p c_g u_{af} + 4\varepsilon_2 (T_g^{(n-1)})^3 \\
\mu &= (1 - \sigma_f) \left[(1 - \alpha_f) R_s + \varepsilon_g R_L \right] + 3\varepsilon_2 \left(T_g^{(n-1)} \right)^4 + \\
&\quad + \sigma_f \varepsilon_1 T_f^4 + \rho_a c_p c_g u_{af} T_{af} - LE_g
\end{aligned} \tag{54}$$

Equation (50) is rewritten in the finite differences in accordance with the well-known Crank-Nicolson scheme. The boundary and initial conditions (27), (53) and (28) are also presented in finite difference form. Such a finite-difference problem is solved at each iteration with the aid of the so-called tridiagonal algorithm (see e.g. Remson et al., 1971). Details are presented in Appendix B.

Once $T(z,t)$ is known, we proceed to the solution of the soil moisture equation (51) with the boundary and initial conditions (7), (27) and (28).

For this we make use of the predictor-corrector equations (suggested by Douglas and Jones (1963) and recommended in Remson et al. (1971) for the type of problems under consideration) again solving them with the aid of tridiagonal algorithm at each iteration. By including a special logical scheme in the iteration process, we provide the satisfaction of the surface boundary conditions (7). Details are presented in Appendix C.

Fig 16.1 shows a simplified flowchart of the soil moisture and temperature calculation at a given time step. In the following we explain it briefly. At the beginning all data, including those referred to the previous time step, are passed on from Box I to Box II. In Box II the equations for the vegetation layer are solved; in the first iteration, as a zero approximation, the values of the soil moisture and of the temperature at the surface are those calculated in the previous time step. Then the values of T_f, E_g, E_{tr} and H_g are passed on to Box III and/or to Box IV. In Box III the equation for the heat transfer is solved and a temperature profile is obtained. This is passed on to Box IV. Successively in Box IV the equation for the soil moisture is solved and a moisture profile is obtained. Finally the values of the surface temperature and moisture calculated, respectively, in Box III and Box IV are passed on to Box II and a new iteration starts. At the end of the iterative process a new time step is considered.

In summary, a time-integration scheme for computing soil moisture and

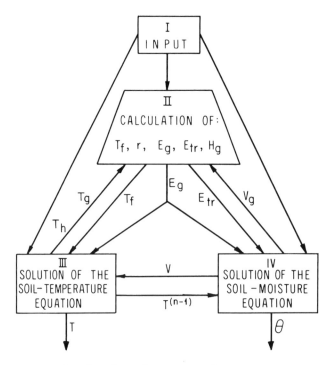

Figure 16.1   Flowchart for soil moisture and temperature computation.

temperature profiles as well as the surface fluxes has been constructed for a one-dimensional soil-vegetation-atmosphere system.

The method needs the following information: data about the march of meteorological elements at the shelter level (wind, temperature, humidity, precipitation), data about the march of the cloudiness and solar radiation, data about some physical parameters of the soil and the vegetation cover whose thickness is assumed to be known and to be less than the height of the shelter level.

The numerical method consists of the Crank-Nicolson predictor-corrector scheme in the form suggested by Douglas and Jones (1963) and Remson et al. (1971), two internal and one external iteration processes. It provides the necessary accuracy and convergency of the solution and is rather economic from the point of view of the computer's time.

ACKNOWLEDGMENTS

It should be noticed that Dr. M.G. Scarpino, from Italy, has taken part actively in completing this paper. She has introduced some essential improvements in the method of the solution of the problem. The authors express sincere gratitude to her. They express also their heartfelt appreciation to Prof. L. Berkofsky for his moral support.

This study has been partially supported by the United States Army, Contract No. DAJA45-84-C-0007.

APPENDIX A
Determination of $(T_f)_j$ and Whether Condensation or Evaporation is Occurring at the Foliage at $t = t_j$

Setting $r = 1$ in (36), we solve the eq. $F(x, 1) = 0$ numerically by the Newton-Raphson method (see Grove 1966):

$$x^{(m+1)} = x^{(m)} - F(x^{(m)}, 1)/\frac{\partial F(x^{(m)}, 1)}{\partial x^{(m)}} \qquad m = 0, 1, \ldots \qquad (55)$$

The iteration process is stopped when

$$\left| x^{(m+1)} - x^{(m)} \right| < 0.1°C \qquad (56)$$

The fact that $\partial F(x, 1)/\partial x$ and $\partial^2 F(x, 1)/\partial x^2$ do not change their signs at $x > 0$ provides the convergence of the iterations for any $x^{(0)} > 0$. After determining x, we compute $b(x)$ by (37).

Further computations depend on the values of $b(x)$.

If $b(x) < 0$, then in accordance with (42) condensation on the foliage is occurring and $T_f = x$.

If $\varepsilon_b > b(x) > 0$, where ε_b is very small (we put $\varepsilon_b = 10^{-5}$), evaporation from the foliage is occurring. However in this case, the evaporation is sufficiently small to neglect it by putting $E_f = 0$. Then we find ζ from (43) and determine r from (16) and (17). [Owing to (21), E_{tr} is negligibly small, as well as E_f]. In this case T_f is so close to x, that it is possible to take $T_f = x$.

If $b(x) > \varepsilon_b$, then evaporation from the foliage is occurring. We denote $x = T_f^{(1)}$. One can show that then $T_f^{(1)} < T_f < T_f^{(2)}$, where $T_f^{(2)}$

is a solution of the eq. $F\left(T_f^{(2)}, \dfrac{\xi}{1 + \xi}\right) = 0$. We turn again to the Newton-

Raphson method, finding $T_f^{(2)}$ from the same iterative formula (55) in which one should substitute $\xi/(1 + \xi)$ instead of 1, as a second argument of the function F. But now it is better to set $x^{(0)} = T_f^{(1)}$.

A criterion for stopping the iterations is the same as (56).

Proceeding to the solution of the eq. (47), we note that the function

$$f(T_f) = \zeta(T_f) - AF\left(T_f, \frac{\xi}{1 + \xi}\right) - B \qquad (57)$$

is continuous and increasing at the interval $T_f^{(1)} < T_f < T_f^{(2)}$. With the help of (21), (30), (44) and (48) one can show that

$$f(T_f^{(1)}) = 1 - B + \Delta t \cdot a_E \sigma_f b(T_f^{(1)})/\theta_{d\max} > 0 \qquad (58)$$

$$f(T_f^{(2)}) = -B < 0$$

Consequently, since $f(T_f)$ is a monotonic function, the solution of the eq. (47), e.g. $f(T_f) = 0$, exists and is unique. To find this solution, we use the so-called "rule of false position or reguli falsi" (Remson et al. 1971), which is presented by the following convergent iteration process

$$T_f^{(n+1)} = \begin{cases} \dfrac{T_f^{(n)}f^{(1)} - T_f^{(1)}f^{(n)}}{f^{(1)} - f^{(n)}} & \text{if } f^{(n)} < 0 \\[4mm] \dfrac{T_f^{(2)}f^{(n)} - T_f^{(n)}f^{(2)}}{f^{(n)} - f^{(2)}} & \text{if } f^{(n)} > 0 \end{cases} \tag{59}$$

where we donote $f(T_f^{(n)}) = f^{(n)}$.

The criterion of stopping the iterations is the same as (56).

APPENDIX B
Numerical Scheme for Solving the Temperature Equation (50)

Since c and λ do not depend on T, the eq. (50) is linear. The boundary conditions (27) and (53) are also linear. Therefore, one can use the well-known Crank-Nicolson scheme, which is absolutely convergent, to provide an accuracy of the order of $(\Delta t)^2 + (\Delta z)^2$ and is amenable for solution via the so-called tridiagonal algorithm (Remson et al. 1971).

Supplementing the time-grid introduced earlier, we shall introduce a uniform space-grid $z = i\Delta z$, $i = 0,1, \ldots N$ and denote $\phi(z_i, t_j) = \phi_{i,j}$, where ϕ is any variable of the problem.

Presenting the eq. (50) in the form

$$\frac{c}{\lambda} \frac{\partial T}{\partial t} = \frac{\partial^2 T}{\partial z^2} + \frac{\partial \ln \lambda}{\partial z} \cdot \frac{\partial T}{\partial z} \tag{60}$$

we replace it by the finite-difference equation in accordance with the Crank-Nicolson scheme and then transform it to the following form:

$$A_i T_{i-1,j} - G_i T_{i,j} + B_i T_{i+1,j} = -F_i \quad (i = 1, \ldots N - 1) \tag{61}$$

where

$$\begin{aligned} A_i &= 1 - 0.25 \ln \left(\lambda_{i+1,j}/\lambda_{i-1,j}\right) \\ B_i &= 1 + 0.25 \ln \left(\lambda_{i+1,j}/\lambda_{i-1,j}\right) \\ G_i &= 2 \left[1 + (\Delta z)^2 c_{i,j}/\Delta t \cdot \lambda_{i,j}\right] \\ F_i &= A_i T_{i-1,j-1} - 2 \left[1 - (\Delta z)^2/\Delta t \cdot \lambda_{i,j}\right] T_{i,j-1} + B_i T_{i+1,j-1} \end{aligned} \tag{62}$$

Equation (61) is solved by tridiagonal algorithm (see Remson et al. 1971).

$$\left. \begin{aligned} \alpha_{i+1} &= B_i / \left(G_i - \alpha_i A_i\right) \\[2mm] \beta_{i+1} &= \left(A_i \beta_i + F_i\right) / \left(G_i - \alpha_i A_i\right) \end{aligned} \right\} \quad i = 1,2,\ldots N - 1 \tag{63}$$

$$T_{i,j} = \alpha_{i+1} T_{i+1,j} + \beta_{i+1} \quad i = N - 1, \ldots 1, 0$$

To employ this algorithm one needs to know α_1, β_1 and $T_{N,j}$.
The latter value is known from (27) $T_{N,j} = T_b$.
To find α_1 and β_1 we have to rewrite (53) in the finite-difference form. Remember that the Crank-Nicolson scheme provides accuracy of the order of $(\Delta z)^2$ with respect to z. Therefore, we use the following representation:

$$\partial T/\partial z\big|_{z=0} = \left(3T_o - 4T_1 + T_2\right) /2\Delta z \tag{64}$$

providing the same accuracy.

Substituting (64) into (53), we come to a linear equation linking T_0, T_1 and T_2. The second linear equation linking these three values is (61) at i = 1. Elimination of T_2 from these two equations yields

$$T = \alpha_1 T_{1,j} + \beta_1 \tag{65}$$

where $\alpha_{1,j}$ and $\beta_{1,j}$ are values of interest:

$$\alpha_1 = \left(4B_1 - G_1\right) / \left[\left(3 + 2\Delta z v/\lambda_{o,j}\right) B_1 - A_1\right] \tag{66}$$

$$\beta_1 = \left(2\Delta z \mu B_1/\lambda_{o,j} + F_1\right) / \left[\left(3 + 2\Delta z v/\lambda_{o,j}\right) B_1 - A_1\right]$$

Note, that in the expressions (54) for v and μ the surface temperature T_g refers to the previous iteration step. Therefore, the computation $T_{i,j}$ by (63) can be considered as a realization of one iteration step, i.e. as obtaining $T^{(n+1)}$.

Substituting the value $T_{o,j}$ obtained from (63), into (54), we proceed to the next iteration step, etc. As a criterion for stopping the iterations we use the inequality

$$\max\left|T_{i,j}^{(n+1)} - T_{i,j}^{(n)}\right| < 0.1°C \tag{67}$$

APPENDIX C
Numerical Scheme for Solving the Soil-Moisture Equation (51)

First, instead of θ we introduce a new independent variable ("Kirchhoff transformation").

$$v = \left(\theta/\theta_s\right)^{b_T+3} \tag{68}$$

Equation (51) takes the form:

$$\frac{\partial^2 v}{\partial z^2} = \frac{\theta_s}{(-\psi_s)K_s b_T} \cdot v^{-\frac{b_T+2}{b_T+3}} \cdot \frac{\partial v}{\partial t} + \frac{2b_T + 3}{(-\psi_s)b_T} v^{\frac{b_T}{b_T+3}} \cdot \frac{\partial v}{\partial z}$$

$$- \frac{b_T + 3}{(-\psi_s)b_T K_s} \left(D_T \frac{\partial^2 T}{\partial z^2} - S\right) \tag{69}$$

The terms in brackets are known, because T for the moment j has been calculated and in the expression (6) for S soil moisture θ is taken from the j − 1 moment.

Eq. (69) is more convenient for the numerical solution than the eq. (51)

inasmuch as powers in coefficients are not so great, although the parameter b_T can be of order of 10 (see Table 2 from Clapp and Hornberger, 1978).

In addition, the second order derivative term is transformed into its simplest form. As was stated earlier, we use the Douglas and Jones predictor-corrector method (1963) for the solution of eq. (69).

First of all, we replace (69) with the system of two finite-difference equations (the first of which is the predictor, and the second is the corrector, following eqs. 3–50a and b in Remson et al. 1971). Then both of these equations are reduced to the standard tridiagonal form.

The predictor is given by

$$A_i v_{i-1,j-\frac{1}{2}} - G_i v_{i,j-\frac{1}{2}} + B_i v_{i+1,j-\frac{1}{2}} = - F_i \tag{70}$$

where

$$A_i = 1 \quad B_i = 1 \quad G_i = 2 \left(1 + h_{i,j-1}\right)$$
$$F_i = 2h_{i,j-1} v_{i,j-1} + \tfrac{1}{2}g_{i,j-1} \left(v_{i-1,j-1} - v_{i+1,j-1}\right) + f_{i,j}$$

$$h_{i,j} = \frac{(\Delta z)^2 \theta_s}{(-\psi_s)b_T K_s \Delta t} v_{i,j}^{-\frac{b_T+2}{b_T+3}} \quad g_{i,j} = \frac{(2b_T + 3)\Delta z}{(-\psi_s)b_T} v_{i,j}^{-\frac{b_T}{b_T+3}} \tag{71}$$

$$f_{i,j} = \frac{b_T + 3}{(-\psi_s)b_T K_s} \left[D_T \left(T_{i-1,j-\frac{1}{2}} - 2T_{i,j-\frac{1}{2}} + T_{i+1,j-\frac{1}{2}}\right) - (\Delta z)^2 S_{i,j}\right]$$

and is followed by the corrector:

$$A_i v_{i-1,j} - G_i v_{i,j} + B_i v_{i+1,j} = - F_i \tag{72}$$

where

$$A_i = 1 + \tfrac{1}{2}g_{i,j-\frac{1}{2}} \quad B_i = 1 - \tfrac{1}{2}g_{i,j-\frac{1}{2}}$$
$$G_i = 2 \left(1 + h_{i,j-\frac{1}{2}}\right) \tag{73}$$
$$F_i = A_i v_{i-1,j-1} - 2 \left(1 - h_{i,j-\frac{1}{2}}\right) + B_i v_{i+1,j-1} + 2f_{i,j}$$

To solve (70) and (72) we use the same formula (63) of the tridiagonal algorithm. It should be noticed that eqs. (70) and (72) are solved successively. First from predictor (70) we find $v_{i,j-\frac{1}{2}}$. Substituting these values into (73), we solve the corrector (72), finding $v_{i,j}$.

The values α_1 and β_1 have to be found from the boundary conditions at the surface (7). To satisfy (7) while computing $v_{i,j}$, we employ the logical scheme, presented in Fig. 16.2.

It should be noted that the values $v_{i,j-\frac{1}{2}}$ relate formally to the intermediate time step $t = t_{j-\frac{1}{2}}$, but they can be interpreted as the first approximation to the values of interest $v_{i,j}$. In this regard, the coefficients figuring in the boundary conditions (7) refer to the j-th moment of time in the predictor as well as in the corrector.

The bottom boundary condition (27) gives

$$v_{N,j-\frac{1}{2}} = v_{N,j} = \begin{cases} v_d < 1 & \text{for dry soil} \\ & \text{or} \\ 1 & \text{for saturated soil} \end{cases} \tag{74}$$

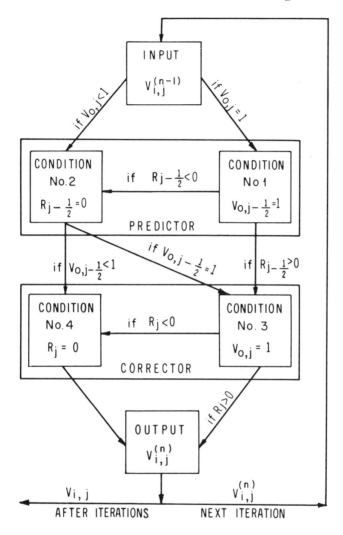

Figure 16.2   A scheme of the calculation of θ
satisfying the boundary condition at the surface.

One can see that an approximate satisfaction of (7) is achieved at the cost of either the predictor, or the corrector, or both the equations having to be solved twice. At worst, the number of computations is doubled.

The value $v_{i,j}$ obtained from the corrector is taken as the input value for the next iteration.

The iterations stop when

$$\max \left| v_{i,j}^{(n+1)} - v_{i,j}^{(n)} \right| < 10^{-3} \tag{75}$$

This criterion provides 1 percent accuracy for θ.

The values α_1 and β_1 corresponding to the conditions No. 1 and No. 3

follow from the last expression of (63) at $i = 1$, rewritten for $v_{i,j}$. We have $\alpha_1 = 0$, $\beta_1 = 1$. To obtain these parameters for the conditions No. 2 and No. 4 one must satisfy the moisture balance equation at the surface when the run-off is absent.

$$R = P_g - E_g + \rho \left(D_\theta \frac{\partial \theta}{\partial z} - K + D_T \frac{\partial T}{\partial z} \right)_{z=0} = 0 \qquad (76)$$

rewritten in the finite-difference form for the moments $t_{j-\frac{1}{2}}$ and t_j.

We carried out the following transformation with (76).

1. Introduced v instead of θ by (68).
2. Replaced the derivatives by the three-point finite-differences, like (64).

After that the procedure of obtaining α_1 and β_1 is exactly the same as in the case of the soil-temperature equation.

For the condition No. 2 we have

$$\alpha_1 = \frac{1 - h_{i,j-1}}{1 + m_{j-1}} \qquad \beta_1 = \frac{M_j + \frac{1}{2}F_1}{1 + m_{j-1}} \qquad (77)$$

where

$$\left.\begin{array}{l} m_j = \dfrac{(b_T + 3)\Delta z}{(-\psi_s)b_T} \cdot v^{\frac{b_T}{b_T+3}} \\[3mm] M_j = \dfrac{(b_T + 3)\Delta z}{(-\psi_s)b_T K_s \rho_w} \left(P_g - E_g - X \right)_j \\[3mm] X_j = \dfrac{\rho_w D_T}{2\Delta z} (3T_{o,j} - 4T_{i,j} + T_{2,j}) \end{array}\right\} \qquad (78)$$

For the condition No. 4 we have

$$\alpha_1 = \left(1 - h_{1,j-\frac{1}{2}} - g_{1,j-\frac{1}{2}}\right) \big/ \left(1 - g_{1,j-\frac{1}{2}} + B_1 m_{j-\frac{1}{2}}\right) \qquad (79)$$

$$\beta_1 = \left(B_1 M_j + \tfrac{1}{2}F_{1,j}\right) \big/ \left(1 - g_{1,j-\frac{1}{2}} + B_1 m_{j-\frac{1}{2}}\right) \qquad (80)$$

The expressions for the run-off are obtained in this way:

$$R_k = M_k - \frac{(b_T + 3)\Delta z}{(-\psi_s) b_T} - 1.5 + 2v_{1,k} - 0.5v_{2,k} \quad \left(k = j - \tfrac{1}{2}, j\right) \quad (81)$$

The constant dimensional factor in front of the expression for R_k is dropped. One must determine only the sign of this expression.

REFERENCES

Baver, L.D., W.M. Gardner, and W.R. Gardner. 1972. *Soil Physics*. John Wiley & Sons, New York.
Camillio, P.J., R.J. Gurney, and T.J. Schmugge. 1983. A soil and atmospheric boundary layer

model for evapotranspiration and soil moisture studies. *Water Resources Research* 19(2): 371–80.

Clapp, R.B., and G.M. Hornberger. 1978. Empirical equations for some soil hydraulic properties. *Water Resources Research* 14(4): 601–4.

Dane, J.H., and F.H. Mathis. 1981. An adaptive finite difference scheme for one-dimensional water flow equation. *Soil Sci. Soc. Am. J.* 45: 1048–1054.

Deardorff, J.W. 1978. Efficient prediction of ground surface temperature and moisture, with inclusion of a layer of vegetation. *Journal of Geophysical Research* 83(C4): 1889–1903.

Dickinson, R.E., J. Jager, W.M. Washington, and R. Wolski. 1981. Boundary subroutine for the NCAR Global Climate Model. *NCA Technical Note.*

Douglas, Jr., J., and B.F. Jones. 1963. On predictor-corrector methods for nonlinear parabolic differential equations. *J. Soc. Indust. Appl. Math.* 11(1): 195–204.

Farouki, O.T. 1981. Thermal properties of soils. CRREL Monograph 81–1. Cold Regions Research and Engineering Laboratory, Hanover, N.H.

Grove, W.E. 1966. Brief Numerical Methods. Prentice-Hall, Englewood Cliffs, N.J.

Haverkamp, R., M. Vauclin, J. Touma, P.J. Wierengas, and G. Vachaud. 1977. A comparison of numerical simulation models for one-dimensional infiltration. *Soil Sci. Soc. Am. J.* 4: 285–94.

Hildebrand, F.B. 1974. Introduction to Numerical Analysis. McGraw-Hill, N.Y.

Iskander, I.K. 1981. Modeling Waste Water Renovation. John Wiley & Sons, N.Y.

McCumber, M.C. 1980. A numerical simulation of the influence of heat and moisture fluxes upon mesoscale circulation. Report N.UVA-ENV SCI-MESO-1980-2 Department of Environmental Sciences, University of Virginia, Charlottesville.

Mintz, Y., P.J. Sellers, and C.J. Willmott. 1983. On the design of an interactive biosphere for the GLAS General Circulation Model. *NASA Technical Memorandum 84973.*

Molz, F.J. 1981. Models of water transport in the soil-plant system: A review. *Water Resources Research* 17(5): 1245–1260.

Nakshabandi, G.A. and H. Konke. 1965. Thermal conductivity and diffusivity of soils as related to moisture tension and other physical properties. *Agricultural Meteorology* 2: 271–79.

Philip, J.R. 1957. Evaporation and moisture and heat fields in the soil. *Journal of Meteorology* 14(Aug.): 354–66.

Remson, I., G.M. Hornberger, and F.J. Molz. 1971. Numerical Methods in Subsurface Hydrology. Wiley Interscience, N.Y.

Schieldge, J.P., A.B. Kahle, and R.E. Alley. 1982. A numerical simulation of soil temperature and moisture variations for a bare field. *Soil Science* 133(4): 197–207.

Sellers, W. 1965. *Physical Climatology.* University of Chicago Press, Chicago.

Sophocleous, M. 1979. Analysis of water and heat flow in unsaturated-saturated porous media. *Water Resources Research* 15(5): 1195–1206.

SEVENTEEN

Wind Erosion

LOUIS BERKOFSKY

ABSTRACT

One of the most difficult problems in soil science is that of determining the rate of soil erosion by wind. The subject is treated empirically by means of the Wind Erosion Equation.

In dealing with the prediction of atmospheric dust concentration by means of mathematical models, a knowledge of the lower boundary condition—the dust concentration in a thin layer near the ground—is needed. This concentration must be related to the erosion rate.

The erosion process consists of three phases: detachment, transportation, and deposition. In this paper, we formulate a simple erosion equation, on the basis of reasonable assumptions about the three phases of the erosion process. Solutions of simplified versions of this equation yield reasonable results. In practise, the nonlinear form of this equation would have to be solved interactively with the atmospheric model to yield ground concentration as a function of time and space.

INTRODUCTION

Erosion is the movement of soil or rock from one point to another by the action of the sea, running water, moving ice, precipitation, or wind. For movement of soil particulates to occur, a threshold level of energy is required. Similarly, a minimum energy level must be maintained to keep the particulates in motion. The erosion process consists of three phases: detachment, transportation, and deposition.

Studies to quantify erosion, i.e., to determine the minimum threshold energy, lead to the concept of a threshold velocity of soil movement. This is the velocity at which aerodynamic forces are sufficient to dislodge particles from the soil and initiate movement. A number of investigators have sought appropriate force balances which lead to threshold velocities. Punjrath and Heldman (1972) balanced shear forces and friction forces. Iversen et al. (1973, 1976) balanced particle weight, aerodynamic lift, drag, moment and interparticle forces. Ishihara and Iwagaki (1952) balanced aerodynamic lift with weight for small grains, and drag force with static frictional resistance for large grains. On the whole, the latter theory agrees well with data for simple monodisperse soils.

The problem of the exact balance of forces required to lift a grain of sand has not yet been solved. In this chapter, we consider the wind erosion problem as starting after a grain has been lifted.

The three modes of soil movement are saltation, surface creep (reptation), and suspension. Saltation is a bounding motion, possibly causing the breaking-up of grains which it strikes, thus leading to production of dust.

The grains in saltation receive their momentum directly from the pressure of the wind on them after they have risen into it. The grains in surface creep remain unaffected by the wind. They receive their momentum by impact from the saltation. Suspension occurs when the fall velocity of particles is smaller than that of the upward velocity of the air. A detailed discussion of these modes of movement is given in a classical book by Bagnold (1954).

In a desert, fine, suspended dust particles are produced by wind erosion. This will be our concern in this chapter. Figure 17.1 shows the relative size and rate of fall of small particles (after Bagnold 1954). It is seen that atmospheric dust particles are of the order $10^{-2} - 10^{-4}$mm ($0.1 - 1.0$ μm). Figure 17.2 shows the threshold friction velocity versus monodisperse particle size (after Chepil 1951). There is a minimum friction velocity that will produce motion in particles about 0.1mm in diameter. Particles larger than

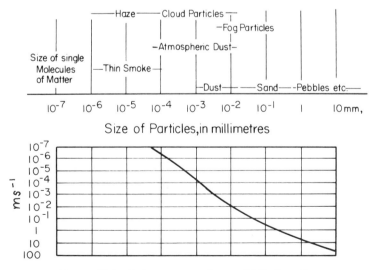

Figure 17.1   Relative size and rate of fall of small
particles (after Bagnold, 1954)

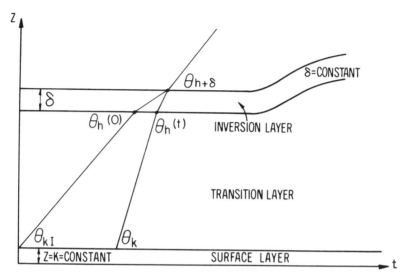

Figure 17.2 Schematic of planetary boundary layer

0.1mm require greater wind speed, presumably because of their greater weight. Smaller particles (atmospheric dust size) also require larger velocities. This results from the following considerations: The Reynolds number, which is the ratio of inertial forces to viscous forces, is given by

$$Re = \frac{D_s V_*}{\nu} \tag{1}$$

(Schlichting 1955), for the so-called laminar (or viscous) sub-layer, where D_s = the thickness of the laminar sub-layer, V_* is the friction velocity, and ν is the molecular kinematic viscosity of air. For purely laminar flow, Re < 5. Then, with $\nu = 0.014$ cm^2 s^{-1}

$$D_s \simeq .07 V_*^{-1} \text{ cm} \tag{2}$$

As the friction velocity increases, the depth of the laminar sub-layer decreases, so that particles will eventually begin to protrude into the more turbulent part of the flow. There they will be exposed to much greater disruptive forces, and these could lead to their removal. For a sufficiently high fixed airflow velocity, one would expect that the erosion rate would initially be high, falling with time towards zero. (Fletcher 1976). Equation (2) shows that the laminar sub-layer will have a thickness of .01 mm when $V_* = 70$ cm s^{-1}. Thus, in order to erode particles of .01mm, a friction velocity larger than 70 cm s^{-1} is required. Such a velocity will also erode larger particles, which, however, will not remain in suspension (see Figure 17.2).

Bagnold (1941) refers to

$$\frac{V_*d}{\nu} = 3.5 \tag{3}$$

where d is grain diameter, as the critical Reynolds number, which distinguishes the conditions under which a surface may be technically either "rough" or "smooth", i.e., (Re)$_{crit.}$ < 3.5 → smooth. Gillette (1982) finds from 74 observations that the erosion Reynolds number

$$\frac{V_*d}{\nu} > 1 \tag{4}$$

always, with a minimum of 1.44 and mode of 31.6. Soil textures ranged from fine clays to coarse gravels.

The problem of the prediction of soil erosion has so far defied analytical solution. Two methods for estimating soil erosion have predominated: the Universal Soil Loss Equation (USLE) and the Wind Erosion Equation (WEQ) (Larson, Pierce and Dowdy 1983). Both equations were empirically derived. In the WEQ, wind erosion is calculated as a function of five factors.

$$E = f(I, K, C, L, V) \tag{5}$$

where E is the potential annual soil loss, I is the soil erodibility, K is ridge roughness (surface roughness and configuration), C is climate (wind speed and duration), L is the field length (the unsheltered median travel distance of wind across a field parallel to the prevailing wind direction) and V is vegetative cover. This equation was designed to predict long-term (ten years or more) soil loss from fields under specific types of crop and soil management. Although erosion estimates obtained with this equation are point measurements, and thus are not exact, it does indicate where potential problems are likely to exist. Moreover, erosion is extremely variable in time. Most of the erosion of susceptible soil takes place during short intervals of high energy availability, and when the soil is not protected.

In formulating a meteorological model for prediction of dust concentration, an important boundary condition is the dust concentration in a thin layer near the ground. In this chapter, we shall attempt to formulate a simple time-dependent lower boundary condition for erosion of dust by wind. Before doing so, we shall describe briefly a simple dust prediction model from which it will become clear how the lower boundary condition enters.

THE DUST PREDICTION MODEL

We have formulated a model in which the planetary boundary layer is divided into a surface layer, a transition layer, and an inversion layer (see Figure 17.3). the surface layer is treated as a constant flux layer of constant depth k, in which the wind is approximated by

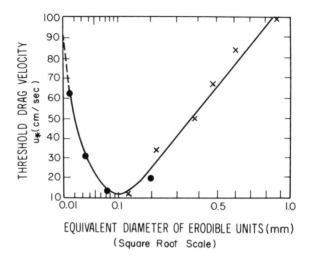

Figure 17.3   Threshhold friction velocity vs. monodisperse particle size
(after Chepil, 1951)

$$V = \frac{V_*}{k_1} \ln \left(\frac{z + z_o}{z_o} \right) \tag{6}$$

where V is wind speed, k_1 is Karman's constant = 0.4, and z_o is the surface roughness. V_* is the friction velocity.

In the transition layer, whose depth is h − k, where h is inversion height, the wind varies according to

$$\left. \begin{array}{l} u(x,y,z,t) = A(z) \; \hat{u}(x,y,t) \\ v(x,y,z,t) = B(z)\hat{v}(x,y,t) \end{array} \right\} \tag{7}$$

where

$$\left(\hat{} \right) = \frac{1}{(h - k)} \int_k^h (\quad) \, dz \tag{8}$$

The potential temperature is given by

$$\theta(x,y,z,t) = \theta_k(x,y,t) + \gamma(t) \, (z - k) \tag{9}$$

where θ is potential temperature, $\gamma(t)$ is the lapse rate $\frac{\partial \theta}{\partial z}$, and is considered to vary only with time. The dust concentration varies according to

$$C(x,y,z,t) = D(z) \, C_k \, (x,y,t) \tag{10}$$

We integrate the appropriate flow equations across the inversion layer of thickness δ. By letting $\delta \to 0$, we derive the interface conditions. These are then used to eliminate inversion height fluxes in the vertically averaged (transition layer) equations. We parameterize surface fluxes by

$$\left.\begin{array}{l}
\overline{(u'w')}_k = - c_d A(k)|V_k|\hat{u} \\
\overline{(v'w')}_k = - c_d B(k)|V_k|\hat{v} \\
\overline{(w'\theta')}_k = c_{Ho}|V_k|(\theta_{GR} - \theta_k) \\
\overline{(w'c')}_k = c_d|V_k|(C_{GR} - C_k)
\end{array}\right\} \quad (11)$$

where (u',v',w',θ',c') are convective scale parameters, c_d and c_{Ho} are transfer coefficients for momentum and heat, θ_{GR} is ground temperature, C_k is dust concentration at $z = k$, C_{GR} is dust concentration in a thin layer near the ground.

We use as closure equation

$$\overline{(w'\theta')}_h = - A_1 \overline{(w'\theta')}_k \quad (12)$$

where $A_1 = $ constant.

We are thus led to the following system of equations:

$$\frac{\partial \hat{u}}{\partial t} - f(\hat{v} - \hat{v}_g) + \left[1 - A(h + \delta)\right] \frac{\hat{u}}{(h - k)} \left(\frac{\partial h}{\partial t} - w_h\right) = - \frac{c_d|\hat{V}|\hat{u}}{(h - k)} \quad (13)$$

$$\frac{\partial \hat{v}}{\partial t} + f(\hat{u} - u_g) + \left[1 - B(h + \delta)\right] \frac{\hat{v}}{(h - k)} \left(\frac{\partial h}{\partial t} - w_h\right) = - \frac{c_d|\hat{V}|\hat{v}}{(h - k)} \quad (14)$$

$$\frac{\partial \theta_k}{\partial t} + \frac{(h - k)}{2} \frac{\partial r}{\partial t} + \frac{\gamma}{2}(w_h + w_k) = \frac{(F_k - F_h)}{\hat{\rho}c_p(h - k)} + \quad (15)$$

$$\frac{(1 + A_1)c_{Ho}|\hat{V}|\theta_{GR} - \theta_k)}{(h - k)}$$

$$\frac{\partial C_k}{\partial t} + \frac{C_k}{(h - k)} \left[\frac{\partial h}{\partial t} - \frac{(w_h + V_g)}{\hat{D}}\right] = \frac{C_d|V|(C_{GR} - C_k)}{\hat{D}(h - k)} \quad (16)$$

$$\left.\begin{array}{l}
\dfrac{\partial \theta_{GR}}{\partial t} = - \dfrac{2\pi^{\frac{1}{2}}}{\rho_s c_s d_1} H_A - \dfrac{2\pi}{\tau_1}(\theta_{GR} - \theta_2) \\[2mm]
H_A = \rho c_p c_{Ho} V_* (\theta_{GR} - \theta_k) - R_{netGR}
\end{array}\right\} \quad (17)$$

$$\frac{\partial h}{\partial t} = w_h - \frac{A_1 C_{Ho}|\hat{V}| (\theta_{GR} - \theta_k)}{\{(\theta_{kI} - \theta_k) + [\gamma(o) - \gamma][r(o) - r](h - k) + \gamma_{inv}(o)\delta\}} \quad (18)$$

In this version of the model, γ (t) is specified.

In this system, $\{A,B\} = 1$, $k \leqslant z \leqslant h$, the horizontal transport terms are absent, F_h, F_k are the fluxes of radiation at $z = h$, k respectively, ρ_s, c_{s}, are soil density, soil specific heat, $d_1 = (k_s\tau_1)^{\frac{1}{2}}$, $k_s = $ soil thermal diffusivity, $\tau_1 = $ period of 1 day, $\theta_2 = $ deep soil temperature, $V_g = $ sedimentation velocity of dust particles. A detailed derivation is given in Berkofsky (1983).

The important point to realize from this system is that the dust concentration C_k at $z = k$ (Eq. 16) depends strongly and inversely on the inversion height, and directly on the ground concentration C_{GR}. Figure 17.4 shows

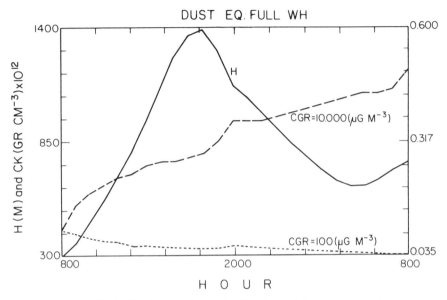

Figure 17.4   Evolution of inversion height and dust concentration

the results of a calculation using the system Equations (13)–(19) inclusively, in which $V_g = -0.1$ cm s^{-1}, corresponding to particles of radius 1 μm.

In that calculation, we assumed values for w_h which varied diurnally. We also assumed C_{GR} = constant = 0, 100, 1000 μg m^{-3}. Both the boundary layer height and the dust concentration evolutions seem realistic, i.e., as the inversion height rises with increased convective activity during the day, the dust concentration at $z = k$ decreases. Further, a large increase in C_{GR}, leading to a persistent upward-transport of dust, eventually increases C_k.

The ground concentration C_{GR} is the quantity related to wind erosion.

In what follows, we derive a simple time-dependent ground concentration equation.

THE EROSION EQUATION

The erosion process consists of three phases: detachment, transportation, and deposition. At the same time that these processes are taking place, there may also exist a source to replenish, at least in part, any losses. The detachment process is what is referred to by aerosol scientists as the resuspension process.

Thus

$$\frac{\partial C_{GR}}{\partial t} \sim \text{Transport} + \text{deposition} + \text{source} - \text{detachment (resuspension)} \quad (19)$$

We parameterize these processes in the following way.

Detachment

We have discussed the laminar boundary layer. The classical picture of the turbulent boundary layer is one in which a region of high shear, which has the characteristics of viscous laminar flow, exists close to the wall. This would imply, for a non-neutral layer, that the Richardson number

$$Ri = \frac{g}{\theta} \frac{\frac{\partial \theta}{\partial z}}{\left(\frac{\partial u}{\partial z}\right)^2} \tag{20}$$

is small, indicative of instability.

We assume that, when detachment takes place, i.e. when V_* is large enough to move 1μm particles, these particles are lifted to a height $z > D_s$ into a region of turbulence and instability. The dust concentration near the ground, $(C_{GR})_{z0}$, thus decreases. We postulate that the rate at which $(C_{GR})_{z0}$ is removed is proportional to the wind shear at $z = zo$:

$$\left(\frac{\partial C_{GR}}{\partial t}\right)_{Det} = - C_d \left(\frac{\partial V}{\partial z}\right)_{z0} (C_{GR})_{Det} \tag{21}$$

where the subscript Det means detachment. Using Equation (6) for aerodynamically rough flow,

$$\left(\frac{\partial C_{GR}}{\partial t}\right)_{Det} = - \frac{C_d V_*}{2k_1 z_0} (C_{GR})_{Det} \qquad Rough \tag{22}$$

Since we are out of the laminar sub-layer. $(C_{GR})_{Det}$ represents the concentration in a thin layer $> D_s$ above the ground: Equation (22) shows that a large value of V_* (corresponding to small particles according to Figure 17.2) would correspond to a large detachment rate.

From Equation (6), we see that the height at which Equation (22) applies, i.e., where $V = V_*$, is

$$z_* = 49z_0 \tag{23}$$

When the flow is aerodynamically smooth,

$$V = \frac{V_*}{k_1} \ln \frac{V_* z}{\nu} + 5.5 \qquad z \gg \frac{\nu}{V_*} \tag{24}$$

$$\left(\frac{\partial V}{\partial z}\right)_{z \sim 0} = \frac{V_*^2}{\nu} \tag{25}$$

so that

$$\left(\frac{\partial C_{GR}}{\partial t}\right)_{Det} = - \frac{c_d V_*^2}{\nu} (C_{GR})_{Det} \qquad Smooth \tag{26}$$

The height at which Equation (26) applies, for $\nu = .014 \ cm^2 s^{-1}$, is

$$z_* \approx \frac{.0023}{V_*} \text{ cm,} \tag{27}$$

which is well within the laminar sub-layer.

Transportation

The horizontal transport has the form, for rough flow,

$$\left(\frac{\partial C_{GR}}{\partial t}\right)_T = - V_{z_0} \cdot (\nabla C_{GR})_T \qquad Rough \text{ (28)}$$

where $|V_{z_0}| = \dfrac{|V_*|\ln 2}{k_1}$, the subscript T means transportation, and ∇ is the vector gradient operation.

For smooth flow,

$$\left(\frac{\partial C_{GR}}{\partial t}\right)_T = - V_{z_*} \cdot \nabla (C_{GR})_T \qquad Smooth \text{ (29)}$$

Deposition

We write

$$\text{Deposition flux} = - V_d C_{GR}, \; V_d > 0 \tag{30}$$

The deposition velocity V_d includes the gravitational settling velocity V_g. The question of the determination of V_d, especially for particles which adhere to leaves (the acid rain problem) is still under intensive investigation (Slinn 1982). Due to the uncertainty involved, we shall simply replace V_d, by V_g in the case of dust.

Thus

$$\left(\frac{\partial C_{GR}}{\partial t}\right)_{Dep} = - \frac{V_g C_{GR}}{(k - z_0)} \qquad Rough \text{ (31)}$$

$$\left(\frac{\partial C_{GR}}{\partial t}\right)_{Dep} = - \frac{V_g C_{GR}}{(k - z_*)} \qquad Smooth \text{ (32)}$$

Source

When the friction velocity is such that small particles are lifted, it will be large enough to lift larger particles, thus initiating saltation. During the saltation process, new dust is produced, some of which is probably deposited immediately and becomes available for detachment (resuspension). We assume that the saltation process produces dust at a rate proportional to that removed by detachment, but opposite in sign.

$$\left(\frac{\partial C_{GR}}{\partial t}\right)_{source} = \frac{\alpha c_d V_*}{2k_1 z_0}(C_{GR})_{Det} \qquad\qquad Rough \text{ (33)}$$

$$\left(\frac{\partial C_{GR}}{\partial t}\right)_{source} = \frac{\alpha c_d V_*^2}{v}(C_{GR})_{Det} \qquad\qquad Smooth \text{ (34)}$$

Here $0 \leqslant \alpha \leqslant 1$.

TOTAL EROSION FLOW

For the total erosion flow, we sum Equations (22), (28), (31), (33) for rough flow and Equations (26), (29), (32), (34) for smooth flow, to obtain

$$\frac{\partial C_{GR}}{\partial t} + \underbrace{\frac{\ln 2}{k_1}V_* \cdot \nabla C_{GR}}_{} + \left[\underbrace{\frac{(1-\alpha)C_d V_*}{2k_1 z_0}}_{} + \frac{V_g}{(k-z_0)}\right]C_{GR} = 0 \quad Rough \text{ (35)}$$

transport   Detachment plus source   deposition

$$\frac{\partial C_{GR}}{\partial t} + \mathbf{V} \cdot \nabla C_{-GR} + \left[\frac{(1-\alpha)C_d V_*^2}{v} + \frac{V_g}{(k-z_*)}\right]C_{GR} = 0 \quad Smooth \text{ (36)}$$

Here, $\mathbf{V}$ is the appropriate vector form of Equation (24).

These equations should be solved numerically, but we first look at some special cases. We will need to know α, to which we will assign a series of values, from $\alpha = 0$ (no replenishment from saltation) to $\alpha = 1$ (replenishment from saltation exactly balances detachment).

Case 1—Detachment Only

$$\frac{\partial C_{GR}}{\partial t} = -\frac{c_d V_*}{2k_1 z_0} C_{GR} \qquad\qquad Rough \text{ (37)}$$

If V_* is independent of t.

$$C_{GR} = (C_{GR})_{t=0}e^{-\left(\frac{c_d V_*}{2k_1 z_0}\right)t} \qquad\qquad (38)$$

For $V_* = 100 \text{ cm s}^{-1}$, $c_d = .002$, $k_1 = 0,4$, $z_0 = 100 \text{cm}$,

$$C_{GR} = (C_{GR})_{t=0}e^{-.0025t} \qquad\qquad (39)$$

Thus C_{GR} will reduce to $1/e$ of its initial value in 400 seconds. This result agrees well with wind tunnel studies of erosion by Fletcher (1976).

The above result indicates a rapid depletion of ground concentration at a point once detachment is initiated. It is likely that horizontal transport, deposition, and production through saltation act to replenish C_{GR}.

For smooth flow, we have

$$C_{GR} = (C_{GR})_{t=0}e^{-\left(\frac{c_d V_*^2}{v}\right)t} \qquad \text{Smooth (40)}$$

Since V_* must be of the order 100 cm s^{-1} for detachment from the laminar sub-layer, erosion from this source is extremely rapid, reaching $1/e$ of its initial value in only 7×10^{-4}s. This result is also in agreement with the wind tunnel findings of Fletcher (1976).

Case 2—Detachment and Source

$$\frac{\partial C_{GR}}{\partial t} = \frac{(\alpha - 1) c_d V_*}{2k_1 z_0} C_{GR} \qquad \text{Rough (41)}$$

$$C_{GR} = (C_{GR})_{t=0}e^{\left[(a-1)\frac{c_d V_*}{2k_1 z_0}\right]t} \qquad (42)$$

The following table gives the time, T, it takes for C_{GR} to be reduced to $1/e$ of its initial value for a number of values of α:

α	T(s)
0.0	400
0.2	500
0.4	667
0.6	1,000
0.8	2,000
1.0	no reduction

These results show that as the amount of dust is replenished through saltation only, a longer time elapses until the initial value of C_{GR} reaches $1/e$ of its initial value.

The results for smooth flow are similar.

Case 3—Detachment, Deposition and Source

$$\frac{\partial C_{GR}}{\partial t} = \left[(\alpha - 1)\frac{c_d V_*}{2k_1 z_0} - \frac{V_g}{(k - z_0)}\right] C_{GR} \qquad \text{Rough (43)}$$

$$C_{GR} = (C_{GR})_{t=0}e^{\left[(a-1)\frac{c_d V_*}{2k_1 z_0} - \frac{V_g}{k - z_0}\right]t} \qquad (44)$$

We use $k = 10$ m.

The following table gives the time (T) it takes for C_{GR} to be reduced to $1/e$ of its initial value.

α	$T(s)$
0.0	417
0.2	527
0.4	714
0.6	1,111
0.8	2,500
1.0	10,000

It is seen that continuous deposition ($V_g < 0$) greatly increases the time needed for C_{GR} to be reduced to $1/e$ of its initial value. The results for the smooth case are similar.

Case 4—Possible Solutions Including Transport, Detachment, Deposition and Source

We consider the one-dimensional linearized form of Equation (34):

$$\frac{\partial C_{GR}}{\partial t} + U\frac{\partial C_{GR}}{\partial x} + AC_{GR} = 0 \tag{45}$$

Here

$$\left. \begin{array}{l} U = \dfrac{\ln 2}{k_1}u_* \\[3mm] A = \left[\dfrac{(1-\alpha)c_d U_*}{2k_1 z_0} + \dfrac{V_g}{(k-z_0)}\right] \end{array} \right\} \tag{46}$$

A solution of Equation (45) is

$$C_{GR}(x_1 t) = (C_{GR})_{t=0}e^{-At}\,f(x - Ut) \tag{47}$$

Equation (47) represents a damped wave moving in the positive x-direction with speed U.

Table 17.3 gives some values of A for various α.

α	$A(s^{-1})$
0.0	.0024
0.2	.0019
0.4	.0014
0.6	.0009
0.8	.0004
0.96	.0000
1.0	$-.0001$

Thus, for $\alpha = 0.0, 0.2, 0.4$ (the saltation source replenishes 0.0, 0.2, 0.4 of the dust removal by detachment), the traveling wave continuously damps with time. When $\alpha = 0.6$, it moves without change of shape. When $\alpha = 0.8, 1.0$ (the saltation source replenishes 0.8 and 1.0 of the dust removal by detachment), the traveling dust wave actually grows with time.

Similar results are obtained for the smooth case.

In actual practise, the erosion Equations (35) and (36) must be used interactively with a complete nonlinear system, for example Equations (13)–(19) inclusive (although horizontal transport is absent in those). Then, from predictions of u and v and the continuity condition of u and v at $z = k$, we can determine V_* as a function of u_k, v_k. This then enables us to determine which size dust particles are erodible, and a dust concentration equation for each size particle is solved. The solution of Equations (35) and (36) at each time step are then used on the right hand side of Equation (16).

CONCLUSION

The problem of dust erosion by wind is extremely complicated, depending on many factors. It has so far not been amenable to analytical treatment. We have formulated what is clearly a very simplified approach to this problem. The method will be subjected to testing with the model herein described.

As noted earlier, most erosion of susceptible soils takes place during short intervals of high energy availability. This suggests that the detachment should probably be treated as a stochastic forcing function whose time scale is much less than that of the flow in which it is imbedded.

REFERENCES

Bagnold, R.A. 1954. *The Physics of Blown Sand and Desert Dunes*. Methuen, London.

Berkofsky, L. 1982. A heuristic investigation to evaluate the feasibility of developing a desert dust prediction model *Monthly Weather Review* 110:2055–2062.

———. 1983. *The Behavior of the Atmosphere in the Desert Planetary Boundary Layer*. Final scientific report to European Office of Aerospace Research and Development, U.S. Air Force, under grant no. AFOSR 0 285.

Chepil, W.S. 1951. Properties of soil which influence wind erosion, 4, State of dry aggregate soil structure. *Soil Science* 2:387–401.

Fletcher, B., 1976. The erosion of dust by an airflow. *J Phys. D.: Appl. Phys.* 913–24.

Gillette, D. 1982. Threshold velocities for wind erosion on natural terrestrial arid surfaces (a summary). Report presented at the Fourth International Conference on Precipitation Scavenging, Dry Deposition and Resuspension, 1982.

Ishihara, T. and Y. Iwagaki. 1952. On the effect of sand storm in controlling the mouth of the Kiku River. Disaster Prevention Research Institute. *Kyoto University Bulletin* 2.

Iversen, J.D., D. Greeley, J.B. Pollack, and B.R. White. 1973. Simulation of Martian eolian phenomena in the atmospheric wind tunnel. In *Proceedings of the AIAA/NASA/ASTM/IES 7th Space Simulation Conference. NASA SP-336. 191–213*.

Iversen, J.D., J.B. Pollack, R. Greeley, and D.R. White. 1976. Saltation threshold on Mars: The effect of interparticle force, surface roughness and low atmospheric density. *Icarus* 29: 381–93.

Larson, W.E., F.J. Pierce and R.H. Dowd. 1983. The threat of soil erosion to long-term crop production. *Science* 219: 458–65.

Punjrath, J.S. and D.G. Heldman. 1972. Mechanisms of small particle re-entrainment from flat surfaces. *Journal of Aerosol Science* 3: 429–40.

Schlichting, H. 1955. *Boundary Layer Theory*. Pergamon Press, London.

Slinn, W.G.N. 1982. Predictions for particle deposition to vegetative canopies. *Atm. Env.* 16: 1785–1785.

PART V

DESERT METEOROLOGY
AND CLIMATE

EIGHTEEN

Effect of the El Chichon Volcanic Dust Cloud on Solar Radiation at Sede Boqer, Israel

ABRAHAM ZANGVIL AND ORAN EINHORN AVIV

ABSTRACT

The dust cloud created by the eruption of the El Chichon volcano in 1982 caused marked effects on solar radiation measured at ground stations in different parts of the world. Measurements of solar radiation at Sede Boqer in Israel revealed considerable changes in the direct and diffuse solar irradiance on clear days beginning in September 1982. The direct beam irradiance showed a consistent decrease of about 10 percent compared to clear day values of the previous year. The diffuse irradiance data showed an increase of about 50 percent. The prominent effects were observed from fall 1982 to spring 1983. Weak effects were still noticeable in the winter of 1983–84 although a tendency back toward "normal" has been evident since then.

The data for the beginning of 1985 shows the beam irradiance to be only 3.3 percent lower than values prior to September 1982, while the diffuse irradiance now reaches values similar to those before September 1982.

INTRODUCTION

On March 28 and April 4, 1982, after being inactive for 600 years, the El Chichon volcano in southern Mexico exploded, blowing off 200m of its cone, and injecting large amounts of ash and sulphur dioxide into the stratosphere. The massive cloud produced by El Chichon was probably 20 times greater than that produced by Mt. St. Helens, and reached a height of more than 30 km.

As a result of strong easterly statospheric winds, the debris from the eruption was carried around the globe in 3 weeks, thus forming a band of debris between 0°N and 30°N. This dust cloud drew the attention of many earth scientists around the world (e.g., Robock 1983; Toon 1982).

In the past, changes of solar radiation due to volcanic dust have been reported (e.g., Viebrock and Flowers 1968). Following the El Chichon eruption, considerable changes in solar radiation have been observed: Spencer and Stewart (1983) reported changes in the radiation in New York in August 1982. Rao and Bradley (1983) noted a drop in the direct beam irradiance and an increase of the diffuse irradiance on clear days in Corvalis, Oregon during November 1982. A similar effect beginning in November 1982 was reported for Fairbanks, Alaska, by Wendler (1984). Hoecker et al. (1985) analyzed variations in the direct beam irradiance attributed to the El Chichon eruption at several other stations in the United States.

In September 1982 a marked decrease in the near noon clear day direct beam irradiance was noticed at Sede Boqer: from about $935 Wm^{-2}$ in the previous several months to about $860 Wm^{-2}$ in September through December (Zangvil and Aviv 1985). This decrease of beam irradiance was accompanied by an increase of the diffuse radiation and also by unusually beautiful reddish sunsets during the fall months of 1982.

So far, to the authors' knowledge, no other accounts on variations in solar radiation due to this dust cloud in Europe or the Mediterranean have been reported. Furthermore the papers mentioned earlier dealt mainly with the initial phase of the dust cloud effect on solar irradiance at the surface. Now, more than three years after the eruption, we feel that it is possible to present a more complete description of the detection of the El Chichon dust cloud effect on solar irradiance at Sede Boqer and also discuss the evolution and the final phases of this phenomenon.

INSTRUMENTATION AND DATA

The solar radiation observatory at Sede Boqer (30°51″N, 34°47″E, 480m above M.S.L.) includes three instruments:

1. An Eppley normal incidence pyrheliometer (NIP) mounted on a solar tracker which measures the direct component of solar radiation.

2. An Eppley precision spectral pyranometer (PSP) which measures the total downward irradiance, or global radiation, in the wavelength band 0.285–2.8μm.

3. An additional PSP equipped with a shade band for measuring diffuse sky and cloud radiation. The data of the diffuse irradiance used subsequently are not corrected for the shade band effect.

A high percentage of data (more than 95 percent) has been retrieved from August 1981. For the period May to July 1981 only about 60 percent of the data are available. All the instruments were calibrated periodically.

Sede Boqer is located in the Negev desert 45 km south of Beer Sheva, the nearest urban center (population about 130,000). The observatory is free from industrial pollution and is therefore ideally located for solar radiation measurements. But since this region lies within the northern margins of the Sahara-Arabian deserts, considerable amounts of dust are raised into the atmosphere by the local winds throughout the year. This is in addition to regional dust storms associated with synoptic systems. This dust makes detecting an effect of the El Chichon dust cloud on the solar irradiance in the Negev more difficult.

Following Zangvil and Aviv (1985), it was decided not to include all the clear days in the analysis (as was done by Rao and Bradley 1983 and by Wendler 1984), but rather to select only the clearest days (usually one or two per month). On these days we expect to find a "window" through the lower tropospheric haze which facilitates the detection of the effect caused by the overlying stratospheric dust. It is assumed that this dust, after being in the stratosphere for several months, has already spread and dispersed in such a way that time and space scales associated with it are much larger than those of tropospheric dust and haze.

For each month, beginning May 1981, the clear days were inspected and the days with the highest average transmissivity (T) between the hours of 11:00 and 13:00 Local Solar Time were selected. The transmissivity is defined as the ratio between the surface measured direct beam irradiance (B) and the extra-terrestrial solar irradiance (B_o). Variations of B_o due to earth-sun distance are taken into consideration. For these days and hours, the average diffuse irradiance (D) and global irradiance (G) were also recorded.

RESULTS AND DISCUSSION

Figure 18.1 shows a time sequence of the clear days' direct beam and diffuse irradiance selected as described above. Prior to September 1982, a rather regular annual variation of B and D is evident. The behavior of B is characterized by a late winter maximum and a summer minimum, while D has an early winter minimum and a summer maximum. The latter character-istic is attributed to the increased turbidity in the summer over our region and the small zenith angle.

As can be easily seen, a marked decrease in B and an increase in D occurred between August and September 1982. The low values of B prevailed throughout 1983 although with a slight upward trend. The values for the first three months of 1984 are atill low but towards the end of 1984 and beginning of 1985 a tendency of returning to the values of 1982 is observed. The low values of B at the end of 1982 and the beginning of 1983 are accompanied by high values of D, about 50 percent higher than the 1981–82 values. In winter 1983–84 values of D are lower than in winter 1982–83 but still higher than in winter 1981–82. Summer 1984 marks the end of the detectable effect on the diffuse radiation. (See also Table 18.1).

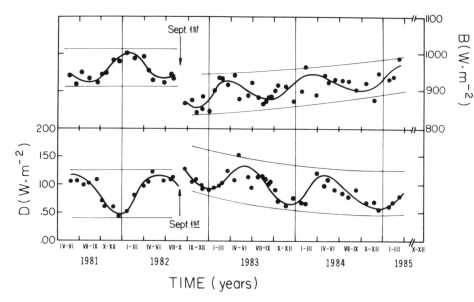

Figure 18.1   Time sequence of the direct beam irradiance (B) and the diffuse
irradiance (D) at Sede Boqer.

A plot of the global irradiance (G) data (not shown) indicates a remarkably regular annual pattern throughout the entire period of our analysis with a minimum of about 570Wm^{-2} occurring in winter, and a maximum of about 1000Wm^{-2} in summer. A closer examination of the data revealed a very light effect of decrease of G during the year following August 1982. The fact that almost no effect was detected in the global radiation is interesting although not entirely surprising. Spencer and Stewart (1983) also reported no change in the global radiation in New York. On the other hand, Rao and Bradley (1983) and Wendler (1984) reported a small decrease in the global irradiance in November 1982. The apparent discrepancy between these measurements and ours can be explained by the fact that in our case both the decrease in beam irradiance and the increase in diffuse irradiance were small compared to their observations.

The time sequence of the clear days' transmissivity (T) is shown in Figure 18.2. In using T we eliminate the large seasonal variations in B (See Figure 18.1) caused by variations in earth-sun distance. Prior to September 1982 the average value of T was about 0.71. A dramatic decrease in T took place between August and September 1982 and continued till the end of 1982. In 1983 the values of T began to increase gradually and by spring 1985 T is approaching the values recorded prior to September 1982.

In Table 18.1 we present the results of comparison between means of four months prior to and after the El Chichon effect was detected.

From Table 18.1 it is evident that the influence of the dust cloud on solar radiation from summer 1984 on, is still detectable in the beam and transmis-

Table 18.1 Comparison of Radiation Data Between Groups of Four Months Prior to September 1982 and after September 1982

DIRECT IRRADIANCE (Wm^{-2})

	Jan.–Apr.				May–Aug.				Sept.–Dec.			
	X	%	σ	N	X	%	σ	N	X	%	σ	N
81	—	—	—	—	937.5		14.6	4	956.6		25.4	5
82	985.0		20.1	4	934.1		9.0	4	862.0	−9.9	17.1	6
83	927.1	−5.9	16.3	5	885.8	−5.3	19.9	6	895.5	−6.4	17.5	6
84	923.1	−6.3	35.0	4	924.8	−1.2	4.1	4	912.3	−4.6	25.6	4
85	952.2	−3.3	31.3	3								

TRANSMISSIVITY

81	—	—	—	—	.714		.011	4	.699		.008	5
82	.721		.009	4	.709		.009	4	.627	−10.3	.017	6
83	.677	−6.1	.019	5	.673	−5.4	.019	6	.658	−5.9	.016	6
84	.675	−6.3	.030	4	.702	−1.3	.006	4	.656	−6.1	.021	4
85	.688	−4.6	.029	3								

DIFFUSE IRRADIANCE (Wm^{-2})

81					103.2		4.5	4	69.5		24.2	5
82	83.6		23.6	4	113.3		6.5	4	104.4	+50.2	13.7	6
83	105.9	+26.7	11.3	5	117.0	+8.1	18.8	6	85.2	+22.6	17.9	6
84	88.5	+5.9	25.9	4	90.8	−16.1	13.5	4	71.4	+2.7	12.7	4
85	70.1	−16.1	8.9	3								

Note: % indicates percentage increase or decrease compared to the data prior to September 1982; σ is the standard deviation; N indicates the number of data.

sivity data, but not in the diffuse irradiance data. This is, as least partly, because the ratio between the standard deviation of the diffuse irradiance to the diffuse irradiance itself is much higher than in the case of beam and transmissivity data.

From the data presented we may assume that the remarkable decrease in direct beam irradiance accompanied by an increase in the diffuse irradiance in September 1982 was caused by the El Chichon dust cloud. The time when the phenomenon was first observed at Sede Boqer is in good agreement with other reported observations of the El Chichon dust cloud. According to the SEAN Bulletin (1982), prior to fall 1982 the dust cloud was confined to latitudes south of 35°N and started to spread northward in fall 1982. The only measurement in our region (to our knowledge) is reported by D'Altorio and Visconti (1983). They observed the stratospheric dust cloud as early as July and August 1982 at a latitude farther north than ours (42°N, 13°E) by lidar. Yet Barth et al. (1982), utilizing the SME 6.3 μm radiance, show that on August 8, 1982, the bulk of the zonally averaged dust cloud was still

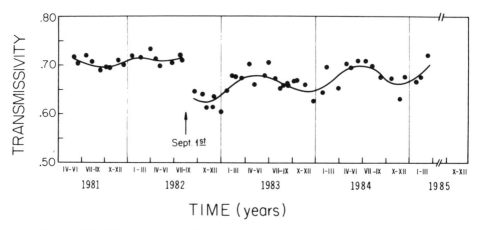

Figure 18.2   Time variation of the transmissivity at Sede Boqer. The arrow is pointing at the remarkable drop in T that had occurred from August to September 1982.

confined within the latitude belt from 30°N to the equator. This is in accord with our observations.

The effect during summer 1984 is still detectable in the beam data but not in the diffuse irradiance data. Toward the end of our observations (March 1985) the beam and diffuse irradiances are returning to values similar to those prior to September 1982 (the beam irradiance is only 3.3 percent lower than "normal" values). This is in accordance with some predictions of the residence time of two to three years of the stratospheric dust cloud pointed out by Robock (1983). We thus conclude that the El Chichon detectable effect on surface solar radiation measurements at Sede Boqer has reached its final phase.

REFERENCES

Barth, C. A., R. N. Sanders, and G. E. Thomas. 1982. Solar mesospheric Explorer measurements of the El Chichon volcanic cloud. *American Meteoroligical Society Bulletin* 63: 1314.

D'Altorio, A., and G. Visconti. 1983. Lidar observations of dust layers' transience in the stratosphere following the El Chichon volcanic eruption. *Geophysical Research Letters* 10: 27–30.

Hoecker, W. H., E. C. Flowers, and G. F. Cotton. 1985. Variation of direct beam solar radiation in the United States due to the El Chichon debris cloud. *American Meteorological Society Bulletin* 66: 14–19.

Rao, C. R. N., and W. A. Bradley. 1983. Effects of the El Chichon volcanic dust cloud on insolation measurements at Corvalis, Oregon (U.S.A.). *Geophysical Research Letters* 10: 389–391.

Robock, A. 1983. The dust cloud of the century. *Nature* 301: 373–374.

Scientific Event Alert Network (SEAN) Bulletin 7, No. 10. 1982. Available from the National Museum of Natural History, Mail Stop 129, Washington, DC 20560.

Toon, O. B. 1982. An overview of the effects of volcanic eruptions on climate. (abstract). *Eos Trans. Amer. Geophys. Union* 63: 901.

Spencer, D. W., and R. Stewart. 1983. Clear atmospheric measurements SEMRTS Region II. *ASRC Publ.* 967. Atmospheric Sciences.

Viebrock, H. J., and E. C. Flowers. 1968. Comments on the recent decrease of solar radiation at the South Pole. *Tellus* 20: 400–411.

Wendler, Gerd. 1984. Effects on the El Chichon volcanic cloud on solar radiation received at Fairbanks, Alaska. *American Meteorological Society Bulletin* 65: 216–218.

Zangvil, A., and O. E. Aviv. 1985. Time variation in solar radiation in the Negev, Israel and its possible relation to the El Chichon volcanic dust cloud. *Journal of Climatology* 5: 363–367.

NINETEEN

A Paleoclimatic Model to Explain Depositional Environments during Late Pleistocene in the Negev

ARIE ISSAR, CHAIM TSOAR, ISAAC GILEAD,
ABRAHAM ZANGVIL

ABSTRACT

The shift from sand to loess deposition and vice versa in the western Negev, Israel, is explained by the south and north shift of the climatic belts during the glacial and interglacial periods, respectively. The southward shift of the subtropical arid belt caused aridity over the Nile catchment basin during the last glacial period, this diminished the supply of sand, but at the same time was connected with the southward migration of the Westerlies belt which brought dust-laden rainstorms to southern Israel over the Libyan Desert, and this caused the deposition of loess.

This model explains also the high anomaly of sulfates in the paleo-water of Sinai and Negev and the special ^{18}O, ^{2}H composition of this water.

1. INTRODUCTION

In a paper by Issar and Bruins (1983) it was suggested that special climatic conditions prevailed during the late Pleistocene in Sinai (Egypt) and Negev (Israel) deserts. During this period, which coincided with the last glacial period (ca 80,000 to 10,000 years BP), most of the rainstorms entered the area from the west and southwest and not from the north and northwest, as is now the case. Due to this special trajectory, these storms were rich in dust, blown from the desert, that was deposited by the ensuing rainstorms all over the Sinai and Negev as pluvio-aeolian sediments. Higher rates of precipitation also caused the formation of Lake Lisan, the precursor of the Dead Sea (Begin et al. 1974) as well as the spread of marshes in the Sinai and Negev (Issar and Eckstein 1969).

These special climatic conditions were explained as a function of the advection of polar air over Europe and the northern Mediterranean. This high caused a southward deflection of the storms approaching the Levant. This deflection caused the storms to enter the continent over Libya.

Other phenomena which were observed in the Negev area and which occurred during the upper Pleistocene, brought the further development of this model and the inclusion of additional phenomena which are described in detail in the following chapters.

SPECIAL DEPOSITIONAL ENVIRONMENTS CHARACTERIZING THE UPPERMOST PLEISTOCENE IN THE NEGEV

This chapter will include a short survey of the various deposits of uppermost Pleistoncene age which occur in the Negev, and their peculiarities will be described. This allows their emplacement in the general model, which will be described in a flow-chart.

The Loess Deposits

The special characteristics differentiating the loess deposits from the other layers deposited during the Pleistocene in the Negev have been discussed by Issar and Bruins (1983). It was shown that they differ also from the present-day dust deposits in their relatively higher clay content. They resemble, however, the composition of present-day dust when it is deposited by rainstorms.

Another important aspect is the salt content of ancient and recent loess deposits as traced in a study of the chemical composition of rain and flood water in the Negev (Levin et al. 1980; Nativ et al. 1983). In these studies, especially in the latter, it has been demonstrated that more salts enter the desert today as aerosols with the rain compared to salts flushed out by floods. This helps the understanding of the formation of a saline topsoil layer in contemporary soil in the Negev. The more ancient loess deposits in the same area show deep calcic gypsum layers without the accumulation of salts at the ancient land surfaces.

An additional difference between contemporary and paleo-loess layers is the deposition versus erosion rates; while the deposition-erosion ratio of paleo-loess layers was positive, contemporary ratios are negative.

This last observation falls within another set of observations that emphasize the difference in depositional environments between the present and upper Pleistocene. It concerns the existence of pluvio-aeolian patches covering the lower part of hill slopes in the Negev highlands. These patches are remnants of an apron of loess deposition that covered the lower parts of the hill slopes and have been eroded since the Holocene to form pseudo-alluvial-fan forms.

Sulfate Anomaly

The loess layers in the highlands of the Negev were found to be character-ized by deep (1.5m–2m) calcic and gypsic horizons. In the area of Beer Sheva these layers were found to be highly enriched with sulfates at a depth of more that one meter. In the same region veins of gypsum were found to penetrate the fractures of the chalks underlying the loess. In the area of Nizana (see figure 19.1) gypsum layers are found that underlie the loess and penetrate into the chalk fractures. We explain the formation of these gypsum layers by leaching processes from the loess layers, which were primarily enriched by sulfate salts. Another high anomaly of sulfates is observed in the paleo-water found in the Nubian-Sandstone aquifers (mainly Kurnub Group, Lower Cretaceous) in the Sinai and Negev (Issar et al. 1972; Gat and Issar 1974). This anomaly is demonstrated in the diagram, representing the sulfate to TDS ratio of the various types of water in Israel, Sinai, and the western desert (see figure 19.2).

Nativ et al. (1983) studied the import/export ratios of rainborne salts under contemporary conditions. The results show that in the majority of cases the composition of the salts is $NaCl$-$CaCO_3$, and in only a few cases the rainstorms contain $CaSo_4$ as the major salt.

It has been found lately that the rainstorms rich in $CaSO_4$ have mainly continental trajectories (Nativ et al. 1985) i.e., are of a west-southwest origin

Aeolian Sands of the Negev and Northern Sinai

Two main groups of active sand dunes are known in Israel and northern Sinai. One composes the inland sand dunes covering the coastal plain of northern Sinai between the Suez Canal in the west, and the northwestern Negev, in the east. The other, a distinct group of active coastal sand dunes, extends parallel to the shoreline, from the eastern part of the Bardawil lagoon in northern Sinai to Tel Aviv, and also in some isolated areas north of Tel Aviv to Haifa Bay. The inland dunes are stabilized toward the north, where they underwent pedogenic development and were covered by coastal dunes (see figure 19.3).

The source of all the aeolian sand, quartziferous in its composition, should be beach sand derived from the Nile River delta by longshore currents (Goldsmith and Golik 1980).

It is very clear from field observations that coastal sand dunes are younger than inland ones. There are some indications of ancient and defunct drainage channels in inland dune areas blocked and covered by coastal sand dunes. The color of the sand in northern Sinai becomes progressively redder the

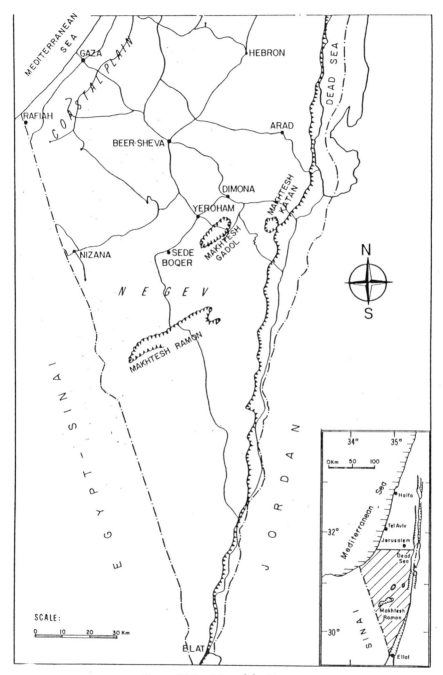

Figure 19.1   Map of the Negev

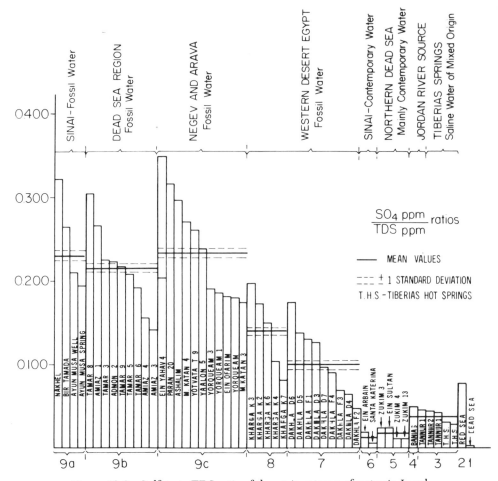

Figure 19.2   Sulfate to TDS ratio of the various types of water in Israel

further inland it is found (Tsoar 1976). Studies of red-color dune sand from other deserts show that sand is reddened by increased age and greater distance of transport (Norris 1969).

Absolute age is ascertainable by archaeological finds. In the Shunera sand dunes of the Negev (see figure 19.3) there is some evidence for attributing upper Paleololthic and Epipaleolithic ages to determine fixed sands (Morris 1985). The surface of the fixed sand dunes of inland dunes found north of the Haluza dune field in the Negev offers abundant implements and pottery with a youngest age as late as Byzantine and the oldest one of Chalcolithic. From the above findings we can conclude that the invasion of the inland sand dunes dates from between 14,000 to 7,000 BP It is possible that this invasion took place in several phases during this long period. It is understood that

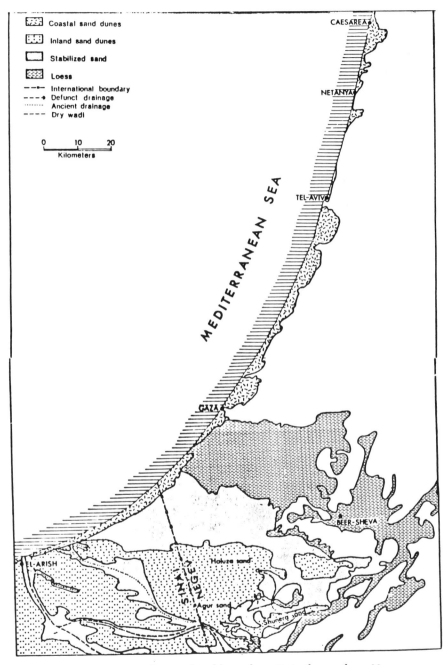

Figure 19.3   Aeolian sand and loess deposits in the northern Negev
and the coastal plain of Israel

during the period from 5,000 to 13,000 BP no invasion of sand occured and that the inland dunes became established. After A.D. 600 and before the nineth to tenth centuries A.D., there was another phase of invasion which still prevails today.

PALEO-CLIMATIC MODEL

In the flow-chart describing this model (see Figure 19.4), the observations listed above are charted as well as those described by Issar and Bruins (1983). As can be seen, the model suggested is that of the southward and northward migration of the latitudinal climatic belts, namely that of the belt of the westerlies modified by the Mediterranean, the belt of the subtropical arid zone over the Sahara, and that of the East Africa Monsoon.

The basic conclusion is that during glacial periods the Negev desert belonging to the geographic belt of the Levant desert enjoyed a more humid climate, while the subtropical semiarid zone in Western Africa was under arid conditions. This shift had two major impacts on the paleo-environment of the Negev and Sinai. First, it brought the dominance of dust-laden rainstorms caused the deposition of the loess layers, as explained by Issar and Bruins (1983). The rainwater was depleted in ^{18}O and deuterium (Gat and Issar 1974) and filled up the Nubian Sandstone aquifers of the Sinai and Negev.

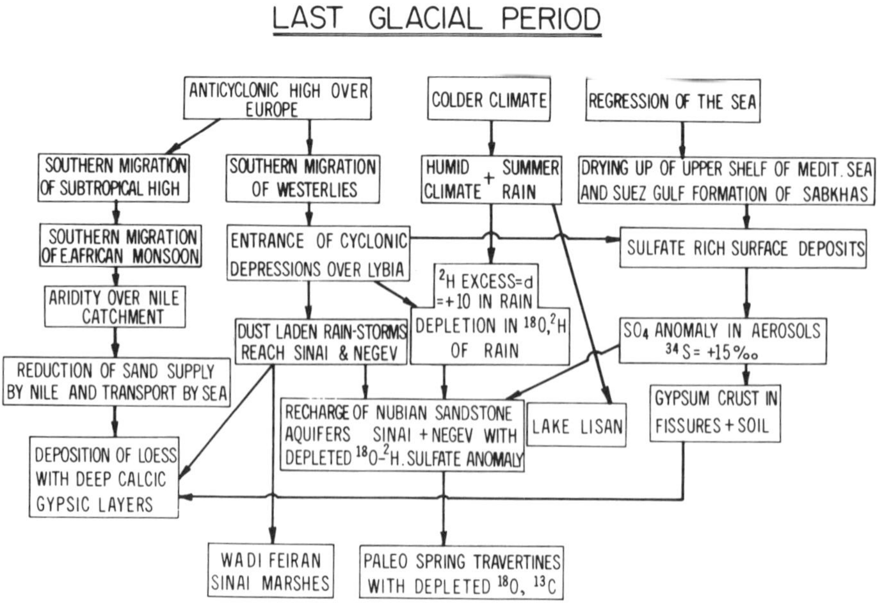

Figure 19.4   Flow-chart of suggested Paleo-climatic model

The high sulfate content of this groundwater is explained by the assumption that the rainwater was also rich in sulfates due to the fact that the glacial period was also a period of the regression of the sea. This caused the formation, on the very shallow shelf all along the northern coast of Egypt, of wide saline marshes that were in the path of the dust rainstorm discussed above. The water of the marshes would have been similar in composition to that of the present Bardawil Lagoon, where a high anomaly of Ca^{2+} and SO_4^{2-} exists, or to upper Pleistocene gypsum deposits found all along the shore of Egypt. It seems feasible that the Suez Gulf at that time also was a saline marsh, as its depth does not exceed 40 meters.

These rainstorms, being rich in airborne sulfates when depositing their dust and salts, caused the leaching of the salts to deeper layers and caused the formation of calcic gypsum layers discussed above. The S isotopic contents of this gypsum of $+15$ $^o/00$ strengthens the assumption that the origin of these sulfates is marine lagoons.

Another environmental impact caused by the shift of the climatic belt was the reduction of the sand supply by the Nile due to the aridity over most of its Ethiopian catchment basin. When this ended, sand dune invasion began to cover the loess layers, the deposition of which was highly reduced.

REFERENCES

Begin, Z. B., A. Ehrilich, and Y. Nathan. 1974. Lake Lisan, the Pleistocene Precursor of the Dead Sea. *Geological Survey*. Bull. No. 63. Ministry of Commerce and Industry, State of Israel.

Gat, J. R. and A. Issar. 1974. Desert isotope hydrology: Water sources of the Sinai Desert. *Geochimica et Cosmoshimica Acta* 38:1117–31.

Goldsmith, V. and A. Golik. 1980. Sediment transport modes of the southeastern Mediterranean coast. *Marine Geology* 37:147–75.

Issar, A. and Y. Eckstein. 1969. The lacustrine beds of Wadi Feiran, Sinai. *Israel Journal of Earth Sci.* 18(1):29–32.

Issar, A., A. Bein, and A. Michaeli. 1972. On the ancient water of the Upper Nubian sandstone aquifer in central Sinai and southern Israel. *Journal of Hydrology* 17:353–74.

Issar, A. and H. Bruins. 1983. Special climatic condtions in the Sinai and Negev during the most Upper Pleistocene. *Paleogeo. Paleocli. Paleoecol.* 42.

Levin, M., J. R. Gat, and A. Issar. 1980. Precipitation, flood and groundwaters of the Negev Highlands: An isotopic study of desert hydrology. Arid Zone Hydrology Investigations with isotope techniques. *IAEA* 3.

Morris, N. 1985. "Terminal Pleistocene Hunters—Gathers in the Negev and Sinai". Ph.D. dissertation submitted to Hebrew University, Jerusalem.

Nativ, R., A. Issar, J. Rutledge. 1983. Chemical composition of rainwater and floodwaters in the Negev Desert, *Israel Journal of Hydrology* 62:201.

Nativ, R., A. Zangvil, A. Issar, and A. Karnieli. 1985. The Occurrence of Sulfate-rich Rains in the Negev Desert, Israel. *Tellus* 37B: 166–172.

Norris, R. M. 1969. Dune reddening and time. *J. Sed. Petrol.* 39:7–12.

Tsoar, H. 1976. Characterization of sand dune environments by their grain-size, mineralogy and surface texture. *In Geography in Israel*. ed. D.H.K. Amiran and Y. Ben-Arieh. IGU, Jerusalem.

TWENTY

Seeing Through
the Desert Atmosphere

NORMAN S. KOPEIKA AND ABRAHAM N. SEIDMAN

ABSTRACT

Imaging through desert and non-desert atmospheres is compared from
the standpoint of interactions of optics and meteorology. Modulation
transfer function (MTF) criteria for image resolution are presented to
describe atmospheric image degradation deriving from atmospheric
background radiation, turbulence, and aerosols. Regression coefficients with which to ascribe relative roles in experimentally observed
image quality are calculated for relative humidity, air temperature,
and windspeed. The last is particularly important in desert atmospheres because of its role in causing desert dust to be airborne. Analysis of regression coefficients in the spatial frequency domain permits
quantitative determination of effects of each meteorological parameter
on atmospheric background, turbulence, and aerosol MTFs sepa-
rately. In this way, insight is gained not only as to the extent to which
each meteorological parameter affects imaging resolution, but also to
the mechanism of the effect.

INTRODUCTION

The interaction of optics and meteorology in determining image quality
obtained from seeing through the atmosphere is complex. When the atmosphere is that of a desert the complexity of interaction is considerably
greater as a result of the airborne desert dust particulates.

In non-desert atmospheres image quality is governed primarily by atmospheric background illuminance and by atmospheric turbulence (Kopeika
1978, 1981). The former serves to decrease contrast in much the same
way as background illuminance from ceiling lights decreases image contrast

on the movie screen in a movie theater. The atmospheric effect is essentially independent of spatial frequency but does vary strongly with wavelength. Atmospheric illuminance results from scattered sunlight and thermal emission of atmospheric gases (Kopeika and Bordogna 1970). The first is primarily visible light whose spectrum is determined by that of the incident solar light and spectral light scattering and absorption properties of the atmosphere. The spectrum of thermal emission of the atmosphere is in the infrared and is determined by air temperature and atmospheric spectral absorption. The scattered sunlight and thermal emission spectra, both of which comprise background atmospheric illuminance or radiance, intersect at about 3 to 4 μm wavelength under normal daytime conditions (Kopeika and Bordogna 1970). It is here that atmospheric background radiance is least and, as a result, so too is image contrast degradation caused by such atmospheric background radiance (Kopeika 1981). In non-desert atmospheres this degradation decreases as wavelength increases from the middle of the visible into the near infrared spectrum. We shall see that in the desert this wavelength dependence is different.

Atmospheric turbulence describes the common situation where atmospheric refractive index fluctuates randomly, thus causing random refractions of light. Light propagating from a point source should be ideally imaged into a point image. However, refractions of the beam, which are random in both time and space, cause the beam finally incident on the receiver to arrive from many different angles, thus smearing or spreading the image of the point source. this spreading is called the system "spead function" and it characterizes the resolving capability of the imaging system including the intervening atmosphere (Levi 1980). The spatial Fourier transform of the spread function yields the optical transfer function (OTF) of the system, which decreases monotonically as spatial frequency increases. It is customary to normalize the OTF by its maximum value, so that the normalized OTF varies between unity and zero. The magnitude of the optical transfer function is called the "modulation transfer function" or MTF. For a sine wave object (rather than point source or object), the system MTF can be shown to be equal to the system modulation contrast transfer function (MCF) (ratio of image plane modulation contrast to object plane modulation contrast) (Parrent and Thompson 1969) The decrease of MTF with increasing spatial frequency signifies contrast degradation at higher spatial frequencies. At some relatively high spatial frequency, system MTF has decreased to such a low value of contrast, that it is below the threshold contrast function of the observer. This means that such high spatial frequency content of the image cannot be resolved by the observer because of the poor contrast. The spatial frequency at which system MTF is just equal to the threshold contrast of the observer defines the maximum useful spatial frequency content of the system. We will call it here $f_{r_{max}}$. Often the threshold contrast of the observer is taken to be two percent, although there is some evidence that it really increases with spatial frequency (Snyder 1973) as shown in Figure 20.1. If Δx and $\Delta x'$ are uncertainties in the object and image planes respectively, and if s and s' are object and image distances respectively, then on the basis of similar triangles

$$\frac{\Delta x}{s} = -\frac{\Delta x^1}{s'} \propto -\frac{1}{f_{r_{max}} s'} \tag{1}$$

where the minus sign refers to image inversion. Since optical magnification M is equal to the ratio of s' to s, the minimum size of resolvable detail in the object plane is

$$\Delta x \propto (f_{r_{max}} M)^{-1}. \tag{2}$$

The greater the useable spatial frequency contact $f_{r_{max}}$ provided by the imaging system, the smaller the object plane detail that can be resolved and the better the imaging system.

For relatively long propagation paths through the atmosphere, system spread function and MTF are limited primarily by atmospheric- rather than instrumentation-limited phenomena (Kopeika 1978).

The contrast degradation deriving from background atmospheric radiance can *also* be considered from the standpoint of spatial frequency domain. Such background illuminance contributes towards dampening of MTF uniformly across the spatial frequency spectrum, as will be shown below. Since MTF decreases monotonically with spatial frequency, such dampening causes the intersection of MTF with threshold contrast to take place at a lower spatial frequency. This decrease in $f_{r_{max}}$ deriving from the dampening

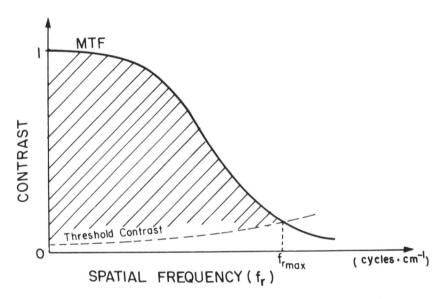

Figure 20.1   Image resolution as defined in the spatial frequency domain.
Shaded area is MTFA.

causes an increase in Δx in (2) and thus a worsening of resolution (Kopeika 1978, 1981).

Spatial frequency domain analysis shows that overall system MTF is equal to the product of the MTFs of each individual component in the imaging system (Levi 1980). This means that the atmosphere can be approached as any other component in the imaging system and an MTF assigned to it. In particular, the MTF describing image degradation resulting from background atmospheric radiance N_A (λ,T) is (Kopeika 1978, 1981; Jensen 1968)

$$M_B\ (\lambda,T)\ =\ \frac{N_o(\lambda,T)}{N_o(\lambda,T)\ +\ N_A(\lambda,T)/\tau(\lambda,T)} \qquad (3)$$

where N_o is object scene radiance, λ is wavelength, and T is thermal emission temperature. $\tau(\lambda,T)$ is atmospheric transmittance over path length z and is equal to

$$\tau\ =\ \exp\ \left[-\ \int_o^z \alpha(\lambda,T,z')\ dz'\right] \qquad (4)$$

where α is the atmospheric extinction coefficient, which is equal to the sum of the atmospheric scattering and absorption coefficients S_a and A_a, respectively. Equation (3) shows that M_B is not a function of spatial frequency. If N_A were zero, then (3) would be unity and there would be no dampening. Since atmospheric background is non-zero, (3) is less than unity, and multiplication of other MTF's by it represents MTF dampening uniformly across the spatial frequency spectrum.

Turbulence phenomena are generally characterized with a refractive index structure coefficient C_n. The MTF to describe relatively long exposure plane wave imaging through atmospheric turbulence is often given by (Huffnagel and Stanley 1964; Fried 1966; Kopeika 1978)

$$<\ M_T(\lambda,f_r)\ >\ =\ \exp\ [-\ 59.19\ (f_e f_r)^{5/3}\lambda^{-1/3}\ \int_o^z C_n{}^2 dz^1] \qquad (5)$$

where f_e is imaging system focal length and f_r is spatial frequency. It can be seen from (15) that the wavelength dependence of turbulence MTF is quite negligible. As a result the wavelength dependence of seeing through a non-desert atmosphere is usually determined by (3) which, in turn, is affected strongly by the wavelength dependence of the atmospheric radiance N_A described above (Kopeika 1978, 1981). For high glare and/or long atmospheric path lengths imaging at even 0.9 μm offers significant improvement in resolution over that obtainable at visible wavelengths (Kopeika 1978).

Background aerosols are normally on the order of half a micrometer radius or less (Patterson and Gillette 1981). Light scattering by them is typically at large angles relative to direction of propagation prior to the scattering because the small size of the scattering particulate relative to incident wavelength limits diffraction effects. As a result of the large scattering angle, the effect of the scatter is essentially attenuation with regard to the initial direction of propagation. However, as scattering particles grow in size, much of the light is diffracted in the forward direction. This is manifested as forward scattering at very small angles relative to the initial direction of propagation. Multiple forward scattering effects cause some forward scattered radiation to be received and imaged together with the unscattered light. This means that the multiple forward scattered component is incident on the receiver from random small angles of arrival with respect to that of the unscattered component. The effect on spread function and resolution is qualitatively similar to that of atmospheric turbulence. Quantitatively, however, scattering exhibits strong wavelength dependences according to the ratio of scattering particulate size to wavelength. The aerosol MTF for the object beam is given by (Lutomirski 1978)

$$M_a(f_r) = \exp(-A_a z) \exp\left[-(f_r/f_c)^2 S_a z\right], \quad f_r < f_c \qquad (6)$$
$$= \exp(-\alpha z) \qquad\qquad\qquad f_r \geq f_c.$$

f_c is a high spatial frequency cutoff, whose value is

$$f_c = a/(\lambda f), \qquad (7)$$

where a is scattering particulate radius. Expressions similar to (6) have been developed independently by Yura (1971) and Ishimaru (1978) for underwater imaging limitations imposed by particulate scatter. These differ from other theoretical developments based on single-scattering approximations that are not limited by a high spatial-frequency cutoff (Kabanov 1968; Ganich and Mukarevich 1972). It is assumed in equation (6) that light received from the object is scattered many times ($\int_0^z s_a(z',\lambda)dz' >> 1$) before reaching the receiver. The spatial-frequency dependence of image degradation by small-angle aerosol scattering is essentially a low-spatial-frequency process, with the high-spatial-frequency cutoff f_c in (6) being proportional to the ratio of particulate size to light wavelength. For ordinary background aerosols $a \simeq 0.2 - 0.4 \ \mu m$, and f_c is consequently too small for the aerosol MTF to be observed with ordinary optics. Very little visible and near infrared light scattering is then in the forward direction. However, soil-derived particulates such as desert dust lifted by the wind usually have a radius of the order of 2 to 4 μm (10), (16), thus increasing f_c by an order of magnitude and enabling the aerosol MTF not only to be easily observed at visible and near IR wavelengths but also to play a dominant role in the wavelength dependence of imaging through the atmosphere (Kopeika et al. 1981, 1982; McCartney 1976). The wavelength dependence of the scattering coefficient can often be expressed as

$$s_a \propto \lambda^{-n} \qquad (8)$$

where n is its maximum value of 4 for pure Rayleigh scattering. The wavelength dependence of (2) is then

$$M_a(f_r,\lambda) \propto \exp\left[-\lambda^{(2-n)}\right] \qquad (9)$$

where (7) and (8) have been substituted into (6). Equation (9) thus suggests considerable wavelength dependence according to the value of n. For n < 2, M_a favors imaging at shorter wavelengths where fall-off with increasing spatial frequency is less rapid. In very clear weather n > 2, and consequently M_a then falls off less rapidly with spatial frequency at longer wavelengths. In this situation, better resolution is obtained at longer wavelengths. The wavelength dependence of the scattering coefficient in (9) is very much a function of meteorological conditions with regard to both soil and the atmosphere. If the soil contains moisture, for example, the resulting adhesiveness of soil particles to one another prevents many from being airborne in the wind, particularly as regards the larger and heavier particles. Good correlations have been observed under dry desert soil conditions between (6) and the time-integral of wind strength in experiments involving imaging through desert atmosphere in both horizontal (Kopeika et al. 1981, Kopeika 1982a) and near-vertical directions (Kopeika 1982b). The time-integral of wind-strength plays a large role in determining both the size distribution and concentration of soil-derived particles that are airborne. Expression (6) affects image quality propagated through the atmosphere particularly in areas where the soil is dry and bare so that particulates can be uplifted by the wind. Hence, it is particularly significant in desert climates.

The three known atmospheric mechanisms of image quality degradation are described quantitatively by (3), (5), and (6). In the visible and near infrared wavelength regions, the background atmospheric radiation is also affected largely by aerosol scattering properties. When scattering particulate radius α is on the order of wavelength size, the magnitude of the scattering coefficient is generally maximum. For $\lambda < a$, the wavelength dependence of S_a displays various maxima and minima. For $\lambda > a$, S_a generally decreases with wavelength according to (8), where n increases with increasing wavelength. It is clear, therefore, that (3) and (6) are both strongly wavelength dependent, and they essentially determine the wavelength dependence of imaging through the atmosphere. We will now proceed to compare imaging in desert with imaging in non-desert atmospheres.

The wavelength dependence of (3) is determined by the ratio (N_A/N_O) and α. For a background deriving primarily from scattered radiation, N_B itself is affected also, largely by α, although wavelength dependence is determined too by that of the background source, which often is the sun. Thus, for non-arid areas where aerosol radii are normally on the order of a fraction of a micrometer, (N_A/N_O) and α are maximum at approximately 0.45 μm. (Kopeika et al. 1981; McCartney 1976; Henderson 1977). In this situation, atmospheric resolution improves as imaging wavelength increases beyond this range, particularly in high glare situations (Kopeika 1978). Image degradation stemming from (3) is least at wavelengths where atmospheric background is minimum. Normally, when aerosol sizes are small as indicated above, optimum background contrast is in atmospheric windows between 2 to 4 μm wavelength (Kopeika 1981). Even imaging at 0.9 μm wavelength offers significant improvement over imaging at visible wavelengths for high glare and/or long atmospheric path lengths.

When the atmosphere contains large concentrations of soil-derived particulates such as desert dust (Patterson and Gillette 1981; Kopeika et al. 1981) a peak in aerosol size distribution is also seen at 2 to 4 μm radius. Such particles scatter near-infrared radiation much more than they do visible radiation (Kopeika et al. 1981; McCartney 1976). Under such conditions, (3) is larger at visible than at near IR wavelenghts, thus indicating resolution improvement at shorter wavelengths (Kopeika et al. 1981). This means that when concentrations of airborne desert dust are relatively high, better resolution is obtained at visible than at near infrared wavelengths—the very opposite result of that typical of non-desert atmospheres (Kopeika et al. 1981). In other words, if near infrared sensors which are advantageous in non-desert atmospheres are utilized in desert atmospheres, they are most likely to be disadvantageous in the dry season.

The small size of background aerosols can be used to explain why the sky is blue in clear weather. Because for such small particulates $a < \lambda$, there is less scattering at longer wavelengths. Hence, in the visible spectrum it is the short wavelength blue light which is scattered most, thus causing the sky to appear blue to us. However, as particulate size increases through haze and fog, their light scattering becomes more spectrally neutral and the sky appears to us to become grayer and whiter. Finally, in the desert where soil-derived particles are so large that $a = \lambda$ in the mid-infrared, light scattering in the visible is maximum at longer wavelengths, and the sky appears to us to be brownish and even reddish in dust storms.

The complex interactions of imaging and meteorological properties of the desert atmosphere are compared further with those of the non-desert atmosphere in the following experiment.

EXPERIMENT

Modulation contrast functions (MCF) at visible and near infrared wavelengths over a 4.15 ground level near-horizontal path (elevation varied from 1 to 5 m) were measured in the northern Negev desert in Beer Sheva, Israel, during a three-year period. The target was a collection of black and white stripes forming normalized spatial frequencies of 4, 9, 10, 13, 20, 28, 40, 83, and 104 lines per milliradian, as described in (Kopeika et al. 1981). Long wavelength-pass filters with varying short wavelength cut-offs were used to measure MCF spectral dependence. The long wavelength cut-off was that of a 700 TV line enhanced infrared response silicon vidicon TV system, at about 1 μm wavelength. Irradiance at the receiver was maximum at about 450 nm wavelength and fell off strongly as wavelength increased, being at 750 nm only slightly more than 10 percent of its peak value at 450 nm. Thus, for shorter wavelength cut-offs most of the detected video current was derived from the visible rather than IR portion of the passed light. Neutral density filters were used to attenuate where needed so that for the lowest spatial frequency, video signal was equal at all wavelengths. Measurement of MCF at the various higher spatial frequencies then yielded to a first approximation the wavelength dependence of imaging through the atmosphere, as described in more detail elsewhere (Kopeika et al. 1981). (Since the target was square wave rather than sin wave, MCF did not equal MTF but was close to it.) Meteorological parameters at the times of measurement were obtained from the local branch of the Israel Meteorological Services, which was situated only about a kilometer from the experimental line-of-sight. Such measurements include surface air temperature, air pressure, wind speed and direction, relative humidity, clouds, etc. Multiple partial regression coefficients between the imaging (MCF) and meteorological parameters were computed (Crow et al. 1958). In the calculations, the parameters are assumed to be normally distributed. Over 3000 measurements were taken. The required averaging or summation of MCF over wavelength or spatial frequency yields 60 to 70 separate cases.

The data was treated as type I in the nomenclature of Crow et al. (1958) because of the possibility of non-independence of some of the time sequential meteorological measurements. In the type I method, the independent variable is taken as measured and only the dependent variable (MCF here) is required to be a stochastic variable. This allows for regression but not correlation calculations, since the latter require independent, normally distributed dependent as well as independent variables. The f-test allowed the examination of the significance of the regression formulae. Because climatic conditions are so different between winter and summer the data have been divided according to season. Winter is cooler, more damp, and rainy at times. Summer is hotter and the soil is quite dry. Moisture in the soil in winter plays a major role in decreasing soil-derived airborne particulate size and concentration. The summer or dry season thus permits an excellent opportunity to study effects of soil-derived particulates upon imaging through a desert atmosphere. The winter season is essentially comparable to a non-desert atmosphere since the atmosphere is freer of desert dust. Winter measurements preclude rain conditions since resolution was too poor then for any measurements.

RESULTS AND DISCUSSION

As a single-value criterion of image resolution, the MCF area (MCFA) is a number convenient to use in much the same way as MTFA (Snyder 1973). MTFA is the area bound by the MTF and threshold contrast function curves in Figure 20.1. Here the summation of MCF measurements at a given wavelength are used as single numerical criterion for image quality at that wavelength. The greater the spatial frequency at which MCF measurements can be obtained, the higher the sum of such measurements. This is proportional to MCFA and is labeled here Σ MCF (λ). Regression coefficients for temperature (T), relative humidity (RH) and windspeed (W) were calculated.

For the winter or rainy season, it was found that

$$\Sigma_{f_r} \text{MCF}_w (\lambda) = a_w(\lambda)\, T + b_w(\lambda)\, RH + c_w(\lambda)W + d_w(\lambda) \qquad (10)$$

Figure 20.2 shows the value of the regression coefficients as functions of wavelength.

Thus, for 780 nm wavelength

$$\Sigma_{f_r} \, \mathrm{MCF}_w(780) = -2.92 \times 10^{-2} \, T_w + 0.69 \times 10^{-4} \, \mathrm{RH}_w \\ + 3.76 \times 10^{-2} \, W_w + 1.48 \qquad (11)$$

where T_w is in °C, RH_w is in percent and W_w is in knots. For summer the subscript s is used instead of w. This figure includes standard error of the mean estimate for the regression coefficients. Solid lines are used for winter and dotted lines for summer.

To calculate regression coefficients of temperature, relative humidity, and windspeed for each spatial frequency, MCF data at each spatial frequency averaged over all wavelengths was used as the criterion for image quality at each spatial frequency. In this way, regression coefficients of these meteorological parameters were calculated at each spatial frequency f_r, i.e., for winter

$$\overline{\mathrm{MCF}_w \, (f_r)} = a_w(f_r)T + b_w(f_r)\mathrm{RH} + c_w(f_r)W + d_w(f_r). \qquad (12)$$

where the overbar refers to averaging over all wavelength intervals. The regression coefficients as functions of spatial frequency for winter and summer respectively are plotted in Figure 20.3. In many cases, MCF at higher spatial frequencies was zero, particularly at mid-day in the summer when turbulence was high. Consequently, some of the regression coefficients for summer in Figure 20.3 do not extend out to high spatial frequencies.

The strong changes in Figure 20.3 indicate the existence of the different MTF mechanisms in the different spatial frequency intervals. This information is obtained in the following way. Background contrast degradation and aerosol MTF are both highly wavelength-dependent, while turbulence is very weakly wavelength-dependent. However, turbulence degrades atmospheric MTF over the whole spatial frequency spectrum (Huffnagel and Stanley 1964, Fried 1966, Kopeika 1978), while aerosol MTF refers only to spatial frequencies less than $f_c = a/\lambda f$. Background contrast degradation is manifested as a uniform dampening over the whole spatial frequency spectrum. As such, background contrast degradation affects adversely resolution of both large and small objects, while turbulence degrades resolution of primarily small objects. Forward scattering degrades resolution of medium-size objects in particular. Thus, at very low spatial frequencies overall atmospheric MTF is limited primarily by background contrast, since turbulence and aerosol MTFs both start at unity at zero spatial frequency. At slightly higher spatial frequencies aerosol MTF begins to make its presence felt. At spatial frequencies higher than aerosol MTF cutoff, overall atmospheric MTF is affected primarily by turbulence. This spatial frequency variation between the various atmospheric imaging degradations makes it possible to utilize spatial frequency information to determine how various meteorological parameters affect imaging through the atmosphere. The

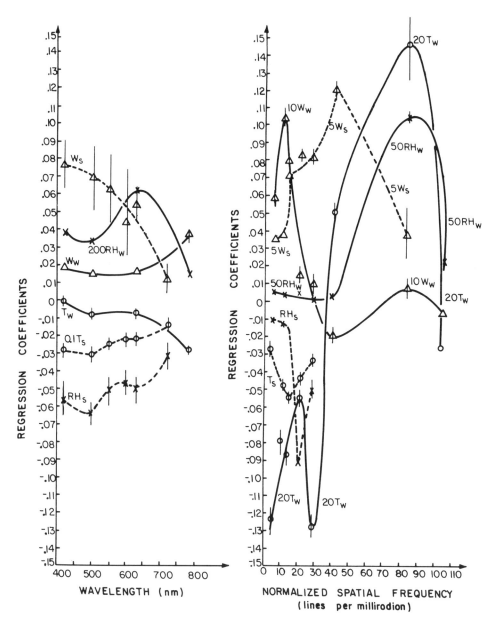

Figure 20.2   Meteorological regression coefficients vs. wavelength.

Figure 20.3   Meteorological regression coefficients vs. spatial frequency.

aerosol MTF high spatial frequency cutoffs in these experiments is on the order of 17 to 30 lines mrad^{-1} (Kopeika et al. 1981; Kopeika 1982a; 1982b).

In winter, Figure 20.2 indicates relative humidity increase and windspeed increase are seen to yield improved imaging through the atmosphere, since these regression coefficients are positive, while air temperature increases are seen to lead to worsening of image quality propagated through the atmosphere. Our measurements and calculations involving relative humidity effects upon imaging through the atmosphere here are opposite to those obtained at microwave frequencies on the basis of turbulence alone (Schiavone 1983). They might, without Figure 20.3, imply some role for forward scattering upon imaging through the atmosphere, as explained in the introduction. However, Figure 20.3 indicates that it is particularly at high spatial frequencies that the regression coefficient for relative humidity is most positive. This means that imaging resolution improvement brought about by relative humidity increase in winter is a result of decreased turbulence degradation in particular. However, turbulence should affect all spatial frequencies, including low ones. The strong dip in the RH_w curve in Figure 20.3 at low spatial frequencies indicates relative humidity increase also increases image degradation via increased atmospheric background and forward scattering effects. This is attributed to increased haze and particulate size as relative humidity increases, and should not be surprising. However, the decrease of turbulence degradation in winter with relative humidity increase, is opposite to that obtained in (Schiavone 1983). The reason is discussed below, after the temperature data are analyzed.

The negative temperature regression coefficient in Figure 20.2 indicates temperature decrease yields improved resolution. As pointed out above this implies decreased temperature gradient improves imaging resolution. This is consistent with turbulence-related phenomena. Temperature decrease, if absolute humidity does not change, implies relative humidity increase. Thus, the negative temperature and positive relative humidity regression coefficients in Figure 20.2 appear to be connected with each other and point to turbulence as a common mechanism in limiting image resolution through the winter or rainy atmosphere. However, Figure 20.3 indicates that at low spatial frequencies the regression coefficient for temperature T_w is negative while at higher spatial frequencies it is positive. Thus, at higher spatial frequencies the T_w and RH_w curves are similar rather than opposite. The very low spatial frequency result implies that increased winter temperature increases background degradation by increasing the background radiance. This shows that the evaporation rate of soil moisture into the air tends to be greater than condensation of haze droplets back into water vapor, thus increasing the number of haze droplets and atmospheric scattering background radiance. This is supported by the second dip of T_w in Figure 20.3 at about 30 lines·mrad^{-1}, corresponding to additional image degradation by forward scattering effects. Similar phenomena seem to characterize summer temperature effects and suggest that negative regression coefficients for temperature stem primarily from forward scattering. However, the higher spatial frequency results in Figure 20.3 indicate image degradation due to turbulence decreases as winter temperature increases. In view of the low spatial frequency T_w results, this may well suggest a decrease in humidity gradient resulting from the known increase in the absolute number of haze droplets as winter temperature increases. This would also be consistent with the rise in the RH_w regression coefficient at higher spatial frequencies. The latter implies that increase in relative humidity leads to decreased image degradation by turbulence (Schiavone 1983). Thus, the similar higher spatial frequency characteristics of both T_w and RH_w in Figure 20.3 suggest the two are related in the manner described here. The spectral dependence of both these curves in Figure 20.2 are not too different either. This result is the opposite of that of (Schiavone 1983) for microwave fading and suggests that in that case turbulence was affected largely by temperature rather than humidity gradient.

The sharp positive peak of winter windspeed regression coefficient at very low spatial frequency in Figure 20.3 indicates that the primary effect of wind on imaging in winter is to disperse haze droplets and thus decrease atmospheric background. This indicates the effect of windspeed in winter is mostly on background and not on turbulence, and that the spectral effect of the W_w curve in Figure 20.2 must be evaluated accordingly. This latter curve indicates background contrast degradation in the near infrared is less than in the visible. This is a common result and indicates airborne desert dust does not play so significant a role in winter imaging. Although the T_w curve in Figure 20.3 indicates some forward scattering effects as discussed above, these are attributed to increased particle size via humidity increase rather than picking up of large desert dust particles by the atmosphere. That the origin of this forward scatter is humidity is supported by the low value of the RH_w regression coefficient at low spatial frequencies as compared to that at high spatial frequencies in Figure 20.3.

While increased windspeed is seen to be favorable to imaging through background haze dispersal, the high spatial frequency dip in Figure 20.3 indicates increased windspeed increases turbulence degradation. This too is opposite to the result in (Schiavone 1983) and is attributed to increased humidity gradient via decrease in number of haze droplets brought about by wind dispersal, and is thus consistent with the RH_w and T_w data in Figure 20.3.

To summarize, in winter increased windspeed and decreased air temperature and relative humidity tend to improve background contrast particularly in the near infrared, while at the same time increasing image degradation via turbulence effects. Forward scattering degradation is attributed to humidity rather than to soil-derived aerosol effects. The background contrast improvement in the near infrared is typical of conditions where soil-derived aerosols do not play major roles, and results from the relatively small size of common background aerosols which scatter much less near infrared than visible light (Kopeika 1978). This description is typical of non-desert atmospheres in the absence of rain.

The summer results in Figure 20.2 show that increased windspeed improves resolution while increased relative humidity and temperature degrade resolution at short wavelengths in particular. Figure. 20.3 indicates strong forward scattering effects involving all three meteorological parameters since they decrease at low spatial frequencies. The fact that the W_s curve in Figure 20.2 is positive rather than negative would appear to result from increased air mixing and reduction of turbulence MTF by wind, as discussed in (Schiavone 1983). The significant effect of windspeed on atmospheric turbulence is indicated by the positive values of W_s at higher spatial frequencies in Figure 20.3. This is in agreement with the microwave results (Schiavone 1983) and is consistent with the winter model presented above. In winter, it is suggested above that increased windspeed increases image degradation through turbulence because wind disperses haze and thus increases humidity gradient. In summer, however, although the early mornings are quite humid, relative humidity decreases very quickly to very dry conditions by about 9 to 10 AM. Windspeed picks up around noon (Kopeika et al. 1981). Thus, in summer, windspeed has little if any effect on humidity gradient and its main effect is only decreased turbulence effects through increased air mixing. Consequently, while the winter result for wind speed disagrees with that of (Schiavone 1983) regarding turbulence, the summer result is in complete agreement and reflects the complexity introduced by desert dust conditions.

The wavelength dependence of W_s is determined primarily by forward scattering effects. Figure 20.2 shows strong degradation of resolution in the near infrared since W_s there drops so sharply. Extension further into the near infrared might even result in a negative regression coefficient despite the positive effect of windspeed on imaging via turbulence reduction. The forward scattering effects in summer brought about by increased windspeed are thus quite significant. This is quite consistent with comparisons of visible and near infrared imaging presented previously for these desert conditions (Kopeika et al. 1981; Kopeika 1982). The average airborne desert dust particle radius in summer is 3 to 4 μm (Kopeika et al. 1981). Because of the large size such particles scatter near infrared radiation much more than they do visible radiation (McCartney 1976). The curve for T_s in Figure 20.3 indicates that increased temperature decreases background contrast and leads to increased image degradation through forward scattering, as in winter. However, Figure 20.2 indicates that while in winter such degradation is primarily at infrared wavelengths, in summer the degradation via temperature is primarily at short wavelengths. The curves for RH_s in Figures 20.2 and 20.3 are similar to those for T_s and suggest the effects of temperature and relative humidity on imaging are related also in summer. Increased humidity in summer degrades short wavelength resolution primarily. In the introduction it was pointed out that the size of haze droplets increases with time for high humidity conditions. Thus, in winter when it is humid for long periods of time the droplets tend to be larger than in summer, when it is humid only for short periods in the early morning. As temperature increases as the day wears on, evaporation of early morning dew is in the form of very small droplets primarily. The dry conditions as the day wears on prevent the size of such droplets from growing in summer. Consequently, background and forward scattering temperature and humidity image degradation tend to be at shorter wavelengths in summer. The long duration of high humidity in winter causes the droplets to grow in size, thus affecting longer wavelengths in particular.

However, the strong winds beginning typically at mid-day in summer (Kopeika et al. 1981) uplift many dry soil-derived particles into the atmosphere. Their large size (3 to 4 μm radius) causes forward scattering image degradation of near infrared wavelengths in particular, as described above and by the W_s curve in Figure 20.2.

The negative relative humidity regression coefficients for summer in Figures 20.2 and 20.3 are opposite from those to be expected from turbulence. In view of the above the main effect of humidity in summer on image degradation is seen to be short wavelength forward scattering effects as can be seen from the strong dip at about 20 lines·mrad^{-1}. Figure 20.2 indicates regression coefficients for relative humidity in summer and winter are of opposite sign. With Figure 20.3 we can see that there is no contradiction since the spatial frequency analysis indicates that the primary effect of relative humidity is on turbulence (high spatial frequencies) in winter and on forward scattering (low spatial frequencies) in summer.

In summary, in desert atmosphere (summer) increased windspeed and decreased temperature and relative humidity improve background contrast particularly at shorter wavelengths. This spectral result is opposite to that of winter (non-desert atmospheres). Increased desert windspeed decreases image degradation via turbulence; however, it increases image degradation significantly via forward scattering effects, particularly in the near infrared, as a result of the relatively large size of soil-derived particulates.

The wavelength dependence of imaging in summer (desert atmosphere) tends to be opposite to that in winter (non-desert atmosphere) over the spectral region used in these measurements. This is attributed to the role of the large soil-derived desert dust particulates airborne in the dry summer season. Their size and concentration increased with windspeed. This causes both background contrast and aerosol forward scattering degradation of image quality to be worst at near infrared wavelengths during periods of high concentration of such particles, such as in the afternoons when windspeed is relatively high. Earlier in the day, when windspeed is low, background contrast and aerosol forward scattering image degradation is worst at shorter wavelengths, as is typical of non-desert environments, because of the small size of aerosols.

Using Figures 20.2 and 20.3, substitution of typical values of temperature, relative humidity, and windspeed into (10) indicates overall image quality as determined by the MCFA criteria tends to be somewhat better at near infrared wavelengths in non-desert and at shorter wavelengths in desert atmospheres.

CONCLUSIONS

A start has been made on predicting imaging resolution in accordance with meteorological prediction inputs, using regression coefficient calculations. These calculations have been carried out to show both wavelength-dependent and spatial frequency-dependent effects of air temperature, relative humidity, and windspeed. Analysis of spatial frequency regression coefficients permits individual determination of effects of each meteorological parameter on background contrast, forward scattering, and turbulence. Thus, we know not only the effect of each meteorological parameter on imaging resolution but also the mechanism of effect. This interplay between wavelength and spatial frequency dependences permits development of a model on a quantitative basis to describe the interrelationships of meteorological and imaging resolution parameters. Although some of the results here disagree with those in the literature (Schiavone 1983) which pertain to non-desert atmospheres, the Fourier spatial frequency analysis permits quantitative explanations here as to the reasons and circumstances for the deviations in behavior from those recorded in the literature. This diagnostic tool should be useful in understanding the interactions between optical and meteorological parameters under different climatic conditions. Here, they have been compared for winter and summer, which correspond to non-desert and dry desert atmospheres, respectively.

REFERENCES

Crow, F.L., F.A. Davis, and M.W. Maxfield. 1958. *Statistics Manual*. Dover.

Fried, D.L. 1966. Optical resolution through a randomly inhomogeneous medium for very long and very short exposures. *J. Opt. Soc. Amer.* 56: 1372.

Ganich, P.Y. and S.A. Makarevich. 1972. The contrast transfer functions of scattering media. *Atm. and Ocean Phys.* 8: 462.

Henderson, S.T. 1977. *Daylight and Its Spectrum*, 2nd ed, Adam Hilger, Bristol, England.

Huffnagel, R.E. and N.R. Stanley. 1964. Modulation transfer associated with image transmission through turbulent media. *J. Opt. Soc. Amer.* 54: 52.

Ishimaru, A. 1978. Limitation on image resolution imposed by a random medium. *Applied Optics* 17: 348.

Jensen, N. 1968. *Optical and Photographic Reconnaissance Systems*. John Wiley & Sons, N.Y., p. 44.

Kabanov, M.V. 1968. The optical transfer function for scattering media. *Atm. and Ocean Phys.* 4: 478.

Kopeika, N.S. 1977. Spectral characteristics of image quality for imaging horizontally through the atmosphere. *Applied Optics* 16: 2422 (1978): 1162.

_____. 1981. The general wavelength dependence of imaging through the atmosphere. *Applied Optics* 20: 1532.

_____. 1982a. The spatial frequency dependence of scattered background light: The atmospheric MTF resulting from aerosols. *J. Opt. Soc. Amer.* 72: 548.

_____. 1982b. Spatial frequency and wavelength-dependent effects of aerosols on atmospheric MTF. *J. Opt. Soc. Amer.* 72: 1092.

Kopeika, N.S. and J. Bordogna. 1970. Background noise in optical communication systems. *Proc. IEEE* 58: 1571.

Kopeika, N.S., A.N. Seidman, I. Denstein, C. Tarnasha, R. Amir, and Y. Biton. 1984. Meteorological effects on image quality: Reconnaissance considerations. In *Airborne Reconnaissance* 8, eds. Paul Henkel and F.R. La Gesse. Proc. SPIE, vol. 496, p. 153.

Kopeika, N.S., S. Solomon, and Y. Gencay. 1981. The wavelength variation of visible and near IR resolution through the atmosphere: dependence on aerosol and meteorological conditions. *J. Opt. Soc. Amer.* 71: 892.

Levi, L. 1980. *Applied Optics, vol. 2*. John Wiley & Sons, N.Y.

Lutomirski, T.L. 1978. Atmospheric degradation of electrooptical system performance. *Applied Optics* 17: 3915.

McCartney, E.J. 1976. *Optics of the Atmosphere*. John Wiley & Sons, N.Y., Chap. 6.

Parrent, G.B., Jr. and B.J. Thompson. 1969. *Physical Optics Notebook*. Society of Photo-optical Instrumentation Engineers, Bellingham, Wash.

Schiavone, J.A. 1983. Microwave radio meteorology: seasonal fading distributions. *Radio Sci.* 18:369.

PART VI

DESERT ARCHITECTURE

TWENTY-ONE

Thermal Performance of a Passive Solar House in the Negev

DAVID FAIMAN AND DANIEL FEUERMANN

ABSTRACT

Data are presented for the first year's thermal performance of a lived-in passive solar house at Sede Boqer, Israel. The house, of adobe construction, was completed during 1982, and monitoring of its performance began in October of that year. It consists of three rooms each with a different passive heating device for winter space-heating (direct gain with storage respectively in a floor and in a wall, and a Rotating Prism Wall). Summer cooling is effected, when necessary, via enhanced passive ventilation.

INTRODUCTION

Sede Boqer is located in the heart of Israel's Negev Highland region at a latitude of about 31° N. The altitude is approximately 500m above sea level, and the annual average temperature is about 18° C. The surroundings consist of arid desert, the annual average rainfall amounting to only 90mm. This climatic combination gives rise to remarkably pleasant summers in the sense that the discomfort of July/August temperature extremes is moderated by very low atmospheric humidity. On the other hand, the damp winter months with their mean temperature of about 10° C give rise to a space-heating problem that is generally exacerbated by poorly designed houses.

It was this situation that prompted the initiation of a research project in 1979 to investigate the possibility of designing an energy efficient house that should not cost more than standard building costs in Israel, i.e., about $500/ sq.m.

By a combination of passive solar design and earth building techniques, both the energy and cost criteria were met. This chapter presents the thermal part of the results in the form of data measured during the first complete year that the house was lived in.

PASSIVELY SOLAR-HEATED ADOBE HOUSE

The experimental adobe house shown in Figure 21.1 is a combined project of the Desert Architecture Unit and the Applied Solar Calculations Unit of the Jacob Blaustein Institute for Desert Research, Sede Boqer. The building is a single-family house with three rooms: a living area, a study, and a bedroom. Figure 21.2 shows the floor plan of the house. Each of the rooms is heated in winter by solar radiation in a different manner.

The living area, which with the kitchen forms one large room, contains a south-facing, double-glazed window of net area 4.08 sq.m. (see Figure 21.3). This window allows the room to be heated in winter by so-called direct gain solar heating, day-to-night storage being effected by a massive adobe floor covered by dark brown ceramic tiles. An exterior blind reduces heat loss during winter nights and prevents unwanted solar gain during summer days.

The study, located in the north of the house, is also heated in winter by direct gain solar heating. A clerestory window in the roof admits solar radiation, and day-to-night storage is effected by a darkened northern adobe wall (see Figure 21.4) of 0.2m thickness, which is separated from the outer envelope (also 0.2m of adobe) by a 0.02m air gap. The clerestory window consists of 3.27 sq.m of double-glazing tilted at an angle of 55° to the

Figure 21.1   View of the Sede Boqer solar adobe house from the south-east.

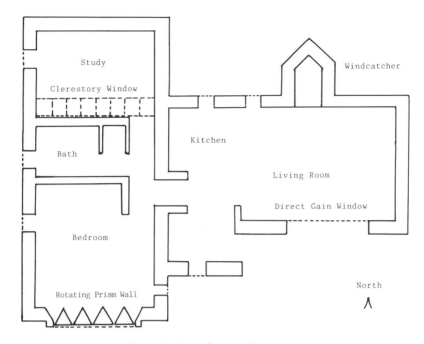

Figure 21.2   Schematic floor plan.

Figure 21.3   Direct gain window and floor storage in living room.

horizontal, this being the angle that maximizes solar collection during the winter months at this latitude. (During the period of data collection reported here, night insulation was not employed with the clerestory window.)

The bedroom is heated by a Rotating Prism Wall (Faiman 1980), double-glazed with a net aperture area of 5.16 sq.m. This device, by design, contains its own storage and night insulation (see Figure 21.5).

An additional feature of the house is a windcatcher tower situated adjacent to the northern wall of the living room. It is used to enhance night ventilation of the building during the summer months.

The building's walls are composed of an outer adobe wall of thickness 0.20m, a 0.02m air gap, and an inner adobe wall of the same thickness as the outer wall. This structure is plastered on its interior and exterior surfaces to produce a wall of total thickness equal to 0.44m.

The roof consists of three different structures. The living and kitchen area has an almost horizontal wooden roof, the study has a north-tilted roof of corrugated asbestos, and the bedroom has a horizontal roof made from concrete beams. The ceilings are thermally insulated.

WINTER OPERATION OF THE HOUSE

The building has been lived in by a married couple since October 1982. During the winter of 1982/1983 the various solar heating devices described above were operated in the following manner.

The blinds of the living room direct gain window were opened at about 7:30 every morning, and closed at about 16:30 each afternoon, when collection of solar energy was considered to be nominally complete in the sense that any further exposure would probably result in a net heat loss back out through the glazing. In the same manner the Rotating Prism Wall was turned into its collection or insulation mode of operation (Faiman 1980), respectively, at these same times of day. The northern study room's clerestory window remained uninsulated all winter because the night insulation was not installed. Backup space heating is provided by electric bar heaters. These were used whenever the inhabitants felt it was necessary.

SUMMER OPERATION OF THE HOUSE

Beginning April 1, 1983, collection of solar energy was reduced by closing the shutters of the living room's direct gain window during the daytime, by rotating the Prism Wall into its insulating mode of operation, and by adding outside blinds to the clerestory window of the study. During the hot summer months of May through September, the house was ventilated at night by opening all windows and vents, and by using the windcatcher.

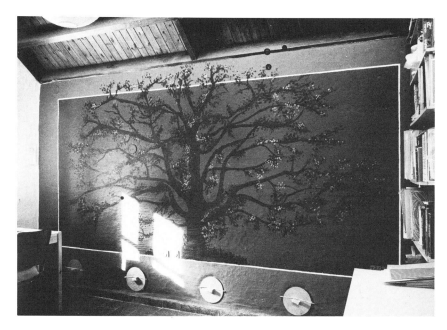

Figure 21.4   Dark mural on northern storage wall of direct gain system in study.

Figure 21.5   Interior view of the Rotating Prism Wall in bedroom.

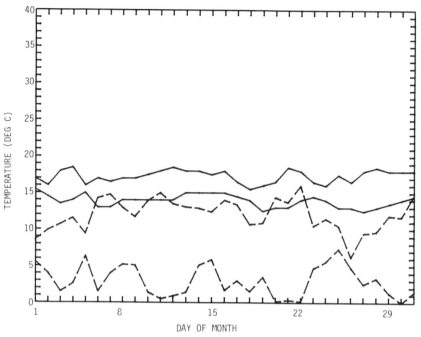

Figure 21.6   Bedroom temperatures for January 1983.

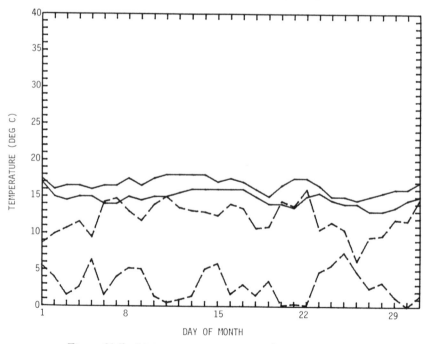

Figure 21.7   Living room temperatures for January 1983.

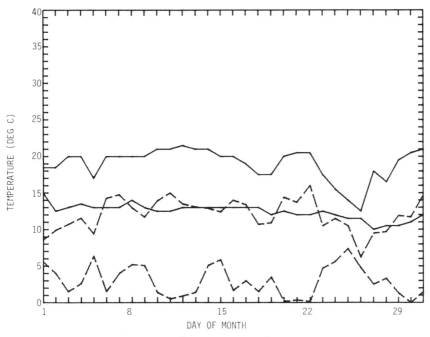

Figure 21.8   Study temperatures for January 1983.

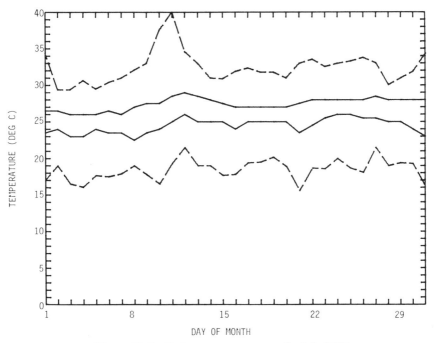

Figure 21.9   Bedroom temperatures for July 1983.

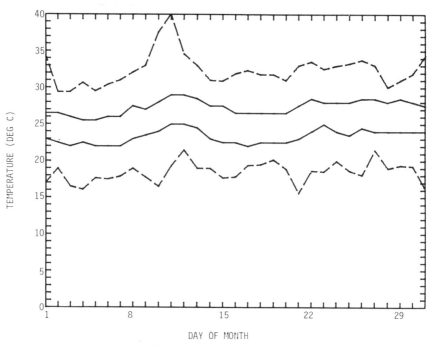

Figure 21.10   Living room temperatures for July 1983.

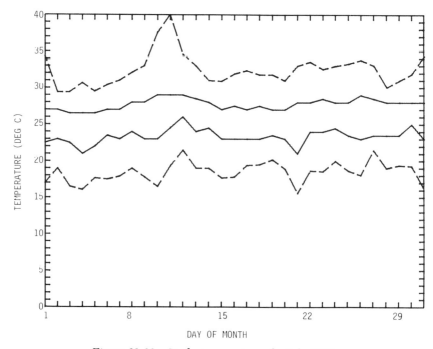

Figure 21.11   Study temperatures for July 1983.

MEASUREMENTS

Three distinct electricity circuits allow for separate measurement of electricity consumption: (1) space heating backup; (2) appliances and lighting; and (3) hot water backup. The three electricity meters were read daily. Measurements of the minimum and maximum temperatures in each of the rooms were taken daily, by means of minimum/maximum thermometers. (Owing to funding problems, an automatic data logger was not available during this first year for recording the output of thermocouples located in various parts of the house. In subsequent years however, all temperatures were recorded automatically.) Measurements of the daily global radiation and minimum/maximum ambient temperatures were kindly provided by the Desert Meteorology Unit of the Institute. The use of cooking gas was monitored by weighing the gas bottles bi-weekly, and the daily readings on two water clocks provided information on consumption of hot and cold water.

RESULTS

A qualitative picture of the building's performance may be obtained from Figures 21.6–11, in which the daily minimum and maximum temperatures of each room (full lines) and ambient (dashed lines) are recorded for the months of January and July. No backup heating was needed for the bedroom, while the living room required only 242 kWh of auxiliary heating for the entire winter. The study was essentially unused in winter evenings, so no backup heating was provided for that room. Its door was closed at night.

Table 21.1 summarizes the monthly average temperatures for each room and for ambient along with the corresponding mean values for the diurnal swings. The temperature swings show the ability of the house to maintain a narrow temperature band throughout the year, with best performance occuring in the bedroom with the Rotating Prism Wall. The study, lacking night insulation, shows the largest temperature swing.

During the summer months the temperature swings are generally larger, since nighttime ventilation is employed to cool the building's mass. The temperature swing in the bedroom is smallest, but its average temperature is slightly higher compared to the other rooms. (The small eastern and western windows of this room seem to provide insufficient nighttime ventilation.)

The building's backup energy consumption is expressed in terms of the solar heating fraction, SHF, defined by

$$\text{SHF} = \frac{\text{net load} - \text{auxiliary heat}}{\text{net load}},$$

where,

$$\text{net load} = (\text{total load}) - (\text{internal heat generation}),$$

Table 21.1 Monthly Daily Mean Temperatures and Mean Diurnal Temperature Swings for the Three Rooms and Building Exterior

	Ambient (Deg C) Mean MDS*	Bedroom (prism wall) (Deg C) Mean MDS*	Living room (d. gain + ins) (Deg C) Mean MDS*	Study (d. gain – ins) (Deg C) Mean MDS*
Nov '82	13.14 ± 5.46	20.72 ± 0.80	20.60 ± 1.43	20.86 ± 2.33
Dec '82	10.20 ± 4.46	18.02 ± 0.94	17.70 ± 1.73	17.88 ± 3.25
Jan '83	7.53 ± 4.54	15.67 ± 0.90	15.61 ± 1.69	15.73 ± 3.28
Feb '83	9.45 ± 4.81	17.25 ± 0.86	16.78 ± 1.71	17.41 ± 2.71
Mar '83	11.93 ± 5.64	18.15 ± 1.01	17.65 ± 1.78	18.81 ± 2.77
Apr '83	15.98 ± 6.48	20.95 ± 0.63	20.66 ± 1.19	20.23 ± 0.81
May '83	20.80 ± 7.62	22.28 ± 1.20	22.47 ± 1.74	22.28 ± 1.90
Jun '83	23.54 ± 7.60	24.27 ± 1.33	24.09 ± 2.01	24.00 ± 2.23
Jul '83	25.45 ± 6.99	25.94 ± 1.40	25.32 ± 2.02	25.54 ± 2.20
Aug '83	25.31 ± 6.64	26.13 ± 1.42	25.44 ± 1.98	25.48 ± 2.22
Sep '83	23.14 ± 6.74	25.77 ± 1.11	24.85 ± 1.92	25.18 ± 1.77
Oct '83	19.57 ± 6.17	24.11 ± 1.05	23.40 ± 1.35	23.45 ± 0.98
< Winter >	10.45 ± 4.98	17.96 ± 0.90	17.67 ± 1.67	18.13 ± 2.87
< Summer >	21.97 ± 6.89	24.21 ± 1.16	23.75 ± 1.74	23.74 ± 1.73

MDS* = mean diurnal temperature swing.

internal heat generation = heat from cooking gas, appliances, lights and occupants.

The results are summarized in Table 21.2. The total load was calculated using the ASHRAE (1977) heating load calculation procedure. The monthly average temperature, i.e., the mean of the three rooms, was taken as the base temperature to determine the load. The conductivity of the adobe walls has not been measured yet, so for the purpose of the present SHF estimates its value was assumed to lie halfway between the minimum and maximum value published in the literature (Cytryn 1957; Rogers 1978), namely, 0.75 W/(m deg K). The so called "sol-air" temperature concept was used to account for the effect of radiation falling on the envelope. The house has the natural color of adobe, which has approximately the same absorptivity as the surrounding sand, alpha = 0.70. Air infiltration was estimated to be one air change per hour.

SHF was found to be 0.95 for the heating season, in spite of an unusually cold winter. The total space-heating energy savings for the five winter months is thus estimated to be 4342 kWh. Detailed experiments on the

Table 21.2   Winter Heating Load Analysis

	Horizontal insolation (MJ/sq. m/d)	Backup heating (kWh/d)	Cooking gas (kWh/d)	Appliances & lighting (kWh/d)
Nov '82	12.25	0	1.324	4.033
Dec '82	10.07	0.874	1.154	4.690
Jan '83	10.76	3.923	0.870	3.923
Feb '83	14.51	1.607	2.343	4.068
Mar '83	18.40	1.558	1.751	3.833

	Occupants (kWh/d)	Heating load (kWh/d)	Net load (kWh/d)	SHF (−)	Collector efficiency (−)
Nov '82	1.7	38.80	31.74	1.0	0.56
Dec '82	1.7	41.13	33.59	0.97	0.64
Jan '83	1.7	43.91	37.42	0.90	0.65
Feb '83	1.7	38.00	29.89	0.95	0.49
Mar '83	1.7	26.25	18.97	0.92	0.32

thermal properties of the building structure are planned for the future, and these will enable us to reduce the uncertainty on the various derived quantities.

It is interesting to regard the entire house as a solar collector and to enquire as to its efficiency as such. We can define an effective monthly efficiency by simply comparing the monthly solar contribution to the heating load, as estimated above, with the amount of solar radiation incident upon all of the collector windows during the same period. For this purpose we have taken monthly daily mean horizontal insolation data for the winter in question and used them to simulate the corresponding figures for south-facing vertical (bedroom and living room) and 55° tilted (study) windows (Erbs et al. 1972). For this purpose an albedo of 0.3 was assumed. Table 21.2 shows the results month by month during the winter months.

One sees that over the entire heating season the average efficiency exceeded 50 percent. This is a good example of a fact that is not widely appreciated in Israel; namely, that passive space heating can take its place alongside solar water heating as a highly efficient way of using solar energy.

Regarding hot water requirements, a roof-top 105 l "bread box" type of solar water heater with a 1.0 sq.m aperture area was used to pre-heat water for a 60 l electrically heated tank inside the house. The total amount of backup electricity that went toward heating water was 158 kWh for the year, with no backup being used during the months May through October. This represents an annual solar fraction of about f = 0.9.

SUMMARY AND OUTLOOK

The preceding paragraphs have described the first year's thermal performance of a passive solar adobe house at Sede Boqer. It is estimated that solar energy supplied 95 percent of the winter space-heating requirements, and together with a measured 242kWh of electrical backup, maintained the interior temperature at an average winter value of 18°C, compared with a mean ambient winter temperature of 10.5°c. The diurnal temperature swing inside the house was small, particularly in the room heated by a Rotating Prism Wall, where this means daily fluctuation was less than +/− 1.0°C. (A detailed discussion of the Prism Wall performance is published in Faiman and Feuermann 1983). During the summer season, interior temperatures were kept close to 25°C via the use of nighttime ventilation and daytime shading; no backup cooling being necessary. Use of a solar water heater resulted in only 158 kWh of backup electricity for domestic hot water requirements.

Based upon 242 kWh of space-heating backup (SHF = 0.95), 158 kWh of domestic hot water backup (f = 0.9) and a further 1509 kWh for lighting and appliances, the entire annual energy needs of the residents amounted to only 1809 kWh instead of an estimated total of about 7673 kWh. A total annual energy figure of 7673 kWh would in fact be typical of many families who live at Sede Boqer, and for those families, winter space heating is indeed the major consumer of the energy, followed (in the case of those without solar water heaters) by domestic hot water.

In the solar adobe house, with water and space heating needs substantially (i.e., greater than 90 percent) provided by the sun, by far the largest consumers of energy were the electrical appliances. These accounted for some 80 percent of the total 1809 kWh of electricity used by the residents during the first year. It is planned for some time in the future to reduce this building to a near zero-energy consumer by the addition of about 10m**2 of photovoltaic cells.

ACKNOWLEDGMENTS

The authors of this chapter were supported by a research grant from the Israel Ministry of Energy and Infrastructure.

The Blaustein Institute for Desert Research wishes to record its lasting gratitude to Ms. Betine Lebeau of London, England, without whose outstanding fund-raising efforts this house could not have been built. Construction was carried out mainly by a team of unskilled volunteers, among whom Ms. Judith Hobbs deserves special credit for her unflagging energies. The project was initiated during the period when Arie Rahamimoff was head of the Desert Architecture Unit. The architectural design of the house was due to Mike Kaplan, adobe construction techniques to Larry Maayan, and the wind-catcher design to Eli Levin-Epstein. The authors are indebted to Dr.

Avraham Zangvil of the Desert Meteorology Unit for kindly furnishing them with accurate local climatic data during the period reported herein.

REFERENCES

ASHRAE Handbook. 1977. Fundamentals, Ashrae, N.Y.

Cytryn, S. 1957. Soil Construction: Its Principles and Application for Housing. The Weizmann Science Press of Israel, Jerusalem.

Erbs, D. G., S. A. Klein, and J. A. Duffie. 1982. Estimation of the hourly, daily, and monthly-average global radiation. *Solar Energy* 28: 293–302.

Faiman, D. 1980. Rotating prism wall as a passive heating element. *Solar Energy* 25: 563–64.

Faiman, D. and D. Feuermann. 1984. Performance details of a rotating prism solar wall. *Energy and Building* 7: 301–308.

Rogers, B. T. 1978. Effect of moisture content on the thermal properties of sun dried adobe. *Proceedings of the 1978 annual meeting of the American section of ISES*, 1978. Denver. Colo., Vol. 2.2.

INDEX

Index